African football migration

Manchester University Press

Globalizing Sport Studies

Series editor: **John Horne, Visiting Professor of Sport and Social Theory, Waseda University, Tokyo, Japan**

Public interest in sport studies continues to grow throughout the world. This series brings together the latest work in the field and acts as a global knowledge hub for interdisciplinary work in sport studies. While promoting work across disciplines, the series focuses on social scientific and cultural studies of sport. It brings together the most innovative scholarly empirical and theoretical work, from within the UK and internationally.

Books previously published in this series by Bloomsbury Academic:

Global Media Sport: Flows, Forms and Futures
David Rowe

Japanese Women and Sport: Beyond Baseball and Sumo
Robin Kietlinski

Sport for Development and Peace: A Critical Sociology
Simon Darnell

Globalizing Cricket: Englishness, Empire and Identity
Dominic Malcolm

Global Boxing
Kath Woodward

Sport and Social Movements: From the Local to the Global
Jean Harvey, John Horne, Parissa Safai, Simon Darnell and Sebastien Courchesne-O'Neill

Football Italia: Italian Football in an Age of Globalization
Mark Doidge

Books previously published in this series by Manchester University Press:

The Greening of Golf: Sport, Globalization and the Environment
Brad Millington and Brian Wilson

Sport and Technology: An Actor-Network Theory Perspective
Roslyn Kerr

Sport in the Black Atlantic: Cricket, Canada and the Caribbean Diaspora
Janelle Joseph

Localizing Global Sport for Development
Iain Lindsey, Tess Kay, Ruth Jeanes and Davies Banda

Mega-Events and Social Change: Spectacle, Legacy and Public Culture
Maurice Roche

African football migration

Aspirations, experiences and trajectories

Paul Darby, James Esson and
Christian Ungruhe

MANCHESTER UNIVERSITY PRESS

Copyright © Paul Darby, James Esson and Christian Ungruhe 2022

The right of Paul Darby, James Esson and Christian Ungruhe to be identified as the authors of this work has been asserted by them in accordance with the Copyright, Designs and Patents Act 1988.

Published by Manchester University Press
Oxford Road, Manchester M13 9PL
www.manchesteruniversitypress.co.uk

British Library Cataloguing-in-Publication Data
A catalogue record for this book is available from the British Library

ISBN   978 1 5261 2026 7   hardback
ISBN   978 1 5261 7199 3   paperback

First published 2022
Paperback published 2023

The publisher has no responsibility for the persistence or accuracy of URLs for any external or third-party internet websites referred to in this book, and does not guarantee that any content on such websites is, or will remain, accurate or appropriate.

Typeset
by New Best-set Typesetters Ltd

Paul dedicates this book to Dianne, Oliver, Oran and Grace and to the memory of his mother, Rosaleen Darby.

James dedicates this book to Siobhan, Zak, Kofi and Kathleen-Ruby.

Christian dedicates this book to Anna, Hannes and Lea.

Contents

Series editor's preface	*page* viii
Preface	x
Acknowledgements	xvi
Introduction	1
1 Theorising African football migration	19
2 The history, geography and regulation of African football migration	40
3 'Producing' African labour for the global football industry	64
4 Speculation in and through football migration	84
5 'Becoming a somebody' through football	104
6 Luck, sackings and involuntary immobility in football	124
7 Navigating liminality in foreign football industries	146
8 Hope and precarity in transnational football careers	169
9 Post-playing-career transitions and struggles	196
Conclusion	222
Bibliography	234
Index	260

Series editor's preface

There is now a considerable amount of expertise nationally and internationally in the social scientific and cultural analysis of sport in relation to the economy and society more generally. Contemporary research topics, such as sport and social justice, science and technology and sport, global social movements and sport, sports mega-events, sports participation and engagement and the role of sport in social development, suggest that sport and social relations need to be understood in non-Western developing economies, as well as European, North American and other advanced capitalist societies.

The series *Globalizing Sport Studies* is thus in line with a massive growth of academic expertise, research output and public interest in sport worldwide. At the same time, it seeks to use the latest developments in technology and the economics of publishing to reflect the most innovative research into sport in society currently underway in the world. The series is multi-disciplinary, although primarily based on the social sciences and cultural studies approaches to sport.

The broad aims of the series are to: *act* as a knowledge hub for social scientific and cultural studies research in sport, including, but not exclusively, anthropological, economic, geographic, historical, political science and sociological studies; *contribute* to the expanding field of research on sport in society in the United Kingdom and internationally by focussing on sport at regional, national and international levels; *create* a series for both senior and more junior researchers that will become synonymous with cutting edge research, scholarly opportunities and academic development; *promote* innovative discipline-based, multi-, inter- and trans-disciplinary theoretical and methodological approaches to researching sport in society; *provide* an English language outlet for high-quality non-English writing on sport in society; and *publish* broad overviews, original empirical research studies and classic studies from non-English sources.

The *Globalizing Sport Studies* series has always been interested in transnational topics and transdisciplinary research. It is therefore immensely pleasing to see the publication of *African football migration* that provides a very timely account based on innovative research and engagement with the latest writing on the subject. Using West Africa as its geographic location, the book is informed by research conducted for over a decade by three authors coming from the three disciplines of anthropology, geography and sociology. It offers a comprehensive overview of the history, networks and institutional structures involved in the migration of young African men and youth in the global game of football.

As with so many other projects conducted since 2019, the COVID-19 pandemic impacted on some aspects of research that were to be part of the underpinning of this book. Most notably, the pandemic put a brake on the movement of those men who relied on intra-regional and international migration, and thus hampered continuing research into their experiences. Additionally, the absence of research findings about the mobility of African women footballers is a direct effect of the restrictions on conducting research in 2020 and 2021. This is admirably accounted for in the preface to the book.

The book overall is a valuable contribution to understanding the various issues that male migrant African football players face and have to respond to, before, while and after they encounter different forms of local, regional and national reaction, including racism, in the foreign leagues in which they play. It offers insights into the precariousness of their careers and makes a great contribution to understanding all the work that goes on behind the making of contemporary football players. In this respect, it will be of interest to teachers, researchers and students in sport studies, African studies, migration studies, as well as sociology, geography and anthropology.

John Horne
Edinburgh, 2021

Preface

Doing research with African migrant football players, past and present, and with African youth who aspire to play the professional game abroad and who pursue this goal with a dedication, diligence and focus that belies their youthful age is a thrilling, rewarding and challenging experience. We have shared aspiring players' excitement and worries about upcoming matches or trials and listened to professional players reflect on the progress of their career trajectory. We have watched from close quarters their efforts and daily toil in exacting conditions. We have been privy to their future hopes for self and family as well as their insecurities and fears of not succeeding, and the sting of shame that this brings. We have also observed the countless challenges, setbacks and victories they navigate in their quest to 'make it' as professional footballers.

The players' stories of overcoming adversity and reaching their goals, and of their career struggles and heartbreak at unfulfilled ambitions, certainly piqued our intellectual curiosities as academics and our more general interest in football and the lives of football players. Indeed, despite uncertainty and precarity and the relentless nature of the physical, psychological and emotional demands that characterise the pursuit of a career in what is an intensely competitive and often unforgiving industry, we cannot deny a little bit of vicarious identification and envy. Each of us played football in our childhoods and dreamt of playing professionally, or more specifically turning out for our respective teams, Liverpool, AC Milan and Borussia Mönchengladbach. However, unlike those who participated in our research, we did not possess the talent, dedication, willingness to make sacrifices or the appetite that we have witnessed first-hand over the years of our research with African footballers.

It is this dedication that African youth and young men show towards the game, and their commitment to securing and sustaining a career in the global football industry, that makes their football migration life projects, achieved or envisaged, deeply fascinating and admirable – and worthy of the academic inquiry that we expose them to in this book. However, this forms only part of our motivation to write a book about African football migration. In keeping with the accelerating flow of talented footballers out of the continent since the 1990s, the academic discourse has gathered pace since the first studies appeared during that decade (see Chapter 1). We believe that this is a timely juncture to offer a comprehensive perspective on the history, structures, geographies, temporalities, networks and outcomes of African football migration and to situate these in the context of the global game.

Without wishing to draw what might appear to some to be naive parallels between the comparatively comfortable labour conditions of three middle-class academics located in universities in Northern Ireland, England and the Netherlands, and those experienced by African footballers, it could be argued that writing a book shares some analogies with their migration project. James Joyce, the famous twentieth-century Irish writer, once said that the craft of writing requires the author to 'be an adventurer above all, willing to take every risk, and be prepared to founder in his effort if need be' (cited in Power, 1974: 45). While Joyce was discussing writing novels, short stories and poetry, his words not only resonate with our experiences of accessing, capturing and chronicling the lifeworlds of African migrant footballers, but also encapsulate what those players must do on an almost daily basis in their efforts to enact and reproduce the transnational mobility required to enter into and sustain a career in the global football industry. Both enterprises – writing a book and chasing what is a utopian, and for most an unrealistic, dream – are unpredictable, all-consuming, arduous, exciting, engaging, promising and, not least if the envisaged outcome is eventually accomplished, intensely rewarding.

As we show in this book, African football migration is a process that connects individuals to networks of actors and institutions that can facilitate (and curtail) their ambitions. Equally, this book is a product of a collective, collaborative effort involving a sociologist, a geographer and an anthropologist. Working together certainly accentuated the positive sides of writing and enabled us to cope a bit more fleet-footedly with the challenges that we encountered along the way. We feel that our various disciplinary lenses, methodologies and writing styles provoked 'outside-the-box' thinking, stimulated our discussions and provided opportunities to learn from each other's expertise and approaches. We believe that this book is stronger and more comprehensive for this collaboration and possesses relevance beyond a single discipline.

Nevertheless, producing this book was a process of unimagined uncertainties. While our research engagement in the field of African football migration stretches back to 2008, most of our writing was undertaken during what was a tumultuous 2020 and early 2021. The wider impact of the COVID-19 pandemic continues to unfold and it is likely that it will have ramifications for the way we live our lives long into the future. A policy brief by the OECD (2020) suggested that the COVID-19 crisis has posed particular challenges for immigrants around the world, pointing to its disproportionate impact on them in terms of health, jobs, education, language training and public opinion. The closing of international borders, a key element in the fight against COVID-19, has also created significant problems for millions of people across Africa whose lives and livelihoods are tied to intra-regional and international migration. According to Teye (2020), travel restrictions and the closing of legal channels for migration are being keenly felt across West Africa, the geographic focus for this book, and may force more people to become caught up in irregular migration and trafficking – practices that encompass football migrants.

In light of this, it will come as no surprise to learn that the pandemic has generated unique challenges for African migrant footballers and those with aspirations to become transnationally mobile professionals. For many, the pandemic put their migration projects on hold (see Chapter 8). Following the initial outbreak, leagues and other competitions were either suspended or cancelled, and those that resumed mostly did so without fans in attendance. This has created pressures on club revenues, leading many to take measures to reduce labour costs. As a consequence, contractual uncertainty for existing migrant players has grown and the number of international transfers has declined for the first time in a decade (Ahmed, 2020; FIFA, 2020a). This has sharpened the precarity faced by African migrant players abroad. But, in a context where clubs are less willing to speculate in the transfer market, it also creates the risk of effectively placing a moratorium on the hopes of countless talented young African players, leaving them bereft of alternative routes to productive livelihoods.

With far less serious implications, COVID-19 also challenged our book project. With offices, nurseries and schools closed during several lockdowns, writing the book became a family affair, and, at times, it seemed better for everyone if we sought peace and quiet away from our makeshift home offices and the demands of home-schooling our young children. Thus, park benches and deserted car parks, locations that we never imagined would be conducive to writing, became regular sites for progressing our manuscript. Travel restrictions made it necessary to adjust the scope of the book to some degree. While a planned fieldwork trip to further interrogate African footballers' migration to South-East Asia was cancelled at the last minute, our enforced immobility also prevented us from conducting planned research with female footballers and other actors relevant in African women's football migration. While we have been able to incorporate primary data on African football migration beyond the prominent Africa–Europe nexus, this book is now entirely about male players – and we cannot deny a certain unease with this.

From this book project's conception, it was our intention to incorporate the aspirations, experiences and trajectories of female African players in a meaningful and sustained way. Having dealt with the challenges of researching men's football almost exclusively over our careers, we knew that the inclusion of girls and women was an ambitious endeavour. Nonetheless, we had begun to undertake research with aspiring African female players in Ghana, conducting initial interviews at a local football academy in 2015 and following up with them at a youth football tournament in Sweden two years later (Darby and Agergaard, 2018). The restrictions imposed by the pandemic meant that it was impossible to add further primary data on the full spectrum of female African players' ambitions, experiences and career trajectories. These constraints on conducting further primary research and an acknowledgement of the limits of the empirical evidence we had already gathered were important in our decision to re-orient our focus to the men's game only.

Our decision to focus on the men's game was also influenced by a recognition of the gendered particularities of African football migration. This is clearly demonstrated in the small but rich body of work that has explored African women's football-related mobilities (see Chapter 1). This scholarship made it clear to us that simply generalising female players' encounters with football migration according to those of male players would be insufficient in capturing the nuances and differences between the male and female experience. There are undoubtedly some similarities between male and female African players. Both possess the requisite talent and ambition, aspire to ply their trade at the highest level, compete with the best players, avail of professional facilities to improve their abilities and, not least, to earn a decent living by playing abroad professionally, and in doing so supporting their families at home (Botelho and Agergaard, 2011). Some of those women who have been able to secure professional careers in Europe have also been confronted with the same challenges posed by racialisation that male players have had to deal with (Engh, Settler and Agergaard, 2017). Uncertainty and precarity also manifest themselves similarly across the post-playing-career lives of male and female African football migrants (Agergaard, 2018; Agergaard and Ungruhe, 2016).

In many other ways, however, football in Africa is deeply contoured by gender, and this impacts aspirations and opportunities for football migration among female players. The infrastructure for girls' and women's football on the continent is much less developed than its male equivalent. Whereas the game has become increasingly popular among girls and women all over Africa, they generally lack access to adequate facilities, professional clubs and leagues as well as sufficient support from local, regional and national governing bodies. Quantitatively, transnational migration for female African players is much less prominent than for their male counterparts and does not have a similar global reach (Agergaard and Tiesler, 2014). For example, in 2020 the number of international transfers of male players from Africa to leagues outside the continent stood at 1,786, generating transfer receipts of almost fifty-five million US dollars. The number of female African players making the same journey in the same period numbered fifty-eight with no discernible transfer fees being recouped (FIFA, 2020a). While there are a growing number of professional leagues and expanding media coverage in the women's game around the world, the fact that it significantly lags behind the men's game in terms of commercialisation and mediatisation, makes migration in women's football much less lucrative and speculative.

A consequence of the challenges noted above is that football migration does not fuel the hopes of female youth players to a degree comparable to male players. It also does not have the same sort of critical implications for their future life projects that it does for a whole generation of boys and young men who increasingly look to football as the one pathway to success, respectable social adulthood and acceptable masculine identities. Given these differences in scale and social meaning, we felt that it was important either to engage deeply with African women's football migration in this book or refrain from it entirely. After many discussions, and in light of the issues for fieldwork imposed by travel restrictions and other pandemic constraints, we chose the latter course. Certainly, a richer and more nuanced understanding of African football migration would have been gleaned by incorporating women's migration. We hope to pursue this further in our future research.

Of course, 2020 was not only the year of COVID-19, with all its restrictions and problematic implications for the global football industry and those who labour within it. It was also a year that appeared to open up new horizons and possibilities in terms of how issues of racialisation and racism, both overt and covert, are confronted within the game. While campaigning against racism has been on the agenda of players and coaches, clubs, supporters, and national and continental governing bodies for some time, structural racism and racialisation in football persists largely unchecked. African football migrants, and Black players more generally, live with the insidious nature of this problem throughout their careers and often beyond. However, football's embracing of the Black Lives Matter movement in the second half of 2020 may instigate more robust, committed efforts on the part of the football authorities and other stakeholders to tackle this issue. The official endorsement of a range of gestures, symbols and practices that support the Black Lives Matter message by a range of national football federations and leagues appears to represent a bigger step towards acknowledging the depth of the problem. Black players have certainly felt emboldened and have been outspoken on the structural and direct racism they experience. Yet incidents involving the use of social media platforms to hurl racist invective at Black players and the largely ineffectual response to this has raised questions about whether the incorporation of the Black Lives Matter movement into professional football will initiate significant, lasting change. At the very least, it has increased awareness of the issue of racism and racial inequality in football and of how much work remains to be done to rid it from all levels of the game. One of our hopes for this book is that it might make a modest contribution to this fight by further raising awareness of the discrimination and hardships that migrant African players encounter over the course of their careers and migration trajectories.

Paul Darby, James Esson and Christian Ungruhe
February 2021

Acknowledgements

There are too many participants and interlocutors who gave so generously of their time to thank individually. Their stories and perspectives can be found across the following pages and we hope that the prominence of their words and insights in the text testifies to their immeasurable contribution to this book. We are indebted to all of you.

Two of our colleagues have significantly added to this book by contributing interview material with aspiring and retiring African footballers: Nienke van der Meij, who wrote her PhD thesis under Paul's supervision and was initially part of this book project but decided to pursue other ventures, and Sine Agergaard, who led the research project on African footballers' post-playing-careers that Christian worked on. Many thanks for your valuable contributions and sharing your insights and interview material with us. There are many other colleagues, friends and family members who have offered support in a multitude of ways in our professional and personal lives during the research and writing stages of this book. They are too numerous to single out but they know who they are.

This book would not have been possible without the support of our current and previous institutions: Ulster University, Loughborough University, University College London, Erasmus University Rotterdam, Aarhus University and the University of Bayreuth. We would also like to thank the various institutions and programmes that funded our respective research projects: the UK Economic and Social Research Council, the European Union's Horizon 2020 research and innovation programme, the Erasmus School of History, Culture and Communication, the Joint Committee for Nordic Research Councils in the Humanities & Social Sciences and the Bavarian State Ministry of Sciences, Education and the Arts.

Much of the book was written in what were unprecedented and extraordinarily trying circumstances. Beyond COVID-19, the exigencies of our jobs and life in general, the arrival of new additions to our families and the loss of loved ones all delayed progress. We thank Tom Dark, our commissioning editor, and his team at Manchester University Press for the latitude they permitted us to finally get this book 'over the line'. Finally, we are grateful to Joe Haining, our copy-editor, for his good humour, valuable insights and going above and beyond to give the manuscript one last polish.

Introduction

Among the growing number of talented young African football players who sought out and secured a career in elite professional leagues across western Europe during the late 1980s and early 1990s, Nii Odartey Lamptey was widely considered as the most prodigiously gifted. His performances as a fourteen-year-old for Ghana at the Fédération Internationale de Football Association (FIFA) U-16 World Championship in 1989, had prompted no less a footballing luminary than Brazil's Pelé to describe him as his 'natural successor' (Oliver, 2008). Having transferred to Europe aged fifteen, he lived up to this promise during spells as a teenager at RSC Anderlecht and PSV Eindhoven. At sixteen he was an age-group world champion, having starred in the 1991 U-17 World Cup, finishing as joint leading goal scorer. He was described by his coach at that tournament, the German Otto Pfister, as the 'best youth player in the world between 1989 and 1992' (interview, 9 February 2008). At sixteen, he made his debut for the Ghanaian senior national team, marking the occasion by scoring one goal and creating another. He went on to win an Olympic bronze medal aged eighteen and by the age of twenty-one he had appeared almost forty times for Ghana. The subsequent trajectory of his career is best described as erratic; it certainly did not reach the heights that numerous football commentators predicted. While he remains one of Ghana's best-known football exports, elements of his biography represent a cautionary tale for those young African boys aspiring to a future abroad as a professional footballer.

At the end of a month-long bout of fieldwork in Ghana researching the role of football academies in the country's burgeoning football export industry, Paul sat pensively on a plastic chair on the tiled front patio of the home of the now retired Lamptey. A chance conversation and some hastily snatched insights into his experiences as a football migrant in the lobby of an Accra hotel two days previously, led to a kind invitation to his house in East Legon, a prestigious residential community adjoining the main campus of the University of Ghana. An hour after our scheduled meeting time Lamptey had yet to arrive, delayed by an engagement at the

Glow-Lamp International School he had founded shortly after the conclusion of his playing career. With his flight back to the UK scheduled to leave Kotoka International Airport later that evening, Paul grew increasingly uneasy. As the late afternoon sun slowly slipped out of view, so too did the prospect of an interview with a man perfectly placed to offer insights and perspectives on how young African males' hopes and dreams of 'making it' as a transnational football migrant are formed, pursued and, for a minority, enacted.

Finally, after two hours of anxious waiting, Lamptey's black SUV pulled into the driveway. Diminutive in height but stocky in stature, he offered polite apologies and invited Paul inside his home, where they exchanged pleasantries and shared thoughts on Ghana's defeat to Cameroon in the semi-final of the 2008 Africa Cup of Nations four days previously. One wall of the spacious living room was adorned with photographs of his playing days and the various trophies and awards he had picked up along the way. As he pointed out his favourites, he lingered over the Golden Ball trophy that he secured as player of the tournament while helping Ghana to its first world youth crown in 1991. This was an appropriate and vivid backdrop to the next two hours of what was an intense and sometimes emotional conversation, during which Lamptey recounted his journey from playing informally on the streets and makeshift pitches of Accra and Kumasi, Ghana's biggest cities, to a professional career that lasted almost two decades, saw him sign for thirteen clubs and spanned eleven countries across four continents. Almost exactly two years after this meeting with Paul, Christian also interviewed Lamptey as part of a separate project on the career and post-playing-career trajectories and experiences of African football migrants in Europe. In sharing with us his insights into a circuitous career that was at times rewarding but often trying, Lamptey broached many of what, unbeknown to us at the time, would become the central concerns of this book.

In keeping with our commitment to foregrounding the *aspirations, experiences* and *trajectories* of male African football migrants and to challenging tropes that depict these individuals as helpless, passive victims of wider macro-structural currents both within the football industry and beyond, we turn much of this introductory chapter over to a 'thick' description of Lamptey's early life growing up in Ghana, his football career and his post-playing-career path. In particular, we focus on how the game featured in his youthful future-making imaginaries before outlining how he was able to enact cross-border and social mobility. We account for his experiences as a football migrant, the routes and nodes he traversed and the nature of his encounters along the way, including those during his post-playing-career return to Ghana. Treated in isolation, his eventful career constitutes a fascinating insight into how professional migrant athletes produce and reproduce transnational mobility, a process that encompasses the multi-directional and entangled dynamics of cross-border spatial mobility and aspirations and enactments of social mobility. However, the purpose of our exposition here is to contextualise and animate the following six core questions at the centre of this book:

1. How have African players become embedded in the global football industry and what are the historical, spatial and regulatory features of their transnational mobilities?
2. What actors, networks, institutions and processes influence Africans' opportunities to produce football-related mobility?
3. How do African youth rationalise their entry into the game and their aspirations for spatial mobility through football?
4. How have African youth encountered, experienced and negotiated the pursuit of football migration, and what are the outcomes?
5. How do African players experience and navigate transnational moves and professional careers 'outside', including irregular football-related migration?
6. What are the post-playing-career trajectories of former African migrant football players and how do they experience their lives after retirement?

Once we have outlined the undulations of Lamptey's personal biography, we reflect on how his experiences as a young footballer in Ghana, his career trajectory as a migrant, professional player and his post-playing-career life speak to these questions.

Nii Odartey Lamptey: a biographical vignette

Much of the media coverage and popular discourse around Nii Lamptey's career tends to focus on the interpersonal and familial relationships that influenced his journey across diverse football settings and the core narrative depicts him as an exploited, passive victim of unscrupulous football agents and a nefarious trade in football labour. These micro- and meso-level interactions undoubtedly helped to contour his career arc, and it is certainly the case that he was ruthlessly exploited in the early stages of his professional life. However, as we contend throughout this book, failing to adequately position Africans' football-related transnational mobility within specific local cultural contexts and wider macro-level currents, and examine how individual agency articulates with these, offers only partial, atomised insights into what is a much more complex reality.

Lamptey's football talents and aspirations were fashioned in a socio-economic environment where opportunities for male youth to secure employment and stable, productive livelihoods were increasingly constricted. By the early 1980s, political and economic instability in Ghana precipitated a succession of military coups and fluctuations in global commodity prices combined with rampant debt had significantly reduced standards of living for most Ghanaians. In a bid to resuscitate the economy, Jerry Rawlings's military government turned to the World Bank and the International Monetary Fund who quickly enacted structural adjustment programmes (SAPs), considered at the time as the antidote to poverty in developing countries. The neoliberal governance that came with SAPs heralded rapid privatisation and unprecedented cuts to state expenditure on public services and social welfare (Konadu-Agyemang, 2000). The outcome was increasing numbers of Ghanaians falling below the poverty line and, with the slashing of public sector jobs, a significant increase in unemployment. A further consequence of this curtailment of public spending, and one that played out in Lamptey's early life, was a rise in the number of children falling out of formal education (Esson, 2016).

Ghana's success in securing its fourth and, at the time of writing, last victory in the continent's premier international football competition, the Africa Cup of Nations, in 1982, subsequent achievements in qualifying for five consecutive U-17 World Championships between 1991 and 1999, winning the tournament twice and finishing runners-up on two other occasions, and their bronze medal at the 1992 Olympic Football Tournament stood in marked contrast to the country's economic fortunes. These victories ensured that the game, immensely popular and well-funded in the period leading up to and immediately following independence, maintained its appeal among local youth (Darby, 2010). This was no less the case for Lamptey. Born in Tema, Ghana's largest seaport, he grew up in the nation's two largest cities, Accra and Kumasi. Lamptey's introduction to football involved playing informal versions of the game among peers. In a television feature on *FIFA Futbol Mundial*, an international weekly football magazine show, Lamptey describes honing his skills as a child during small-sided games, referred to in the local vernacular as *muchendae*. These games were played in the street or on patches of waste ground in local communities, attracted adult interest and were frequently accompanied by betting. Victorious teams and talented players often benefited from small gestures of benevolence and gratitude from those who had successfully wagered on the outcome. This became a way for children to acquire small amounts of money that helped them negotiate their daily existence. For Lamptey, it was an early introduction to the potential of the game as a source of income and an insight into how he might translate his athletic capabilities and skills into financial capital.

An unstable family life and parental abuse focused Lamptey's mind on becoming self-sufficient as he navigated what was a precarious childhood.

He has spoken openly about the neglect and ill-treatment he suffered at the hands of his mother and father. His parents divorced when he was aged eight; when his mother remarried, he moved from Accra to Kumasi to live with his father, who was an alcoholic and disapproved of his son's participation in football. Fearful of the beatings his father frequently dispensed, Lamptey often slept rough on the streets (interview, 11 February 2008). Without parental guidance or encouragement, he attended school only infrequently and soon joined the growing ranks of youth dropping out of formal education. As had been the case in Accra, he filled his days playing football. He regularly turned out in school football competitions and performed with such distinction that his non-enrolment in school was overlooked (Acheampong, 2020). While the game offered escapism, it also provided material support and a small measure of security. His abilities in street versions of the game brought him to the attention of local coaches in the more organised Colts system of youth leagues and he was offered the chance to reside in or 'camp' with a Muslim football club, Kaloum Stars, albeit on condition that he converted to Islam. While this exacerbated his difficult relationship with his Christian father, it afforded him a place to live and a modicum of stability.

None of this is to suggest that his engagement with youth football constituted a carefree antidote to an unstable upbringing. Despite its popularity, and in contradiction to the painting of football as an escape from poverty for youth in African settings, playing the game beyond the school setting was, at this time, strongly associated with poverty and social deviance, and those who played were frequently socially stigmatised (Esson, 2016). Indeed, footballers in Ghana were, and among older generations still are, often referred to as *kobolo*, a Gã word that has found its way into almost all the Ghanaian languages (the plural is *koboloi*). It has become a common term reserved for children who drop out of school, are believed to be heading towards a life of vagrancy and who lack communitarian instincts or impulses (van der Meij and Darby, 2017). In short, and as Cobblah (2011) has observed, to be a *kobolo* is to be considered a 'good-for-nothing'. This perception was reinforced by the fact that the best players tended to come from low-income communities and had little formal schooling. As a consequence, middle- and high-income families were often loath to allow their children to play football outside of the school environment. Such was the level of faith in education as *the* route to social mobility, poorer parents, including Lamptey's father, frequently expressed displeasure when their children prioritised football over school. Reflecting back on this stage in his life, Lamptey recalled the pejorative meaning of this label, explaining that 'nobody want[s] to [be] *kobolo*, you don't have a home' (interview, 17 February 2010).

While playing in the Colts system, Lamptey had not given much consideration to football as a potential career path, and the prospect of moving overseas to play professionally did not register as a possibility: 'At that time, I was playing football for fun. I was very young. I didn't know anything' (interview, 17 February 2010). This may appear at first glance to be implausible given the weight of football-related migration in the future-making projects of a rapidly increasing number of young footballers in Ghana and elsewhere on the continent (Ungruhe and Esson, 2017). However, it is reasonable to presume that Lamptey's perspective reflected the fact that while emigration more generally was becoming increasingly prominent for Ghanaians, given the economic downturn of the 1970s and 1980s, it was not as entrenched a feature of young footballers' mindset or disposition as it was to become in subsequent years (Quartey, 2009). Lamptey also had few fellow football-playing compatriots to aspire to. While prominent in other parts of North and West Africa, migrating through football was relatively rare in Ghana at this time, inhibited as it was by a protectionist outlook on the part of the government and national football association (Darby, 2010).

Some members of the victorious Ghanaian team that won the 1978 Africa Cup of Nations, including former African Player of the Year Abdul Razak and his teammates Emmanuel Quarshi and Haruna Youcef, had moved to clubs in the United States, Egypt and the United Arab Emirates (Versi, 1986). However, Europe remained uncharted territory. This began to change, albeit only in a modest fashion, by the mid-1980s with several players moving to Belgium where clubs had utilised the country's networks to sign players from its former African colonies (Lanfranchi and Taylor, 2001). Abedi Pelé and Tony Yeboah, who subsequently came to be recognised as path-breakers for future generations of Ghanaian football migrants, made what were low-profile transfers in 1986 and 1988, respectively, the former to French second-tier side Niort and the latter to 1. FC Saarbrücken in Germany's 2. Bundesliga. However, with migration far less associated with football in Ghana as it was to become from the 1990s onwards, Lamptey's understanding of what the game might offer in terms of his future was not explicitly informed by the exploits of transnationally mobile football-playing compatriots.

The extent to which football migration featured in how Lamptey thought about his future was soon to be transformed by a conflation of circumstances. A return to Accra when his father remarried, saw him sign for Young Corners, a local youth side, and from there he quickly attracted the attention of the selectors of the national youth team who were putting together a squad for the 1989 U-16 World Championship in Scotland. As has since been the case with numerous Ghanaian and other African migrant players, making a national squad and participating in international competition was a pivotal moment in affording Lamptey the visibility necessary to produce transnational football mobility (Carter, 2011; Engh and Agergaard, 2015). His performances in Scotland piqued the interest of a number of overseas clubs, but the presence of the Nigerian international Stephen Keshi on the roster of leading Belgian outfit RSC Anderlecht placed them in prime position to secure his signature. With a long tradition of recruiting African players, their interest in bringing him to Belgium was relayed via a Nigerian representative of Keshi who travelled to Ghana while Lamptey was in camp with the junior national team. Keshi, one of the highest-profile African players at that time, featured prominently in the conversation and his personal interest in seeing the young prodigy join him in Belgium clearly left an impression, convincing Lamptey that his future lay beyond Ghana. Lamptey recalled the circumstances in the following terms:

> Yes, after that tournament there were so many clubs that were interested in me, Anderlecht, Vasco de Gama, Rangers ... but the country wanted to keep us together, they did not want anybody to go so they had all our documents, our passports. Stephen Keshi was playing in Belgium at that time for Anderlecht and he was known already in Africa. So Anderlecht said 'We want this boy so if you can, go for him'. He sent his local agent from Nigeria and he came to Ghana here. He came to the camp. We spoke and because Keshi said he wanted me to play I was so happy ... He gave me his card and he gave me some small money and then he left and then two weeks later we break camp and we have to go [on] holidays for about two weeks and I refused to go back to camp. I thought, 'No, I will go, I will go to Lagos [to meet the agent]. I want to go and play professional football.' So, the small money that I had, I gathered it and I went to the station and advised the driver that I don't have a passport but I want to go to Lagos. (Interview, 11 February 2008)

Without informing his parents or any family members, relying on his bonus money from the World Youth Championship and armed with only a business card, Lamptey persuaded a taxi driver to take him to Lagos, a journey that required three illegal border crossings. On arrival, Lamptey was able to contact Keshi through his representative. Within a matter of days, he embarked on another illegal journey northwards to Europe, this time with a fake Nigerian passport, posing as Keshi's son. Lamptey recounted how his journey from Nigeria to Belgium materialised:

> After I arrived in Lagos, I gave the card to the taxi driver and it was easy for him to take me to the guy's house ... and the wife called him and said 'You have a visitor'. She mentioned my name and I was here. On the phone he was shouting. Within twenty minutes he came back home and then when he called Keshi in Belgium and said 'Lamptey is here', and then Keshi said 'Are you sure?', so he spoke to me and I said 'Yes Keshi, I'm here'. Luckily, Nigeria were

playing some qualifier ... I watched the match that day so Stephen Keshi came and we met and went to the hotel. I was there and he made some few calls when I was with him and then in some few hours I had a Nigerian passport, and after the match we flew to Belgium. (Interview, 11 February 2008)

In actively producing mobility and traversing a route that took him from Accra to Belgium, via Togo, Benin and Nigeria, Lamptey displayed the resilience, ingenuity and tenacity gleaned from his experiences of living on the streets of Kumasi. However, though his stay was legalised with the help of officials from RSC Anderlecht, thus ensuring that he could sign for them (Acheampong, 2020), Lamptey was ill-prepared for life in Brussels and initially struggled to adjust: 'At the beginning I wanted to come back home ... I was homesick but I did not tell anybody. I don't know anybody, I just left the country and here I am in Belgium' (interview, 11 February 2008). Living at the Anderlecht clubhouse proved isolating for a young Lamptey and he found it difficult to acclimatise to the weather, food and culture (Acheampong, 2020). Supported by Keshi, who had gone through similar experiences, Lamptey slowly adapted to his new environs and the demands of the European game, and aged just fifteen he made his senior debut for Anderlecht, marking the beginning of what were two fruitful years with the club.

In the first move of his professional career, Lamptey was loaned to the Dutch giants PSV Eindhoven for what was another highly productive spell, one that suggested an illustrious career in the European game was in the making. However, when PSV baulked at the transfer fee required to make his loan move permanent, his club career began to stall. He moved to England, initially on loan to Aston Villa and subsequently a permanent transfer to Coventry City. During his two seasons in the English top flight his playing opportunities were limited by a combination of the physical demands of the English game and regular international commitments with Ghana; ultimately, he featured in only sixteen league games. Following an argument, a twenty-one-year-old Lamptey also become estranged from the Black Stars, Ghana's national team, playing his thirty-eighth and final international game in 1996 (Rice-Coates, 2017).

The decline of Lamptey's career in this period was partly a consequence of significant difficulties off the field of play, not least those connected with the highly exploitative five-year contract brokered by his Italian agent, Antonio Caliendo, who was among the most recognised football intermediaries at the time. As Lamptey made his first steps into Anderlecht's senior team, Caliendo was able to tie him into this deal by promising him more lucrative contracts with bigger clubs in the future (Kaper, 2019). It has been suggested that young African players in this period willingly acceded to unfavourable terms in the first professional contract they signed because they viewed these deals as a foothold in the European game, and believed that once they had proven themselves, they would possess more bargaining power in subsequent contract negotiations (Broere and van der Drift, 1997; Darby, 2000a). This perspective is suggestive of strategic forms of agency on the part of young African migrant players, but in Lamptey's case his lack of education and youthful naivety meant that he did not fully understand the terms or implications of the contract he was signing, a contract that he subsequently learnt gave Caliendo control over his onward transfers and granted him a generous share of earnings. Initially refusing to talk about his agent during the interview with Paul, Lamptey relented and described his contractual relationship in the following manner: 'So all those years can you imagine that I was just playing football for my agent. I mean, maybe my salary was just increasing, but no signing-on fee. It was terrible. I did not know anything. My education was very bad' (interview, 11 February 2008).

Given that Lamptey was transferred three times in the two seasons between 1995 and 1997, the absence of a signing-on fee, a standard way in which clubs incentivise players to sign for them, is revealing of how he was effectively duped by his agent. His agent's actions, treating him as a tradeable financial asset, undoubtedly held back Lamptey's career and took it in unproductive directions. Otto Pfister, his coach at the 1991 FIFA U-17 World Cup, was very clear on this, arguing that he was 'treated like a piece of meat' by intermediaries: 'He was the most incredible, world-class player who was just wasted because everybody around him was just trying to continuously get something out of him instead of encouraging him to play good football' (interview, 9 February 2008).

With his career trajectory in Europe seemingly in decline, an unconventional transfer to Latin America did little to revive Lamptey's career. However, it was not until he attempted to broker a move from Unión Santa Fe in Argentina back to Anderlecht, that Lamptey became aware of the exploitative nature of his contract with his agent. He turned to the Argentine Football Association, and with their help he was able to extricate himself from his relationship with Caliendo. Lamptey explains how events unfolded:

> I wanted to go back to Anderlecht because I thought I still belonged to Anderlecht. So, when I called, the secretary said, 'No, you don't belong to us. You belong to Caliendo.' I called him at work and said I'm going to Ghana and that I called Anderlecht. Then he became nervous ... so he came down to Buenos Aires and we had a chat and then I called the Argentinean football federation and they said, 'Well, you're free. If you don't have a contract, then you are free.' So, I saw him and he said that I should sign for him, I should sign and he'll be paying me until he finds a club for me, but I refused. So, we had a big fight and then I left there and came to Ghana. And that is where I became free. For all that while I was just playing football for him. (Interview, 11 February 2008)

Released from his contract, it might have been expected that Lamptey would have been able to resurrect his career. However, following his unproductive spell in England and a brief period with Venezia in Italy's Serie B, his visibility and perceived worth had diminished. Unable to attract suitors from the higher echelons of the club game, his mobility became circuitous and was concentrated in lower-level leagues. In an eight-year period beginning in 1997, he moved to clubs in Turkey (Ankaragücü), Portugal (União Leiria), Germany (Greuther Fürth), China (Shandong Luneng) and the United Arab Emirates (Al Nasr Dubai). Lamptey's stay at each club rarely lasted more than a season as he sought opportunities to maximise his earnings. He also experienced personal tragedy along the way, losing four-month-old son Diego to a lung disease while in Argentina and his daughter, Lisa, at the same age to the same disease while playing with Greuther Fürth. He also struggled to adapt to some of the cities he moved to, citing language difficulties as an issue, particularly in the early stages of his career (interview, 11 February 2008).

Reflecting its widespread prevalence in European football in this time period, Lamptey also encountered racism. He experienced racist abuse from opposing fans while in Belgium, but it was in Germany that this issue featured most prominently in his career. Fans of his team, Greuther Fürth, were supportive; however, he was frequently subjected to racial slurs and insults from opposing supporters. He was able to ignore much of the racial vitriol emanating from the terraces (interview, 17 February 2010), but the racism he experienced in his daily interactions with some teammates was more difficult to overlook. As he recounted:

> You know, your own teammates, maybe you enter to the dressing room, you say '*Morgen*' [German for 'morning'], nobody will mind you. But then their colleague will come and say '*Morgen*', everybody will answer. You know it's painful ... Maybe you play on the pitch, they don't want to pass you, they don't want to give you a pass because maybe you are Black ... So all these things make things difficult in Europe. (Interview, 17 February 2010)

Somewhat ironically, his stay at the club in southern Germany was, with the exception of his time at Anderlecht, the most elongated single-club stint of his career, but it was also to herald the end of his playing days in Europe. Following his sojourns in China and the United Arab Emirates, respectively, Lamptey returned to Ghana to sign for Asante Kotoko before seeing out his career in South Africa with Jomo Cosmos.

While the final two moves of his career reflected a desire to continue playing for as long as possible, his return to Africa also allowed him to put in place plans for his post-playing-career life. Following his retirement from the game in 2008, Lamptey resettled back in the nation of his birth, and in what was an unorthodox move for a retired footballer, he established a junior school, the Glow-Lamp International School. Lamptey's motivation was partly rooted in a lingering bitterness about his own lack of formal schooling and his belief that he could have achieved much more in his career and avoided some of the difficulties he encountered had he been better educated. However, his account of the rationale behind his investment in the school is replete with discourses of reciprocity and a sense of himself as socially responsible and a 'caretaker' of youth:

> I did not have a good education when I was growing up. My education was bad and I was very poor and due to that I suffered in my career. I could not understand what I was reading, I was signing things that I did not understand and due to that I lost so many things in life. It's painful and I don't want my children or other children to go through that experience. Because of that I decided to start the school so that people will benefit from it. For me, the best thing that you can give your child is a good education. (Interview, 9 February 2008)

Beyond establishing the school, setting up a cattle and sheep breeding farm on the outskirts of Accra and investing in a range of small businesses, Lamptey, like many other high-profile former migrant players, became involved in the development of the local game. He has taken up a range of roles in this regard, acting as a media commentator, an adviser to the Ghana Football Association (GFA), a coach in the domestic league with Sekondi Eleven Wise, and in 2010 he established a residential youth football academy in the port city of Elmina. As with his school, he framed his investment in the Glow-Lamp Soccer Academy as part of his desire to 'give back' (Acheampong, 2020; Adams, 2018). Nonetheless, the potential economic opportunities that come with developing young Ghanaian football players who are eager to pursue a professional career 'outside' and acquire the trappings of acceptable male adulthood, will not have been lost on a man whose own football career and spatial mobility, circuitous and challenging as it was, ultimately enabled his own social mobility.

Reflecting on Lamptey

This biographical vignette reveals a career trajectory that followed a tumultuous and at times unconventional path, one that might lead some to conclude that Lamptey's experiences are exceptional or atypical in the context of African transnational football migration. His sojourns in and encounters with football markets around the world certainly occurred at a unique juncture in the history of African players' transnational mobilities. As we show in Chapter 2, African players had performed with distinction in the elite football leagues of former colonial powers from as early as the 1910s, most notably in France, Portugal and Belgium. However, it was not until the early 1980s that they began to traverse European borders in more discernible numbers, a trend that accelerated significantly during the 1990s (Alegi, 2010; Darby, 2000a; Lanfranchi and Taylor, 2001). Lamptey constituted part of this transformative period in the flow of African football resources into the European game and further afield and given the profile and reputation he acquired, particularly in the early years of his transnational football career, he can be considered one of the trailblazers of what has since become a much larger outflow of football labour from Africa.

The sourcing, refining and export of African football talent for the global football industry has changed significantly since Lamptey moved to Anderlecht as a fifteen-year-old boy. In chapters 2 and 3, we illustrate how these processes have become much more systematic, speculative, geographically diffuse and have been subject to attempts to more tightly regulate some of the more nefarious elements, particularly the trafficking of minors. However, conceiving of Lamptey's journey as entirely novel or as shaped by forces and factors specific to the time period or the unique personal circumstances within which he carved out a career in the game, brings with it the risk of ignoring the continuities between his transnational mobility and that of the almost 150 Africans who were playing professionally in France by the late 1930s (Murray, 1996), the many migrants who so enriched Portuguese football from 1949 onwards (Cleveland, 2017) and, indeed, all of those Africans who have since traversed the globe in their efforts to fashion a livelihood from professional football. While this book does not seek to tease out or compare the continuities between African migrant footballers across different historical time periods, the value of beginning this study by retelling the story of how Lamptey negotiated his career lies in its foregrounding, vividly in our view, of the core issues and themes that we explore in the chapters that follow.

What we see in Lamptey's biography and what we explore throughout this book, is the interplay between aspirations for and the enactment of spatial mobility through football and the economic, socio-cultural, interpersonal, familial and football contexts in which they are forged. His story provides a revealing window into the myriad forces and dynamics that undergird and shape African football migration and the barriers and challenges that migrant players navigate in their efforts to produce and sustain their mobility. For example, it sheds light on how macro-structural forces, particularly persistent economic inequalities between Africa and the Global North accentuated by the advance of neoliberalism, have created the sort of material conditions in African cities, towns and villages that directly influence the future-making imaginaries and projects of children and youth. In Lamptey's words and actions we also see how the uneven political economy of the global football industry drives the almost relentless pursuit of football-related mobility among increasing numbers of African youth.

The contrast in opportunities to extract a livelihood from football in Ghana and Belgium or between the top league in Senegal and France helps to explain why young, talented African players seek to escape the local football scene on the continent. It also reveals much about why they are prepared to work so hard and go to such lengths in their pursuit of a livelihood from the game. In Lamptey's relationship with Stephen Keshi, we also see how successful, high-profile African migrant players frequently represent a template for young players to follow or idols to aspire to. In his relationship with his agent, we become attuned to how the global football industry can expose young African players to unscrupulous actors who seek to profit from their ambitions and talent. The impact of this relationship on Lamptey's career also reflects the reality of most African players' careers, which are disproportionately played out in lower-level leagues, often require frequent moves to reproduce and sustain mobility, involve difficulties in adapting to foreign climes and are characterised by precarious employment conditions, most notably in the form of low wages and short-term contracts (Poli, 2006a).

In Lamptey's biography, we glimpse the significance of football mobility as a resource for acquiring the sort of social and cultural capital that allows male youth and young men to negotiate a whole series of cultural norms and socially constructed expectations around transitioning from the life phase of youth into social adulthood. In particular, it sensitises us to how a career as a migrant professional footballer enables young men to achieve respectable masculinity and fulfil obligations to family and wider social networks by becoming a 'social giver' (Martin, Ungruhe and Häberlein, 2016). The import of a range of meso- and micro-level actors in providing access to and shaping the material and subjective experiences of Africans' transnational football migration is also writ large across the account of Lamptey's career. What his story reinforces, however, is the fact that African football migrants are social actors who exercise strategic forms of agency in their decision making and actions and who exhibit perseverance, resilience, ingenuity and 'judicious opportunism' (Johnson-Hanks, 2005) in order to acquire and reproduce the livelihoods and cultural capital that accompanies football-related mobility. The post-playing-career phase of Lamptey's story also illuminates the fact that migrant footballers have lives after their retirement. Some become influential in creating opportunities for African youth to enter into transnational football circuits. Others engage in philanthropic activities or support projects that equip African youth with other forms of capital that help them navigate, or at least aspire to, futures beyond football. However, other ex-migrant players experience a range of occupational and personal challenges once their playing days have concluded and many face uncertain and precarious future life courses.

These are among the central concerns of this book. In dealing with them, the book makes a novel contribution to our understanding of sport migration and, more specifically, the complex mobilities of African football players. By engaging with wider sociological, geographical and anthropological literatures on migration and youth mobilities, we also highlight the value of sport as a lens for extending our understanding of the drivers, meaning and experiences of migration and transnational mobility for male African youth and young men more generally.

Methods, localities, scope and ethics

Two core principles underpin the nature of the ethnographic approach that we have employed in our research. Firstly, we follow Marcus's (1995: 96) contention that it is imperative to trace the social formation or object of study 'across and within multiple sites of activity'. Our focus on the mobilities of African footballers, both within and beyond their nation of birth, and how these are rationalised, given meaning and experienced, necessitated multi-sited fieldwork. Thus, much of the empirical data that informs our analysis of the aspirations, experiences and trajectories of African migrant footballers has been gleaned from extensive, multi-sited ethnographic engagement across multiple settings in Ghana, Kenya, South Africa, Sweden, Denmark, Norway, France, Germany, England and Thailand. Key to our multi-sited approach was acknowledging the multifarious social dynamics that emerge between migrants' places of origin and destination contexts, and to examine the transnational interconnectivities that characterise their relations (see Schiller, Basch and Blanc-Szanton, 1992; Vertovec, 2009).

The second principle stems from Levitt and Glick Schiller's (2004) observation that, alongside multi-sited fieldwork, the study of migration should be conducted longitudinally. Thus, our ethnography has been ongoing since January 2008 and has been characterised by both long and short bouts of fieldwork ranging from one week to nine months, totalling two years in duration. This has involved participant and non-participant observation alongside over two hundred in-depth interviews as well as countless informal conversations with young football players and their family members, migrant players at various stages in their careers, football academy owners, directors and coaches, club officials and coaches, football administrators, player agents, journalists and a whole host of other stakeholders who make up the football industry in Africa and beyond.

While our methodological approach facilitated a wide range of vantage points through which we could come to better understand African football migration and the lived experiences of African football migrants, both aspirant and actual, we selected Ghana as the key locale for our data collection and for exploring the research questions at the centre of this book. The rationale for this is fourfold. Firstly, the country has come to feature as one of the most prominent exporters of African football labour to Europe and further afield since the new millennium and, as such, it is firmly entrenched within and illuminates the wider dynamics of the African/global football migration industry. Secondly, and beyond football, Ghana is a country with a deeply rooted and long-standing culture of migration (Black, King and Tiemoko, 2003; Quartey, 2009; Twum-Baah, 2005). As a result of a significant proportion of its citizens possessing what Kalir (2005) refers to as a 'migratory disposition', Ghana represents an ideal case for deeper exploration of football-related migration. Thirdly, we argue that some of the experiences and trajectories of Ghanaian migrant players and those who aspire to a professional career abroad, are broadly generalisable to other African settings, particularly in West Africa. Finally, and partly in recognition of Ferguson's (2006) advice to avoid totalising conceptualisation of 'Africa' as homogenous or undifferentiated, we seek to uncover how African football migration is contoured by local cultural particularities in one setting.

While we make extensive use of the unique, in-depth insights into transnational football migration from Ghana that emerged from our ethnographic fieldwork, we position these within secondary materials, academic and journalistic, that address football migration from elsewhere on the continent. This allows us to broaden the geographic scope of the book and examine football migration from other African contexts, mainly the continent's geographic west. In our fieldwork and engagement with participants, we followed the principles of research integrity and good scientific practice of the funding organisations and respective institutions to which we were and are affiliated. All participants who appear in this book gave their active consent to the interviews and our procedures regarding data collection, analysis and dissemination. Since African migrants in (and outside) Europe are generally considered a 'particularly vulnerable group' according to European Union (EU) research guidelines (European Commission, 2020), we treated the personal information of our research participants in a confidential manner to ensure their anonymity and integrity.

Where we refer to publicly known African players, coaches or other actors in the game and whose career trajectories, including problematic experiences and encounters, have been widely discussed in the media or other academic works, we use their full names (as in the case of Nii Lamptey). In these cases, we carefully considered any potential personal or professional ramifications, and we are content that no harm will arise from narrating their experiences in this book. All remaining participants and organisations are attributed pseudonyms, unless otherwise stated. Overall, all our research participants were informed verbally or in written form about our respective research goals, methods, data handling and dissemination plans. In order to provide the maximum degree of individual safety and comfort, they were further assured of the right to withdraw from our research at any stage.

Overview

The first chapter opens by situating this book within the wider academic discourse on African football migration. Thereafter, it sets out the broad interdisciplinary, analytical framework that we employ to explain the aspirations, experiences and trajectories of African migrant players. The theoretical and conceptual tools that we introduce and sketch out here enable us in subsequent chapters to account for the structural, macro-level determinants and geographical patterning of this process. At the same time, they also help us to explain the practices, subjectivities, agency and (im)mobilities of players and how these have been impacted by wider structural forces, localised cultural norms and beliefs, as well as the ambitions and actions of a whole host of football, and non-football, institutions, stakeholders, actors and intermediaries operating across macro-, meso- and micro-scales.

Chapter 2 examines how Africa has become integrated into the global football marketplace for players. More specifically, in setting out how and why the continent, but particularly West Africa, has become a key exporter of football labour, we unpack the history, geography and changing regulatory features of this process. Chapter 3 examines the key nodes of the African football export industry, and in doing so, it outlines the primary sites that young players typically access and navigate as they pursue a career as a transnationally mobile, professional football player. Given their centrality as the dominant production and export node in this industry, the chapter focuses on the rise and diversity of football academies and explains the divergent philosophies and business models that they adopt.

The next three chapters draw on primary data from our ethnographic fieldwork to detail and explain how young Africans' football-related migratory projects are formed, negotiated, curtailed, enacted and experienced. Focusing on the Ghanaian context, Chapter 4 traces how the post-independence football industry there was transformed from a nationalist social development project where the idea of emigrating to play football did not circulate widely, into a business characteristic of 'millennial capitalism' (Comaroff and Comaroff, 2000). As we show, this resulted in the rapid growth of an export-oriented infrastructure for Ghanaian football and intense speculation over playing talent involving a multitude of actors, ranging from the players themselves, to clubs, football associations, card dealers, managers and recruitment agents.

Chapter 5 examines the rationale behind African youth entering into and transitioning between a series of nodes in the local football industry that they hope will lead to transnational football migration. In so doing, we tease out the economic and cultural drivers that influence their decisions to pursue football as a professional career and a potential source of transnational mobility. Chapter 6 concentrates on how young Ghanaian players experience youth football and academy life and the strategies they deploy and the resources they draw on as they work towards becoming professional migrant footballers. We also examine how these young players encounter, respond to and seek to overcome an inability to translate their considerable physical, emotional and oftentimes financial investments into securing a professional contract abroad and a concomitant 'involuntary immobility' (Carling, 2002).

The next three chapters illuminate players' border crossings into and out of the professional football industry, with a particular focus on European and South-East Asian settings. Chapter 7 follows a number of African players as they make their first tentative steps from academies and clubs in Africa to football markets abroad. We explore their experiences of navigating these moves, both those that are considered conventional, including transfers from academies or feeder clubs, and those that are more unconventional and involve self-organised, highly speculative journeys that can and do expose aspiring migrant players to exploitation and fraudulent actors. Chapter 8 focuses on the various challenges that African migrant players encounter and navigate as they seek to reproduce career mobility in Europe and South-East Asia. Some of these challenges contour the African migrant experience more generally, and include adjusting to a different climate, food, language and culture. Others though, are more specific to football and incorporate the particularities of the football environment, culture, expectations and playing styles of any given club or league. We also interrogate African footballers' social position abroad, particularly their racialisation and experiences of racism in European football industries and how they respond to this.

Chapter 9 explores how African migrant players plan for, manage and negotiate the conclusion of their football career. We show how a neglect of formal education and the absence of other dual-career possibilities frequently limit alternative occupational opportunities for migrant players, resulting in precarious livelihoods characterised by financial difficulties and a declining social status. These can generate significant and (often interconnected) obstacles for players' post-playing-career trajectories, not least by creating a 'status paradox' (Nieswand, 2014), which is a discrepancy between one's social status abroad and at 'home'. However, in keeping with the rest of this book, this chapter illustrates the resourcefulness of African football players as they seek out other ways of reproducing their social mobility and status when their professional playing career concludes, not least by investing in businesses and housing at home and making strategic decisions around remaining abroad or returning to Africa.

In the final, concluding chapter, we highlight what this book reveals empirically and theoretically about African football migration and, by implication, the field of sport migration, and how this connects to the wider literature on migration and youth in Africa more generally. In so doing we argue that the significance of this study extends beyond the narrow confines of sport migration. It makes a much broader contribution to our understanding of how African youth and young men develop migratory aspirations, work towards these, secure and sustain careers abroad and how they navigate their transnational lives. We finish this chapter by outlining emerging key topics for future research in the field of African football migration.

1

Theorising African football migration

Introduction

In setting out the broad theoretical approach and conceptual tools that we employ in this book, this chapter opens with an overview of the state of academic inquiry into transnational African football migration. Our aim is not to engage in an exhaustive review of the extant literature. Rather, we provide a flavour of those issues and themes that have featured on the research agendas of a growing number of scholars working in this field. The focus of our treatment of this literature is on the schism between studies that have emphasised structural, macro-level determinants and those that have foregrounded the experiences and subjectivities of migrating, or aspiring, African players and how these articulate with the local cultural milieus within which they are embedded. The purpose of unpacking this debate is to illustrate that adequately and comprehensively explaining transnational African football migration, in all its temporal phases and complexity, requires an expansive, interdisciplinary theoretical approach. In the second half of the chapter, we sketch out such an approach, one that we argue accommodates a macro-level perspective of the forces both within and beyond the football industry that impact players' migratory projects with analyses of the micro-level agency of these players and how it is influenced and shaped by more localised social, economic and cultural dynamics.

Scholarly perspectives on African football migration

The acceleration of African football migration since 2000, its framing as a process that is deleterious to the game in Africa and, particularly, its intersections with exploitation, irregular migration and human trafficking, has spawned significant interest among journalists, non-governmental organisations and policy makers both within football and outwith (Bale, 2004; Darby, Akindes and Kirwin, 2007; Donnelly and Petherick, 2004; Poli,

2006b). The same period has also witnessed the emergence of a fledgling but growing corpus of multi- and interdisciplinary work that has examined the historical, economic, geographical, social, cultural and sporting dimensions of the mobilities of African football players. Combined, this work provides insights into the decision making and career trajectories of these athletes and the aspirations of those who seek to follow in their footsteps. It tells us much about how players' motivations, decisions and experiences are impacted and shaped by a complex nexus of economic conditions, localised social and cultural norms, actors, intermediaries, institutions and policies operating across macro-, meso- and micro-level scales. It also reveals that the geographical routes that Africans have traversed in pursuit of a sustained career in professional football are diverse, involve intra-national, regional and transnational mobilities that incorporate South–North and South–South movements and encompass regular and 'irregular' forms of mobility.

Beyond examining those who have been able to produce transnational mobility via a contract of employment in the professional football industry, studies have highlighted the problematic experiences of African players in the European football industry, particularly in relation to precarious career courses (Ungruhe, 2018a) and racialisation that frequently characterise their sporting sojourns (Engh, Settler and Agergaard, 2017; Scott, 2015; Ungruhe, 2014). Simply put, while the extant research makes clear that the outcomes of football migration for a minority are characterised by the immense financial rewards and global stardom that come with reaching the highest echelons of European football, the majority experience much more modest, transient and complicated careers (Poli, 2006a).

The research in this field has also begun to address the experiences and subjectivities of those who have been unable to translate their desires and investment of bodily capital into football-related mobility (van der Meij, Darby and Liston, 2017), and whose trajectories get 'stuck' along the way (Büdel, 2013; Hann, 2018; Kovač, 2018; Ungruhe and Büdel, 2016). The findings of this work lay bare the fact that of the countless young players who dream of 'making it' or at least securing a foothold in the professional game 'outside', only a tiny proportion succeed and the reality for the rest is involuntary immobility and uncertain, precarious futures. This work has not only attended to a lacuna in the sport migration literature on the failure of aspiring migrant athletes to produce transnational mobility (Agergaard and Ryba, 2014) but has also responded to growing calls in the wider field of migration studies for research that examines immobility (Arango, 2004; Jónsson, 2011; King, 2012). This concern for the unwanted outcomes of pursuing transnational football mobility has also encompassed important research on those who have been exposed to 'irregular' football-related migration and trafficking (Esson, 2015a, 2020; Esson and Drywood, 2018).

Research since 2010 has taken the scholarship in other novel empirical and theoretical directions. For example, van der Meij (2015), van der Meij and Darby (2014, 2017) and Onwumechili and Akpan's (2019) studies on internal football migration in Ghana and Nigeria, respectively, have drawn attention to the importance of family and household livelihood strategies as mediating influences in this process and how it features as a precursor, real or perceived, to international migration. This widening of the geographical scope of the work is also reflected in research that has examined migratory flows from Africa to Asia and the Middle East as well as those that are intra-continental (Abe, 2018; Akindes, 2013; Cornelissen and Solberg, 2007; Darby and Solberg, 2010; Mukharji, 2008; Poli, 2010a; Rehal, 2015). Adding a further important perspective on this process, Acheampong (2019) and Acheampong, Bouhaouala and Raspaud (2019) have explored the 'give back' practices of African migrant players in Europe, specifically how they have invested into communities in their countries of origin. In doing so, these scholars have begun to uncover how migrant players engage in processes of 'social giving' which have become important in enabling the transition from the social category of youth to adulthood across West Africa and elsewhere on the continent (Martin, Ungruhe and Häberlein, 2016).

This wider developmental potential of football migration and the football academies that play a key role in enabling it, have also been subject to academic scrutiny (Darby, Akindes and Kirwin, 2007; Dubinsky and Schler, 2017, 2019). The experiences and career paths of female African football migrants have also, somewhat belatedly, begun to feature in the literature, with studies outlining the range of constraining and enabling variables at play in their migratory journeys (Agergaard, 2018; Agergaard and Botelho, 2014; Darby and Agergaard, 2018; Engh and Agergaard, 2015; Engh, Settler and Agergaard, 2017). In addition to work on players' motives for returning to Africa at the conclusion of their playing career (Kyeremeh, 2020), emerging scholarship on the post-playing-career trajectories of African players, specifically those who have played in Scandinavia, and the ambivalent forms of precarity they experience points further to the original and heterogeneous directions in which the research is moving (Agergaard and Ungruhe, 2016; Ungruhe and Agergaard, 2020a, 2020b, 2020c).

This growth in the field and the traversing of new and diverse avenues of investigation has reflected the intellectual interests, disciplinary proclivities and associated methodological approaches of the increasing number of scholars who have turned their attention to African football migration. A common thread underpinning this work has been a shift from a macro-structural-level approach to one that seeks to unpack the meso- and micro-level dynamics that shape football-related mobilities. This is accompanied by an examination of how these dynamics are experienced in the geographical locales and cultural settings within which they occur. It should be acknowledged that this shift was initially observed in wider studies of sports labour migration, with Carter's (2011, 2013) anthropological interventions particularly prominent. While not seeking to downplay the significance of the structural contexts within which sport migration takes place, Carter called for much more focus on migrating athletes themselves and the ways that they negotiate and navigate through local conditions in both sending and receiving contexts. For him, much of the existing scholarship did not do this sufficiently, and he argued that 'the major works on sport labour migration … somehow do not have anyone actually moving through space' (Carter, 2011: 7).

Although not necessarily prompted by Carter, the research on African football migration has become more concerned with the lived experiences and subjectivities of migrant and aspiring players and how their actual or desired mobility is forged within the local contexts they inhabit. This analytical shift has reflected some of the wider distinctions in the field of migration studies between historical-structuralist perspectives that ascribe migration to unequal, macro-structural relations between the Global North and South, and approaches that seek to illuminate how the agency of individual migrants determines why they move, how they move and where they move to (Massey *et al.*, 1993; Hammar and Tamas, 1997; Castles and Miller, 1998). Much of the early work on the migration of football labour from Africa, mainly to Europe, tended to follow the former perspective. In drawing on Marxist-inspired theories such as dependency and world system, the analytical optics were pointed predominantly at macro-level dynamics – not least the uneven nature of the global economy and financial disparities within the global football industry – that encouraged young African players to envisage and actively seek out opportunities and futures beyond their nation of birth (Bale, 2004; Darby, 2000a, 2007a, 2007b; Lanfranchi and Taylor, 2001). As such, the migration of African footballers was mainly conceptualised in terms of neocolonial relations and as a process that reflected the domination of 'core' recruiting nations in Europe over 'peripheral' exporting countries in Africa.

This approach to what was at the time an unresearched field, was useful in illustrating a general picture of the economy, patterns and logic underlying this migration process. However, these pioneering studies have been subsequently criticised as portraying, albeit inadvertently, those with the motivation and requisite abilities to become professional footballers abroad as passive pawns, lacking in human agency and responding mechanically to structural forces over which they had little or no control. This was partly a consequence of the fact that the actual lived experiences, careful planning, strategic decision making and resourceful actions of migrant and aspiring migrant players, and how these were informed by local cultural norms and values, were largely overlooked. African migrant footballers clearly operate in a wider economic and structural context and within broader transnational migratory flows that do much to shape their professional career trajectories and aspirations. However, by reducing their decisions and actions to economics, pre-existing routes or the vagaries of supply and demand dynamics in the global football industry alone, the early work was overly deterministic and concealed a wider set of localised social and cultural dynamics that impacted the mobilities of African players. It also downplayed the fact that those considering, attempting to produce or actually engaged in migration through football are agentic social actors who possess the capacity to imagine and act strategically to navigate a path towards achieving their hopes of a better future.

The limitations of this early work have been oft-expressed, not least by the authors of this book. In building towards the theoretical approach that we employ in this study, it is useful to briefly outline the key elements of our critique. Reflecting on his early forays into this field via Wallerstein's (1974, 1979) and Frank's (1969) classic analyses of the asymmetrical nature of global development, Darby (2013b: 44) argued that the importance of local contexts and actors and the agency of players 'makes adhering to and applying a rigid core-periphery framework to a dynamic, multi-faceted process problematic'. In expanding on this point, he observed that such an approach 'constrains us to think about the trade *only* in terms of one-directional economic exchange between a dominant, powerful core and a weak, dependent periphery while also overlooking how local actors respond to global processes' (Darby, 2013b: 44). Darby's co-authored work with Nienke van der Meij (Darby and van der Meij, 2018; van der Meij and Darby, 2014, 2016, 2017) was also rooted in an acknowledgement of the need to move beyond the constraints of a macro-level, economistic approach and it positioned the imaginaries, hopes and actions of young African players squarely within local socio-cultural conditions and relations. More specifically, it explored how meso-level actors (not least family members), locally constructed social norms around intergenerational reciprocity and notions of migration as a family livelihood strategy contoured the football-related (im)mobilities of academy players in Ghana.

Esson's (2013, 2015a, 2015b, 2015c, 2016, 2020) work on both the regular and irregular migration of West African football migrants has been central in pushing for more nuanced, locally grounded and player-centric research in this field. While acknowledging that historical-structuralist theories were and still are 'somewhat appealing', he notes that 'these approaches yield top-heavy determinist accounts that are inattentive to the agency of human actors, particularly the players themselves' (Esson, 2015c: 48). In addition, he suggests that the earlier work 'usually focuses on the practices of European institutions', and as a result, migration 'is viewed from a European perspective' (Esson, 2015b: 1383). In seeking to address these deficiencies and develop a richer understanding of why and how young West Africans pursue football-related mobilities, much more interpretive weight is placed on the rationales underpinning decisions to migrate through football. This has been a critical intervention because, as Esson (2015c: 54) observes, 'ignoring the perceptions of young West African footballers, and viewing migration and mobility as being distinct from broader social relationships, hinders our understanding of African football migration and the agency of the young people involved in this migration process'. Thus, his work has enhanced our understanding of how the migratory aspirations of young West African footballers are informed by local cultural meanings associated with spatial mobility, how their investment of bodily capital in football constitutes an entrepreneurial strategy for navigating the uncertainty and constrained life chances facing them in neoliberal contexts, and how they deploy individual autonomy and resourcefulness in this process. By focusing on these issues, Esson's scholarship has not only yielded rich empirical insights but has also brought research on African football migration into conversation with wider debates on development, mobility and youth agency in the Global South.

Esson's concerns with the macro-structural approach have also been articulated by Ungruhe. In his critique of this work, he argues that African football migration has been framed from a Western perspective which has depicted migrants as 'victims of global economic inequality, exploitative connections and caught up in a modern continuation of colonial links' (Ungruhe, 2016: 1769). While he welcomes the shift to approaches that are more sensitive to the micro-level, he asserts that there remains 'an analytical gap between the ambitions and experiences of migrating players and economic power relations on the one hand and the socio-cultural embedding of the transnational connections in football migration on the other' (Ungruhe, 2016: 1769). His work sets out to connect the imaginaries and lived experiences of young West African football talents to locally embedded socio-cultural understandings of social and spatial mobility. This is particularly prominent in his analyses of the career courses of African players in Scandinavia (Agergaard and Ungruhe, 2016) and Germany (Ungruhe, 2018a), and his studies on why young African men cling to the hope of 'making it' as professional players in Europe, despite the precarity and exceptionally long odds they face in trying to translate this into reality (Ungruhe and Büdel, 2016; Ungruhe and Esson, 2017). It is also apparent in his analysis of the differential reasons for the migration and non-migration of footballers from East and West Africa (Ungruhe and Schmidt, 2020).

We have not been alone in taking the research beyond the early important but somewhat reductive and deterministic analyses. Other scholars have offered interpretations that account for players' agency in directing and negotiating their own pathways and how these are shaped by the socio-cultural contexts they leave and arrive at. For example, Büdel's (2013) study of the travails of Nigerian footballers in Istanbul highlights the complex interplay between these migrants' experience of hardship, including fraud, informality, financial difficulties and injuries, and their ability to act and search out opportunities in the football industry. Engh (2014) and Engh and Agergaard's (2015) research on how female Nigerian migrant players in Scandinavia seek to sustain and reproduce transnational mobility demonstrates the capacity of migrant players to manoeuvre within power geometries of race, class, gender, nationality and religion. Cleveland's (2017) work on the transnational trajectories of African footballers who traversed a range of routes across the Portuguese colonial empire between 1949 and 1975 also offers important insights into the agency of players and the embedding of migratory practices in particular socio-economic, political and cultural settings. Indeed, in foregrounding the calculated nature of players' (and families') migratory decision making and the creative strategies they employed to produce mobility from the colonies to the metropole, Cleveland (2017: 16) contends that his study 'echoes the work of scholars who have dismissed reductive characterisations of African migrant footballers in Europe as "merely tools of European owners", thereby dispelling notions of these athletes as casualties of alleged exploitation'.

Collectively, these innovations in how the transnational migration of African footballers is approached and theorised have significantly enhanced our understanding of this migratory process and the practices and experiences of those involved. However, Carter's (2011: 190) view that 'there is so much more to be done' in understanding transnational sport migration and the experiences of mobile athletes is especially apt in the case of African footballers. Their migratory projects are intensifying and the terrain on which they seek to enact mobility is shifting and taking novel turns. As neoliberalism tightens its grip across the continent, increasing numbers of youth are eschewing other livelihood projects and turning to the game as a vehicle for realising their hopes of a better life. The transnational routes that they target, and traverse, are becoming more diffuse, touching down in the increasing number of countries where the game offers opportunities for an income, modest or otherwise.

Ongoing regulatory change in the global football industry, specifically the possibility of new rules governing the international movement of minors, has the potential to open up more opportunities for transnational football migration (Mason *et al.*, 2019; Yilmaz *et al.*, 2020). This will likely further concretise perceptions of football as a realistic avenue of social and economic betterment among African youth. Since around 2010, the efforts of intermediaries operating at local, national and international scales whose actions can both enable and constrain players' mobility have intensified as they seek to capitalise on these developments. The recruitment networks through which players move have also lengthened and thickened and the institutional arrangements and partnerships designed to facilitate the flow of the continent's most talented youth have taken on new forms, perhaps most notably in the case of African actors or academies purchasing clubs in Europe.

As this migratory process, and the experiences of players therein, takes on new dimensions and becomes more complex, this field of study must also develop, make empirical contributions to knowledge and continue to move in more theoretically cogent directions that are more interdisciplinary than has been the case to date. In making this latter point, we are mindful of Carter's (2011: 191) claims for the primacy of an anthropological perspective in sport migration research, one that he sees as 'absolutely essential'. There is no doubt that his work and other anthropological studies have greatly enhanced our knowledge of sports-related mobilities (Besnier, 2015; Besnier et al., 2018; Besnier, Calabrò and Guinness, 2020; Guinness, 2018; Haß and Schütze, 2019; Hann, 2020; McGee, 2015; Müller, 2013; Rial, 2016; Schieder and Presterudstuen, 2014). However, Klein (2007), an anthropologist himself, has cautioned that pursuing one disciplinary lens in ways that may invalidate others can lead us into unhelpful disciplinary ghettoes that straitjacket our understanding of complex social processes such as sport migration. This view is echoed in Maguire and Falcous's (2011) observations of the research on sport migration. For them, 'the essential point remains, no one discipline alone ... explains all aspects of the phenomena. Instead of denigrating or misrepresenting any one approach a dialogue between advocates of different disciplines is required' (Maguire and Falcous, 2011: 3).

Vigorous academic debate between or within disciplines is to be welcomed and, as the preceding discussion has shown, it has contributed to more empirically robust and theoretically sophisticated work on transnational African football migration. However, disciplinary polemicising, particularly around the value of macro- or micro-level approaches or agency–structure binaries, has the potential to close up potentially fruitful analytical avenues in the study of sport migration. This has long been observed in the development of migration theory more generally, not least by Bakewell (2010: 1689) who contended that 'attempts to develop a robust body of migration theory have been thwarted by a structure–agency impasse'. This monograph traverses this impasse by employing an interdisciplinary, multi-level and temporal approach that emphasises the articulations between structure and agency at particular periods or moments of possibility and transformation, what Johnson-Hanks (2002) refers to as 'vital conjunctures', in the lives and career trajectories of African migrant players. More specifically, a 'vital conjuncture' is 'a socially structured zone of possibility that emerges around specific periods of potential transformation in a life or lives' (Johnson-Hanks, 2002: 871). This concept is used later in the book to examine the specific and momentary configuration of structures within the football industry, while maintaining recognition of young people's agency. The analytical framework that we now propose accommodates the interplay between the macro-, meso- and micro-level dimensions of transnational African football migration, is attuned to the socio-economic and cultural contexts within which it is embedded and attends to the agency of those social actors who engage in or aspire to football-related mobilities.

Transnational African football migration as a global production network

Our theoretical entry point is the interdisciplinary field of global production network (GPN) research which encompasses the cognate global value chain (GVC) perspective. We do not intend to present a deep excavation of this framework. Rather we proceed in this section by sketching out its core elements and highlighting how we use it in this study. The voluminous literature that falls within the GPN canon has its roots in Hopkins and Wallerstein's (1977, 1986) work on commodity chains and Gereffi's seminal studies on GVCs (Gereffi, 1994, 1995, 1996, 1999, 2001; Gereffi and Korzeniewicz, 1994). The latter explores the fragmented but coordinated nature of the global production, distribution and consumption of goods, commodities and services across a range of industries, including, but not limited to, agriculture, electronics, clothing and the automotive industry. Much of this work has employed a heuristic model that examines: the *input–output structures*, or technical components of global production; the *institutional structures* within which the chain or sectors of the chain operate and the agents, agencies and policies that impact on production; the *territoriality* or space through which the chain operates; and the *governance structures* or relations of power between 'lead firms' and other entities in the chain.

Advocates of the GVC model have argued that it allows for nuanced analyses of global political economy (Collins, 2005; Friedland, 2011; Watts and Goodman, 1997). However, critics have raised questions about its theoretical or explanatory value and the extent to which it adequately makes visible and enables consideration of all actors across the production–export chain (Kaplinsky, 2001). Those supportive of a network-centred approach have been particularly vociferous, and in the early 2000s their critique led to the emergence of the GPN framework, the first iteration of which was labelled 'GPN 1.0' (Coe and Yeung, 2019). At its core, GPN theory seeks to capture and explain 'the nexus of interconnected functions and operations through which goods and services are produced, distributed and consumed' (Henderson et al., 2002: 445). It has extended the GVC model in three important respects. Firstly, it views global production as much more dynamically structured, involving horizontal, diagonal and linear interconnections and multi-directional power relations between firms and actors in the Global North and South (Coe, Dicken and Hess, 2008; Coe and Hess, 2013; Dicken et al., 2001; Gibbon and Ponte, 2005). Secondly, while GVC research approaches production from the top down, concentrating its analysis on 'lead' firms at the apex of the chain, the GPN perspective argues for the importance of studying *all* actors in the network, including micro-enterprises and individuals that operate at its base (Kelly, 2013). Thirdly, the notion of 'embeddedness' has become a key analytical construct for GPN analysts, with proponents increasingly emphasising the importance of understanding 'the social dynamics of production' and 'how production networks are embedded in particular kinds of social and power relations' (Philips et al., 2014: 431).

Taken together, these developments are illustrative of a perspective more attuned to the social, political and cultural contexts 'on the ground' within which global production processes are situated and the heterogenous outcomes for the people and places incorporated within GPNs. Despite this, concerns have lingered that the potential for a bottom-up, critical route into explaining global production was not being fully realised in the GPN 1.0 literature (Bair, 2008). A particular issue was the lack of sustained consideration of labour and the failure to conceptualise it as anything other than merely a factor of production, subordinate to the needs of global capital (Coe and Jordhus-Lier, 2011). This issue has begun to be addressed through revisions to GPN work, collectively referred to as 'GPN 2.0', which has brought it into dialogue with a range of fields including labour geographers' research on workers' agency (Coe and Hess, 2013; Coe and Yeung, 2019; McGrath, 2018). While this convergence of labour agency and GPN work is in its infancy, it has illustrated that, irrespective of the industry concerned, a full understanding of global production needs to consider workers, particularly those who labour at the margins of production networks, as sentient, reflexive, agentic actors rather than as passive victims or powerless and expendable inputs to production (Coe and Jordhus-Lier, 2011).

These emerging concerns within GPN research for the socio-cultural embeddedness of production networks, and the forms of agency enacted by those who labour within them, especially those in the Global South, accentuate the value of theorising transnational African football migration through the prism of GPNs. Indeed, both the GVC and GPN perspectives have been productively employed in studies of sport migration, specifically on baseball migration from the Dominican Republic to the United States (Klein, 2011, 2014), the production and export of African football labour (Darby, 2013b; Poli, 2005), and on child recruitment and mobility in the global football industry (Esson *et al.*, 2020; Mason *et al.*, 2019; Yilmaz *et al.*, 2020). However, these frameworks have not been used uncritically or without qualification. While acknowledged as useful in setting out a structural level view of how sport migrants are produced and move through space, the GPN and GVC models have been combined with other concepts to enable more fine-grained analysis of meso- and micro-level dimensions.

This is precisely how we proceed in this book. In short, we consider African football migration as part of a larger production network in the global football industry. The primary purpose of this production network is to facilitate the flow and circulation of talented football labourers who might help satisfy the sporting and economic imperatives of leagues and clubs around the world, but particularly in Europe. In the two chapters that follow, we use the GPN framework to illuminate how African football players have come to represent a key human resource in the global football industry. In Chapter 2, we chart the historical evolution of this process, map its spatial dimensions and provide an overview of the changing regulatory frameworks within which it has operated. In Chapter 3, we set out the key anatomical features or nodes of Africa's transnational football migration industry, paying particular attention to football academies as prominent sites of production. Throughout the rest of the book, and with an eye on the GPN concern for embeddedness, we utilise a range of concepts that have interrogated the cultural foundations of migration in Africa, the relationship between social and spatial mobility there and the ways in which migration features as a strategy for youth to navigate neoliberal contexts across the continent. This allows us to present more of a bottom-up perspective on African players' experiences and encounters across multiple local and transnational nodes of the football industry.

Mindful of the shifting focus from the macro-level to more localised, player-centred analyses in the scholarship on African football migration outlined earlier, we feel it is necessary to make two important qualifications to our use of the GPN framework in this study. Firstly, utilising a perspective and conceptual language that focuses on inert commodities such as agricultural produce, clothing or electrical components might seem like an unusual and somewhat reductionist place to begin when seeking to make sense of the imaginaries, trajectories and mobilities of living, sentient, social actors and their embeddedness in localised socio-economic and cultural contexts. Clearly, footballers are not inert objects or raw materials. Nor are their career aspirations and trajectories wholly dictated by the needs and caprices of those actors and institutions whose business it is to produce and trade talented players in the global football industry. Rather, they are reflective, agentic beings who engage in practices, and manoeuvre, strategise and actively pursue opportunities that might lead to entry into the professional playing ranks of this industry. Furthermore, unlike coffee, clothing or the components of an electrical circuit, the production of a highly skilled, tradeable football player is a much more complex, elongated, non-linear and embodied process that is characterised by highly uncertain and heterogenous outcomes. The same is true for athletes elsewhere in the professional sports industry. As Klein (2014) notes of Dominican baseball players pursuing a professional career in the United States:

> A ballplayer is brought into the production cycle as a boy (a prospect) and becomes a man by the time he reaches completion as a professional ... The trajectory or production path is never wholly predictable, as the player who is being fashioned may move forward in the projected path or may deviate – for good or bad – in any number of ways. He may also leave the chain at one place and return to it in another and in some partially altered way. (Klein, 2014: 20)

As subsequent chapters reveal, these sorts of non-linear trajectories are writ large in the experiences of African migrant footballers and for the overwhelming majority of aspirant players, their recruitment into and navigation through a club, academy or training programme designed to develop their talent into a saleable commodity fails to yield the desired transnational football mobility (van der Meij, Darby and Liston, 2017).

Given the obvious distinction between an inert commodity and agentic footballer, questions might arise as to the compatibility of a GPN approach with this study. However, in keeping with Klein's framing of Dominican baseball players, we argue that professional footballers are not only central in the production of this industry's commodity (as labourers) but they actually constitute the core commodity that is produced, exported and consumed. Brackenridge (2010: 3) captures this view perceptively, arguing that young people either in or on the cusp of professional football constitute 'both worker, a unit of labour, and a commodity, to be traded in international markets'. Other research has shown that young footballers in the Global South, including in West Africa, who play at an amateur level and are unsalaried, understand themselves as *workers* who have embarked on a *career* that requires them to hone and refine their bodily capital into a saleable commodity (Esson, 2013; Meneses, 2013). Additionally, the regulatory systems governing labour within the global football industry, not least provisions that require 'training compensation' to be paid to clubs that train young players who progress into the professional game, further commoditise players and transform them into potent financial assets for clubs (Darby, Esson and Ungruhe, 2018), an issue that we explore in detail in Chapter 4. In short, conceiving actual or aspirant transnationally mobile African football players as both labourer and commodity enables us to consider them within the ambit of the GPN literature.

The second qualification is that engaging with a perspective that examines global production systems might be interpreted as a return to macro-structural analyses that we have previously acknowledged offer only partial insights into the transnational mobilities of African players. However, using the GPN framework does not necessarily involve prioritising industry-level institutions and actors over the lived experiences and subjectivities of migrant football players and the local cultural contexts in which their desires for mobility are fashioned. In chapters 2 and 3, we do use the GPN perspective to present a 'big picture' skeletal outline of the complex networks through which African footballers are produced and become mobile, how these networks are configured or structured organisationally and geographically, the myriad actors and institutions involved and the legal frameworks that regulate player mobilities. However, alongside its value in terms of enabling this sort of industry-level mapping, the ways in which the GPN perspective approaches global production fits well with our focus on the imaginaries, strategies and transnational mobilities of African players. A concern for the localised socio-cultural dynamics within which production occurs and an attentiveness to the agency of those who frequently labour under difficult, precarious conditions at the extremities of production networks are particularly important in this regard.

Social navigation, social infrastructure and African football migration

The incorporation of workers' agency into analyses of GPNs is useful in how we think about the forms of agency enacted by African footballers as they imagine, work towards, produce and sustain transnational mobilities in the professional game. For example, in their analysis of mineworkers in South Africa, Bezuidenhout and Buhlungu (2011: 257) defined labour agency as a concept that can be 'formal or informal, individual or collective, spontaneous or goal directed, sporadic or sustained'. Viewed in this way, the everyday micro-level practices of African footballers are replete with agency that takes different forms and produces differing outcomes depending on the circumstances and settings within which they occur. Acknowledging this is critical in eschewing depictions of young, aspiring African footballers as passive, powerless victims and in considering them as resourceful social actors. That said, while a number of researchers have incorporated disaggregated notions of workers' agency into their analysis of GPNs (Carswell and De Neve, 2013; Kelly, 2013; Lund-Thomsen, 2013; McGrath, 2013), their work does not neglect the broader structural constraints on workers' capacity to reshape the conditions under which they labour. Lund-Thomsen (2013) in particular is careful to acknowledge that labour agency is not only enabled and constrained by the 'vertical' structures of GPNs but also by horizontal dimensions such as the embeddedness of workers in local places, institutional contexts, communities and households. This is an important point when we consider how young people across the African continent enact agency in the pursuit of migration through football. In particular, it highlights the fact that the realisation of their ambitions is enabled and constrained not only by the vertical organisational structure and regulatory features of football's GPN but also by the localised socio-cultural and economic conditions and meanings that contour their everyday lives.

In seeking to explain this complex interplay between agency and structure in the lives of aspiring or transnationally mobile African footballers, we are drawn to the concepts of social navigation and social infrastructure. The term 'navigation' is fairly common in the social science lexicon and is taken to refer to how people act in difficult or uncertain circumstances and how they attempt to move through structural constraints towards better positions. Our usage is informed by Vigh's (2009) conceptualisation of social navigation in his study of how young urban men in Guinea-Bissau attempt to build better lives. In defining social navigation, he employs the idea of 'motion squared' or 'motion within motion' to explain how social actors engage in 'the act of moving in an environment that is wavering and unsettled' (Vigh, 2009: 420). Social navigation then is a type of creative, youthful agency that entails calculated, resourceful and judicious decision making and actions in unstable environments. For Vigh (2009: 420), conceptualising social navigation in this way 'grants us an analytical optic which allows us to focus on how people move and manage within situations of flux and change'. Crucially, it also draws attention to how the continuous interaction between social actions and the wider social environment within which individuals are positioned informs how 'we act, adjust and attune our strategies and tactics in relation to the way we experience and imagine and anticipate the movement and influence of social forces' (Vigh, 2009: 420).

A social navigation perspective has been usefully employed to describe youth agency in a range of African settings beyond Guinea-Bissau, including in

Ghana (Langevang, 2008), Cameroon (Waage, 2006) and Sierra Leone (Finn and Oldfield, 2015). It has also been applied to how Ghanaian youth aspire to a football career abroad and how they negotiate involuntary immobility (Esson, 2015b; van der Meij and Darby, 2017). Collectively, this work reveals that despite living in environments characterised by socio-economic insecurity and labour market restructuring that curtails their life chances, African youth exhibit resourceful and entrepreneurial forms of agency through their everyday decisions, choices and practices. In applying a social navigation perspective in this book, we contend, like Vigh (2009), that in order to understand how actors navigate environments that are unsettled and wavering, it is crucial to understand the wider social and cultural conditions within which they are embedded and how this influences the tactics and strategies employed by young people. This echoes the advocacy in GPN research for studies that explore the horizontal embeddedness of production in particular social and cultural settings and how this impacts the decisions and practices of labourers.

Alongside our use of social navigation, we use the concept of social infrastructure to examine both the discursive and socio-material conditions that shape people's everyday practices and then to identify how these practices enable people to negotiate structural constraints to improve their life chances through football migration. Social infrastructure denotes the ways in which socio-material relations within society are created and maintained through the actions of people (Simone, 2004). Influenced by McFarlane and Silver (2017), we pay particular attention to three dimensions of practice within a people-oriented conceptualisation of social infrastructure. *Consolidation* refers to the practices of those seeking to attain a more secure social or economic position through football. *Coordination* is the capacity to organise social, economic or political activities in the football industry through a more consolidated position within this domain. *Speculation* is the practice of envisaging and acting into the future by taking calculated risks about how to accrue social mobility through football.

Social infrastructure then becomes a way to better account for the mobilities and geographies of life in the margins of football's GPN. Utilising an 'infrastructure' lens also offers a novel way to qualify some of the implicit mechanistic tendencies of GPN approaches, and to tease out some of the lesser-known multi-scalar relations enabling the production of talent (cf. McGrath, 2018). This allows us to provide insights on structures at a macro scale, while remaining attentive to the myriad interpersonal relationships enmeshed within mediating drivers of African football migration – that is, the factors that 'enable, facilitate, constrain, accelerate or consolidate migration' (van Hear, Bakewell and Long, 2018: 932). More specifically, we employ the term 'drivers' to denote an assortment of relational factors that generate the structural elements influencing the social contexts in which football migration is possible.

In this book, we argue that while football migration has unique characteristics and dynamics, it should not be viewed as distinctive from other forms of spatial mobility in Africa, and that it needs to be understood as rooted in the same contexts that drive these wider mobilities. To proceed in this way, it is necessary to bring insights from African football migrants and those with hopes of becoming mobile through football into conversation with the wider scholarship on the lived experiences of African youth, how they navigate a path to social mobility and respectable adulthood, and the significance of spatial mobility in this process. In bringing this chapter to a close, we begin to tease out how this scholarship informs our analysis of African football migration.

Localising transnational African football migration

Migration is a deeply rooted cultural practice in African societies, one that has been productively analysed via a 'culture of migration' lens. This concept has been employed by a range of scholars to explain migrant motivations and how they are constructed by focusing on the socio-cultural meanings attached to the process of leaving one's home to live elsewhere (Boswell, 2008; de Haan and Rogaly, 2002; de Haas, 2010; Kandel and Massey, 2002; Rigg, 2007; White, 2009; Wilson, 2010). This research has shown that it is not only the potential of economic gains and increased professional opportunities that underpin the desire to migrate but also the social prestige or status attributed to migrants by those in the sending context. It also illustrates that the acquisition of the markers of such status, or at least a belief that they can be achieved through spatial mobility, can lead to migration becoming a deeply embedded social norm (de Haas, 2010), giving rise to the prevalence of a 'migratory disposition' (Kalir, 2005). This disposition is tied to a perception that the possibility of improving one's future life chances while residing at 'home' is highly unlikely (Hernández-Carretero and Carling, 2012; Jónsson, 2008; Simone, 2005; Kleist, 2017).

It is hardly surprising that this concept has been used to explain the rationales of migrants, or aspiring migrants, in Africa. Bluntly stated, Africa is a continent with a culture of migration *par excellence*. Quantitatively, both internal and international migration are hugely prominent. This is because in African contexts mobility is 'engrained in the history, daily life and experiences of people' (de Bruijn, van Dijk and Foeken, 2001: 1). Regional migration has been an important livelihood strategy among young men since the early twentieth century, and this continues apace with growing numbers of young males and females moving from rural communities to industrial centres, cities or other urban settings to find work, marriage partners, educational opportunities and participation in perceived modern lifestyles (Adepoju, 1998; Ungruhe, 2010, 2011; Whitehead, Hashim and Iversen, 2007). Equally, there are increasing numbers of young people from all over the continent migrating or aspiring to migrate to Europe, North America and elsewhere (Adepoju, 2006; Kleist, 2017; Nyamnjoh, 2013; Nyamnjoh and Page, 2002). As a consequence, migration constitutes a deeply rooted, everyday practice in Africa, challenging popular notions that it is driven solely by precarity and desperation in African settings (Beauchemin, 2018; Flahaux and de Haas, 2016).

For Klute and Hahn (2007: 1), the value of a 'culture of migration' lens is that it involves 'orienting our research towards the meanings of migration for migrants themselves'. This resonates with how we seek to theorise transnational African football migration. Not only does applying this concept position players and their perspectives at the centre of our study, it also allows us to more fully explicate the non-economic dimensions of football migration and to further challenge depictions of players as passive and non-agentic, moved by and at the mercy of global economic inequalities. In short, we propose that a 'culture of migration' lens is appropriate to explain the significance of African youth migrating, or aspiring to migrate, through football. More importantly, our use of this concept encourages us to situate these processes within the social and cultural meanings of mobility for youth and the relationship between social and spatial mobility in African societies.

In order to make sense of transnational African football migration in this way, we follow studies on youth in African contexts that have focused on its dynamic and relational characteristics, and that have illustrated how generational positions such as childhood, youth and adulthood are neither natural, fixed nor predetermined but arise out of socio-cultural contexts and power relations (Christiansen, Utas and Vigh, 2006; Honwana and De Boeck, 2005; Johnson-Hanks, 2002). Thus, youth is not primarily defined by age, by a certain stage of psychological and biological development or by legal standards, but rather is a fluid category that reflects local sociocultural understandings of social status and of one's position (and self-positioning) in the life course. Hence, we use the term 'youth' to refer to those (young) people whose specific social, economic and cultural capital as well as their individual social relations assign them to a particular position in society that implies certain rights and duties, moral and social expectations, experiences and means that differ from those of adults and children (Ungruhe, 2018b). On the one hand, youth are those who are beyond the life phase of childhood with its rather limited degree of social, political and economic responsibilities, ambitions and autonomy (Honwana, 2014; Langevang, 2008). On the other, while youth have not (yet) reached the sphere of social adulthood and the responsibilities and recognition connected to it in their society, their various forms of capital and social relations hold the promise of achieving social maturity in the near future (Hann, 2018; Jeffrey, 2010, 2012; Thieme, 2018).

Conceptualised in this way, 'youth' constitutes a generational position that young people inhabit, move within and seek to escape. Their experiences of this position, the meanings they attach to it and the strategies they employ in negotiating it are shaped by the interplay between their agency and the wider socio-economic and cultural contexts in which they are located. Across the African continent, radical restructuring of economic and social life, heralded by neoliberal reforms introduced in the 1980s, has had a pronounced impact on youth. In particular, young people have experienced forms of marginalisation that have seen their life chances restricted, opportunities to acquire the social and economic markers of adulthood constrained and their aspirations to participate in and feel connected to a perceived modern global youth culture curtailed (Alacovska, Langevang and Steedman, 2020; Esson, Amankwaa and Mensah, 2020; Thieme, 2018). The fact that around two-thirds of the African population are referred to as youth and children according to the African Union (cited in Martin, Ungruhe and Häberlein, 2016) indicates that these experiences are widespread across the continent.

Studies of the uncertain and ambivalent futures faced by youth in the neoliberal era have employed notions of 'crisis', hopelessness and decline as metaphors to describe their life chances (Richards, 2005; Cruise O'Brien, 1996; Hansen, 2005; Resnick and Thurlow, 2015). The social category of youth as it is lived in African settings has also been depicted negatively as involving a time of 'waithood' (Honwana, 2014), of being 'stuck' (Sommers, 2011) or even as 'social death' (Vigh, 2006b). While acknowledging the creative potential of youth, this work tends to reproduce a sense of youth as powerless and passive and in doing so underplays the hopeful imaginaries of young people across the continent, how they plan and set out to fulfil these imaginaries and the agentic practices they engage in (Martin, Ungruhe and Häberlein, 2016; Oldenburg, 2019; Ungruhe, 2019; Ungruhe, Röschenthaler and Diawara, 2019). As Enria (2018: 117) argues in her study of the place of youth in labour markets in Sierra Leone, characterising youthhood in a predominantly pessimistic manner can 'obscure from analytical view the complexity, dynamism and creativity of the navigational now'. The predominant negative connotation of the lifeworlds of youth in African settings reflects a general trend in academic and public discourses to think of Africa through a lens of crisis. Such a predisposition is particularly problematic since it manifests the oversimplified and stereotypical notion of African inferiority and otherness. It is precisely such an 'African crisism' that we want to challenge through our in-depth exploration of young African football talents' trajectories and transnational mobilities. In doing so, our use of the concept of social navigation helps us to avoid overly bleak, sobering depictions of African youth. Without overlooking the very real structural constraints posed by the economic and political contexts in which they live, a social navigation perspective allows us to bring into analytical focus the creative choices and actions of young football players as they seek out and pursue new pathways towards their imagined futures.

In accounting for the rationales of migrant and aspiring African footballers and how these are embedded in local cultural contexts, we also take cognisance of the literature on how youth in Africa acquire the social, economic and cultural markers of respectable adulthood as part of a process of 'social becoming' (Ansell et al., 2018; Honwana and De Boeck, 2005; Langevang and Gough, 2009; Waage, 2006). This research has illustrated that social adulthood is characterised by the achievement of higher social standing in one's environment and that it brings with it an increase in both authority and social obligation. Marriage and social reproduction often constitute the most important threshold to maturity with educational and economic success also critical. Possessing the means to become a 'social giver' (Martin, Ungruhe and Häberlein, 2016) and to take responsibility for one's extended family are equally important in reaching social adulthood (Coe, 2020; Kabeer, 2000; Langevang, 2008; Martin, Ungruhe and Häberlein, 2016). This is particularly the case for youth and young men for whom becoming a 'giver' and being able to provide for one's family are critical features in the reproduction of acceptable masculinity (Esson, Amankwaa, and Mensah, 2020; Hann, 2018; Ratele, 2008; Wignall, 2016).

Viewed through this research, the allure of football for African youth is not simply that it represents a mere distraction from a precarious present and uncertain future or as a way to fill time in a period of suspension between childhood and adulthood. This may well be the case for those who do not possess or are unlikely to develop, the athletic prowess necessary to play at a standard that offers access to recruitment networks or nodes where they can pique the interest of potential overseas suitors in the football industry. Rather, as we show in this book, it has increasingly become the case that talented young players across the continent, but predominantly in West Africa, are investing their bodily capital in the game. This is due to the perceived possibilities football offers for spatial mobility, as a strategy for circumventing the blockages to social becoming and the futures they aspire to.

Our analysis of the growing stock placed in transnational football migration as a route to social becoming by African youth is also underpinned by research on the ways in which spatial mobility in Africa and elsewhere in the Global South has come to be seen as emblematic of social status, and a central component of strategies to better one's life (Howard and Boyden, 2013; Gough, 2008; Jua, 2003; Nyamnjoh and Page, 2002; Porter et al., 2010; Salazar, 2011). Rooted in a long-standing culture of internal labour migration in Africa, moving from a rural environment to an urban one is understood to form part of a 'rite of passage' towards what are envisaged as better futures and social adulthood (Thorsen, 2006). For youth in African urban settings, embarking on international migration to Europe or North America is viewed as involving a similar kind of transition (Langevang and Gough, 2009; Nyamnjoh and Page, 2002; Simone, 2005). Beyond the longer-term hopes of contributing to social adulthood, internal rural–urban and international migration has also taken on significance as a way of satisfying the more immediate needs of participating in a perceived modern, global youth culture. For many young people across the continent, connecting themselves to this culture and enjoying a modern life phase of adventure, freedom, pleasure and consumption – and with it, acquiring social status in the here and now – are as important as figuring out pathways to future social adulthood. With access to and participation in this youth culture often restricted for contemporary African youth, the lustre of spatial mobility for young people becomes enhanced (Bleck and Lodermeier, 2020; Thorsen, 2006; Ungruhe, 2010).

Beyond the role of spatial mobility in enabling individualised forms of social advancement, the migration of young people is often undergirded by the needs and aspirations of the family. In this, the cultural norm of an intergenerational contract becomes visible (Bleck and Lodermeier, 2020; Coe, 2012; Kabeer, 2000; Roth, 2008; Twum-Danso, 2009; Whitehead, Hashim and Iversen, 2007). This is a deeply embedded social norm that operates across West Africa and is rooted in the principles of reciprocity and entrustment. In Ghana, for example, in return for the support of parents, older siblings or relatives, youth are expected to conform to culturally produced obligations to support the family. The requirement to live up to these obligations becomes more acute as they get older and achieving the means to meet them is a vital part of the journey towards adult respectability and 'becoming a somebody' (Coe, 2012; Langevang, 2008; Ungruhe and Esson, 2017). Informed by some of the wider scholarship on the role of families or households in migration (Massey et al., 1993; Tiemoko, 2004), de Haas (2010: 246) argues that migration frequently constitutes a household livelihood strategy 'to diversify income sources and overcome social, economic, institutional development constraints in the place of origin'. This literature is also important in localising transnational African football migration and it helps us to demonstrate in subsequent chapters how locally embedded, collectivist social norms around intra-family relations contour aspirations for and experiences of pursuing a career in professional football abroad.

Conclusions

This chapter has introduced and outlined the constituent parts of the interdisciplinary theoretical framework that we employ in this book. This framework enables us in chapters 2 and 3 to position transnational African football migration within the structures and dynamics of the global football industry, an industry like others where the mobility of labour is often contoured by wider global economic disparities. As we have argued, however, a macro-level, industry-centric perspective, important as it is, is insufficient in adequately capturing the complexity of the motivations, movements and experiences of African players at various temporal stages in their football-related migratory projects. Thus, we have pointed up some of the more prominent concepts and research that underpin how we make sense of the lived experiences and subjectivities of African youth and adults as they seek to produce and sustain transnational mobility through football.

Our player-centric perspective is also concerned with how these individuals use football to navigate through localised, often challenging socio-economic and cultural conditions. Our analysis of their career trajectories from Chapter 4 onwards is, therefore, brought into conversation with wider writing on, for example, what it is to be a youth in African settings and how to become an adult, the cultural meanings of spatial mobility for young people and the importance of familial obligations in creating and pursuing routes to future lives and livelihoods. The ground that we cover in this chapter is by no means exhaustive and it has not been our intention to undertake an excavation of each and every piece of research or concept that we use in subsequent chapters. While we have focused on the core elements of our framework, we leave space in subsequent chapters for introducing other ideas that usefully illuminate particular dimensions of transnational African football migration and that complement our broad theoretical approach.

2

The history, geography and regulation of African football migration

Introduction

Sitting in a shaded courtyard at the administrative offices of Liberty Professionals FC, a Ghanaian Premier League club based in Dansoman on the outskirts of Accra, Cecil Jones Attuquayefio, the club's technical director, set out an illuminating overview of the emergence and evolution of transnational football migration in Ghana:

> I remember very well, before the overthrow of the president [Kwame Nkrumah in 1966] nobody from here went outside to play football. We thought football was going to grow in this country to be equal to outside but after the government was overthrown, there were few opportunities for us to go abroad. Some teams in America wanted players but the authorities at that time didn't believe that football in America was played under the auspices of FIFA. So, we were prevented from going. There was even a signed policy that said that people were not allowed to go, but some went to America, about five players … The government felt that these players were not serious about the national team and they were not invited to play for the national team when they left … The American embassy felt that it was wrong for the authorities to force a player against his will so we were more relaxed about it but it was difficult. (Interview, 20 January 2009)

Beyond the Ghanaian government's prohibition of player migration at this time, Attuquayefio also highlighted the perspectives of players themselves and, in particular, their concerns about what migrating through football might involve:

> I remember one particular player [Ibrahim Sunday], who went on to become the captain of the Black Stars, who left for Germany. The players were not happy to see their teammates go away. Then, there were no proper arrangements. We had a situation where the feeling was that players were going into slavery and that players were being smuggled out of the country to play in another country. People did not trust one another in that regard because there were no regulations and the clubs would make it very difficult for a player to go. (Interview, 20 January 2009)

As Attuquayefio recalled, however, during the 1980s and 1990s, a recognition of the potential financial rewards of players' migration for clubs and footballers, clearer regulation of international transfers and enhanced opportunities for young Ghanaian players to make their abilities visible to potential overseas employers in the football industry prompted a more sustained outflow of Ghanaian football talent:

> Then, the clubs realised that if you allow a player to go you could get money for them and that would put you in a strong position and they changed their perception and realised that it would be better to negotiate with other teams. That also became possible when FIFA introduced transfer regulations ... Yes, I remember Kuffour and his group, the group that played in the [1991] World Cup at U-17 level, a lot of them went abroad, to Italy when they won ... The football public were happy that by playing in that level of competition, they had the opportunity to go away. Even though the money they were going to receive in their clubs was small, they were going to earn more than they were in Ghana. (Interview, 20 January 2009)

Highly venerated in Ghana and much respected in football circles around the continent, Attuquayefio was well positioned to offer this astute assessment. Born in 1944, he played for a number of Ghana's most prestigious club sides between 1962 and 1974, and spent almost a decade representing the national team, the Black Stars, with whom he won the 1965 Africa Cup of Nations. As well as holding senior positions in the GFA, he had a long and illustrious career as a coach in the domestic Ghanaian game and at international youth and senior level, managing Ghana's U-17 and U-23 teams, acting as assistant coach to the Black Stars and leading Benin to the Africa Cup of Nations in 2004. As such, he had direct encounters with the processes, individuals and events depicted in his account.

While what Attuquayefio describes in this excerpt relates to Ghana, a country whose players were relative latecomers to football fields beyond their nation of birth, his recollections speak to the intersections between African football migration and the evolution and politics of the game elsewhere on the continent. In his referencing of the place of America as a destination for some of the country's first transnationally mobile footballers and their subsequent migrations to Europe in the late 1980s and early 1990s, we begin to get a sense of the spatially dispersed nature of Ghanaian players' career trajectories. The changing regulatory context within which these careers have been constrained and enabled is also writ large in this account. It is these three themes – the historical, spatial and regulatory dimensions of African footballers' transnational mobilities – that constitute the focus of this chapter.

While subsequent chapters engage in more fine-grained analyses that localise African players' aspirations, experiences and trajectories in the particularities of the social, cultural and economic milieus within which they are fashioned, this chapter and the next take a wider view. Both chapters harness the core tenets of the GPN framework to garner analytical purchase on Africa's, and more specifically West Africa's, status as a critical production and export centre in the global football labour market. In the next chapter, we identify and describe the key production sites or nodes where African youth hone their bodily capital and through which they hope to enact transnational mobility as professional football players overseas. Before then and in keeping with the emphasis in the GPN canon on the territorial distribution of products or commodities and the institutional and regulatory environment that shapes how production and export proceeds, this chapter examines the spatial dynamics of transnational African football migration from the colonial period through to the twenty-first century and accounts for the changing regulatory context within which the mobilities of African players have been produced and reproduced.

The pervasiveness of football in Africa

The vaunted social and cultural significance of football in contemporary African societies and its place in the migratory projects of youth are deeply rooted, extending far beyond the increasing media-fuelled ubiquity of the game, back into Africa's colonial past. While a detailed treatment of the game's social and political development on the continent is not necessary here, a historical sensitivity to its introduction and growth in African societies is important in understanding why it is such a pervasive cultural practice and has featured so prominently in the consciousness of generations of young Africans as they imagine and plot their futures. Diffused to the continent as part of the wider European colonial project in the late nineteenth and early twentieth centuries, football quickly captured the imagination of indigenous populations and acquired mass popular appeal (Alegi, 2010; Darby, 2002; Stuart, 1995; Mangan, 1998). It is difficult to generalise about the specifics of these processes in a geographical setting as vast and culturally diverse as Africa. However, there were some common features that led to football supplanting existing, pre-colonial cultures of games, sports and dance, and becoming the continent's pre-eminent sporting pastime.

In the late nineteenth and early twentieth centuries, European educators and the schools they established were instrumental in introducing the game initially to African elites who quickly took to it partly to acquire the higher social status that accompanied cultural imitation of their colonial 'masters' (Darby, 2002; Stuart, 1995). Contact with European settlers, traders and soldiers was crucial in the downward diffusion and dissemination of football to the labouring classes in rapidly expanding industrial, urbanised settings. A belief in the perceived civilising and educative capacity of football led to Christian missionaries promoting the game as part of the broader missionary impulse and as a vehicle to recruit local people to churches (Mangan, 1998). The view that the provision of constructive, rational leisure opportunities would help instil positive character traits in African colonial subjects was also shared by colonial administrators; they organised and promoted football clubs and leagues as a method of minimising tendencies for the expression of anti-colonial resentment and maintaining the colonial order, particularly in crowded, industrialised cities (Darby, 2000a).

Beyond the influence of colonial administrators, churchmen, educators, traders and settlers in the game's growth and popularisation, Africans quickly appropriated football for their own ends in ways that enhanced its growing prominence in the continent's sporting landscape. The game's emerging status as a site for anti-colonial sentiment and the articulation of nascent nationalism in the post-war period in North Africa, the Belgian Congo, Tanzania, Zanzibar, Ghana, Nigeria and Algeria was particularly important in this regard (Alegi, 2010; Boer, 2006; Darby, 2013a; Fair, 1997; Fates, 2004; Hawkey, 2009; Lema, 1989; Martin, 1991; Ndee, 1996; Versi, 1986). In his survey of the relationship between football, nationhood and the movement for independence in late colonial Africa, Stuart (1995: 34) summarised the central argument of the small, but important, historiography on football in Africa by pointing to the fact that the game became 'an embodiment of the political aspirations of the African people' and was utilised as an 'expression of defiance towards the state and of independence from their colonial oppressors'.

As independence movements came to fruition across the continent, the game's radical political pedigree further stitched it into the fabric of African cultural and political life. In the immediate post-colonial period, some of the leaders of newly independent African nations, not least Kwame Nkrumah, the Ghanaian father of pan-Africanism, invested financially and ideologically in football as a vehicle both for national and continental unity and for pursuing recognition in the post-colonial world (Darby, 2013a). The establishment of national leagues, the development of continental competition and investment in national teams, identified as important in mobilising youth around a common sense of national identity, aided the continued upward trajectory in the game's popularity.

An expanding African constituency within FIFA from the late 1950s onwards ensured that international tournaments, particularly the World Cup and newly instituted international youth competitions, better accommodated African national teams, and their participation and successes contributed further to the embedding of football as one of the continent's most prominent social practices (Darby, 2002, 2005). While local domestic leagues in the late twentieth and early twenty-first centuries have been beset with financial and management issues that have at times constricted their growth (Onwumechili, 2020), the influence of television has further propelled the game's status in Africa. The expansion of television audiences, a consequence of de-regulation and technological improvements in the 1990s, saw the continent become an important television market, and a range of transnational media conglomerates and satellite broadcasters fed the growing appetite for coverage of elite European leagues and of migrant African players participating in these leagues (Alegi, 2010; Akindes, 2010; Akpan, 2020). As was clear in the excerpt of the interview with Cecil Jones Attuquayefio that opened this chapter, the migration of the most highly skilled African players was intimately entwined with this broader social and political history of the game. Furthermore, the growing popularity and pervasiveness of football in the consciousness of children and youth, mainly male but increasingly female, and their understanding of the game as a potential route to spatial and social mobility has been due in no small measure to the long-standing and spatially diverse transnational mobilities of African players that we now unpack.

Football migration in colonial Africa

A useful starting point in seeking to understand the history and territorial configuration of colonial, post-colonial and contemporary transnational African football migration is to recognise that both the aspiration and enactment of this highly prized form of mobility has been unevenly distributed across the continent. Players from a range of regions, particularly western, northern, southern, Lusophone and Central Africa, featured to varying degrees in the outflow of migrant football talent during the colonial and post-colonial periods. However, what contemporary transnational football migration from Africa reveals is that in the early twenty-first century it is spatially concentrated, emanating predominantly from core production and export 'zones' in West Africa; however, at the same time, the destinations where African players arrive and circulate through have become geographically diffuse (Darby, 2000b; Poli, 2006b). Our intention in highlighting these regional differences up front is not to render insignificant the football-related mobilities from outside those regions or countries that are prominent in the export trade. Rather, foregrounding these differences enables us to avoid producing overly generalised, homogenising perspectives of 'Africa' and 'African football migration' and to acknowledge not only the diversity of the continent but also the multifarious and context-specific social, economic and cultural drivers of transnational football migration (Darby and Solberg, 2010; Ungruhe and Schmidt, 2020). Emphasising territorial difference also justifies our disproportionate coverage in the remainder of this chapter and the next on those regions and countries that both at the time of writing and historically have been focal points for football migration.

The roots of African football migration can be located mainly in the coastal west and northern stretches of the continent, with players from these regions having migrated beyond their national borders to play in foreign fields, predominantly in Europe, for over a century. It should come as no surprise that the initiation and early development of this process was heavily contoured by colonial encounters. This was particularly the case for players from Francophone Africa, most notably those from the French North African territories of Algeria, Morocco and, to a lesser extent, Tunisia. By 1938, more than 140 had sought out playing opportunities in the French game following its professionalisation in 1932, many of whom combined their athletic endeavours with study or other forms of work (Lanfranchi and Taylor, 2001; Murray, 1996).

Unlike these early migrants, Moroccan-born Larbi Ben Barek constituted what Lanfranchi and Taylor (2001) described as 'a new type of African import', given that his transfer to Marseille in 1938 was his sole reason for moving to France. His uniqueness extended to the fact that he was the first African-born player to represent France, making his debut for the national team just four months after his arrival in the 'motherland' and quickly becoming a 'French icon' (Lanfranchi and Taylor, 2001). In doing so, and as an outworking of the French colonial policy of Gallicisation or the assimilation of those from colonial territory into the French metropole (Albertini and Wirz, 1982), Ben Barek paved the way for the numerous African players who have subsequently played for France (Darby, 2000b). The route from Francophone North Africa to the professional game in France continued to be well trodden after the Second World War, with seventy-six Algerians, thirty-four Moroccans and seven Tunisians making the journey northwards between 1945 and 1962 (Barreaud, 1998).

Although the tradition of Senegalese players in France extends back to the signing of Raoul Diagne by Racing Club de Paris in 1930, it was in the post-war period that players from Francophone West Africa, particularly Côte d'Ivoire, Mali and Cameroon began to populate the rosters of French clubs; by 1960 their number exceeded forty. All were effectively French citizens before their move, and while for some, education was the primary reason for their migration, others moved specifically to take up opportunities to play football professionally (Alegi, 2010; Lanfranchi and Taylor, 2001). That they did so was a consequence of their own personal ambitions, the attractiveness of cheap labour for French clubs in the austerity of the post-war period and the exemption of players from the colonies from a rule, instituted in 1955, that banned foreign players from the French game (Dubois, 2010).

The other primary destination for African migrant players during the colonial era was Portugal. While not as quantitatively significant as the outflow of North and West African talent to France, those players who did make the move captured the imagination of football fans in the colonies and made a significant contribution to the fortunes of the clubs that recruited them. Temporally, their entry into the Portuguese game lagged behind the migration of their counterparts from Francophone Africa. Although a few players from Lusophone Africa had moved to the metropole prior to the Second World War (Alegi, 2010), it was not until the 1950s that appreciable numbers moved from Portugal's 'overseas territories', particularly Mozambique and Angola (Cleveland, 2017). This reflected the unfolding political and racial history of the game in Lusophone Africa. Despite being racially segregated, football was popular among indigenous populations and the establishment of African leagues and clubs in the 1920s and 1930s provided an organised structure for their participation. The subsequent de-racialisation of the game, uneven as it was, and the initial entry into the lower reaches of formerly whites-only leagues as a precursor to joining elite colonial leagues and clubs, furnished local players with the cultural, linguistic and sporting traits that would later ease their transition to Portugal. Critically, it also provided a platform for talented players to make visible their abilities and potential prior to the lifting of restrictive rules on the transfer of players from the colonies to the metropole (Cleveland, 2017).

A decline in the performances of the Portuguese national team and a desire on the part of domestic teams to sign players from the colonies led to Antonio Salazaar's regime liberalising the regulations on player transfers; from 1949, Portuguese clubs were officially free to recruit Africans. While this immediately led to an active and at times aggressive search to mine African talent, it should be recognised that local players were more than mere athletic fodder but rather engaged in shrewd, calculated and highly strategic practices and decision making that sought to extract maximum benefits from the opportunities that had been opened up. As Cleveland cogently observed:

> The players and their parents hardly conducted themselves like star-struck, pliable rubes during the negotiatory process in which they were engaged. Many played rival suitors off one another, declined clubs' initial approaches in the hopes of receiving improved offers, or simply rebuffed overtures. Moreover, many of the guardians of their talented sons foresightedly prioritised life beyond football, which prompted many African players to eschew the major clubs in favour of Académica de Coimbra, where they could pursue both the sport and their studies ... In this fashion, African prospects were actively shaping their own football and post-football futures. (Cleveland, 2017: 99)

Facilitated by the Indigenous Peoples Rule, which granted 'assimilated' status to culturally 'Europeanised' Africans, some of the most exceptional migrants went on to represent Portugal, earning international acclaim in the process. For example, following his transfer to the Lisbon-based club Belenenses in 1951, Mozambique-born Lucas Sebastião da Fonseca, popularly known as 'Matateu', acquired considerable renown not only for his scoring exploits for his club but also while earning twenty-seven caps for Portugal. Matateu's successes, and summer tours especially to Mozambique and Angola by Portuguese clubs, encouraged further recruitment from the colonies, and by the early 1960s around thirty had migrated. Béla Guttmann, the veteran Hungarian coach of Benfica, was a strong proponent of this colonial resource and he was particularly pro-active in drawing on the rich pool of talent that it provided in his pursuit of domestic and European honours. Indeed, four of the team that brought Benfica its first European Cup success in 1961 – Jose Aguas, Costa Pereira, Joaquim Santana and Mario Coluna – hailed from either Mozambique or Angola (Darby, 2007a). Coluna was also notable for his international career which saw him represent Portugal on fifty-eight occasions and captain them at the 1966 World Cup. The lynchpin of that World Cup team was undoubtedly his fellow Mozambique-born teammate Eusebio da Silva Ferreira, known globally as Eusebio, who was naturalised shortly after signing for Benfica in 1961 (Armstrong, 2004a).

While the unwillingness of British clubs to countenance signing African players during the colonial period made African football migration to Britain a quantitatively less significant process than was the case in France or Portugal (Vasili, 1995), those that moved did so via imperial connections. As early as the 1910s, Egyptians who had moved to Britain mainly to study were signed by British clubs. White South Africans were also prominent in the English game in the same period, coming to the attention of English and Scottish clubs during their tours of South Africa in the late 1920s and 1930s. Most of those who moved already possessed or were easily able to acquire British citizenship, thus smoothing their transition into the British game. For example, Liverpool held the registrations of six such players at one time and Charlton Athletic were also active in recruiting South African-born players, signing at least thirteen in the post-war period (Alegi, 2010). One of the most famous South African exports in the colonial period, Bill Perry, signed for Blackpool in 1949 from Johannesburg Rangers, playing with Stanley Matthews and claiming an FA Cup winners medal in 1953 before making three appearances for England (Glanville, 2007). His success whetted the appetite of English clubs for South African talent, and between 1956 and 1961 three Black South Africans – Steve Mokone, Gerry Francis and Albert Johanneson – were recruited by English clubs.

Despite liberal legislation, particularly the British Nationality Acts of 1914 and 1948, which effectively granted British subjects from the Empire and Commonwealth unhindered rights to enter Britain, football immigration from Britain's imperial possessions in West and East Africa was largely absent (Darby, 2010; Ungruhe and Schmidt, 2020). Apart from the presence of the Ghanaian Arthur Wharton, who moved to England in 1882 to train as a Wesleyan Methodist minister before turning his attention to a full-time football career for clubs in the north-west of England and the Midlands, British clubs were too insular to view a burgeoning West African football scene as a potential talent pool (Lanfranchi and Taylor, 2001). However, after a tour of Britain by a Nigerian representative team in 1949, a number of Nigerian players who came to England for work and study were signed by English professional and amateur clubs. For example, Tesilimi Balogoun joined the Midlands league club Peterborough United before signing for Queen's Park Rangers, while his teammate Etim Henshaw, captain of the touring side, returned to England to study and signed for Cardiff Corinthians (Vasili, 1995).

Post-colonial mobilities

African players continued to move to Europe in the immediate post-colonial period, and by the mid-1970s there was a steady flow of talent to France and Belgium. In France, this was best exemplified by the Malian Salif Keita, who excelled at Saint-Étienne following his transfer in 1967. He was followed by other footballing luminaries such as Jules Bocande from Senegal, the Algerian Rabah Madjer and the Cameroonian duo Roger Milla and Joseph-Antoine Bell, all of whom helped pave the way for a more sustained influx of Africans into French football in the 1980s. By 1960, around thirty players from the Belgian Congo had signed for clubs in Belgium's top two divisions before this route was effectively closed in 1962 by the Zairean authorities for over fifteen years with the imposition of regulations that allowed them to control international transfers of local players (Lanfranchi and Taylor, 2001). This protectionist stance was extended in advance of the 1968 Africa Cup of Nations when Mobutu's government not only bought out the contracts of Congolese players in Belgium and repatriated them but also passed legislation that placed a complete moratorium on transnational player mobility (Poli, 2006b; Goldblatt, 2007).

Similar efforts to curtail migratory aspirations and possibilities for African players were apparent elsewhere. For example, as the words of Cecil Jones Attuquayefio at the start of this chapter illustrated, in the late 1950s and 1960s the newly formed Ghanaian government, led by Kwame Nkrumah, viewed footballers as national assets who should enrich both the domestic game in Ghana and the national team by remaining at home (Darby, 2010). With high-profile talent, particularly from the former French colonies, continuing to leave the continent, the Confédération Africaine de Football (CAF), established in 1957 to oversee and direct the continent-wide development of the game, introduced a rule in 1965 that prevented African national teams from fielding more than two overseas-based players at any one time in international fixtures. While this did not constitute the sort of outright ban on migration that was experienced by players from Ghana or Zaire in this period, it was designed to encourage players to stay at home and prioritise winning national team representation and success rather than chasing a career abroad. However, the rule did little to persuade players to forgo the rewards of a professional career overseas, and with African teams forced to pick from a weakened pool of players for international competition, it was rescinded in 1982 (Rednege, 1998). Zaire's position on player migration had been reversed four years previously, and this, alongside liberal citizenship laws that enabled adults with three years' residency to be naturalised, was key in the re-emergence of Belgium as a destination for African migrants.

These more conducive conditions contributed to a sustained, quantitatively significant flow of Africans entering the European game from the early 1980s. In Belgium, for example, almost 130 Africans played in the top two divisions between 1985 and 1995 (Lanfranchi and Taylor, 2001). This rate of increase was apparent elsewhere on the continent in the same period, and by the mid-point of the 1990s the number of migrant players plying their trade in first- and second-tier European leagues was estimated at more than 350, with the majority hailing from West Africa (Gleeson, 1996). This was significantly aided by a combination of factors linked to the political economy of football locally and globally, the increased visibility of African football players to potential European suitors and regulatory changes across both the African and European football landscape, not least the Bosman ruling by the European Commission (EC) in 1995. These will be discussed later in this chapter. At this juncture, it is sufficient to say that, combined, these developments, particularly where they intersected with favourable immigration policies in a range of European countries, effectively lessened barriers in terms of accessing and pursuing a career in European football and contributed to a further surge in the number of African players making the move northwards. Indeed, at the turn of the new millennium, the number of African migrant footballers across all levels of the professional European game had increased to almost one thousand (Ricci, 2000).

As the export trade in African players gathered pace in the 1980s and 1990s, the mobilities of these footballers increasingly encompassed markets beyond Europe. For example, intra-continental migration saw players move to other African states that were considered to be feeder nations to the European market (Alegi, 2010). African footballers also moved to South and South-East Asia in this period. For example, the Nigerian David Williams was the first African to play in India, moving to East Bengal in 1979 (Mukharji, 2008). He was followed to the Calcutta Football League by his compatriot Chima Okeria and three other Nigerians who arrived there in the mid-1980s. Following a ten-year hiatus without recruiting African players, the period between 1995 and 2000 saw a further fifteen, mostly Nigerians and Ghanaians, sign for clubs in this league (Mukharji, 2008). Cameroonian players, not least the much-lauded former international Roger Milla, were recruited by clubs in Indonesia as early as 1993 following the lifting of a ban on foreign players (Poli, 2010a). Quantitatively, these flows were less prominent than the movement of players to Europe. However, as we illustrate shortly, in the first two decades of the new millennium South and South-East Asia have become important migratory routes for African footballers.

Mapping contemporary transnational African football migration

It is difficult to glean, with any precision, the exact numbers of expatriate African players worldwide who have moved primarily for football reasons since 2000 or to accurately map all of their points of origin and destination. However, there are a number of invaluable sources of data that enable us to construct a clear picture of both the expanded volume and spatial dimensions of transnational African football migration in this period. The CIES Football Observatory, headed by Raffaele Poli, who has contributed significantly to the study of African football migration, is most notable, especially their 'Atlas of Migration'. This online tool maps the international flow of players in 147 leagues across 98 national football associations, including the majority of African federations (CIES, 2020). While its scope is impressive, the Atlas does not cover all of the routes that male African footballers traverse, nor does it incorporate all of the leagues that expatriate players are playing in at the time of writing. As such, it furnishes only a partial view. Nonetheless, it remains the most comprehensive resource for understanding the geography and volume of contemporary transnational African football migration. The primary conclusions to be drawn from the data provided by the Atlas are twofold. Firstly, the spatial configuration of sending regions and countries was as concentrated in 2020 as it was in the colonial and immediate post-colonial periods. Secondly, while Europe remains the primary destination, the range of national leagues within and beyond this continent that have become incorporated into the mobilities of African footballers is more diversified than it has been at any other point in the history of this process.

In terms of mapping points of origin, as of May 2020, 70 per cent of the 2,022 African expatriate players whose trajectories are recorded in the Atlas hailed from West Africa, with the five primary exporting countries – Nigeria, Ghana, Senegal, Côte d'Ivoire and Mali – accounting for three-quarters of the total number of 1,410 football migrants from the region and 52 per cent of the continental figure. A more comprehensive study published by the CIES Football Observatory that captured data for the 2014/15 season from 458 leagues across 183 countries, further testifies to the pre-eminence of these five nations in the export of football labour, with Nigeria being one of only five countries worldwide where the number of expatriate players in that season exceeded five hundred. Along with Senegal, Côte d'Ivoire and Ghana, it was among the top fifteen exporting football nations globally, and combined, these four countries represented the origin of 1,706 African footballers abroad at this time (Poli, Ravenel and Besson, 2015). Cameroon, geographically located in the west of the continent but economically, politically and in terms of football administration situated in Central Africa, also forms part of this group, and in the five seasons from 2015 it has been positioned either fifth or sixth on the list of primary African football labour exporters (CIES, 2020).

While few other African countries produce anything close to this number of players who move abroad specifically for football-related reasons, there are pockets of reasonably significant transnational player mobility emanating from elsewhere on the continent. For example, North Africans, and specifically those from the five countries of the Maghreb, constitute just under 10 per cent of the total number of African footballers abroad as of May 2020, with exactly two-thirds of these being nationals of Algeria, Morocco and Tunisia. France is prominent in these migratory flows, albeit not the primary destination, with Spain topping the list for Moroccans and Algerians while most Tunisian expatriate players can be found in South Africa. Given the strength of the professional game in Egypt and the salary levels available, comparatively fewer Egyptian players tend to migrate compared to their counterparts elsewhere in North Africa. Indeed, these same features combined with liberal visa requirements make Egypt a key nodal point for intra-continental migration in football. This is especially the case for players from countries south of the Sahara. However, inasmuch as the Egyptian game provides better remuneration opportunities than these migrants might have expected had they remained at home, most see the country as a stopping off point on what they hope will be a northwards career arc that will see them advance into European football (Groves, 2012).

The Premier Soccer League (PSL) in South Africa functions in a similar way, and players from across the continent, but particularly from southern Africa, are attracted by the opportunities it offers for a professional career. Indeed, excluding players from South Africa and Angola, the primary destination for migrant footballers from all other countries in the region is South Africa, which in 2020 housed 53 per cent of the region's 150 expatriates. This migratory route is particularly prominent among Zimbabweans, with 80 per cent of the country's forty-one migrant players resident in the South African game (CIES, 2020). A similar trend can also be observed in Zambia. While it did appear that there was an emerging migration channel opening up between Zambia and Belgium in the late 1980s, the collapse of the local league in the early 1990s saw intra-continental migration involving Zambian players become well-established (Chipande, 2016). By the mid-2010s, almost half of the country's twenty-six expatriate players were registered with clubs in South Africa. Aside from South Africa, the Moroccan, Tunisian and Egyptian top-flight leagues have also proven attractive to migrant Zambian players (Chipande, 2016). The Congolese club TP Mazembe, bankrolled by the Katanga province mining industry, has also been able to offer the sort of salaries that enabled them to sign three Zambian internationals, Given Singuluma, Nathan Sinkula and the former captain Rainford Kalaba, along with a number of Ghanaian and Ivorian players. The strength of the PSL tends to limit the emigration of South Africans to only the most exceptional (Darby and Solberg, 2010), and of the twenty-nine playing abroad in 2020, Portugal, France and Belgium were the three main destinations.

Beyond Cameroonian players, football migration from Central Africa is comparatively small, constituting only 4 per cent of transnationally mobile African players, with most being nationals of Gabon, the Democratic Republic of Congo and Congo, countries that have a longer history of exporting players. East Africa resides at the bottom of the list of football labour exporting regions, comprising only 3 per cent of the total number of African expatriates accounted for in the CIES Atlas. Sport migration from the region is much more pronounced in track and field and middle-distance running (Bale and Sang, 1996; Chepyator-Thomson and Ariyo, 2016), and there is a much smaller pool of highly skilled football talent relative to other parts of the continent. This is a consequence of a comparatively weak football tradition and structural weaknesses in the national and local administration of the game relating to finance, governance and leadership, all of which hinder a systematic approach to youth player development (Njororai, 2009, 2019; Rintaugu, Mwisukha, and Onywera, 2012). The comparative absence of a wider culture of migration from the region to Europe or the United States has also contributed to and produced what Ungruhe and Schmidt

(2020) refer to as widespread 'voluntary immobility' among local footballers in East Africa. That said, Johansen's (2013) study of Kenyan football migration does reveal a migratory aspiration on the part of many young players, albeit in the twenty years since 1990 he estimates that only 120 were able to enact or have actively pursued transnational mobility and relatively few have moved to European clubs.

In terms of the points of arrival for African football migrants, Europe remains the primary importer and is undoubtedly the preferred destination for the vast majority of migrant players (Poli, 2010a). As we show in subsequent chapters, the 'big five' leagues of England, Spain, Germany, France and Italy are especially prominent in the migratory imaginaries of young aspiring footballers. The number of expatriate footballers generally in these leagues has grown exponentially since the mid-1990s and Africans have been prominent in this rise. For example, aside from the flow of European players, Africa is second only to Latin America in terms of exporting football labour to these leagues. In the period between the 1995/96 and 2005/06 seasons, the percentage of Africans as a proportion of the total number of foreign players in the 'big five' rose from 10.6 to 16.2 per cent. By this latter season, France was the primary destination for African migrant players, accounting for 57 per cent of the total, with long-standing transnational routes from Côte d'Ivoire, Senegal and Mali being particularly well-travelled. France was followed by England (20 per cent), Italy (11 per cent), Germany (9 per cent) and, finally, Spain (3 per cent) in this list (Poli, 2010d).

Outside these leagues and reflecting a shared colonial history and well-established transnational migratory channels, Belgium and Portugal have maintained their status as prominent destinations for African players. Alongside this continuity in the spatial configuration of player flows into Europe, it should be noted that the routes pursued by African players have diversified significantly since 2000. For example, migration to northern and eastern Europe is growing, and within these regions Africans tend to be more highly concentrated in middle- and lower-ranking levels of competition (Poli, 2010a). An indication of the wider diversification of this process beyond Europe can be found in the number of destinations internationally that African players are spread across. While players from Côte d'Ivoire, Senegal, Mali and Cameroon are highly visible in France, nationals from each country play professionally in a large number of leagues around the world. As the CIES Atlas (2020) reveals, players from Côte d'Ivoire are present in fifty-four of the ninety-eight associations represented in the data, while for their Senegalese, Cameroonian and Malian counterparts, the numbers of destination countries are fifty, forty-six and twenty-eight, respectively.

The other major trend in the contemporary geography of African football migration has been the increase in the number of players drawn to leagues across Asia, especially in South-East Asia and the Indian sub-continent (Abe, 2018; Akindes, 2013; Mukharji, 2008; Poli, 2010a; Rehal, 2015). Although small in number, the existing studies exploring these mobilities have contributed much to our understanding of how and where African players are distributed across these regions. The majority of those who travel eastwards to play football hail from the geographic west of the continent. As noted earlier, the trailblazers of these routes were predominantly from Nigeria and Cameroon, and they tended to pursue emerging migratory channels to India and Indonesia. This continued in the early years of the 2000s, and by 2006 thirty-five footballers from ten African countries, twenty-three of whom were Nigerian, signed for clubs in the Calcutta Football League (Mukharji, 2008). Reflecting the growing professionalisation of football and the lifting of restrictions on signing foreign players in South-East Asian countries, 'several dozen' Africans were playing in leagues across the region by the close of the first decade of the new millennium (Poli, 2010a: 1002).

Drawing on data from team rosters gleaned from the websites of leagues and clubs in South and South-East Asia, along with newspaper articles and interviews with football officials and journalists, Akindes (2013) provides a more up-to-date picture. For example, his study illustrated that in 2010, 108 players from seventeen African countries were officially contracted with teams in Bangladesh, India, Indonesia and Vietnam. Reflecting earlier patterns, most were from Nigeria (forty-five) with Cameroon the second most significant exporter (nineteen). They were followed by Liberia and Ghana, which contributed thirteen players each to the total number of African football expatriates. Based on his analysis of data from the 2012 season, Akindes (2013: 691) also identified clubs in Singapore, Thailand and Nepal as important recruiters of African talent with 'recommendation-type supply channels' prominent in facilitating these mobilities. Rehal's (2015) study on African players in the Philippines also shows a not insignificant presence of African players in the two-division professional league there. Aided by liberal immigration rules in the country and the low barrier of entry into the local club game, during the 2013 season fifty-three Africans, mainly from West Africa, had been recruited by fourteen of the twenty professional teams.

East African footballers, especially those from Rwanda, Uganda and Kenya, have also been travelling eastwards to countries such as India, Malaysia and Singapore, albeit still in relatively small numbers (Akindes, 2013; Johansen, 2013). Within these spatial mobilities, Kenya emerged as a 'hub' through which players from elsewhere in Africa frequently transited until stricter visa regulations imposed by Asian governments put an end to this in the second decade of the twenty-first century (Ungruhe and Schmidt, 2020). It should also be noted that beyond those migrant players formally contracted to clubs in South and South-East Asia, many other aspiring African youth travel to these regions without a contract offer but rather avail of existing networks of friends and acquaintances in their pursuit of a foothold in the game there (Akindes, 2013; see Chapter 7).

African players' mobilities also encompass the countries of the oil-rich states of the Persian Gulf, which are increasingly perceived to offer those aspiring to a move to Europe a potential stepping stone, or for those more established migrant players coming towards the end of their careers, a final pay-day (Poli, 2010a). The establishment of the Aspire Academy in Qatar, part of the country's wider use of sport for enhancing its international image (Brannagan and Giulianotti, 2015), has created a novel dimension to the geographical patterning of the transnational migration of African footballers, illustrating the continually evolving nature of this process. Aspire is a multi-sport academy but its focus is on football, and since it started recruiting African minors to its parent facility in Doha in 2005 it has brought up to twenty young hopefuls per year to the Qatari capital and its sister academy in Senegal. Recruitment is conducted via its 'Africa Football Dreams' project, which consists of a talent-scouting network covering ten African countries, mainly the prominent football labour exporters in West Africa but also including Kenya, Rwanda, Uganda and Tanzania (Poli, 2010d). Once players turn eighteen, the most talented have the opportunity to move either to KAS Eupen in the Belgian First Division or Cultural y Deportiva Leonesa in the Spanish second division, clubs that are owned by the Aspire Academy (Esson et al., 2020). Beyond Aspire and Qatar, professional clubs in Saudi Arabia have also been active in recruiting players from North Africa, particularly Algeria and Morocco, while the United Arab Emirates (UAE) has emerged as an attractive destination for Tunisian players (CIES, 2020). Footballers from West Africa have also been observed travelling to the UAE on short-term visas in the hope of landing a contract with a professional club, despite the limited odds of actually securing one (Pelican, 2014).

Two other destinations for African players merit a brief mention, namely China and the United States. China's Football Development Reform Plan (2015–2025) has seen significant investment in local youth player development and this forms part of President Xi Jinping's drive to overhaul the domestic game and transform the Chinese national team into a World Cup winner by 2050 (Beech, 2014; Phillips, 2017). Alongside this, from around 2015 clubs in the Chinese Super League began flexing their considerable financial might to recruit foreign players, arguing that this would make the league more attractive and competitive and, in doing so, would contribute to President Xi's aspirations (BBC Sport, 2017). However, there were concerns that pathways for local talent were being closed up, and in 2017 the league tightened quotas that reduced the number of foreign players permitted to sign for Chinese clubs from four to three and a 100 per cent tax on international transfer fees was introduced (BBC Sport, 2017). Nonetheless, a number of high-profile African players, including Didier Drogba, Cédric Bakambu, Asamoah Gyan, Gervinho and Obafemi Martins among others, signed for prominent Chinese clubs. While most of these African imports were entering the latter years of their playing careers, they were doubtless attracted by the ability of Chinese clubs to pay some of the highest salaries in the world game.

As was highlighted earlier, a number of African players availed of opportunities to play professionally in the original North American Soccer League in the United States which operated between 1968 and 1984. The inauguration of Major League Soccer (MLS) in 1995 and its subsequent growth has seen the United States remerge as a destination for African migrant players. Ghanaian players have been prominent in this renewed but small flow of talent. In the 2020/21 season, nine Ghanaian players were playing for MLS clubs while a further ten featured on the roster of teams in the country's second tier, the United Soccer League Championship (*Transfermarkt*, 2021a, 2021b). Among these players were established internationals such as Harrison Afful and Jonathan Mensah as well as a string of young players who moved to the United States via the Right to Dream academy in Ghana, which has a series of partnerships and links with US schools and colleges (see Chapter 3). Attractive salaries, a competitive level of play and the opportunity to combine football with education all account for the growing number of African players in the US.

Regulating the international transfer of African football labour

The transnational mobilities of African football players to football markets around the world have been governed and shaped by a range of rules, regulatory frameworks and legislation both within and external to the football industry. As the preceding discussion has begun to illustrate, these have intersected at particular historical junctures in ways that have both enabled and constrained the mobilities of those with the talent and ambition to pursue a professional football career abroad. For example, the alignment of legislation that granted assimilated status or citizenship for 'subjects' of France and Portugal's African territories with rules introduced to govern the recruitment of non-national talent by domestic football clubs in both countries eased the migration of appreciable numbers of African players. At the same time, the prevailing inward-looking culture and attitudes to foreign talent that were evident among clubs in England and Scotland meant that there were considerably fewer opportunities for those from Britain's African colonies to play professionally there despite liberal immigration legislation that granted them unhindered rights of entry. Barriers in countries of origin also emerged in the early post-colonial period with the introduction of protectionist regulations designed to curtail what was considered to be a 'loss' of talent to Europe by a number of African states and CAF.

While the lifting of these sorts of restrictive policies in origin countries in the late 1970s and 1980s might have removed one set of impediments to their career ambitions, prospective African migrant players still had to negotiate a whole plethora of legislative and regulatory barriers to entry into the high-profile European leagues that they most aspired to play in. However, access to these leagues was, and remains, dependent on meeting the immigration conditions required to live and work in the countries concerned. This is complicated by the presence of a wide variety of approaches to migration management and divergent procedures around securing a residency visa and work permit across EU member states. While the overall approach to labour migration is a selective one (Adam and Devillard, 2008), most EU countries do include provisions to accommodate prospective athletic migrants. However, there is variance across the EU in the specifics of these provisions and in how visa and work permit applications for professional athletes are processed. This not only makes the European immigration apparatus difficult for African players to navigate but it also renders some European leagues more or less attractive and accessible points of arrival (Lembo, 2011).

As well as divergent immigration regimes across Europe, African players have also had to traverse an evolving and initially restrictive regulatory framework within the football industry that was designed to limit the number of non-nationals in European leagues. The Union of European Football Associations' (UEFA) '3 + 2' rule was notable in this regard, allowing European clubs to sign only three foreign players plus two who had five years of uninterrupted residency within a national jurisdiction. Following two challenges to this rule in the European Court of Justice (ECJ) in 1973 and 1976 and discussions between the EC and UEFA in 1978, clubs were permitted to sign as many foreign players as they liked but the number who could be fielded in UEFA competitions remained restricted. As observed earlier, African players were moving to a number of European countries in this period, including to those within the then European Economic Community, but this rule clearly squeezed the number of Africans that European clubs were inclined to recruit and they tended only to sign players with proven abilities. The EC, convinced that the '3 + 2' rule contravened Article 48 of the Treaty of Rome, which guaranteed freedom of movement for EU workers, continued to press UEFA for the removal of the 'nationality clause' in its transfer regulations but UEFA and its member associations were unmoved, and throughout the 1980s they largely ignored both the EC's and the European Parliament's calls for change. With the threat of a legal challenge looming, UEFA reached a compromise with the EC that would see its rules on non-nationals apply only to the top-division leagues of its nineteen member associations from January 1992. The implications of this for prospective African migrant players was that it lifted restrictions on their movement into the lower tiers of the European leagues. However, much more radical changes to UEFA's transfer system were afoot, and these, combined with the massive growth of revenues in the European domestic game, would soon transform player movement, including from Africa, to football markets across Europe (European Commission, 1995).

The ECJ's Bosman ruling of 1995 and its implications for international football transfers have been thoroughly outlined elsewhere and it is not necessary to detail its genealogy and finer points (Dabscheck, 2004, 2006). In short, it had two major provisions, namely the removal of the nationality clause and the ending of the requirement for clubs to pay a transfer fee for players who are out of contract. Alongside a surge in revenues from the sale of television broadcasting rights for the leading domestic leagues in Europe and UEFA competitions (King, 2003), these changes to the transfer system had a major role in heralding an exponential increase in demand for and recruitment of African football labour by clubs across Europe. As the financial might of Europe's leading clubs expanded, so too did their appetite for the world's best players, and high-profile African migrant players were benefactors of a three- to fourfold increase in gross expenditure on salaries across these leagues between 1995 and 2000 (Poli, 2006b). African players in general were increasingly sought-after and moved to clubs from lower divisions and leagues outside the 'big five'. The reasons for this were both financial and regulatory.

The deep disparities in salary levels available across the professional game in Europe created what Poli (2006a) described as a 'dual labour market'. While elite clubs could lavish large sums on salaries, those in leagues that experienced more modest revenue growth but an increase in operational costs had to think more creatively about building a squad that would allow them to be competitive. The abolition of the '3 + 2' rule accelerated this process because it created a scenario where a club could invest in developing and training a young player only to lose them to a larger European team for little or no financial recompense. This effectively disincentivised these clubs from developing homegrown talent and instead they became much more pro-active, speculative and youth focused in their approach to player recruitment.

With African national teams performing with some distinction at world tournaments at youth and senior level in the 1980s and 1990s, lower- and middle-ranking European teams increasingly looked to what they considered as a plentiful, highly skilled and cheap talent pool in Africa (Darby, 2000). This had a dramatic impact on the scale, demography and geography of African football migration. As observed earlier, in the five years between the Bosman ruling and the turn of the millennium, the number of African migrants in Europe increased almost threefold (Lanfranchi and Taylor, 2001). Their distribution in the European game became more diverse during the late 1990s and through the 2000s and they tended to be concentrated outside the 'big five' leagues. In order to maximise opportunities for potentially lucrative transfer fees, African players were invariably recruited at a much younger age than their European counterparts. All of this is well captured by Poli:

> The relative over-representation of African players in the last four levels of European competition indicates the need of less well-off clubs to recruit 'low cost' players abroad. This occurs also in the context of a strategy based on speculation, in which financially weak and middle-ranged European clubs aim to buy young footballers in Africa in order to resell them at a higher price to richer clubs. (Poli, 2006a: 284)

It is critical to point out that these economic and regulatory changes in the European professional football industry also induced what were predatory, ethically problematic and at times illegal recruitment practices in Africa by clubs and a host of other actors and intermediaries, both European and African (David, 2004; Drywood, 2016; Hawkins, 2015). As will be discussed later in this book, this rendered young African players susceptible to exploitation and abuse and opened up emergent forms of illicit transnational football migration including trafficking *in* and *through* football (Esson, 2015a; Poli, 2010c).

In response to the rapidly changing regulatory environment governing player transfers into European football and partly motivated by a well-intentioned desire to better protect minors – especially those from Africa and Latin America – from exploitative recruitment practices, FIFA instituted a new international framework to oversee all player transfers in football. FIFA's Regulations on the Status and Transfer of Players (RSTP), introduced in 2001 and modified in 2005, 2009, 2015 and 2018, govern the mobility of players worldwide, but a number of its provisions have been particularly germane to Africa's embeddedness in football's global production networks. For example, Article 19, which prohibits the international transfer of minors (defined as players under the age of eighteen), was included in the RSTP partly because of growing concerns in the late 1980s and early 1990s about the exploitative treatment encountered by African minors in the European football industry (Darby, 2000b; Darby, Akindes and Kirwin, 2007; Donnelly and Petherick, 2004). As will become clear in the next chapter, this rule had the unintended consequence of further concretising an emergent, but what has since become the critical, site or node in football production and export networks linking Africa and Europe, namely football academies. Despite the overriding concern with the protection of minors in Article 19, the academy node in Africa contains segments that continue to expose youth to exploitative practices and negative experiences that impinge upon their rights as enumerated in the United Nations Convention on the Rights of the Child (Mason et al., 2019).

The inclusion of what is referred to as the 'solidarity mechanism' in FIFA's RSTP has also been significant in the emergence of academies and other sites for youth player development in Africa. This 'mechanism' encompasses a set of rules relating to the payment of compensation to clubs involved in the training of young players who go on to be transferred into and within the professional game. Under these rules, compensation is payable for training costs incurred during the period commencing from the season the player's twelfth birthday falls in, up to the season in which they turn twenty-one; payment becomes due when they are registered as a professional for the first time or they transfer between clubs of two different associations before the end of the season of their twenty-third birthday. The calculation of the costs arising from the training and education of a player is based on the training cost of the new club of the player multiplied by the number of years that they spent with their former club. The training cost is a standard set fee established by confederations and national associations through the categorisation of clubs from category one, the highest training cost, to category four, the lowest (Esson et al., 2020).

The 'solidarity mechanism' is motivated by a desire to ensure that clubs, including those at grassroots youth level who have been involved in training a player, are financially compensated and are thus able to reinvest in the talent development cycle. As with Article 19, this provision has had ramifications both for young African players and those actors and institutions involved in their training. In terms of the former, countless child players across the continent, but particularly in West Africa, have seen their talent and desires to play professionally abroad become commodified and transformed into a potential source of revenue for clubs, agents and a range of other intermediaries involved in football's GPN (Esson, 2015b). For those who run or invest in local youth clubs and academies, a regulated system for training compensation has contributed to a prevailing understanding of youth football as business. European clubs' recruitment drive in the African football market post-Bosman has cemented this view.

In Chapter 4, we illustrate how financial speculation and domestic trading of child players in Ghana has intensified since the 1990s as academy and club owners vie for the next young star to sell to a wealthy foreign club (Dubinsky and Schler, 2019; Ungruhe and Esson, 2017). For those clubs and academies that sit outside or on the fringes of transnational production networks, their goal is to sell a player to segments of the network where an international transfer is more likely, and in these cases the 'solidarity mechanism' offers at least some promise of a financial return. As highlighted in the next chapter, all of this has not only increased the number of actors and institutions establishing youth football academies and clubs in Africa but has also diversified their organisational forms and the scale at which they operate.

One final site of regulation in football's GPN that has impacted the trajectories of young African players relates to the activities of player agents, individuals who are ostensibly responsible for handling the interests of players and representing them in contract negotiations with a buying club and potential sponsors. These individuals have emerged as powerful actors in the player transfer market, acting as a bridge between players and clubs (Poli, 2010d). However, regulating these intermediaries in football has been a challenge because of the transnational and cross-jurisdictional nature of their activity (Rossi, Semens, and Brocard, 2016) and this has contributed to the entry into the profession of individuals who prioritise financial gain over the best interests of the players they represent. The account of Nii Lamptey's career that opened this book is a case in point, but countless other African migrant players have fallen victim to the predatory actions of unscrupulous agents and there have been long-standing concerns about the exploitation they have suffered (Broere and van der Drift, 1997; Darby, 2000b, 2010).

In an attempt to improve legal and ethical standards and more tightly regulate the profession, FIFA introduced a licensing system in 1994 that required all player agents to meet certain minimum requirements, including the completion of certified training and the passing of an agents' exam. However, by 2009 it had become clear that only 25–30 per cent of international transfers were actually conducted by licensed agents, and ongoing problems with the activities of those working in this field, including the continued exploitation of child players (European Commission, 2009), led FIFA to reform the system. The outcome of this reform process was a new framework, the Regulations of Working with Intermediaries (RWI), introduced in 2015. While this did appear to offer some additional protection in mitigating the exploitation of young players, the RWI effectively de-regulated the agent market by abolishing the licensing requirement to practise the profession.

In place of a centrally administered licensing system, intermediaries were simply required by the RWI to provide proof that they did not have a criminal record and to register with a national football federation. This effectively lowered professional standards and enabled unqualified individuals to operate in the player recruitment domain (Yilmaz *et al.*, 2020). As Tom Vernon, the founder of the Right to Dream academy in Ghana, explained, this had potentially serious implications for young aspirant African players. From his perspective, not only did it exacerbate their risk of being exposed to intermediaries with malign intent but it also led to practices that threatened the stability of their academy training, and ultimately their prospects of being able to secure a professional contract overseas (interview, 19 June 2018). Indeed, in the three-year period between the introduction of RWI and our interview, players and family members at this particular academy had been offered financial inducements by intermediaries to break their ties to the academy and enter into representation agreements that would open up opportunities for the intermediary to profit from a future overseas transfer. These sorts of cases and widespread criticism of RWI have led FIFA to acknowledge that the new framework has not worked in the ways intended and they have initiated a reform process that is focused around reinstating agent licensing and better protecting child football players from financial exploitation at the hands of agents. At the time of writing, these reforms were ongoing and their impact on African football migration remains to be seen.

Conclusions

This chapter examined how African football players have become incorporated into the football industry's GPN, and more specifically, it unpacked the historical, spatial and regulatory features of this process. The spatial dimensions of transnational African football migration reveal that it has historically been clustered around a small number of core talent production centres in West Africa and key export markets in Europe. Long-standing transnational ties, often but not exclusively rooted in colonial history, have been key and they continue to have a significant influence on the geography of player mobilities. However, the first two decades of the twenty-first century witnessed not only a dramatic increase in the volume of African players plying their trade abroad, but also a much more diffuse spatial distribution across the European football industry and to emerging professional leagues in South and South-East Asia and the Middle East. These diversified paths traversed by African talent have been influenced by players' willingness to look beyond traditional markets to earn a living from their footballing abilities.

As we show in chapters 7 and 8, the mobilities that incorporate these paths are infused with strategic forms of agency and are often pursued because they are believed to offer alternative routes into more prestigious, financially rewarding markets in western Europe. However, they have also been contoured by wider structural and regulatory changes in the professional football industry, not least those initiated by the Bosman ruling. A changing landscape for the local game in Africa, one that has increasingly become oriented around producing and exporting its most promising talent, has been equally significant. In order to fully expound the imaginaries, experiences, agency and trajectories of African youth as they encounter and navigate a network of local development pathways or nodes that they hope will enable, or at least move them closer to, entry as contracted workers in the global football labour market, it is critical that we proceed with an understanding of how these nodes are structured and organised.

3

'Producing' African labour for the global football industry

Introduction

On a Saturday morning in Medina, a northern suburb of Accra, the capital of Ghana, around twenty U-12 Colts teams and their coaches gather to take part in a football tournament organised by one of the most prominent academies in the country. Reflecting the pervasiveness of European football on African satellite television networks, the teams bear monikers such as Manchester United, Anderlecht, Lazio and Juventus. However, the facilities for the day's proceedings could not be further removed from those enjoyed by young players at these illustrious clubs. A single school pitch hosts the entire tournament and its bone-hard, dusty, crevice-filled surface necessitates consummate technique to perform even the most basic skills. Before each match, the young trialists are corralled in front of the watching scouts who visually appraise height and weight to garner a rough approximation of their age. The checking of birth certificates and school records will wait for another day.

The taut atmosphere is punctuated by the jocular banishment of a handful of players whose physique plainly reveals them to far exceed the permitted age limit. Viewed from the shade of a tented, pitch-side vantage point, where Paul sits with academy staff to observe the matches, the competition is intense and most participants highly skilled. Vociferous neighbourhood residents line the pitch perimeter to watch the contests unfold. Some stand atop an abandoned car to gain an unobstructed view. Others seek shade under a nearby acacia tree, rushing to the side-line when shouts from the crowd alert them to a goal scored, an exciting passage of play or a controversial incident.

Eventually, the teams are whittled down to four semi-finalists. As the tournament nears its conclusion, tension builds, the pace of play quickens and the concentration of the players involved becomes palpable. The stakes are clearly high. In this tournament though, the spoils are not a title, medals, sporting pride or bragging rights. The sole objective for the participants is to impress the watching scouts enough to win through to the next stage of the academy's recruitment process, a month-long residency in the more salubrious surrounds of the academy facility. Here, players' physical capital, football technique and tactical nous, along with their educational level and 'character', will be more comprehensively evaluated.

As the day's events unfold, pitch-side conversations with players and coaches reveal that the academy hosting the tournament is well known. While it offers recruits opportunities to study in the United States and England, it is its success in producing players who have secured contracts with professional football clubs overseas and represented Ghana at youth and senior level that is of most interest to the young hopefuls. For the trialists, a place at this academy is understood as a potentially transformative juncture in their lives, one that is laden with possibilities to move them closer to fulfilling their aspirations and translating their football-related imaginaries into reality. Elsewhere on the continent similar scenes have played out on countless occasions as young aspiring players vie for a foothold or seek out more advantageous positions in African football's production networks. Not all nodes of the local football industry are as prestigious or well renowned as that described in this vignette, nor have they developed the sorts of clearly defined transnational networks through which graduates of this particular academy migrate. However, a trial for a high-end academy, a seemingly nondescript local youth team or one of the thousands of makeshift neighbourhood academies that increasingly populate the grassroots football landscape on the continent is often approached with the same level of commitment and intensity by the young protagonists.

In the chapters that follow, we interrogate how and why African youth pursue a future as a professional footballer beyond the confines of their nation and continent of birth and explore the nature of their encounters with and experiences of both the local and global football industry. In order to make sense of these encounters, a structural view of the key junctures or nodes they must traverse and navigate in their quest to secure a football contract 'outside' is required. As argued in Chapter 1, the GPN framework offers an appropriate analytical scaffold for such an enterprise. Drawing on its focus on the input–output structures that enable the production of a finished commodity, this chapter examines the primary nodes through which the initially untrained abilities of young African players might be shaped into a highly skilled form of labour, one that can assume significant monetary value and is potentially exportable to football markets beyond the African continent.

Production and export nodes in African football

The honing of raw talent, the development of technical skills, the acquisition of tactical knowledge and the building of the resilience, resolve and application required to access and sustain a transnational career in professional football are complex and temporally elongated processes. These typically begin in early childhood and continue well beyond the securing of a first contract as a professional player. As observed in Chapter 1, unlike other manufacturing industries, the production of football players, and of athletes more generally, is riven with uncertainty and there are no guarantees that entry into production nodes will translate inexorably into transnational mobility or a sustained career abroad. The social, cultural, economic, physical, psychological and market variables involved in processes of talent identification and development in football are too numerous and unstable for this to be the case. As a consequence, only a small proportion of those young players who enter Africa's football production networks actually progress to a professional career; for the vast majority, the normative outcome, even for those trained over an extended period of time at the best-equipped academies with the most direct channels to the global football industry, is involuntary immobility (van der Meij, Darby, and Liston, 2017). Nonetheless, aspiring African players will invariably encounter or be recruited into a series of local nodes where their abilities are progressively developed, and their readiness to move from one node that might be considered informal and ad hoc to another that is more performance-oriented and explicitly focused around producing talent for the export market, is subject to almost constant surveillance and evaluation.

At the base of the production network lies an embryonic node which constitutes the entry point in terms of children's early engagement with football. It is characterised by informal, organic play with peers, siblings or other family members in improvised spaces in local neighbourhoods. While undoubtedly linked to the long-standing cultural pervasiveness of football on the continent and the stardom achieved by its most successful football exports, the initial attraction of the game to children in Africa is not significantly different to its appeal for their counterparts elsewhere in the world who are drawn in by the opportunities it offers for movement, physical activity, sociability, escape from chores or schoolwork, and simple enjoyment. While these incipient sites of interaction with the game sit outside the more formalised elements of football's GPN, they are crucial in stimulating the flow of young players into this network (Darby, 2013b; Poli, 2005). If players are enamoured by the game and proficient, and are provided with suitable support and encouragement, they are likely to become involved in more organised youth football structures.

Children's exposure to football and their entry into locally embedded production networks also occurs via their experiences in the context of both primary and secondary schools. Within education systems in most countries around the world, including in Africa, it is a legal requirement to provide opportunities for physical education (PE) (Hardman, 2008). However, it is important to recognise that there is geographical variance across the globe in terms of the relationship between statutory requirement and actual practice. In the context of prevailing economic conditions and funding constraints on the education sector in Africa, there are questions around the status of PE in education systems and the allocation of curriculum time, but also in terms of the numbers of adequately trained and competent teachers and the suitability of facilities.

These issues notwithstanding, competitive games-based sporting activities tend to dominate PE curricula in Africa. This reflects a post-colonial model that saw the content of PE in schools become aligned to sports development and aspirations on the part of newly independent countries to use competitive sport in nation-building processes and the pursuit of international prestige (Amusa and Toriola, 2010). As noted in the previous chapter, football featured prominently in this regard and this, along with the wider popularity of the game, has ensured that it is a staple both of curriculum PE and inter-schools sports competition in Africa. As UNESCO (2010) has acknowledged, the place of competitive sport activities on PE curricula around the world introduces children, of all sexes, to a performance sports discourse that sets some on the path to pursuing a professional career in sport. Thus, participation in football via this schools node often constitutes a platform for children in Africa to progress to or be recruited into other sites in football's production networks.

As with schools football, the organised youth game represents an important site where young players refine their skills and develop aspirations to pursue a professional career abroad. This level of the game involves a vast network of clubs and leagues affiliated to national football federations across the continent and caters for a range of age groups outside the youth structures of professional clubs. In West Africa, organised youth leagues are growing to cater for an increasing appetite for the game at this level. In Chapter 4, as part of our wider analysis of how African youth encounter this node of football's production networks, we describe in much more detail the emergence and organisational features of a system of Colts or amateur youth leagues in Ghana, one that is peerless across the region.

The academy node

Football academies, defined in the broadest terms as facilities or programmes that aim to identify, develop and often export talent to external football markets, are a critical node in the game's GPN (Darby, Akindes and Kirwin,

2007). Their significance in this regard was apparent in a report by FIFPro, the global professional players union, which revealed that 55 per cent of U-18 players worldwide with a professional contract had entered the professional game through an academy (FIFPro, 2016). There is considerable variance, internationally, in how football academies are structured and operate and how they engage with young players, and this is no less the case in Africa. All have a primary focus on football training but many also require children to pursue formal education, either on-site or in local schools. Some academies are entirely residential and involve players living on-site away from the family home. Others are non-residential with young players continuing to live at home while making frequent visits to the academy facility to train and play matches. The typical age of recruitment is ten to twelve years of age but younger children and those aged up to eighteen also take up academy places. Some involve training on a part-time or time-limited basis while others are full-time and operate all year round (Mason *et al.*, 2019).

Academies have long been a feature of African football. For example, a number of leading Portuguese clubs such as Sporting Lisbon, Benfica and Porto invested in training facilities and coaching provision in Mozambique and Angola during the late colonial era as part of their efforts to source and nurture talented players (Darby, 2006). As will be discussed in the next chapter, coordinated youth football development in post-colonial Ghana can be traced back to the launch of the Academicals in the early 1960s by Ghana's first Director of Sports, Ohene Djan. This initiative, in some ways a prototype for modern football academies, was comprised of the country's best secondary school and college players who were recruited from inter-regional schools competitions for extended periods of training and to participate in tours. The Academicals programme formed an important part of the drive to improve the standards of both the domestic club game and the national team. In doing so, it contributed to the broader use of football in Ghana for the purposes of national unity and achieving international recognition (Barimah, 2017; Darby, 2013b; Quansah, 2001).

Since the early 1990s the number of academies in Africa, particularly in the west of the continent, has expanded considerably and these have taken a variety of forms. Some segments of the academy system are focused on facilitating the recruitment and development of talent for the domestic game, and clubs that compete in local professional leagues run youth academies that mainly prepare players for participation at this level (Onwumechili and Perry, 2020). However, the best players can use these club academies as a springboard to an international transfer. Opportunities to participate in local league competition often provide players with their first taste of senior football; as such, these leagues represent a site where aspiring players' abilities and competitive instincts are further refined and made visible for potential overseas buyers. Other local club academies operate more transnationally and seek specifically to produce talent in one national context with the aim of exporting it to another. While some in this category function independently, others have entered into partnership arrangements with European clubs and essentially operate as 'farm' or 'feeder' academies/clubs. These sorts of arrangements are most common in West Africa (Darby, Akindes and Kirwin, 2007).

Other forms of academy structures exist throughout the continent. These include: academies established and operated by European teams as an exercise in 'off-shoring' talent production; academies that are privately sponsored by high-profile former African migrant players, local businessmen or corporations, or a combination of these actors; and charitable or social enterprise-oriented ventures that combine football and education and have wider, often development-related, objectives beyond producing footballers. The production of young players is also augmented by national federations, some of whom operate national football centres of excellence which are oriented around training players for national youth teams and, ultimately, for senior national squads. These are very much elite youth development programmes and often complement the training that players receive at other academies. Opportunities to represent national youth teams in international competition is not only important for players' technical development but also affords them the sort of visibility in the international market that might enable them to secure a professional contract overseas (Engh and Agergaard, 2015). For example, the success of African youth teams in winning four of the first six editions of FIFA's biennial U-17 World Cup, inaugurated in 1985, was pivotal in increasing awareness of the potential of young African talent among European clubs and talent speculators, and ultimately in facilitating the transnational mobility of some of those players who featured in these tournaments (Darby, 2000b).

It is important to recognise that this broad typology is fluid in the sense that some academies have, at various stages of their existence, belonged to one or more of the categories outlined above and that the transnational relations that connect some to the global football market vary in density and form. Furthermore, the boundaries between academies in different categories are permeable and players are often recruited from one form into another or traded between them as part of their trajectory within the game's GPN. Given their centrality in football migration, and in order to illustrate their variability and complexity, a deeper exposition of those academies that have a track record of producing and exporting players is warranted. To undertake this, we focus on notable academies in three of

The Ivorian 'blueprint'

As noted in the previous chapter, Côte d'Ivoire has a long and sustained tradition of producing and exporting highly skilled football migrants. The MimoSifcom academy, part of the Ivorian club Association Sportive des Employés de Commerce (ASEC) Mimosas, is the most well renowned in the country in terms of consistently producing football labour for the top end of the European market. Founded in 1994 in Sol Béni in M'poutu, a small village close to Abidjan, by the former French international Jean-Marc Guillou and the president of ASEC, Roger Ouégnin, MimoSifcom was one of the first structured football academies in sub-Saharan Africa, and since then has become considered the blueprint for many of the academies established throughout the continent. The recruitment process is extensive, involving the screening of up to thirty thousand hopefuls for a typical annual intake of around eighteen players aged between twelve and fifteen. The academy, which runs on a residential basis and provides both a football and academic education, has proved highly effective in producing a steady stream of talent for ASEC Mimosas' senior team, facilitating much success in domestic and intercontinental competition. However, the most talented 'academicians', as they are commonly called in Abidjan, are sold on to European teams, and many have gone on to represent leading clubs in the 'big five' European leagues as well as the Ivorian national team (Marsaud, 2001).

The route into the European game for academy graduates has fluctuated over time and has been expedited by a number of personal relationships and transnational ties to clubs in Europe. Indeed, the establishment of the academy was made possible by an initial investment from the French team AS Monaco, whose signing of former ASEC Mimosas player Youssuf Fofana in 1985 and the quality of his performances during his eight-year spell in the principality had convinced them that the Ivorian club represented a potential source of highly skilled talent (Jones, 2006). This investment was short-lived, largely because of the difficulties associated with securing work permits for players seeking to enter the European game directly from Côte d'Ivoire. However, this complication was addressed when Guillou fronted a consortium that invested in a Belgian club, KSK Beveren, and subsequently became manager in 2001. His appointment to this role opened up a transnational route into Europe for a steady stream of illustrious ASEC graduates, including Yaya Touré, Emmanuel Eboué, Arthur Boka, Gervinho, Romaric and Boubacar Barry. Following a three-year residency in Belgium and the acquisition of EU citizenship, their onward transfer to more elite leagues in Europe was much less problematic than it would have potentially been without the link between ASEC and Beveren.

In some cases, the career trajectories of the most talented graduates were also aided by further sets of transnational ties instituted by prominent figures who had been involved in the ASEC academy. For example, Guillou's close relationship with Arsène Wenger, who was his assistant at the French club Cannes in the early 1980s and who subsequently managed Arsenal in the English Premier League, underpinned the signing of an agreement between Arsenal and Beveren that granted preferential access to ASEC academy graduates who had signed for Beveren (Jones, 2006). Following a dispute and subsequent falling out between Ouégnin and Guillou over ownership of ASEC, the academy formed a partnership with the English league side Charlton Athletic in 2006, and this facilitated the transfer of a number of players who were subsequently loaned to clubs in Belgium and Scandinavia where work permit regulations are much less stringent than in England (Ornstein, 2008).

The Senegalese approach

Prior to the establishment of the Ligue Sénégalaise de Football Professionnel in 2008, football in Senegal was structured around a largely amateur national league and off-season regional tournaments involving neighbourhood clubs, the so-called *navétanes* teams, which started in the 1950s and became increasingly popular in the decades that followed (Hann, 2018). By the early 1990s, *navétanes* football was becoming increasingly organised and 'professionalised' and some high-profile Senegalese migrant players launched their European careers directly via these teams (Baller, 2014). However, in the same period a number of football academies emerged and have since become the primary node in the production and export of Senegalese talent.

One of the most notable is the Dakar-based Collège Africain Sports-Études (CASE), originally named the Centre Aldo Gentina, which was founded in 1992 by the former president of the Senegalese Football Federation and Minister of Tourism, El Hadj Malick Sy. This academy was a collaborative project that saw AS Monaco invest in a local league team, J'eanne d'Arc, in return for preferential access to the most talented trainees. Once it expanded its recruitment across Senegal in 1993, CASE began to produce a steady stream of players not only for European clubs but also for Senegal's national youth and senior teams. For example, six graduates of this academy were selected for the Senegalese squad that reached the quarter-final of the 2002 World Cup (Ndiaye, 2001). An expansion of its provision to incorporate other sports and academic education in 2004 coincided with the ending of the relationship with Monaco, and this led CASE into a range of partnerships with local and foreign companies and the introduction of registration fees for recruits (Schokkaert, 2016). While it still produces players for the professional football industry, mainly in France, its links with a number of colleges in the United States and Canada have seen it offer athletic scholarships in a range of sports to its graduates.

Of the other academies that produce migrant Senegalese players, those established by or associated with former professional footballers are noteworthy. While some have a broader social agenda and incorporate opportunities for education, they all provide a platform for entry into professional football abroad. For example, Alizé Elite Foot, established in 2000 by a number of retired Senegalese international players including Idrissa Thiam, who played professionally in France, creates pathways into education with the support of an anonymous partner in the US. Nonetheless, the focus is on establishing networks with French and other European clubs to facilitate trials and transfers for its most promising recruits. Génération Foot, founded in the same year by Mady Touré, a Guinean player who had also previously played in France, has been a particularly productive node in the transfer of players from Senegal to Europe, mainly France. This has been facilitated in large part by a partnership with the French club FC Metz, but public endorsements by high-profile migrant ex-players, such as the Togolese former Arsenal player Emmanuel Adebayor and the Senegalese ex-international and Génération Foot graduate Babacar Gueye, have also helped. Reflecting the strength of their relationship, five of the thirteen graduates who transferred abroad in the 2011/12 season were signed by Metz (Schokkaert, 2016).

While CASE, Alizé Elite Foot and Génération Foot are important fixtures in the topography of Senegalese football, the Diambars Institute is perhaps the best known and most professionally run academy in the country. It was opened in 2003 in Dakar by Saer Seck, then vice-president of the Senegalese Football Federation, along with Patrick Vieira and Bernard Lama, two former French internationals of Senegalese and French Guianan descent, and Jimmy Adjovi-Boco, a Beninese ex-international. With support from UNESCO, the French and Senegalese governments and a range of multinational corporations including Adidas and Air France, Diambars's reputation in terms of combining education with elite football training quickly grew. While it was established ostensibly to improve the level of both football and education in the country and to create a route into the professional game abroad, the institute was also underpinned by a humanitarian, development-oriented inflection and functioned as a platform for those who had acquired financial security from the game to 'give something back' (Manzo, 2007). This was prominent in how Patrick Vieira rationalised his involvement in the project:

> I wanted to go back and start a project there. I wanted to do something for the country and to use football – everyone loves football there – as a means to educate kids ... We tell them how hard it is to become a professional footballer. Perhaps only one or two will succeed. That's why their education matters. (Cited in Cowley, 2005: 20)

While Diambars's business model is rooted in raising revenues from patrons' donations, sponsorship and leasing its facilities, developing and selling players is central to its financial sustainability, with transfer fees and solidarity payments associated with transfers recouping 25–30 per cent of operational costs (Akindes, 2013). This has been aided by the development of close transnational ties to a number of professional teams in France and in Norway where its players have acquired visibility through participation in prestigious international youth tournaments. Indeed, of the nine international transfers involving Diambars graduates in the 2011/12 season, four left for France while five signed for Norwegian clubs (Schokkaert, 2016).

The academy 'system' in Ghana

The academy node in Ghana has evolved into one of the most institutionalised in Africa, as befits a nation that has consistently ranked in the top five exporting countries of African football labour since the 1990s. As observed earlier, coordinated youth football development, initially oriented around producing talent for the local game, has been a feature of the Ghanaian football landscape from the 1960s onwards. In the next chapter we detail the evolution of this process in order to contextualise our exposition of the subjectivities, experiences and trajectories of twenty-first-century Ghanaian youth as they pursue a professional football career abroad. Alongside this inward-facing infrastructure for youth player development, the early 1990s witnessed the emergence of an academy system in Ghana that was considerably more export-oriented and has been hugely influential in fuelling the football dreams of young boys across the country.

As is the case elsewhere in West Africa, academies in Ghana are not uniform but rather are comprised of a variety of arrangements ranging from linear, vertically structured transnational set-ups that create clearly discernible pathways to professional football in Europe, to small-scale micro-enterprises that sit at the margins of but feed into more organised production networks. In terms of the former, two of the most prominent were the Feyenoord Fetteh Football Academy and Red Bull Ghana. The Feyenoord academy was launched in 1999 following an agreement between officials of the Dutch parent club in Rotterdam, the Ghanaian Sports Ministry and local tribal chiefs in the town of Fetteh on Ghana's Cape Coast. Based on the ASEC model, Fetteh Feyenoord operated on a residential basis, combining academic as well as football education. Red Bull Salzburg, the Austrian component of a growing portfolio of football clubs owned by the Red Bull business empire, initiated a similar academy in 2008. According to Herman Kern, former General Manager of what became known as Red Bull Ghana, they invested around six million euros in a state-of-the-art facility in Sogakope in the country's south-eastern Volta Region (interview, 1 June 2011).

In our interviews, staff at both academies pointed to engagement in education and some wider philanthropic work as evidence of a humanitarian impulse in their operations. However, their primary purpose was to identify, source and transfer talented Ghanaian players to the parent club, or at least enable a financial return on their investment by selling players elsewhere. As Karel Brokken, General Manager of the Feyenoord academy, observed: 'The number-one objective of course is forming a few boys for Feyenoord. That's the reason for the academy … It is about getting a return on the investment' (interview, 30 January 2008). Gareth Henderby, former chief scout at Red Bull Ghana, painted a similar picture, confirming that its primary aim 'is to try to produce professional footballers' (interview, 26 August 2010).

In pursuit of their objectives, both Fetteh Feyenoord and Red Bull Ghana operated in a similar fashion to other academies in West Africa. They typically recruited boys aged between ten and fourteen via local, regional, national and transnational recruitment networks and through organised trials, referred to locally as 'justifies'. Once recruited, the 'production' process was focused on technical, tactical and physical football development and the readying of players culturally for the European market. This latter process saw foreign language skills placed at the centre of the school curricula and efforts made to inculcate character and personality traits deemed by academy staff to be important in securing and maintaining a career in European football. In cases where young recruits did not fulfil their promise, they were released, whereas those who demonstrated potential either for the parent club or as a saleable asset were retained. Leading up to the point where they could legally transfer internationally, their contact with the parent club in Austria and the Netherlands, respectively, intensified via participation in tournaments, trials and/or training placements before a decision was made on their future.

Largely as a consequence of the limited success in producing players for the export market, Feyenoord withdrew sponsorship from its academy in 2009, although it continued to offer technical support and funded participation in tournaments in the Netherlands (van der Meij, 2015). Relaunched as the West African Football Academy (WAFA) by its new owner, the Dutch agricultural entrepreneur Henri Wientjes, who had a number of long-standing business interests in Ghana and elsewhere in West Africa, its trajectory soon intersected with the Red Bull project. Bedevilled by what was at times a fractious relationship with the local chiefs and residents of Feivie, the village where the academy was situated, combined with issues around internal management and the failure to produce a single player for Salzburg's senior team, Red Bull closed the academy just six years after it opened (Kainz, 2015). Eager to maintain a footprint in Ghana and extract some return on its investment in the academy facilities, the organisation negotiated an arrangement that saw WAFA take over the site. According to its former technical director, the late, venerated Ghanaian coach Sam Arday, a loose partnership was formed with Red Bull Salzburg that granted access to WAFA graduates (interview, 17 August 2015). This eased the transfer in 2016 of two former academy players, Samuel Tetteh and Gideon Mensah, to FC Liefering, a feeder club for Salzburg who play in the second tier of Austrian football. It also enabled Salzburg's signing of Majeed Ashimeru a year later and their recruitment of two eighteen-year-olds, Daniel Owusu and Amankwah Forson, in February 2021 (Gallwey, 2018; Opoku Amoako, 2021). Aside from these five players, WAFA have since 2016 transferred players to clubs in a wide range of countries in Europe but also to teams in the US, Canada, Tanzania, Côte d'Ivoire and locally within Ghana.

Other European clubs have been active in establishing transnational channels in Ghana. For example, in 1999 the Dutch giants Ajax Amsterdam invested almost six million euros in purchasing a 51 per cent stake in the then Premier League club Obuasi Goldfields in order to use it as a site for sourcing and developing players. This venture was short-lived, with Ajax ending their investment in 2003; according to Francis Oti Akenteng, a former coach at the club, this was because of what were perceived to be limited returns for the parent club (interview, 31 August 2010). In the mid-2000s, the Danish Superliga team FC Midtjylland brokered a relationship with local club FC Maamobi United that was designed to provide access to young Ghanaian talent. However, Midtjylland quickly decided that Nigeria offered better, less competitive recruitment opportunities than Ghana and pulled out of their relationship (personal correspondence with Jacob Ebsen Madsen, 28 May 2010). Meanwhile, in 2011 FC Utrecht from the Netherlands became the first European team to set up a presence in the country's Northern Region, partnering with Abdulai Alhassan, a Ghanaian former migrant player, in establishing an academy in Tamale.

Alongside these African-European academies there are a range of locally initiated and operated projects that recruit and develop young Ghanaian talent for international markets. However, while Dubinsky and Schler (2019: 249) acknowledge their role in this regard, they argue that such ventures, including the Mandela Soccer Academy in Accra, the Unistar Academy based in Kasao on the outskirts of the capital and the Kumasi Soccer Academy in Ghana's second city 'embrace a starkly different agenda', one that employs football for engendering varying forms of local development. The other key local segment of the Ghanaian football production network are clubs in the domestic leagues, particularly those run by wealthy local entrepreneurs, colloquially known as 'big men' (Esson, 2015c; Pannenborg, 2010). Some of these clubs, referred to locally as 'one-man shows' because of the influence of a single, influential owner, have become important nodes in facilitating transnational mobility for aspiring players.

At the outset of the 2000s, Liberty Professionals FC were the most prominent example of a 'one-man show'. This club was founded in 1996 by the late Alhaji Sly Tetteh, a former player in the local game, who worked as an adviser to a number of Ghanaian clubs in the early 1990s, helping them to sell talented players abroad. Rather than operate on the fringes of a network that was dominated by overseas interests and offered limited access to Ghanaians, Tetteh inserted himself in a much more central manner. With the support of a group of local investors, he purchased a third-division club, Accra All Stars, which he renamed Liberty Professionals FC, after Liberty University of Lynchburg, Virginia, in the United States where he had studied. The club employed a number of experienced local coaches and put in place an extensive nationwide network of scouts that allowed it, in Tetteh's words, to 'go to the root' and capitalise on intimate knowledge of talent at the base of the production network (interview, 26 January 2009).

For a period, Liberty Professionals FC were highly successful in the trade and located, developed and exported players such as Michael Essien, Asamoah Gyan, Sulley Muntari, John Paintsil, Derek Boateng and Emmanuel Addoquaye Pappoe, all of whom played in elite European leagues and were a key part of Ghana's squad at the 2006 World Cup. Plans to expand the academy following the acquisition of a large tract of land in Dodowa, an Accra suburb, and discussions with a number of clubs in the top French and Italian leagues were halted when Tetteh died suddenly in September 2011. Without Tetteh's vision and oversight, the club struggled financially and in sporting terms, and have since been far less active in the football export market (Ayamga, 2019).

No exposition of the Ghanaian academy system would be complete without reference to Right to Dream, a not-for-profit charitable venture that was established by Tom Vernon, an English social entrepreneur, in 1999. Initially located in Dawu in Ghana's Eastern Region in a rudimentary facility consisting of a single pitch, one classroom and basic dormitories, the academy is now based at a purpose-built campus in New Akrade nestled on the banks of the Volta river. Right to Dream has a wider philosophy and ethos that sees it place considerable stock in formal education, character development and engagement in a range of development-related initiatives, not least promoting access to education and sustainable livelihoods for women (interviews with Tom Vernon, 1 February 2008 and 15 August 2015). An on-site school, partnerships offering full scholarships at elite boarding schools and colleges in the United States, a bespoke character programme and the launch in 2013 of the first residential football academy for girls in Africa have been key in this regard (Darby, 2013b; McGee, 2015).

Despite this wider remit, Right to Dream was originally conceived of and continues to function as a football academy in a conventional sense, and it shares many of the characteristics of other organisations that make up this node of the game's GPN. It recruits children, normally from age ten upwards, from Ghana and elsewhere in Africa to fully residential scholarships of up to six years' duration. Since its inception, over sixty graduates have gone on to play professionally in Europe and the United States with many representing Ghana at youth and senior level. In 2010 Right to Dream began to develop clearly delineated transnational pathways for graduates by entering into a long-term collaboration with Manchester City, an arrangement that has facilitated financial investment estimated at one million euros per year, coach exchanges, training placements for players and, for the most talented, an opportunity to sign professionally for the club. While twelve graduates had joined the English club by the 2019/20 season, at the time of writing none have yet featured in the first team and have instead either been sent on loan to continue their development at smaller clubs in Europe with whom Manchester City have ties or have been sold.

Other transnational relationships have been developed over time but the most significant in terms of creating a pathway into European football for its graduates, and better protecting its investment in academy trainees, was Right to Dream's acquisition in December 2015 of the Danish Superliga team FC Nordsjælland via a group of investors led by Vernon. Since the inception of this unique node in African-European football production networks, there have been sustained, transnational exchanges of knowledge, institutional philosophies and practice designed to enable the transition of young Right to Dream and FC Nordsjælland players into the professional game in Denmark and beyond. What senior management at FC Nordsjælland have dubbed, the 'international academy' is critical in this regard and it involves regular two-way exchanges of Danish and West African players to both sites for periods of up to three months. These exchanges also involve combined FC Nordsjælland–Right to Dream teams participating in prestigious youth competitions mainly in Europe but also in Asia. The rationale for the 'international academy' in terms of preparing Right to Dream students for the European football environment was explained by

Jan Laursen, FC Nordsjælland's former Sports Director and, since January 2021, club chairman:

> We try to get them here as much as possible so they have the best chance to adapt into the first team and to the way of life here ... so when you arrive here it's not your first visit to Europe or Denmark and you've been here in the winter also so you know it's going to be very dark and cold. Just to be aware of the difficult aspects of it so you're being prepared is a big help ... We invest heavily in travelling and being here as much as possible. It makes a big difference for the young players so they are as well prepared both off the pitch but on the pitch, how we train and how we play. It's a big investment in trying to give as many kids as good a chance as possible. (Interview, 22 October 2018)

By the 2019/20 season, eight Right to Dream graduates had signed for FC Nordsjælland. It is anticipated that their experiences in the Danish game will add to their value in the transfer market and enable a move to more elite European leagues. This approach reflects a business model primarily focused on making a profit from developing and selling young talent and reinvesting in this process. Indeed, in July 2020, nineteen-year-old Mohammed Kudus, who had already represented the Ghanaian national team, transferred from FC Nordsjælland to the Dutch giants Ajax Amsterdam for a fee of nine million euros, with performance-related add-on payments included in the fee structure (Narkortu Teye, 2020). Right to Dream has been subject to academic and journalistic critique in terms of its interventions in the wider moral politics of development (McGee, 2015), and in how it manages the football-specific career trajectories of its students and graduates (*Der Spiegel*, 2018; Haslov and Brock, 2018a, 2018b). However, within the context of Africa's export-oriented football industry, it continues to be viewed as a template for others to follow in terms of producing and exporting highly skilled football labour (see Chapter 7).

The informal sector

Alongside the formal academy system in Senegal, Côte d'Ivoire and Ghana, and elsewhere on the continent, there is a sizeable informal sector that operates at its fringes. This sector is comprised of a range of entities and actors that seek to produce players that can be traded to other academies, domestic clubs or, occasionally, directly to the international market. Some are little more than neighbourhood youth teams run by coaches who invest their own, often limited, capital in the running costs associated with football at this level. They tend to be motivated by a communitarian impulse and a concern for local youth, and a hope that they may play some role in 'uncovering' a star player and receive some financial recompense for this. Others are more strategic in their pursuit of the financial remuneration that developing and trading football labour can bring and try to imitate some of the more 'professional' practices and structures they observe in the formal academy sector. For example, some establish recruitment networks that extend beyond the local neighbourhood and enlist young players from a much wider geographical area. Those recruited from further afield typically leave the family home to live with relatives close to the academy or are accommodated in small, rudimentary facilities or 'club houses' built by the academy owner. Both types of informal academies tend to provide a loosely structured football education, often from poorly qualified coaches. According to Isaac Addo, former General Secretary of the GFA, beyond registering with regional or national governing bodies in order to play in official youth leagues it is a largely unregulated sector (interview, 27 January 2009).

These types of academies abound throughout the continent and can be found in the major cities of most West African countries. In Senegal, for example, at the beginning of the new millennium there were as many as 160 training centres registered with the Association of Football School Managers of Senegal, which was founded in 1995 (Mahjoub, 2003). As a consequence of Senegal's success in reaching the quarter-final of the World Cup in 2002, the number of informal academies rapidly grew with the Fédération Sénégalaise de Football estimating that almost three hundred had been established in Dakar (Schokkaert, Swinnen, and Vandemoortele, 2012). They are equally numerous in Accra, with one estimate suggesting that towards the end of the first decade of the new millennium there were as many as five hundred (McDougall, 2008). While they are a quantitatively significant feature of the football industry in West Africa, it is rare that these sorts of informal academies will have formed the transnational relationships that can facilitate the direct transfer of players abroad. Nonetheless, they are an important conduit through which young players can access more transnationally connected, organised academies.

The links between this sector and the more structured academies are multifarious. Some owners will act as scouts for larger academies, accruing a 'finders' fee' for bringing promising talents to their attention, some of whom they will have recruited into their own set-up. Others enter into arrangements that see them act as feeder clubs, identifying and training young players who may subsequently move to an organised academy. As the vignette at the start of this chapter revealed, other youth teams or academies also insert themselves into the trade by entering teams or putting forward their most talented young charges for trial events organised by the larger academies. This has been augmented by the organisation of tournaments for non-affiliated academy teams from across West Africa by unofficial bodies, such as the Confederation of African Football Academies, which provide opportunities to assess a large pool of young talent at a single venue (Darby, Akindes and Kirwin, 2007).

This informal sector also offers opportunities for a variegated network of local scouts, intermediaries and talent speculators to insert themselves into the trade in young African footballers. As we detail in the next chapter, the youth game in Ghana has become increasingly populated by actors, typically young males, who seek to profit from youth talent through varying forms of financial speculation. This can serve to lubricate the flow of talented players from this peripheral end of the football production network to more transnationally organised nodes. However, at the same time, aggressive recruitment practices and competition can also undermine and threaten the sustainability of localised investment in youth football development at this level. As Kwame, co-owner of an informal academy in Ghana, explained:

> We are having problems with the managers because we go outside to bring the boys to the camp. We train them and when they become good, they [card dealers] just want to come and take them and pay them shit money which is very bad ... You need to be careful because some of the managers can just come up and say 'I want to take your player to trial', and before you realise, they sell the player and take all the money.

His colleague Kudos added:

> The only way really that this can happen is if you take the boy to a different region before you can do that, because if you come for my player and you take him somewhere local then you can trace him and get my boy back. I will produce the boy's licence. But some managers have been doing this, taking a boy from a team in the north and bringing him down to the south. (Interview, 4 February 2008)

This type of commodification of their embodied talent and the financial speculation that accompanies it can be exploited by young players to navigate to more advantageous positions in the game's production network from which they may be more likely to enact transnational mobility. However, it is also important to emphasise that it can also seriously curtail their prospects by exposing them to illicit, nefarious practices, including trafficking, an issue that we address in the next chapter.

Border crossings and the post-playing-career node

Without exception, the objective of every young footballer that we engaged with during our research who were situated in and navigating their way through the production nodes described above was to leave their home countries and secure a professional contract 'outside'. Most aspired to follow in the footsteps of those star players whose careers had taken them to the elite echelons of the 'big five' European leagues. However, our interviews with numerous young players revealed how these aspirations change over time. As the players neared the age at which they could transfer abroad, they began to better understand the opportunities available in the global football industry. They also started to grasp how their place in particular production sites impacted on these opportunities, and many became more realistic and flexible in terms of where their first transnational border crossing might take them.

This is borne out in the spatial distribution of contemporary African football labour outlined in the previous chapter, which clearly shows that players have become increasingly open to moving to leagues of much lower standing in order to gain a foothold in the professional football industry. In Europe, a key factor in this process has been the ongoing recruitment drive in Africa by clubs from middle- and lower-tier leagues, initiated by the Bosman ruling, which has led to a relative over-representation of African players in lower levels of competition (Poli, 2010a). The emergence of academies in Africa established by or operated in conjunction with European clubs, discussed earlier, has also contributed to careers that encompass clubs in middle-ranking European leagues in countries such as the Netherlands, Austria, Belgium and Denmark. As opportunities to earn a living from the game have expanded beyond Europe, the geography of African players' transnational mobilities has diversified further, taking them to championships in, for example, South and South-East Asia, destinations that are unlikely to have featured in their imaginaries as they plotted and worked towards initiating their migratory projects.

Transferring to more modest leagues does not reflect an acquiescence on the part of African players to a relatively nondescript career at the periphery of the football industry. This is frequently the outcome for those who move to these sorts of markets, but the decision to take their football labour to these fields should be read as a strategic form of mobility. While pockets of the football industry outside Europe do offer the prospect of earnings not available in their country of origin, these types of moves are motivated by a desire to bolster their visibility and further develop their attributes in ways that might enable onward step-migration to more high-end, lucrative European markets (Poli, 2006a, 2006b, 2010a). However, progressing to nodes in more prestigious national settings in the professional game is a process imbued with uncertainty and unpredictability. Improving on the quality and output of their football labour in order to attract the attention of more esteemed employers in higher-profile leagues has proven difficult for African migrant players; for most, their career paths tend to be characterised either by stagnation or a downward trajectory rather than progression to higher-level leagues or financially stronger clubs (Poli, 2010a). As we discuss in chapters 7 and 8, this is partly a consequence of the frequently challenging contractual conditions under which they labour as well as the rigours of adjusting to and settling in what players often experience as culturally, and frequently linguistically, alien contexts. The fact that, on average, they tend to make their first move abroad at a younger age than their counterparts from South America and Europe likely plays into this scenario, making them less prepared to cope with the wider challenges associated with migration (Poli, 2010a).

While GPNs involving inert commodities or services typically have a life cycle that ends with consumption, those involving athletic labour can be circular and involve a post-playing-career node. We see this in those instances where retired migrant players return home, utilise the intellectual, financial and cultural capital accrued during their career overseas and reinsert themselves back into the production network by setting up or investing in academies or football clubs. Abedi Pelé, Ghana's most decorated football export and three times African Player of the Year, is a case in point. Following an illustrious career that took him to Switzerland, Germany, Italy and, most famously, France in the 1980s and 1990s, Pelé returned to Ghana in 2000. Armed with significant footballing knowledge and expertise and, equally importantly, first-hand experience of the networks that facilitate football migration in various European countries, Pelé established his own club, FC Nania, and set up a youth academy that not only produced talent for the club but also became a fruitful conduit for exporting players, including his three sons, André, Jordan and Ibrahim, all of whom transferred from Nania to European clubs. As is evident in our description of the academy node in West Africa earlier in this chapter, inserting oneself into the trade in African football players in this way is a common practice among those who have had successful transnational careers in the game. In Chapter 9, we further discuss these practices as well as the range of other post-playing-career lives and livelihoods that African football migrants cultivate.

Conclusions

Over the course of the last two chapters, we have employed a GPN framework to set out an industry-level perspective on how and in what ways Africa and African football players have been integrated into a global market for the professional game's core commodity, football labour. This has involved presenting a detailed overview of the complex assemblage of networks, nodes, actors and institutions through which transnationally mobile African footballers are fashioned and exported, and how this has changed through time. It has also encompassed an account of the spatial dimensions of players' mobilities and the frameworks and rules that regulate their cross-border movements. As we acknowledged in Chapter 1, setting out these structural, territorial and regulatory features offers only partial insights into what is a complex, multi-faceted process. While African players' aspirations for and enactment of transnational mobility are a product of the internal dynamics and logic of the local and global football industry, they are equally an outcome of the multifarious aspirations and agency of African youth, the wider socio-economic milieus within which they struggle to survive, their understandings of the relationship between social and spatial mobility and their sense of responsibility for extended family and significant others.

This is not to suggest that the sort of GPN-inspired, industry-level mapping that we have undertaken in these previous two chapters is at odds with our emphasis in the rest of this book on unpacking the imaginaries, agency, subjectivities and experiences of African players as they negotiate local and transnational nodes of the game's production network. Nor are we saying that it conflicts with our intention to expound on how this process is informed by localised social, economic and cultural currents. As we argued in Chapter 1, developments in the GPN literature have seen this perspective become more attuned to the social and cultural 'embeddedness' of production. It is also increasingly attentive to the social dynamics that impact the margins of the network and has come to conceive of workers as agentic, sentient social actors rather than as passive inputs to production. These developments in how GPNs are approached align with the more fine-grained, player-centric analyses that we undertake across the rest of this book. More specifically, in the next three chapters, we use Ghana as a case study to explore how youth rationalise their entry into football and how this is influenced by the structural context of the Ghanaian football industry, the nature of their encounters and engagement with the game, and the outcomes of their efforts to use it as a source of transnational mobility and to 'make it' as a professional player. Over the subsequent, and final three, chapters of this book, we examine how African players experience and navigate transnational moves and professional careers 'outside' and interrogate their post-playing-career trajectories, lives and livelihoods.

4

Speculation in and through football migration

Introduction

> My name is Tommy Howe. I am a football scout. You could say that my job is to look for greatness. I came here expecting to find it. I just didn't expect to find so much of it. I've travelled the world in search of talent and I can't ever remember seeing the game played so beautifully. Here, give a man half the chance, and he takes it. I guess it is true what they say. There is a drop of greatness in every man. (Gray, 2010)

The opening quote is the voiceover from a Guinness television advertisement directed by Greg Gray titled 'Scout', aired to coincide with the 2010 World Cup in South Africa. In the advert, a white, male, European football talent scout goes to 'sub-Saharan Africa' to find the next football star. The advert does not specify the country or countries where Tommy Howe is conducting his search, but it was filmed in Kenya. The advert depicts Howe driving around 'Africa' and witnessing brilliant football performances wherever he goes, before concluding with the revelation that his chauffeur is the star player he was searching for all along. This is a fantastic and fortuitous outcome for the driver because, as we show in chapters 7 and 8, realising transnational mobility via a contract with an overseas club, preferably in Europe, constitutes the most sought-after outcome from the bodily, emotional and financial investments that young African players and a range of actors make as they seek to 'become a somebody' in the football industry. This chapter aims to outline the structural context young players in Ghana encounter as they try to turn their ambitions into reality. Moreover, we seek to reveal a range of lesser-known actors that play a key role in the circulation of talent within football's GPN. In doing so, we utilise the concept of social infrastructure to generate a more grounded and relational understanding of African football migration that is attuned to the interplay between the subjectivities of a multitude of actors within the football industry and global and local processes of socio-economic change.

In the first half of the chapter, we provide a brief overview of the historical and contemporary footballing context in Ghana. To be clear, providing a detailed history of Ghanaian football migration is beyond the scope of this chapter. It is also a topic that has been covered elsewhere (Darby, 2010, 2013b). However, we provide this historical context because it is important to acknowledge the contrast between past and more recent migratory trends in the men's game. It also allows us to situate our analyses in the next three chapters within a longer temporal register to illustrate how contemporary migration drivers are the outcome of post-colonial processes. The second half of the chapter then addresses the commercial dimension, which emerges from this context, and uses a social infrastructure approach to reveal highly speculative behaviour among a range of actors seeking to consolidate their position and coordinate activities within the football industry.

While conscious of projecting a stereotypically dystopian picture of football in African contexts, we acknowledge the historical highs and contemporary lows that have blighted and are blighting Ghanaian football. We contend that viewing the challenges facing Ghanaian football and migratory trends as a symptom of an 'African culture of mediocrity' is reductive. Instead, these challenges should be understood as indicative features of 'millennial capitalism' (Comaroff and Comaroff, 2000), a state of affairs constitutive of the dominating neoliberal global agenda that has led, among other things, to a shift from an emphasis on social welfare to individual gains. This shift fuels the speculative behaviour alluded to above, which in turn drives player mobility and migration within key nodes in football's GPN.

Local articulations of a global game

Kwame Nkrumah, Ghana's first post-independence president, recognised the capacity of football to mobilise Ghanaians around a shared identity, and the value of sporting victories for creating and instilling national pride (Darby, 2010; Fridy and Brobbey, 2009). President Nkrumah sought to develop the sporting infrastructure and advance social development through sport, and he appointed Ohene Djan as Sports Czar within a year of taking office (Alegi, 2010). Importantly for football, together they established the Ghanaian Amateur Football Association (GAFA). In their quest to build a solid foundation for Ghanaian football at both an international and domestic level, the GAFA was also affiliated with CAF in 1957 and FIFA the following year. Amid a backdrop of early independence excitement, a national amateur league was formed in 1959. In 1961 Nkrumah and Djan created Real Republikans, a 'super club' inspired by the legendary Real Madrid side that won five consecutive European Cups from 1956 (Alegi, 2010; Fridy and

Brobbey, 2009). Furthermore, in a gesture bristling with pan-African symbolism and evidence of the President's belief that football was a positive means of demonstrating Africa's potential, the Ghanaian national team adopted the sobriquet 'Black Stars', a reference to Marcus Garvey's famous shipping line (Darby, 2010).

During that same period the Black Stars went on a European tour, playing matches in Germany, Austria, Russia and England in 1962, and Spain and Italy the following year (Alegi, 2010). In spite of the success of the national team and the establishment of a national league, at youth level the sport was still struggling for prestige; while the standard of football was reasonably high and the game was popular, football was merely considered one of many recreational activities. President Nkrumah began the process of developing the footballing infrastructure and assisting youth academies by investing in and improving facilities for U-14 and U-17 youth competitions, known locally as Colts league football (Esson, 2016). At the same time, national policies supported the belief that education was a prerequisite for individual social mobility and national development. Football clubs then, as they do now, would often sign players from the age of eight upwards, seeking to develop and nurture their talent. The intention was that the player would later graduate and play for the senior team. For clubs with small operating budgets this was (and remains) a cost-effective way to supplement the main playing squad.

Crucially, and as discussed in Chapter 2, the movement of players was internally oriented. Despite the amateur nature of the game, from the early post-independence period through to the late 1980s, most male Ghanaian football players were happy to remain 'at home'. Only one notable player migrated during the Nkrumah reign, Charles Kumi Gyamfi; however, his transfer in 1960 to the German club Fortuna Düsseldorf was seen as a patriotic gesture achieved at the President's behest. Given the success of West Germany, world champions in 1954, Nkrumah believed that familiarity with German coaching techniques and playing styles would benefit the Ghanaian men's national team (Darby, 2010).

The key reasons for this commitment to the development of a national football industry were threefold. Firstly, within and beyond football, Ghana's future appeared promising. Consequently, in the period following independence, football players appeared to be masters of a relatively secure career. The game was amateur, yet they were still known to live comfortably if not necessarily extravagantly by twenty-first-century standards. State support for football at the amateur and juvenile level for boys, together with opportunities for continent-wide competition, meant that despite interest from foreign clubs, the vast majority of players did not consider plying their trade abroad. Players were traded locally between clubs, but even at the highest amateur level it was rare for significant transfer or registration fees to change hands over a player (Fridy and Brobbey, 2009). The players were valued for their performances on the pitch rather than any potential commercial worth. Secondly, the government sought to adopt protectionist policies that often acted as a barrier to emigration (Darby, 2010). Finally, and linked to the previous point, unlike France and Portugal, British clubs were parochial and reluctant to look beyond their shores for talent (Darby, 2007a).

For the majority of male Ghanaian youth playing in the early post-independence period, football was not considered the default career choice. Jordan Anagblah, former vice-president of the GFA (successor to the GAFA) and chairman of the Greater Accra Regional Football Association, explained how football's popularity often failed to detach it from connotations of poverty (interview, 29 March 2011). Its low status among the majority of Ghanaians was altered only for very talented players, and for many people education remained the priority.

Our point here is that, in sharp contrast to the perspectives we provide in this and the next two chapters, football's popularity in pre-1990s Ghana did not render it immune from negative perceptions. Accordingly, as Herbert Adika, the man credited with spotting and nurturing the talent of Abedi Pelé, notes below, a career in football was seen as being subordinate to a good formal education and attributed a low social status, to the point of being associated with social deviance and *kobolo*, a term Lamptey made reference to in the opening chapter:

> In my secondary-school time, we were playing boxing, athletics, tennis ... rugby and basketball ... [Of] these five disciplines, all of us were asked to join one of them. So, if you are not a good footballer, you can do something. If you come from a very respectable family, you will want to continue with your education rather than go into football, and people who played too much and were on the street were what we call *koboloi*. (Interview, 28 March 2011)

Nkrumah's investment in football inevitably left the sport exposed to the fluctuation of political tides. Engulfed in a storm of economic uncertainty, his popularity began to wane in the mid-1960s. The ending of his rule following a military coup in 1966 resulted in a long period of economic and political instability. Accordingly, it appeared unlikely that Ghanaian football would continue to benefit from state support. General Ankrah's government could not risk being associated with institutions aligned with Nkrumah's reign, so the new regime reversed football initiatives or let them stagnate (Esson, 2016). Dr Busia was then elected Ghanaian head of state in 1969, but until General Acheampong replaced him in another military coup in 1972, football remained a low political priority (Darby, 2010). This considerably weakened the footballing infrastructure at all levels of the game.

A notable social development through football policy formulated during the Nkrumah era was the aforementioned national youth programme, the Academicals, which consisted of secondary-school students competing at local, district, regional and national level. The formation of this initiative served multiple purposes. Firstly, it was a method of funnelling so-called *koboloi* boys into the education system. The Academicals encouraged aspiring footballers to attend school and improve their chances of being selected by a decent amateur team. This approach proved mutually beneficial for the development of the sport by improving the standard of play. As noted by Herbert Adika, the best amateur clubs could watch the Academicals to easily identify the best players:

> When we had the Academicals, let us say only thirty or forty years back, we can easily identify the quality players by our local standard, and you can easily identify quality players and mention them in any locality that you go. But presently, everybody thinks they can play football, and often they are not even the good types. (Interview, 28 March 2011)

Secondly, in an attempt to dislodge its association with socially deprived children and *koboloi*, the Academicals served the role of popularising football among education-conscious households. As a precursor of the relationship between social and spatial mobility in football, albeit of a short rather than extended nature, the Academicals also offered the additional benefit of travel. As noted by Jordan Anagblah:

> In those days I, for instance, played for the Academicals and we even had a national team because back then we didn't have under-seventeen, twenty or twenty-three, so it encouraged those elite students who, like me, were good both academically and at football. We just played for fun and you are motivated because you will get the chance to travel to the neighbouring countries. So, while your classmates are in school, you can come back and say you went to Nigeria to play, and it is like you have become a hero instantly. They say, 'Oh, so you have travelled to Nigeria by flight? Oh, so you have gone to the airport?' You felt happy that you have impressed people. (Interview, 29 March 2011)

In spite of political and civil unrest during the 1970s and 1980s, all appeared well at international football level when Ghana managed to lift their fourth and, at the time of writing, last Africa Cup of Nations title in 1982, having also won the tournament in 1963, 1965 and 1978 (Alegi, 2010). However, at the domestic level, the physical infrastructure and policies conceived or implemented during the Nkrumah regime were further abandoned and disregarded, with pitches and equipment allocated for Colts league football being particularly inadequate (Esson, 2016). The commitment of leading

Ghanaian football players to remain in the country was tested by the uncertainty seeping through society, attributable to a declining economy and rising unemployment. Therefore, while Ghanaian players were still relatively less visible compared to their contemporaries from former French and Portuguese colonies, several high-profile path-breakers emerged during the late 1970s and 1980s (Darby, 2010). A handful of players, such as Ghanaian ex-international George Lamptey (no relation to his namesake, Nii), made moves to the North American Soccer League (Lamptey, 2021). In Europe, the German-born Anthony Baffoe played for several clubs in Germany's 1. and 2. Bundesliga between 1982 and 1992. Abedi Pelé's distinguished career in French football began in the mid-1980s, while Tony Yeboah, who would go on to play in the top leagues in Germany and England, emerged in the late 1980s. These path-breakers paved the way for players like Nii Lamptey who, as we highlighted at the outset of this book, had a peripatetic football career that touched down in multiple continents from the 1990s onwards.

Organising and monetising football

In an era where the 'grand design' for development was enacted through neoliberal SAPs and marketisation (Black, 2010), the GFA attempted to make changes to professionalise football in line with these philosophies. In 1993, all teams in what was then the national amateur league were made to register as limited liability companies, float shares on the Ghana Stock Exchange, have a physical secretariat and present audited accounts at the end of each football season (Pannenborg, 2010). Accordingly, those involved in Ghanaian football were encouraged to diversify their revenue streams and adopt business-like structures such as establishing a board of directors and appointing a CEO.

The name of the league was also changed to reflect its new status: it became the Ghana Premier League, with an additional two-tier semi-professional league structure later introduced in 1995. In the new format, the Division One League, comprising three zones of sixteen teams (forty-eight in total), sits beneath the Premier League. The top two teams from each zone compete in an end of season play-off with the winners promoted to the top tier in place of three relegated teams. This era of professionalism is associated with the emergence of high-profile club owners, often referred to as 'big men' (Esson, 2015c; Pannenborg, 2010). The men's amateur game, meanwhile, consists of a national second division, divided into regional zones, while a third division was later created to cater for the growing demand for club football. In 2012 the GFA launched the National Women's

League. Up to that point, organised girls and women's football had been played at a regional level with relatively little coverage or support. This was despite stellar performances by the Ghanaian women's national team, colloquially known as the Black Queens, at multiple international tournaments. This included winning the CAF African Women's Championships in 1991 and making three consecutive FIFA World Cups between 1999 and 2007. Alongside this team success, there were also individual accolades. For example, Alberta Sackey and Adjoa Bayor won the CAF African Women's Footballer of the Year award in 2002 and 2003, respectively.

The period from 2011 was clearly a busy one in terms of attempts to develop Ghanaian football. Efforts were made to launch a new regulated and official national Colts league (including U-12, U-14 and U-17 categories, which were subsequently changed to U-13, U-15 and U-17). In March 2011, while registration was still taking place, the GFA regional office in Accra estimated that seven hundred clubs in twelve regional zones would take part, with 240 of these located in the capital, spread over eleven districts. The precise number of registered youth players for that season was unknown; however, teams could register upwards of twenty players per age category. GFA executive Evans Amenumey estimated the number of registered youth players in Accra alone to be in the region of twenty to twenty-five thousand (interview, 29 March 2011). In autumn 2019, the GFA announced that player registration fees for all Colts clubs across the country would be scrapped in order to ease the financial burden on club owners (Sienu, 2019). Sadly, as we demonstrate below, at the time of writing the Colts league is in disarray, having not been able to procure adequate funding or support for decades. This has become a topic of heated debate in the Ghanaian news media (Adamu, 2020; Ghana Soccernet, 2019; Kwafo, 2019). Former Black Stars captain Stephen Appiah has argued that the downturn in the national team's performances at all levels since the senior side's World Cup exploits between 2006 and 2014 can be attributed to the decline of the Colts league (GhanaWeb, 2019). Asamoah Gyan, one of Appiah's successors in the captain's role, has also expressed concern about the situation:

> I started with the Colts level. A lot of players who played for the senior national team, they (also) started from the Colts level. I recently found out that there's no more colt football in Ghana and that is something I want to do [something about]. (Cited in *Ghanaian Times*, 2020)

Despite this downturn in the administration of the juvenile leagues, and for reasons we will discuss below, since the early 2000s the number of youth team clubs and academies throughout the country seeking to enter the football industry, particularly in Accra, has continued to rise. Reports estimate that as of 2019 there were close to one thousand Colts clubs in Ghana

(Sienu, 2019). As discussed in the previous chapter, this increase in youth clubs and academies reflects a broader trend that has been taking place throughout Africa for some time. Similar to the Premier League, the demographic of club owners at the amateur and Colts level has changed post-1991, becoming characterised by youth in their mid-twenties to mid-thirties who see owning and managing a football club as a form of employment (Esson, 2015c), a point we address further below. This is expressed vividly by the founder and owner of the renowned Kumasi Sports Academy (KUSA), King James Asuming, who openly admits his intentions for establishing a youth academy were not purely altruistic. He acknowledges how it was a means for socio-economic consolidation by interacting with multiple nodes of the GPN (youth academy, senior club and national team): 'Through this I can be popular or a big man, because once most of the players in the national team are from your academy you also become a big person or a popular person' (Dubinsky and Schler, 2019: 255).

Corporate investment at the highest level of Ghanaian football was proving beneficial to the GFA and senior national team, but at the time of writing, semi-professional football in Ghana had reached a state of crisis. There were two factors at play here. Firstly, a corruption scandal in mid-2018 resulted in the dissolution of the national football association (GFA) after the president, Kwesi Nyantakyi, was caught on tape accepting a huge cash gift from an undercover reporter. The same report exposed more than one hundred West African referees and football officials who engaged in bribery to influence games over a two-year period between 2016 and 2018 (BBC News, 2018). Secondly, the COVID-19 pandemic derailed the 2019/20 season, leading to its cancellation in June 2020. While the subsequent Premier League season did start in late 2020, domestic football has continued to be disrupted by the ongoing pandemic and had only partly resumed by the time we finished this book in April 2021. COVID-19 notwithstanding, what went wrong? Why did professionalisation along neoliberal lines that was supposed to re-invigorate Ghanaian domestic football result in such dramatic stagnation and dysfunction? How has this structural context shaped the internal and transnational migration of Ghanaian players? We now look at the commercial imperatives within Ghanaian football to address these questions.

Risk and reward in juvenile football

To readers familiar with the political economy of football in African contexts, the depiction of Ghanaian football provided above probably evokes long-standing concerns raised within FIFA, CAF, human rights groups and sections of the liberal European press. These actors propose that the health of football in Africa is dependent on addressing a 'culture of mediocrity' at the heart of the game's political economy (Mahjoub, 1992, cited in Darby, Akindes and Kirwin, 2007). These discourses share similarities with the 'criminalisation thesis' used to explain the alleged failures and inadequacies of African states (Bayart, Ellis and Hibou, 1999). This thesis argues that African social networks and practices undermine rational economic institutions, as the former are underpinned by dishonest cultural predispositions, a lack of separation between private and public spheres and a validation of cunning (see Goodfellow, 2020; Meagher, 2005 for a counter narrative). To some extent, Ghanaian football is indeed struggling to develop an economically effective political economy due to intrinsic dysfunctional 'cultural repertoires', namely a propensity towards clientelism and dishonesty. On the topic of clientelism, Kurt Okraku appeared to foresee the impending corruption scandal when, as head of the Ghana League Clubs Association (GHALCA), he stated:

> The systems don't really work like it works in Europe. It is very difficult. I hope you understand what I am saying. There is a lack of human resource. I mean, the quality is simply not there. People in football have still not come to accept that football is science and that it is not about who is my friend, who is my brother or who is my sister. It is about who has the capacity to deliver. Until we accept this philosophy, things will never change. People aren't accepting this fact that football is science and this affects everything. It affects decision making, it affects organisation, it affects the intangible assets, it affects everything. (Interview, 14 February 2011)

It is not only at the executive level that such issues are prevalent. During what began as a casual discussion after training with U-17 players at Barracks FC, a Colts league club based in Osu (Accra) regarding their career aspirations, James was informed by several players – who became increasingly aggrieved as the conversation escalated – that one of the biggest obstacles to footballing success in Ghana is endemic clientelism. They described how young players are exposed to inappropriate practices including 'refreshing' (bribing) referees to fix results and avoid relegation, falsifying player registration documents to make players appear younger and paying officials to change passport details. It was also explained that it is particularly with regard to international migration that above-mentioned 'big men' are able to use their financial and political clout to influence team selection in national youth sides and, in doing so, ensure that their players gain the much-coveted international exposure offered by FIFA youth tournaments. As also noted in Chapter 2, this improves the player's international visibility (cf. Carter, 2011; Engh and Agergaard, 2015) and enhances their chances of being spotted by foreign recruiters and of gaining a lucrative transfer overseas.

The role of 'big men' in this process represents an example of why we argue here that people constitute a critical form of infrastructure within the context of transnational football migration and in the football industry more generally. The 'big man' plays a crucial role as a mediating driver of migration, in that through consolidating their position within society, they enable and take on a coordinating role and facilitate migration by providing financial and material resources. As we show below, they are not the only actors that fit this description. This interest in the Colts league and elite youth football among 'big men' has arisen despite the above-mentioned challenges facing the organisation of the game at this level, because money circulates in Ghanaian football primarily through player transfers within but preferably out of Ghana (see also Pannenborg, 2010). A key contributing factor of this situation is that the fragile economic state of the Ghanaian football industry means that some clubs are unwilling and/or unable to offer players the financial remuneration, contractual and health security, and training facilities that will encourage them to stay in the domestic leagues. As we show in subsequent chapters, this is compounded by a pervasive migratory disposition within Ghanaian society more broadly. The majority of players in the league earn less than two hundred US dollars per month, a sum that does not compare favourably to a graduate working in the Ghanaian civil service. Nii Lamptey articulated this point:

> We're in a state in Ghana ... no club can pay you even one hundred dollars a month ... I have a family. I have to buy clothes. I have to eat. Somebody pops up, 'I have a club for you in India, they will pay you two thousand dollars a month'. Do you think I will stop? I will go. (Cited in Darby, 2010: 36)

These economic struggles in the men's game filter down into the youth leagues because, as alluded to in Chapter 3 and further illustrated below, youth academies are increasingly positioned as 'extractive ventures' within football's GPN, underpinned by a motivation to identify and sell talent on the international, ideally European, transfer market. The appointment of the Brazilian João Havelange as FIFA president in 1974 was key in this regard. Havelange was elected on a manifesto that promised an increase in political, financial and technical support for football in Africa and developing countries more broadly (Darby, 2002). A key consequence of this was the allocation of more places for African teams at the World Cup finals. The improved profile that this allowed the African game to acquire in the international arena was amplified by the exceptional performances of African sides at the U-20 and U-17 world youth championships, which were also introduced during Havelange's presidency in 1977 and 1985, respectively. These performances began to undermine racial stereotypes of African players as merely 'natural footballers' who relied on their instincts and enhanced physical attributes but lacked the tactical wisdom and discipline to compete in the elite echelons of the international game (Bale, 2004; Lanfranchi and Taylor, 2001). Significantly, the success of African teams at world senior and youth levels effectively showcased the potential of African talent to European clubs and induced the 'demand' for African players in Europe.

It is in this context that Ghana's first FIFA male youth tournament success, in the 1991 U-17 World Championship, came to be considered the watershed moment in terms of transforming Ghanaian football migration on more commercial and speculative rationales (Acheampong, Bouhaouala and Raspaud, 2019; Ungruhe, 2016). The tournaments constitute a 'predisposing driver' (van Hear, Bakewell and Long, 2018) in that they contribute to the creation of a context in which migration is more likely. As Jordan Anagblah observed, following the national youth team's success in 1991, youth football became less about developmental discourses and patriotism, and more a business opportunity:

> The change started in 91 when they introduced this Coca-Cola under-17 games and when those players moved to Europe. Before then players moved to Europe, but nobody knows how much they have been bought for and what goes into it. But when these players were bought and sent to Europe then everybody gets to know that there is money in this thing and that is when people started to struggle for it in Ghana. (Interview, 29 March 2011)

The desire among club owners in the semi-professional and amateur ranks to 'struggle' to find the next young star who might be sold to a foreign club, as a form of speculation, was expressed by a range of our research participants. Ernest Kuffour, the founder of the Unistar Academy, based in Ofaakor, a town located forty kilometres west of Accra, was a case in point. He had previously worked abroad as an accountant before deciding to return to Ghana to establish a commercial foothold in the local football industry. Describing himself as 'an ardent football supporter' and having had previous experience in football administration with Accra Hearts of Oak, one of Ghana's biggest clubs, Kuffour put together a group of Ghanaian investors, including Samuel Addo, a successful Kazakhstan-based businessman who became president of the academy. With initial set-up costs estimated by Kuffour to be close to one million US dollars and annual running costs of 300,000–350,000 US dollars, Kuffour and Addo set about establishing partnerships with clubs 'outside' in order to facilitate the sale of players. This was articulated by Kuffour in the following terms:

> We want to develop partners outside. We want to talk to clubs ... They will come in and help the marketing of the players so that if we develop players, they will come and pick what they want and we can sell the others to clubs that need players. That's the kind of partnership that we are looking for. (Interview, 3 June 2012)

It is worth highlighting here that similar commercial imperatives take place in girls and women's football both in Ghana and more widely (Agergaard, 2018; Agergaard and Botelho, 2014; Agergaard and Tiesler, 2014). King James Asuming, the previously mentioned academy owner, has been very outspoken about the potentially lucrative market that is women's football in Ghana. As Dubinsky and Schler note:

> He [King James Asuming] believed that he could pioneer the development of a girls' team as a way of increasing the revenue of his academy ... Marketing campaigns and promotional materials highlight the stories of those recruited to national teams, such as Blessing Shine Agbomadzi, the academy's women's captain who won the national MVP award in 2015, and was subsequently called up to the national U-17 team. Blessing is also featured in the academy's TV commercial wearing her national team jersey. King claimed that these efforts to leverage Blessing's success generated interest in the academy, and his phone was flooded with calls from interested parents and children following the launch of the commercial. King's reputation and revenue all grew along with children's registration to KUSA. (Dubinsky and Schler, 2019: 258)

Similar to the elite echelons of Ghanaian football, the demographic of club owners in the Colts league has also undergone changes. While high-profile actors like King James Asuming grab the media headlines, the reality is that they are the outliers. The real change is characterised by the predominance of so-called 'small boys' who see owning and managing a football club as a form of employment (Esson, 2015c). The term 'small boy' is not intended to depict the physical stature of these individuals, rather it is an idiom commonly used in Ghana to portray an individual's social status relative to his age. In this instance, it is used to highlight how many of the club owners in the Colts leagues lack social markers associated with normative notions of adulthood, such as home ownership, formal employment and financial independence. On this topic, GFA executive Evans Amenumey explained how these young club owners often struggle financially:

> Times are changing and people also have to change to meet the situation. Before things were not at all like this thing. Now most of these small boys who even organize this juvenile league are unemployed. Some push truck and some help building contractors to carry concrete just to pay referee fees and transport. (Cited in Esson, 2015c: 51)

As noted above, the GFA is well aware that the costs of running a Colts team is a challenge given that a notable difference between 'small boys', who make up the vast majority of owners, and 'big men' is their respective financial strength. During a meeting at the GFA regional office in Accra in 2011, as the Colts league was being reformed, James obtained details,

Table 1 Costs associated with men's amateur and Colts leagues

Activity	Fee (Ghana cedis, GHC)
Registration card	
Second Division	5.00 (per player)
Third Division	5.00 (per player)
Colts	3.00 (per player)
Administration fee	
Second Division	–
Third Division	–
Colts	40.00 (per team)
Officiating fee	
Second Division	35.00 (per team/game)
Third Division	20.00 (per team/game)
Colts	22.00 (per team/game)
Disciplinary offences	
Second bookable offence (two yellow cards)	30.00 (per offence)
Red card	40.00 (per offence)
Travel	Variable

outlined in Table 1, regarding some of the official fees associated with managing an amateur men's and Colts league club.

Perhaps unsurprisingly, these costs have increased with inflation and currency devaluation since 2010. For example, a registration card for a Colts player doubled in price from 5 to 10 Ghana cedis in the decade to 2020. For context relative to wages, Ghana's daily minimum wage, which was 10.65 cedis (1.94 US dollars) in 2019, increased by 11 per cent to 11.82 cedis (2.16 US dollars) in 2020. As Sienu (2019) points out, the GFA's plan to abolish registration fees for players in the Colts leagues should significantly reduce the cost associated with running a club. This financial relief is welcomed by club owners, because taking ownership of a football club carries significant administrative and financial obligations. In addition to these official fees, youth team players are also known to ask for boots, training kit, water, win bonuses and even money for school examinations. The idea of clubs having thirty players for each category, and therefore at least ninety registered youth players in total, might seem excessive. However, it chimes with research that has found that Colts club owners often seek to register as many players as they possibly can (Esson, 2015c). We discuss the reasons for this in more detail below but in sum, young players are seen as commodities with the potential to generate profit when transferred.

Money through movement in football

The speculative disposition among some, but not all, club owners matters for our understanding of how Ghanaian youth are embedded within football's GPN. It illustrates how, within the general economic organisation of world football, Ghanaian players are not only a human resource in the sporting sense for their respective clubs. They are also a potential source of capital, attributed valuations according to their performances and marketability. Crucially, this financial value is virtual when the player is under contract or, in the case of youth, registered with a particular club. However, it becomes real when a player is transferred or sold from one club to another. As noted in Chapter 1, when we view a commodity as something produced and offered for sale in a market and then consider the empirical functioning of the capitalist football industry, the notion of the footballer player as a commodity, first theorised by Poli (2005), appears logical. Moreover, if young football players are viewed as commodities, it is because they resemble the definition suggested by Appadurai that:

> commodities are things with a particular type of social potential that they are distinguishable from 'products' ... and other sort of things – but only in certain respects and from a certain point of view ... it is definitionally useful to regard commodities as existing in a very wide variety of societies though with a special intensity and salience in modern, capitalist societies. (Appadurai, 1994: 78)

We agree with Poli's (2005) concern that while the term 'commodity' depicts how players are transferred and sold, it fails to convey the fact that, unlike typical commodities, a key distinction here is human agency. The case of Ghanaian football provides insights on how this process of player commodification in youth leagues and at the earlier stages of playing careers means footballers are now far more intricately linked to practices of commercial speculation and economic exploitation, as people seek to consolidate their social position through the movement of players. Somewhat ironically, international transfer regulations introduced by FIFA in 2001 to curb this speculative behaviour have arguably exacerbated it. These regulations sought to minimise the movement of minors within football by deterring clubs from signing players under the age of eighteen. One of the associated rulings stipulated that clubs involved in the training of players between the ages of twelve and twenty-three must receive financial compensation from the buying club (FIFA, 2020b). This has financial ramifications, because if a highly talented player is transferred to a professional club in a major league, the compensation could potentially be worth tens if not hundreds of thousands of euros.

These changes taking place in football at the global level are thus being interpreted and put to use in locally specific ways by club owners both in the semi-professional but also the junior ranks of the game, as they seek to consolidate their economic position through the sport. In light of the 2001 FIFA regulations, the labour and investment spent on a youth player is now an objective quality of said player. To further illustrate this point, the following passage from Marx's *Capital* is quoted in full:

> Every product of labour is, in all states of society, a use value; but it is only at a definite historical epoch in a society's development that such a product becomes a commodity, viz at the epoch when the labour spent on the production of a useful article becomes expressed as one of the objective qualities of that article, i.e., as its value. (Marx, 1971: 67, cited in Appadurai, 1994: 83)

We thus begin to see how financial risk, which has always been crucial to the growth of capitalism but has become more pervasive (Comaroff and Comaroff, 2000), plays an important role in the migration of young Ghanaian players. Following this line of investigation enables us to tease out some of the lesser-known multi-scalar relations founded on the speculation of talent through seemingly mundane and everyday objects in the football industry. For example, a youth player's football association registration card now acts as both a financial instrument and contract between the club and the player. Therefore, if the player is sold for a fee later in his career, the club holding or present on a card can receive compensation. This explains why club owners in youth football are keen and willing to register the maximum number of players at each age category.

The registration card is an example of how, under contemporary forms of capitalism, 'production appears to have been superseded, as the *fons et origo* of wealth, by less tangible ways of generating value' (Comaroff and Comaroff, 2000: 295). Possession of the card becomes a strategy for mitigating the risks associated with investing time and money in a club and a player, while simultaneously allowing for the creation and circulation of money. In this sense, the growing reliance on the registration card mirrors that of securitised products and contracts, allied to a transaction-driven mode of contemporary capitalist financial activity. A player's registration card can be likened to a financial bond, purchased with the hope of maturing as the player does (see also Esson, 2016). Significantly, uneven power dynamics between individuals and institutions results in club owners in the Colts divisions being 'cheated' by their counterparts in the semi-professional ranks. The following extract from an interview that James (JE) conducted with Jordan Anagblah (JA), illustrates this development (interview, 29 March 2011):

> JE: So, if I want to sign your player, what would I do?
> JA: You approach me and say 'I have seen your player training and he looks good', and tell me you are interested and then we will bargain until we agree on a price, what your pockets can meet and what I think is okay.

> Then I will transfer the card to you and write a transfer letter transferring him from my club to your club, and then we thrash out a percentage for the future, so that when he leaves your club for another club, whatever money arises you will give me a percentage of it. That is how it goes.
>
> JE: What about the players, do they sometimes not want to change teams?
>
> JA: No, you cannot force the player to leave. Often, he will rather request to move – he will go to you before the other manager will come. You don't tell the player to go to speak to someone else; you don't need to force the player, rather they will force you to transfer them.
>
> JE: So in juvenile football, there is this much money?
>
> JA: Oh yes! My brother, it is just like the senior team, I am telling you. They get cheated when senior teams look for their players, but between the juvenile leagues, among their peers, they will not let someone cheat them. Between their peers they are strong on collecting their money, but when the big clubs come they will just give the player out because the player's mother or father is giving pressure. So they will give the card before the money is paid.

In Chapter 5 we examine the role of family in the social infrastructure of football migration in Ghana, but in the final part of this chapter we want to draw attention to a lesser-known issue. It is not just club owners involved in consolidation and speculation through young football talent. Third parties such as 'managers' and 'card dealers' now also engage in commercial speculation by purchasing player registration cards. They seek to become owners of the player's registration, taking on a coordinating role, influencing to whom the registration belongs and where the player can ply their trade, and gaining the power to sell the player when it is deemed most financially expedient. These speculative practices are a localised version of third-party ownership, a controversial practice that has become part of the global economic organisation of world football, particularly in South America (Esson *et al.*, 2020; Lindholm, 2016; Mason *et al.*, 2019; Melero and Sorion, 2012; Meneses, 2013; Yilmaz *et al.*, 2020).

During a focus group discussion with youth team players from Barracks FC, they explained to James how they were willing to sign a contract with a 'manager', apportioning them a percentage of their future earnings. When quizzed as to what the player-to-manager ratio would be, Kwadwo said 60:40, Badu said 50:50 and Phillip said 60:50 (this is not a typo). One may wonder how such an arrangement benefits the player. Managers are key coordinators, but they are also seen by players as being able to help them consolidate their position. As Ben from Austin Texans FC in the Colts league also explained:

> Some of my friends have managers but it is not an authorised manager, it is just somebody who sees you play and likes the way you play. I don't have

right now, but I want one [a manager] because they will help with boots, kits, food and transportation in and out. You've worn out your boots? They will buy a fresh one for you. (Interview, 24 April 2011)

At a bare minimum, the manager provides boots and training equipment for the player, but as indicated above he will also supplement them with a daily allowance, usually of less than five cedis. This modest sum can in fact be sufficient for two meals. In a context where players and their families are struggling financially, this has the potential to be a significant symbolic and material gesture. Crucially, the manager also provides collateral for the player to attend the tournaments and trials that are considered critical in the quest to secure a lucrative transfer abroad. They may even secure the player and their family a signing bonus when the player changes teams. They are, therefore, both a mediating driver of migration and a source of daily sustenance. Conversely, individuals known as 'card dealers' are concerned solely with the continuous movement of players, and may have links to or enjoy prominent positions at a club. Card dealers are, to some extent, unique in that they simultaneously embody consolidation, speculation and coordination. They will purchase a registration card independently or in partnership with another person, each with their respective percentage according to their financial input. During a conversation with the manager of Barracks FC about some of the financial challenges the club was facing, he explained how some of this was due to card dealers within the organisation:

Eddie [Barracks FC's head coach], I know he has his percentage in so many players. He part-owns lots of players so it is in his interest to move players around. He made Barracks FC buy a few players when he first arrived that he said he needed, so they spent eight hundred cedis here and one thousand cedis there and we later found out he [Eddie] part-owned the players. (Interview, 19 April 2011)

The empirical insights provided above demonstrate how the movement of young players is now crucial to the financial sustenance of the Ghanaian football industry, albeit in an unhealthy and speculative way. This movement is financially advantageous to a variety of actors, including the players themselves, as well as so-called 'small boys' trying to earn an income by owning a club and trading young footballers domestically or on the international transfer market. Football academies are, therefore, simultaneously growing in number and also becoming progressively geared towards the grooming and export of young players to foreign clubs, ideally those in Europe (Darby, Esson and Ungruhe, 2018). This is an important point because, as we show in subsequent chapters, Europe is the preferred destination of young players. We therefore have a situation where the structural logic of the Ghanaian football industry promotes mobility both as a speculative strategy and for career progression, which aligns with the migratory disposition of young Ghanaians. Yet in reality, the ability of young players to migrate to European leagues is often constrained, thereby fostering a sense of involuntary immobility.

Mobility through football at the grassroots level can take place via interactions between locally based actors; however, an international transfer requires the intervention of someone with links 'outside'. Given that the primary objective for players and club owners was securing a transfer to a European football club, encounters with those proclaiming to have connections to this particular geographical region takes on added significance. Problematically, while players at established elite academies like Right to Dream deal with professional clubs and registered agents in accordance with FIFA's transfer system, clubs in the Colts league are likely to encounter persons malevolently claiming to be talent scouts or certified agents with connections to foreign clubs. These intermediaries are associated with a form of trial known in full as a 'Justify your inclusion' or in short as a 'justify'.

In Ghanaian football, a 'justify' is a term used to describe a trial where players compete for a place in a team – that is, you are given an opportunity to justify your inclusion in the squad. These events can range from amateur Colts teams looking to rejuvenate their line-up, all the way through to the Ghanaian national youth team where players from across the country take part in trials to secure a spot in the national side. A 'justify' is, therefore, not a problem in and of itself. Rather, the issue is a contemporary twist on this form of trial. The intermediaries described above set up a 'justify' either in conjunction with a club or independently, based on the proviso that they can engineer a transfer for the best players to a foreign club in exchange for cash. The extent to which these controversial forms of 'justify' are occurring is an area that needs further exploration, and we return to this topic in Chapter 6. One prominent Ghanaian example was reported in the *Daily Guide* as follows:

> AMBITIOUS GHANAIANS were scammed into thinking they had trials at football clubs in Mauritius last year, a DAILY GUIDE SPORTS investigation has uncovered. The players were sent with the promise of a trial abroad and cheated out of thousands of Ghana Cedis for the privilege. When they arrived in Mauritius, there was no such 'invitation' and some have been imprisoned for staying illegally in the country. Our source says the footballers were not of a high standard. An email from Nazeer Bowud, Treasurer of the Mauritian FA dated 25th March, 2010 says: 'There is unfortunately some wrong minded "agents" in Ghana who organize these types of trip for footballers to Mauritius and promise them to use Mauritius as a hub to transit to Europe.' ... The fraud continued, and a fake invitation obtained by DAILY GUIDE SPORTS for one Rama Dela Kobla Kudulo states he will be considered 'in the context

> of skills evaluation and eventual recruitment' … The invited player in this case, Rama Kudulo, wanted to take up the offer and would have were it not for the advice his former coach gave. The prospect of a successful football career is extremely attractive to young Ghanaians, and this desire was exploited. 'He was very disappointed when he got to know and I showed him online. I made him promise he wouldn't go ahead,' Baltisser [the former coach] explained. (Coe and Wiser, 2011)

Unfortunately, as revealed in this case, some intermediaries are able to convince players and their families to hand over large sums of money in the hope of securing a transfer abroad.

Coaches, particularly in the Colts league, clearly occupy a pivotal and potentially influential role as coordinators within the football industry, not only because of their ability to recruit talent but also because intermediaries, card dealers and managers, as well as legitimate actors at elite academies, usually express their interest in signing a player through these coaches (van der Meij, Darby and Liston, 2017). The coach typically liaises with the player and his parents or guardian. The role of coaches, however, extends beyond that of being channels of information. They are often influential when parents are not convinced about the merits of their son signing or playing for a club or an academy, a point which has been made in other West African contexts (Armstrong, 2004b; Hann, 2020).

As alluded to earlier with the example of Eddie at Barracks FC, the mediating role that Colts team coaches play may be influenced by a personal interest given the financial benefits that might accrue from transferring one of their players to an academy. But this is not always the case. For example, Lewis, a coach at an elite academy, explained how he had to convince the parents of a player named Sharif to permit their son's move to a residential academy. Their worries about their son's wellbeing and education if he was living away from home were understandable and reflected concerns about the safeguarding of children in the football industry (Mason *et al.*, 2019). Eben, a coach at Sharif's Colts team, agreed to help Lewis to convince Sharif's parents to allow the move but he did not do so for his own financial benefit: he saw the move as an opportunity to improve Sharif's quality of schooling. Eben gathered a group of players together to visit Sharif's house and explain to his parents the positive educational and social aspects of academy life and the opportunities it offered beyond football.

This concluding example is an important one, because it introduces an important set of actors in the footballing landscape, to which we will dedicate some attention in the next chapter: a player's family and social network. It also points to a further point we will explore later, which is that despite the prevalence of speculation and financialisaton, the social infrastructure of Ghanaian football is also shown to be informed by an ethics of care.

Conclusions

Using Ghana as a case study, this chapter sought to demonstrate the importance of contextualising African football migration geographically and historically. This approach enabled us to highlight a range of actors, networks, institutions and processes that influence opportunities to produce football-related mobility in and from the African continent. Significantly, we outlined the ways in which the shift from a socialist developmental philosophy, to an era where the meta narrative for economic development is neoliberal marketisation, has understandably transformed how the Ghanaian football industry and the actors within it function. Football is now a business and driven primarily by a profit motive. Financial speculation over players is now a core feature of the game, and the country's success in the 1991 FIFA youth championship is considered the watershed moment in the positioning of player migration as a means to generate surplus value. Accordingly, the number of amateur clubs and youth academies seeking to enter the football industry is rising as players, especially youth, are more intricately linked to money. Ghanaian football is subsequently in an era of financialisation, with speculation centred on male youth players and their registration cards. Consequently, the movement and migration of players within Ghana and beyond is encouraged as part of speculative strategies. In the next chapter, we examine how this situation informs young people's engagement with the game and their decision to embark on a career in football.

5

'Becoming a somebody' through football

Introduction

In April 2016 Christian was invited to watch a football match between two local U-17 youth teams in rural southern Ghana, a two-hour drive east of Accra. The boys of the hosting team were attached to a German-Ghanaian non-governmental organisation (NGO) which takes care of children and youth from low-income families and provides education and leisure-time activities. The conditions were challenging. The red-hot sun was blazing and the pitch was in bad shape, an unlevelled mix of sections of grass and sand, sprinkled with stones. Shortly before kick-off the NGO team donned their green and white jerseys bearing the name of a small club from southern Germany who had donated the kit. The players listened intently to their coach's instructions. He organised his boys in a 4-4-2 formation, particularly stressing the role of the midfielders to create chances for the strikers and to support the defenders when under attack.

When the match started, the coach pointed to two or three players who were his biggest talents, suggesting Christian should keep an eye on them. Among those picked out was sixteen-year-old Mensah. Selected as one of the midfielders, his technical abilities and ease in possession of the ball were clear. However, he struggled with the physical style of the opposing team and the bad condition of the pitch. Mensah found it difficult to control the ball and his passes seldom reached his teammates. Eventually, Mensah's team lost by three goals. Yet, as he frustratedly told Christian after the match, he was sure that in more favourable conditions he and his teammates could have shown their technical style and close control, and outplayed their opponents.

Sitting in front of a shady fence next to the pitch and talking to Mensah about the match in particular, football in general and his situation at the time and future ambitions, it became obvious that playing football meant more than merely being his favourite leisure-time activity. Mensah wanted to become a professional footballer, preferably with one of the popular clubs in Europe. In the present, however, Mensah was one of the dozens of underprivileged children attached to the NGO. Since his father had died some years previously and his mother was unable to take care of him, the NGO paid the expenses for his education. At the time, he was attending an eighteen-month course in information and communications technology (ICT) in a nearby town where he stayed with his two elder brothers in a small room. It was his own choice to take the course, but during the conversation with Christian, it seemed that it was not something that Mensah wanted to pursue or saw as a potential future career path. Mensah's passion was football and, like thousands of boys and young men in Ghana and other West African countries who are inspired by successful role models such as Didier Drogba, Michael Essien and Asamoah Gyan, he dreamt about playing in Europe. This dream, however, is one that is exceptionally hard to realise and the vast majority, including Mensah, fail to achieve it (Ungruhe, 2016).

In this chapter we aim to reveal how youth in contemporary African contexts increasingly perceive and rationalise their entry into the local game within their biographical planning in an era of neoliberal governance, a form of planning that they hope will enable them to 'become a somebody' in the guise of a transnationally mobile, professional footballer. We also introduce a range of interpretations and representations of football that shape this project of individual and social becoming. This enables us to tease out the 'migration drivers' that influence young people's decision to realise social and spatial mobility through football. In keeping with contemporary theoretical currents in migration studies, the term 'drivers' is used here to denote a broad assortment of relational factors that generate the structural elements influencing the social contexts in which individuals consider emigrating. Migration drivers shape both the wider context within which a person's aspirations and desire to migrate are fashioned as well as the ways in which people make decisions about whether or not to be mobile (van Hear, Bakewell and Long, 2018). Here we focus on what are known as 'predisposing drivers', which 'become manifest in structural disparities between migrants' place of origin and place of destination, both being shaped by the global macro-political economy' (van Hear, Bakewell and Long, 2018: 931).

The first part of the chapter uses the Ghanaian case to examine in more detail young people's perceptions of, and rationales for, entering the football industry. Building on insights in Chapter 4, we illustrate how football migration is now seen as a vehicle for social mobility and an alternative pathway for youth to attain a sense of respectable adulthood and fulfil intergenerational obligations to family, alongside wider social expectations around cultures of giving (Martin, Ungruhe and Häberlein, 2016) and spatial mobility in (im)mobile West Africa. Subsequently, we focus on this social dimension of Ghanaian football, particularly familial relationships and their impact on young people's experiences in football and their migration strategies. The overarching argument is that individuated understandings of African youth's efforts to 'make it' abroad and 'become a somebody' through football are reductive in their treatment of the structural conditions that 'drive' this form of migration. Instead, we adjust our scalar register and conceptualise these efforts as a collective practice, 'a social negotiation of hope' (Ungruhe and Esson, 2017), among a large cohort of young people in Ghana, inflected with an ethics of care. Through adjusting our analytical lens, more locally embedded and fresh perspectives on the strategies young people in a range of African contexts deploy to 'become a somebody' through football migration emerge from the conceptual and empirical shadows.

'Becoming a somebody' through football

The exchange below between James and Mrs Bannerman (KB), the headteacher at a private school on the outskirts of Accra, continues the discussion on football versus education from the previous chapter and encapsulates several key themes covered in the first half of this chapter. The interview was instigated by a coach at one of the Colts clubs at which James conducts research. The coach recommended that James speak with Mrs Bannerman about the relationship between football, education and social mobility in order to help him understand a puzzling pattern of behaviour he observed at the clubs:

> KB: Well, originally, in Ghana football was mainly for vagabonds and street boys, so that any parent at all who has a child playing football was considered a disadvantaged person who cannot academically make it. That was the perception. We had something called 'gutter to gutter' and they normally played the football on the street. There is a gutter here and one over there and you played between.
>
> JE: I remember coming to Accra in the early 1990s to visit my grandmother, and I was playing football with some boys and she called me inside and stopped me.
>
> KB: Yes, exactly, because football was seen as being meant for vagabonds or those who could not go to school. So if you are to study the situation very well and I am zeroing in on Ghana, the very first batch of people who actually made it in the football world were not very well educated. But around say 1990 some of them started coming back home in grand style – you saw somebody on the street before and now he is acting like he has made it. The blow it started doing to the education of those people

is that this told them, 'if you cannot go to school, you can make it in football'. (Interview, 22 April 2011)

During post-training discussions with players across our case study clubs, the topic of education often surfaced. At Future Icons FC, several players intimated that they had taken the decision not to enrol at a senior secondary school, to 'drop out' and instead pursue a career in professional football. As children they had entered the formal education system not just because it was compulsory but on the understanding that it would eventually lead to formal waged employment and improve their life chances. At Barracks FC, players explained that the main issue was the payment of tuition fees, and their families' inability to meet costs associated with continuing their education. James was informed that what could be considered as minor outlays, such as buying stationery or replacing school shoes they had outgrown, became major factors in their decision to 'drop out'. Nevertheless, the players stressed that they were keen to continue their education later. These discussions seemed to corroborate Langevang's observation that young people in Accra rarely receive the education they wish for in a continuous or linear manner, rather 'they enter school, drop out, work for a couple of years, and then begin formal or informal education again' (Langevang, 2008: 2044).

When the subject of 'dropping out' was mentioned to players at Austin Texans FC and Barracks FC, James was met by a similar response to that at Future Icons FC. Players were aware that many of the semi-professional Ghanaian teams did not have youth academies and would therefore scout the amateur and Colts divisions, in the hope that the players they found would represent Ghana in U-17 and U-20 FIFA youth tournaments. This makes the period between fourteen and eighteen years of age a key time to obtain visibility (cf. Carter, 2011) and a potentially lucrative transfer abroad, a point we also addressed in chapters 2 and 3. This situation appears to epitomise the key time-space that Johnson-Hanks (2002) envisioned when describing the concept of 'vital conjunctures', circumstances which lead to the reassembling of particular material bodies in time and space while conveying the crystallisation of structural forces (Jeffrey, 2010; Johnson-Hanks, 2002).

The puzzling aspect of the players' responses was that, despite the consistent narrative about 'dropping out' due to affordability, it became apparent that actually, when an opportunity to attend senior secondary school arose, it was not taken up, being overlooked in preference to football. This was notably the case at Barracks FC, where a fundraising campaign enabled twenty-one academy players to enrol at a prestigious private senior secondary school, the one where Mrs Bannerman was the headteacher. However, only four attended regularly and the remaining seventeen were eventually expelled for absenteeism and disruptive behaviour (see also Esson, 2013). Mrs Bannerman argued that a loss of faith in the value of formal education allied with a belief in football as a way to improve their life chances was the fundamental issue:

> If they say they are not going to school because of money it is not really true but it is a nice excuse. If you go down to the beach you will see boys playing there but if you give them a uniform to go to school, see how fast they will run away. They just use it [fees] as an excuse because they think there is no future in schooling but there is in football. There are some who are genuine. There are some who want to work and study and you see they are coming from disadvantaged homes but they tried. Others you can tell they don't want to stay but when focused will make it. (Interview, 24 April 2011)

When probed beyond their initial, often vociferous claims to want to attend school, all but one of the seventeen Barracks FC players who were expelled ultimately admitted that education was no longer considered an avenue worth pursuing. Two main reasons were cited. The first related to the personal satisfaction and joy they encountered when playing football compared to studying. The second was rooted in a calculation about the potential return on their investment in education and how this might improve their life chances. Although the Ghanaian economy has grown at a rate of between 5 and 11 per cent between 2010 and 2020 (Gough *et al.*, 2019; Obeng-Odoom, 2013), much of this growth is tied to the discovery of oil and gas, the long-term effects of which for economic growth and the job market are uncertain (Amankwaa, Esson and Gough, 2020; Darkwah, 2013). Meanwhile, three decades of neoliberal reforms have resulted in a scenario whereby the informal sector constitutes an estimated 80 per cent of the economy and dominates the employment landscape (Amankwaa, Esson and Gough, 2020). In this context, the supply of educated labour is considered to exceed demand, and perceptions of 'qualification inflation' has fuelled a belief that returns from education are in decline or are insufficient (Esson, Amankwaa and Mensah, 2020; Rolleston and Oketch, 2008), particularly among those from low-income families who often struggle to pay the fees for post-primary education.

Consequently, the long-standing popular belief in Ghanaian society that investing in one's human capital via formal education is a prerequisite for individual social mobility and national development has lost credibility among many young people and some adults. This was, as Mrs Bannerman alluded to, the harsh reality underlying the players' disinterest in, and their decision to 'drop out' of, secondary schooling. Ekow, a seventeen-year-old player at Barracks FC on the brink of joining the senior team, explained how he sacrificed his plans to become an architect in favour of pursuing a career in football:

> Well, let me put it this way, from the way I see things, I think of Europe and see myself arriving in Europe. I see the houses, the cars, and I know the salaries that the players are earning at the end of the month. That drove me to forget about everything and move out of mind everything that I had learnt about becoming an architect. Because in my head I want to become a footballer, it is like a dream. I didn't want to know about going to school anymore, all I knew was that I had to play football and make it big. (Interview, 8 May 2011)

This quote from Ekow brings us back to the vignette at the start of this chapter with Mensah. A few days after the match, Mensah called Christian to greet him and to talk about football. It was still early in the morning and Mensah had already finished his daily training session. Besides playing occasional friendly matches for the NGO team, Mensah was registered with a club in town which takes part in the local youth league. Their regular morning training sessions allowed him to combine his football ambitions with his ICT studies. Mensah was about to leave for his classes when he called Christian. When Christian commended him for his seriousness towards both football and education, Mensah quickly put it into perspective and confirmed what Christian had already guessed: 'I concentrate on football', he said, 'the ICT is second. I like it but I don't have the passion for it like I have for football. I want to make it as a footballer'. When Christian asked him why he decided to take the course then, Mensah replied: 'The people at the project [the NGO] told me it was good to know something. Many footballers have a business beside so when they end their football they can go back to it and have something [to make a living]' (see Ungruhe, 2016). Here, note how Mensah's prioritisation of football over education, in this case vocational training, chimed with the mindset of other youth in the Colts league that James encountered. His case also attests to an important issue that shapes football migration: namely, informality and precarity in neoliberal urban African contexts.

Entrepreneurs of self

While striving to achieve his dream of becoming a footballer, Mensah was struggling to make a daily living. He relied mainly on a share of his two elder brothers' earnings but also some limited opportunities for casual work that arose during gaps in his training and education schedule. None of them had regular work and, as for many other day labourers in town, it was hard to get by. 'We support each other', Mensah explained to Christian.

'When someone gets some work then he shares the money with us and takes care of things.' Their mother was not able to care for them. She stayed in a small room at the other end of town, struggling to get by herself. 'We are boys, we don't want to be a burden for her. We have to find our own way' (see Ungruhe, 2016). Mensah and his brothers concisely articulate a phenomenon noted by scholars of young people's experiences in African contexts, which is the idea that young African subjects must take responsibility for their own future life chances (cf. Gough and Langevang, 2016; Hann, 2020; Honwana and De Boeck, 2005; Martin, Ungruhe and Häberlein, 2016; Simone, 2005; Waage, 2006). In the context of Ghana, and many African nations with histories of socialist structures, this is a relatively new subjective disposition (Akyeampong, 2018). It has largely replaced the idea that individuals exist within extended communities, and in the post-independence era of President Kwame Nkrumah's social developmentalism, the idea that the state would assist in welfare provision (Amankwaa, Esson and Gough, 2020; Langevang, 2008).

The adoption of neoliberal modes of governance has produced a different form of subjectivity, one in which an individual is obliged to take greater responsibility for their future. The inculcation of this new idea of individual responsibility has a history, and it is a narrative that can be closely associated with the suite of ideas typically bracketed together under the banner of neoliberalism. Given the difficulties and even hardships involved in Mensah's dream of becoming a professional player abroad and having the possibility of an alternative at hand (the ICT course), the question of why he, like so many youth across the continent, remained committed to a career in football comes to the fore. Mrs Bannerman's comments at the outset of the previous section are informative here because they resonate with findings from studies on African football migration which contend that African youth are inspired by the circulating images of European professional football (Esson, 2020; Hann, 2020; Poli, 2010a; van der Meij, 2015), where the success of a few outshines the failures of many. Those same path-breakers who moved to Europe in the late 1980s and early 1990s, who we introduced in Chapter 4, were significant in this regard. Their accomplishments, and those of players who followed in their wake, shifted perceptions of what it means to be a footballer, not just in terms of football's association with deviant forms of behaviour, as addressed in Chapter 4, but also at an ontological level.

Mrs Bannerman, Mensah and the players at our case study clubs also demonstrate why assuming that youth only aspire to become footballers and migrate in pursuit of stardom and wealth provides no more than a partial picture of what is unfolding in Ghana, and elsewhere on the African continent. Such assumptions do not account for how the predisposing drivers informing this decision are the outcome of a complex assortment of motivations within a specific context. Thinking through the empirical accounts above helps us unpack why some male youth in Ghana, and other African contexts (Hann, 2018, 2020; Šašková, 2019), are turning to a career in football. The decision is based on their engagement with, and reinterpretation of, normative understandings of neoliberal conduct and human capital circulating within society. As mentioned earlier, formal education has long been promoted in Ghana as one of, if not the, most appropriate form of human capital investment. However, while the male youth we met agreed that those with appropriate human capital are able to take control of their own productivity and wealth creation, they refuse to be constrained by Ghanaian society's limited interpretation of what appropriate human capital is and can do.

In a society where youth like Mensah and his brothers are being constructed as personally responsible for discovering solutions to life's challenges, they perceive the West African footballer who turns his sporting ability into productive human capital and migrates to a well-paid European league, where he will get a maximum return on his ability, as the embodiment of resourcefulness and self-reliance. He is tantamount to a Foucauldian 'entrepreneur of self', 'being for himself his own capital, being for himself his own producer, being for himself the source of his earnings' (Foucault, 2008: 226). Better still, in a society where monetary success is viewed as an inherently masculine trait (Adinkrah, 2012; Langevang, 2008; Ungruhe, 2010), the glitz and glamour associated with professional football in Europe and, since the 2002 World Cup in Japan and South Korea, Asia (Akindes, 2013; Poli, 2010a), provide a pathway to a respectable notion of manhood. Yet, and perhaps more importantly, football is seen as providing youth with an opportunity to do more than hustle just to make ends meet, unlike education. It offers a way to 'become a somebody' and live up to socially acceptable understandings of adulthood. In the next section, we further investigate the social background and embedding of migration within aspirations for social mobility in West African contexts. This further teases out the role of predisposing migratory drivers and their links to social mobility in relation to football in Africa.

(Im)mobile West Africa

In order to better understand the role of predisposing migratory drivers and their links to social mobility in relation to Ghanaian football migration, it is conceptually useful to locate this form of movement within the culture of migration as introduced in Chapter 1. This enables us to place African football migration within a framework of migratory experiences among young people in African settings more broadly (Ungruhe, 2016: 1778). Doing so makes it apparent that the predisposing drivers associated with football migration, such as gaining social status and supporting one's family, are in fact crucial for the decision to migrate among young people all over the continent (Christiansen, Utas and Vigh, 2006; Honwana and De Boeck, 2005; Simone, 2005). The socio-cultural embedding of international migration has, according to Grätz (2010), become a 'period of the lifecycle that may be compared to an initiation rite'. Rather than a phenomenon that is merely the cause or effect of crises, migration is an everyday and ordinary practice that reflects a dream of a good life, particularly among the young generation (Ungruhe, 2016).

Thus, whereas realising international migration within but preferably outside of the continent is seen as helping young people to improve their life chances and social status, not being able to migrate has the counter effect. A young person becomes unable to share stories, symbols and commodities associated with the mobile and 'modern world' (Langevang and Gough, 2009; Nyamnjoh and Page, 2002; Ungruhe, 2016). This also reduces their potential to adopt the position of a 'giver' – that is, someone who has consolidated their position and can take on a coordinating role in symbolic and material gestures. The idea of attaining the position of a 'giver' is a strong motivation and a driver behind understandings of future making in West Africa (Martin, Ungruhe and Häberlein, 2016). Being unable to migrate therefore excludes young people from gaining social status among peers, the family or the wider community (Esson, 2015c; Hann, 2018; Langevang, 2008).

The ability to migrate is also implicated in gendered notions of social becoming. In Ghanaian society, for example, high expectations and tremendous pressure are placed on young Ghanaian men to be successful in material terms, reproducing a sense of monetary success as an inherently masculine trait (Esson, 2013). This coalesces with perceptions that migrating through football provides a means to identify with, and demonstrate forms of, hegemonic masculinity associated with living in a manner colloquially known as the 'X-Way' (the Extraordinary Way). Here, the X-Way denotes the attainment of higher social status through displays of conspicuous consumption, such as wearing designer clothes, eating in exclusive restaurants, living in private residential estates and driving high-end cars. The emergence of the Internet and social media has also made it easier for images of such lifestyles to circulate within society. However, access to images and insights into the lives of young men who are able to live the X-Way does not guarantee one's participation in this lifestyle. For many, the X-Way thus becomes 'an economy of goods that are known, that may sometimes be seen, that one wants to enjoy, but to which one will never have material access' (Mbembe, cited in Ferguson, 2006: 192). This is because the X-Way life is often obtained by harnessing spatial mobility, which is easier said than done.

The discrepancy between the desire to be spatially mobile and the ability to realise this results in a scenario akin to what Carling (2002) famously conceptualised in his study on emigration from Cape Verde, as 'involuntary immobility'. Involuntary immobility in West African contexts is connected to social (im)mobility and, arguably, a 'social moratorium' that can lead to what Vigh (2006b) refers to as 'social death'. If we apply this to the context of African football migration, we are reminded of the popular saying among young migration aspirants in Senegal, *Barça ou Barzakhe* ('Barcelona or death'), meaning get to Europe or die in the Mediterranean on the way (Ungruhe, 2016). This saying also shows why the concept of involuntary immobility has gained such currency since 2000; in the early twenty-first century the practicalities and feasibility of international mobility have remained stubbornly challenging. Some would argue it has become more difficult for those seeking to travel safely and officially outside of the African continent (Andersson, 2014; Carr, 2015; Papada *et al.*, 2020; Schapendonk and Steel, 2014). Accordingly, while spatial mobility can be a means of enhancing a person's material condition, not everyone has an equal chance of harnessing the benefits of mobility to improve their life chances.

Youth in West African settings live in a context 'characterized by ever-expanding connection and communication' (Ferguson, 2006: 192), but they are acutely aware that as existing immigration borders are being solidified, new borders are being erected. The 'accelerated closure of the West' in the form of tightened immigration rules has fostered the perception that it is almost impossible to acquire a visa using official channels (Langevang and Gough, 2009). On the one hand, as Ungruhe (2016) notes, acknowledging migration as a social norm and conceptualising spatial mobility in African societies as a 'culture of migration' indicates a deeply rooted cultural practice of migration. In this sense, the notion of 'Mobile Africa' points first and foremost to a youthful Africa since it is mainly youth who move and 'try their luck' away from home. On the other hand, however, the 'culture of migration' and 'Mobile Africa' reflect the crucial social implications of status at stake and, in particular, questions of positioning in society for the young generation in contemporary African settings.

Becoming a 'giver'

We now take these broader insights and return to Ghana and the case of Mensah. For him, helping his family was an integral part of his aspiration to become a professional player in Europe. Spatial mobility and social mobility are inextricably linked. Mensah told Christian, 'When I get a club in Europe ... I will think of my brothers and support them and also create a chance for them to play again'. Besides helping his brothers, Mensah also thought of his mother and hoped to use his income to raise her poor living standards: 'I will support my mother and take the burden from her' (see Ungruhe, 2016). In expressing these aspirations, Mensah is becoming an 'entrepreneur of self' and speculating that he will be able to transform and achieve a consolidated position from which he can use his contacts and enhanced financial resources to take on the role of a 'social giver'. The fact that those statements are indeed (but certainly not without exception) turned into practice when a player embarks on a career abroad is exemplified by the case of Kwame.

Kwame, a Ghanaian player in his mid-twenties who has played for a few professional clubs in various European and African countries, used up to a quarter of his monthly earnings as remittances for his family. Over several years, he sent a monthly sum of approximately five hundred US dollars to his parents to secure their livelihood, to take care of the school fees of his siblings and to cover expenditures for medical treatment when his mother suffered from a severe illness. From the money that Kwame saved during those years, he bought a plot of land outside Accra on which he aspired to build a family home. Thus, it did not come as a surprise when Kwame revealed 'the money aspect to help [my] family' as one of his main motives to play football in Europe (interview, 20 April 2016).

Kwame's case illustrates how the idea that migration through football can be rewarding in a range of ways is not confined to youth. Changing perceptions of football, as also noted by informants in this and the previous chapters, has resulted in a situation where family members from a range of generations may actively support a young person's attempts to migrate (see Agergaard and Botelho, 2014, for similar findings regarding the women's game). This behaviour is why scholars argue that individuated understandings of migratory decisions are problematic. Instead, migration can and should be conceptualised as part of a household livelihood strategy to diversify income streams and mitigate the constraints in origin contexts (de Haas, 2008). This point about adjusting the scale at which spatial and social mobility operate can be taken beyond the household level when it comes to African football migration. As Künzler and Poli (2012) have shown, investing in and increasing the quality of social relations is an equally important feature of an African migrant's success. Work by Acheampong, Bouhaouala and Raspaud (2019) examining how Ghanaian football players contribute to their communities of origin using the capital gained through their migration, known as 'give back behaviours', is informative in this regard.

By considering the broader and more general approaches to youth migration in West Africa, this and the previous section have shown how football migration practices are deeply embedded in local understandings of spatial and social mobility. Doing so allowed us to point out that football migrations in Ghana are not individual projects of a player but are part of a 'culture of migration', a discursive space of negotiating meanings of neoliberalism and (im)mobility. It is, however, worth acknowledging that in Ghana, the association between football and spatial mobility has to be understood in the footballing context outlined in Chapter 4. In that chapter we documented how the political economy of the Ghanaian football industry is structured around transfers between clubs within the country but ideally internationally. This is because the circulation of players within Ghanaian football is financially beneficial to clubs, players and a plethora of speculators. Football academies and clubs are, therefore, not only increasingly prevalent in Accra and other parts of West Africa, but also progressively geared towards the grooming and export of players to foreign clubs through an expanding spatial field of talent scouts and recruitment agents (see also Darby, Akindes and Kirwin, 2007; Poli, 2010a). This spatial mobility through football is not only tied to transfers. Competing in international tournaments and trials also provides openings to overcome involuntary immobility. In the next section, we examine in more detail the myriad social pressures that Ghanaian youth are exposed to as part of the process of 'becoming a somebody' through football in (im)mobile West Africa. More specifically, we focus on familial dynamics and how they shape young people's decision to enter the football industry and the agency they deploy to do so.

Speculative reciprocity in youth football

As James stood by the side of the pitch taking notes and making observations during what appeared to be a routine early morning training session at Barracks FC, he was approached by Aksel, a Danish volunteer coach working at the club. Aksel explained how Dodzi, one of the players out on the training pitch, had just been offered a contract by a professional team in China. Given that James's research was on the migration of African football players, Aksel assumed he would be interested to find out more. James was somewhat surprised by this news, and Aksel innocuously touched upon why, when he intimated that he had serious reservations about the authenticity of the contract offer. The reason for Aksel's scepticism was that although Dodzi was hard working and dedicated, he was far from the most talented player. In fact, Dodzi was probably one of the weakest players in the squad and had yet to be registered with the club. James was also further intrigued as to how he had managed to procure a transfer, given that he was certain Dodzi had not mentioned recently attending a trial or 'justify your inclusion' in any of their previous conversations.

After training, Dodzi signalled for James to come and talk to him privately. Dodzi disclosed that Aksel and James were the only people at the club he had confided in, and he asked James not to tell anyone else about his situation, for reasons later elaborated upon. He then suggested meeting at an Internet cafe in Osu later that day, so he could talk more about his transfer and a dilemma he was facing. When James arrived, Dodzi, accompanied by his senior brother, explained that he was unsure about whether or not to inform Barracks FC of the offer from China. Until this point, Dodzi had not signed a registration card with a club in Accra, even at Colts level. At the age of fourteen, with his family's backing, he 'dropped out' of formal education and opted for a career in professional football. However, almost three years of attending trials at various local Colts clubs without actually signing for one represented a clear indication of Dodzi's limited footballing ability. Dodzi was now concerned that signing a registration card with Barracks FC would make him less attractive to the club in China, as in accordance with FIFA regulations they would have to pay compensation to his former club. Dodzi and his brother also assumed that James, as someone from 'outside', was familiar with and knew how to navigate bureaucracy associated with international travel. However, James explained that, unfortunately, he would be unable to assist Dodzi with his dual dilemma. James was unfamiliar with visa and social security number application processes, and it would represent a conflict of interest to advise Dodzi as to whether he should inform the club of his situation. Although visibly disappointed, Dodzi understood and accepted James's reasons and thanked him for listening to his plight.

James then asked Dodzi to recount how this situation had unfolded. He realised he was correct in his recollection that Dodzi had not previously mentioned attending a 'justify': Dodzi had not met the scout on a football pitch in Accra, rather he had met him online. Dodzi explained how he had uploaded a curriculum vitae detailing his football biography and a promotional video (recorded using his mobile phone) showcasing his skills to a football recruitment website, which he believed was used by professional clubs to find players. Dodzi was then contacted via social media by an agent who claimed to have seen his profile on the recruitment website. After exchanging a handful of emails, the agent offered Dodzi a contract with a professional Chinese football team worth four hundred thousand US dollars per season for three years. It was from this seemingly innocuous online encounter that Dodzi was able to procure his supposed transfer.

At this point in his research, James had yet to hear of the mobilisation of football trafficking victims taking place online. However, James was somewhat sceptical about the likelihood of a professional football club offering a multi-million-dollar contract to a player based on video footage taken on a mobile phone. Dodzi agreed to show James a copy of the contract and the email exchanges with the agent. James entered the agent's name into a well-known Internet search engine, and one of the first hits was a link to a website highlighting that this individual was a known fraudster, not just in football but in the sports industry more generally. His modus operandi involved contacting athletes, coaches, physiotherapists and so on with offers of contracts with various sporting institutions around the world, in exchange for a commission. Dodzi had yet to make any payments to the agent and was grateful that he had been made aware of this deceit, albeit he was understandably disappointed that his dream of a professional contract was no longer a reality. Despite this setback, Dodzi informed James that this experience would not prevent him utilising the Internet to achieve his goal, remaining adamant that he would continue looking for transfer opportunities online.

We began this section with Dodzi's story as a way to bring the current and previous section into conversation with each other. There are of course clear connections to the highly problematic conduct introduced in Chapter 4. In this case, the agent who contacted Dodzi is engaging in duplicitous behaviour by preying on the aspirations of young people in the football industry. It is reflective of speculative criminal behaviour within and through football associated with human trafficking (Mason *et al.*, 2019; Ungruhe, 2016). We also see how regulations over training compensation and registration play on the minds of young players as they navigate the football industry. However, and more importantly for the discussion that follows, we get a glimpse into how family members shape young people's journey through the football industry. While not being in a consolidated position, nor being able to act as coordinator, Dodzi's brother took an active role in overseeing his brother's course of action when an 'opportunity' to attain spatial and social mobility through football arose. This is because Dodzi's decision to pursue a career in football was part of a household livelihood strategy to diversify their income sources. Family, both biological and extended, are key actors within the social infrastructure informing dynamics within football's GPN. In the discussion that follows we examine in more detail how Ghanaian youth in the football industry make sense of, adjust to and cope with familial expectations as they try to 'become a somebody'.

'In Ghana, if you are invited to a trial, like the final trial, the coaches will bring them [the players]. There will never really be a parent or a family member who brings them. It will always be a coach or somebody' (van der Meij and Darby, 2017: 1587). These are the reflections of a staff member at an elite Ghanaian football academy during a discussion about the involvement of family members in the academy recruitment process. The coach was uncertain about the cause of this situation, but suspected it to be a cultural quirk specific to Ghana. He noted that in his experience, family members of potential recruits from neighbouring West African countries were not only present but actively engaged in recruitment events. In reality, the situation is more nuanced, and research on familial relations in Nigerian football points to similarities between both settings (Onwumechili and Akpan, 2019). As shown in Chapter 4, coaches in the Ghanaian context engage in coordination, and rather than family members, are much more prominent in facilitating participation in trials and liaising with academies.

The presence of Dodzi's brother at the meeting with James to discuss his potential transfer opportunity in China indicates, however, that family members' physical absence during recruitment events conceals the important role that they play. This is particularly the case for those who are enthusiastic about the prospect of a family member playing professional football as part of a household livelihood strategy, an idea introduced in the previous chapter. In these instances, family members provide emotional and practical support for their relative as they pursue their dream of a career in the game. For example, when Dickson had a chance to participate in a month-long training camp to prepare him for a trial at an academy, his uncle was very supportive. On numerous occasions, he brought his nephew from Tema to Accra, a journey that can take up to two hours depending on traffic, to ensure that Dickson would attend training. In moments of difficulty when Dickson was close to giving up on a football career, his uncle urged him to continue. One of the ways in which he tried to motivate Dickson was by tapping into discourses around social mobility associated with living the X-Way, discussed above, for example by pointing to high-profile Ghanaian players in Europe and the lifestyle that Dickson would miss out on if he gave up training.

These actions on the part of Dickson's uncle were clearly linked to an understanding that securing a place at an academy was a stepping stone to a career in the European game. To some extent, it therefore constituted a form of speculation through an ethics of care. This resonates with postcolonial scholarship in African contexts which has posited that care should not necessarily be seen as a type of altruism (McFarlane and Silver, 2017). In other instances, family members intervene in an even more direct fashion, particularly those who have personal connections in the football industry and who, through a consolidated position, are able to exploit these connections and coordinate a trial for a child or sibling. Family members also provide financial, material and emotional support by, for example, buying new training gear and kit or providing transport to trials (van der Meij, Darby and Liston, 2017). It becomes evident how a 'manager' taking on these responsibilities could alleviate financial pressure on a household, as described in Chapter 4. It is worth noting that familial support is often accompanied by expectations about the material benefits the family will eventually accrue as a result of a player's football career. It is also worth highlighting that players who receive support and encouragement are at an emotional and material advantage compared to those whose family members discourage them from playing football, a subject we now turn to.

Given the trappings of fame and fortune associated with professional football, and its affiliation with social mobility, it may come as a surprise that some players participate in the academy recruitment process in calculated and sometimes covert ways. Yet a number of studies have provided detailed accounts of young players encountering hostility from family members and how they have negotiated or circumvented the reluctance of parents, siblings or relatives to allow them to participate in a trial or recruitment tournament (van der Meij and Darby, 2014; van der Meij, Darby and Liston, 2017). One such account involved a player called Simon who was fully cognisant that his mother would not champion his participation in a trial or recruitment tournament for an academy place. She had previously expressed fears about her son's involvement in football. His mother's primary concern was that his dedication to and investment in football would undermine his education, leaving Simon at risk of the stigma attached to becoming a *kobolo*, the vagabond stereotype Nii Lamptey and Mrs Bannerman alluded to in the Introduction and at the start of this chapter, respectively. Rather than asking his mother for permission to attend, knowing there was a high chance of refusal, Simon made sure his engagement in recruitment events was kept private: 'I always run. ... I would send my bags, my items to my coach, and if I am moving, they don't know that I am moving. I respect my mum, and if she said no, I have to accept, because she is the one taking charge of everything' (quoted in van der Meij and Darby, 2014: 172).

These actions are significant because they offer a stark contrast to the findings in Chapter 4, where we illustrated the intense speculation taking place in relation to youth players in Ghanaian football. Simon's case shows how not all actors are seeking to consolidate their position, and/or engage in speculative behaviour, via young people's mobility in and through football. Thus, when an offer of terms to join an academy is made to a player, intra-family negotiations often take place. These negotiations are shaped by intra-familial power dynamics influenced by hierarchies dependent on the intersectionality of characteristics such as gender, age, educational and occupational status, financial independence and material contribution to the household (Esson, Amankwaa and Mensah, 2020; Brown, 1996; Lloyd and Gage-Brandon, 1993; Nukunya, 2003). These factors are also accompanied by the key values underpinning intergenerational relationships in Ghana, namely respect, responsibility and reciprocity (Twum-Danso, 2009).

Even in cases where family members appeared to be unanimously in favour of a player's engagement in football and supportive of their aspirations to join an academy and pursue a professional career, disagreements can arise. The case of Ebo is illustrative in this regard. With potential future benefits for the family in mind, some members of Ebo's family had been closely involved in his football development and supported him as much as possible in the expectation that he would respond in kind should he go on to play professionally. Their actions can be viewed as a form of speculation that was bounded in reciprocity. When academies began showing interest in Ebo, his older brother Jacob became increasingly influential in offering guidance and advice. Through his seniority in the family hierarchy, Jacob was able to take on a coordinating role, which reflected the fact that older siblings often play a crucial part in decision-making processes in the household in Ghana and elsewhere in West Africa (Brown, 1996; Nukunya, 2003; Wrigley-Asante, 2011).

Jacob considered joining an academy to be a significant stepping stone in his younger brother's career development, not least because, as he saw it, at academies players could concentrate fully on their football development and in the process enhance their prospects of 'making it' as a player abroad. When they were on the verge of agreeing contractual terms with the academy, there was still one obstacle to overcome: Ebo's mother. Even though she offered Ebo financial and emotional support, she was not convinced about him joining an academy because she still harboured concerns about his education and felt that pursuing his schooling was a safer option to secure her son's and the family's future welfare. As we showed earlier in the chapter, education retains a privileged place in Ghanaian society despite a growing disconnect between achieving educational success and securing employment (Gough *et al.*, 2019). This view has been particularly prominent among mothers because in Ghana, and elsewhere on the continent, they will become much more dependent on the care provided by their children in later life (Hoffman and Pype, 2016; McQuaid *et al.*, 2020; van der Geest, 2016; Wignall *et al.*, 2019). As a result of this dynamic, the decision-making process required careful negotiation between Ebo's mother and other family members. In this negotiation, the academy's provision of education assumed utmost importance. As Jacob elaborated:

> Since she really loves education so much [more] than the football, we had to convince her more with education stuff. So we made her know that all syllabus we are using here, it is the same thing over there. There is no difference. So then I made some examples to my mummy. I have two advanced boys in my area, so I called them and then they had to let mummy know. And mummy

said, 'Okay, fine, if there is education, my ward can go'. (Cited in Van der Meij and Darby, 2014: 170)

To some extent, Ebo was fortunate that the intra-familial negotiations only involved his nuclear family. In other cases, players are not so lucky in this regard, and members of the extended family, such as grandparents, aunts and uncles, become active in discussions. This becomes a particular issue where one family member is viewed as blocking an opportunity (van der Meij and Darby, 2017). This was the case when, at the age of twelve, Gyasi was recruited by an academy following his performance in an informal match. His parents had long held conflicting positions on his football aspirations. Gyasi noted that:

> Because my mum doesn't want me to play football and my father wanted me to play football, when I was selected for this academy, they were arguing. My father said that I have to go to the academy, and my mum said that she doesn't disagree, but when I go to the academy, will I be going to school? She wanted me to go to school and my father said, even if there is no school there, if that is what I choose to do, I choose to play football, so if I get a football academy, I should just go. ... And my mum said she would not agree, and this was a big issue. (Cited in Van der Meij and Darby, 2017: 1590)

The issue was eventually resolved when a member of Gyasi's extended family entered the discussion and managed to persuade his mother that an academy place was a fantastic opportunity not to be spurned. Here, someone in a consolidated position due to their social status outside of football used their power to coordinate Gyasi's opportunity to potentially improve his life chances.

In some cases, family members remain uncompromising in their view of the merits, or lack thereof, of joining an academy. The case of a youth player called Cudjoe provides a good example of such a scenario. When Cudjoe was nineteen, he left the family home to play a match against one of the academies without telling his parents. Cudjoe explained that his father was explicit about not wanting him to play football under any circumstances. Instead, like Ghanaian parents who associate football with limited opportunities for improving one's life chances, Cudjoe's father wanted his son to go to school. However, unexpectedly, Cudjoe played so well during the friendly match that the academy's technical director pleaded with Cudjoe to stay with them rather than return home.

At this time, Cudjoe was over eighteen years of age and thus, from a legal perspective, did not require his parents' consent to join the club. However, as we noted above, the key values underpinning intergenerational relationships in Ghana are respect, responsibility and reciprocity (Twum-Danso, 2009). His father's insistence that football was not the correct path for his son remained steadfast. As Cudjoe explained, 'Because I love my father so much, I don't want to do anything that [would make him] disown me or something like that' (cited in van der Meij and Darby, 2017: 1590). Cudjoe, quite understandably, feared that pursuing a career in football could significantly damage the intergenerational relationship he had with his father and, wary of his father's response to the academy's invitation, he was strategic in how he went about telling his parents of his decision to pursue a football career:

> At first, I contacted my mum, because she always understands me. I called my mum and said 'Mum, this is what is happening, but I can't explain things on the phone. So the best thing I want you to do is to contact my manager.' And I contacted my manager to go and see my parents to convince them. … At that time, my father did not want to listen to anybody. … He was even calling my former manager [all] sorts of names. He said 'This is child abusing'. This is what he told my former agent. He even reported him to the police. (Cited in Van der Meij and Darby, 2017: 1590)

The conflicts that occurred in Cudjoe's case have to be understood in the context of expectations shaping the relationship between parents and children, a set of circumstances and dynamics characterised by respect and obedience. Cudjoe's father did not perceive familial dynamics to be functioning as social norms dictated that they should. However, despite the impact that it was likely to have on his relationship with his father, Cudjoe decided to stay at the academy because he saw it as a once-in-a-lifetime opportunity to achieve social and spatial mobility. Whether a place at a football academy truly represents the beginning of a viable means to attain spatial mobility, ideally in the form of passage to Europe, is debatable. But it is clear that this decision to take the risk to find out fuels intra-familial conflicts. What some family members deem a welcome opportunity to engage in a form of speculative reciprocity, might be contested by others who view education as the most realistic way for young people to secure a viable household livelihood strategy.

Conclusions

This chapter extended our understanding of how African youth rationalise their entry into the game. We explored the varied perceptions and representations of football as a form of enjoyment and sociability, a means to escape from poverty and a route to fame and fortune. With regard to the latter two points in particular, football and its association with social and spatial mobility was found to offer youth in Ghana, and other neoliberal African contexts, a means to adopt the position of a Foucauldian 'entrepreneur of self' (Foucault, 2008). This is because their life chances and opportunities to 'become a somebody' are deemed to be reliant on their ingenuity and bodily capital in a world where support from the state is unlikely to be forthcoming. Furthermore, Ghanaian society places high expectations and considerable pressure on young men to be successful in material terms, reproducing a sense of monetary success as an inherently masculine trait.

Football migration is now seen as a way to meet and potentially exceed the social expectations placed on young people. These subjective positions are also entangled in and shaped by social norms and dictates regarding intergenerational relations and an ethics of care. Young people's ability to use football migration as a way to attain social mobility for themselves and/or as part of a household livelihood strategy was shown to be dependent on the interplay between speculative dispositions and reciprocity within the family. Accordingly, although operating within neoliberal contexts that encourage individuation, the migratory drivers informing aspirations to 'become a somebody' through football are part of a more collective endeavour constitutive of a 'social negotiation of hope'. In the chapter that follows, we focus on how young people navigate the football industry as they pursue these aspirations of football migration.

6

Luck, sackings and involuntary immobility in football

Introduction

James's alarm was set for 6.20 a.m. so he could attend a 7 a.m. training session at Barracks FC. It was therefore a surprise when Ricardo (a Swiss volunteer coach at the club) rang and woke James just before 6 a.m. to inform him that a match involving a senior third-division team had been arranged for that morning. It was assumed that the game would be held at the club's home ground, but James was told just before he left that it was an away match and the bus would be leaving at 7.45 a.m. The travelling party stood around waiting until 9.00 a.m. with no reason given for the delay. James eventually found out that they were waiting for some prison guards. With hindsight, this should have been a warning sign for what was to come. The transport arrived – a prison service bus designed to seat a maximum of forty people. However, with youth team players and spectators joining the group, it numbered closer to sixty.

The bus was uncomfortably packed, with people sharing seats and laps. Somewhat understandably, given the circumstances, there was a prayer before the journey began. The bus ride lasted over an hour and some of the players (many of whom were standing throughout) were unhappy with the arrangements, believing the conditions would leave them fatigued for the match. Nonetheless, the passengers appeared in good spirits, laughing and joking for the most part. The destination, of course, turned out to be a prison, and the travelling party were all shocked that Coach John had failed to pass on this rather pertinent piece of information. Indeed, he had spent the morning repeatedly telling players who had enquired not to worry about the opponents, and just to focus on themselves.

Coach John explained that the match against the prison team took place 'most years' as part of a sports day at the penal facility. James found it interesting that none of the players had heard of this tradition, that none of them seemed to know who the opponents were and that, in spite of this, they did not really seem to mind. There was further confusion upon arrival at the prison when staff took all phones and cameras from the visitors and placed them back on the prison service bus along with, but separate from, everyone's bags. The players were then sent to the staff canteen to get changed, not before a moment of panic when it appeared that the team kit had been forgotten.

It was now past 11 a.m. and the players, many of whom had been up since at least 6 a.m., were hot, tired, thirsty and irritable. Frustratingly, they had left their money (if they had any) on the bus and found themselves sitting in a canteen without the means to purchase any food or drink. In the prison itself, James was captivated by how lively and jovial the atmosphere was. The visitors watched a volleyball match between the inmates and guards at around midday (the inmates won) before the football match finally started at 1 p.m., an odd choice of kick-off time given the heat. Despite only being able to have a very basic warm-up, the visiting team still managed to take the lead in the first half, although they did eventually lose 2-1 to the 'Prison All-Stars'. Overall, the day represented a fascinating, if somewhat surreal, experience. It was due to begin with a routine training session but ended up as a football match in a prison surrounded by thousands of inmates, with hardly a guard in sight.

Incidents as bizarre as the prison trip did not happen on a daily basis during the research visit; however, it allowed James to momentarily experience the unpredictable nature of the footballing landscape within which youth in Ghana are attempting to forge a career. In Chapter 5, we discussed the pervasiveness of involuntary immobility in African football and why it is compounded by the ways in which structural conditions inside the football industry interact with the migration infrastructure beyond it. In this chapter, we use a 'social navigation' approach (Vigh, 2009) to examine the unwanted but normative outcome of involuntary immobility (cf. Carling, 2002), and unfulfilled footballing aspirations within this unpredictable landscape. We do so by exploring contrasting ways in which male youth in African contexts attempt to overcome the factors that constrain migration through football so that they can 'become a somebody'. We continue to engage with the concept of speculation (McFarlane and Silver, 2017), as introduced in Chapter 1 and used in Chapter 4, to denote the practice of envisaging and acting into the future by taking calculated risks about how to accrue social mobility through football. In doing so, the chapter provides rich insights on how a player's location within football's GPN has implications for the way these constraints, and endemic neoliberalism-induced precarity, manifest themselves.

In the first half of the chapter, we provide a detailed portrayal of the agency of young players in Ghana's Colts league as they mediate the uncertainty surrounding football migration, an uncertainty that, as highlighted in the previous chapters, shapes and is shaped by social and migration infrastructure. We illustrate how African football migration is shaped by the comingling of spirituality, race and gender. We then shift attention to the experiences of players who have been unable to become transnationally mobile due to being 'sacked' by their elite academy. Crucially, this discussion allows us to reflect more substantively on an overlooked issue in scholarship on African football migration: namely, the emotional dimension of trying to migrate through football as evidenced in young people's narratives of 'shame' and familial relations. Emotions offer insight into young people's agency, aspirations and social relationships (Blazek and Windram-Geddes, 2013). As such, emotions can be seen as a generative lens to approach intersections of youth and transnational mobilities (Judge, Blazek and Esson, 2020). Furthermore, the insights from players 'sacked' from their academy enable us to tackle an oft-overlooked point in academic treatments of African football migration, which is that attempts to achieve transnational migration through football are tied up in internal migratory dynamics and (im)mobilities.

'Trying your luck' in the Colts league

The idea that young people have agency 'has become a type of mantra within the social sciences' (Jeffrey, 2012: 245); however, a key finding emerging from the literature on children and youth is that the form and nature of this agency is complex. For example, young people's agency in African contexts may not take the form of open resistance to structural constraints. Furthermore, agency is discovered or performed during specific moments in their life course. In relation to 'performing' agency, 'trying your luck' was a popular expression used by young players at clubs in the Ghanaian Colts league and semi-professional ranks, connoting a disposition, a temperament and associated forms of practice. Notably, references to luck and providence also emerged during fieldwork and interviews with young migrants in France from Cameroon, Guinea and Côte d'Ivoire as they discussed their football biographies. As McKinnon (2014) observes, luck is typically conceived as something beyond an actor's control. However, as we show below, the expression 'trying your luck' articulates a tension between uncertainty and hope with respect to young people's future making, which is palpable in Africa (Martin, Ungruhe and Häberlein, 2016; Simone, 2005). More specifically, the expression denotes a belief that while the future is shaped by dynamics beyond one's control, it can also be influenced by the actors themselves through directed effort.

To some extent, 'trying your luck' bears the hallmarks of 'managing' in Ghana (Langevang, 2008), and resonates with the Creole expression *dubriagem* that is used in Guinea-Bissau, denoting 'to get by or get the best out of a situation' (Vigh, 2006a: 117), *débrouiller* in Cameroon (Waage, 2006) and 'hustling' in Kenya (Thieme, 2018). These expressions are used by young people in their respective countries to describe agency as it relates to improvisation – that is, using readily accessible resources and amending strategies and plans according to opportunities and constraints. The forms of agency that they enact entail attempting to make calculated risks and behaving in a judicious manner, despite often lacking the privilege of being able to base these calculations on discrete and stable variables. When placed in the context of sport migration, these articulations of agency offer a striking resemblance to Besnier's observation that young people in Global South contexts often see sport as a way to exponentially improve their financial position on the basis of relatively minimal start-up capital, both in a social and economic sense, relative to the rewards on offer. Specifically, Besnier (2015: 852) notes that 'for most, the enchantment of "fabled futures" that sport migrations engender is illustrative of a "casino capitalism", the magical emergence of wealth from nothing, which many see as a signature feature of the turn of the millennium'.

While unique in their geographical and temporal configurations, these conceptualisations of youth agency in African contexts are broadly constitutive of a form of 'social navigation' (Vigh, 2006a, 2009). This theoretical optic focuses attention on how social forces shape people's agency as they negotiate their immediate social and spatial positions. It encourages an examination of how those same social forces dialectically inform people's imagined social and spatial positions within contexts mired in uncertainty. 'Trying your luck', as we outline below, is a speculative form of social navigation deployed by male youth as they try to actualise migration through football and overcome involuntary immobility. It resonates with the concept of migrant visibility, 'wherein a migrant's social location within hierarchies of race, class, gender/sex, religion, nationality shapes possibilities for exerting agency over and within these social hierarchies' (Engh and Agergaard, 2015: 7). So, what are the key elements of 'trying your luck'? The short answer is money, engagement with the spiritual realm and fully utilising one's bodily capital/natural skill.

Money: 'Oh, come and pay'

The first element of 'trying your luck' speaks to a wider perception that, in many African contexts, money enables a person to circumvent and overcome almost any obstacle and unexpected situation they are likely to encounter or to, as Thieme (2018) would say, 'get by and get things done'. To be clear, we are not referring solely to, or perpetuating stereotypes about, corruption.

Money is needed to get by and get things done in the world of football at an everyday level, facilitating necessities such as buying new boots and training equipment, covering transport costs associated with attending matches, refreshments when at the match and treatment for injuries. However, and perhaps more importantly, money is a key element of 'trying your luck' because it affords young African footballers the chance to make and realise opportunities that will place them a step ahead of their peers who are also aspiring to migrate through football but are more financially constrained (see also Hann, 2018; Šašková, 2019). For example, some academies require fees to be paid; money, therefore, enables fee-paying players to more readily negotiate entry into this key node of football's GPN, a node that is perceived as a route to transnational migration (see Chapter 3).

Money also does not need to be in the player's or their family's possession; it can also relate to the financial power of their club owner if they are a 'big man'. This is most evident, as discussed in Chapter 5, in relation to interactions with influential intermediaries and talent scouts, particularly in terms of attending trials and being able to act on the outcome. However, the role of luck, and the need to harness it, takes on an added dimension for coaches and players in the Colts league and lower amateur ranks of the game when it comes to trials. This is because of the potential financial pitfalls associated with this activity, especially when there is an international element. Herbert Adika, a former GFA executive, noted how self-proclaimed talent scouts often hold trials that are far from meritocratic, with players asked to make a payment to secure an opportunity at a foreign club:

> The person will say 'oh, come and pay one thousand cedis' [to get an opportunity] and you will see people rushing to pay. Then you ask yourself how? Where did you get the money? A seventeen-year-old, you are not working, but you have been able to acquire one thousand cedis for a trip you don't even know if it will come off. (Interview, 28 March 2011)

In addition to drawing attention to questions about how young people, typically from low-income backgrounds, are able to raise such sums of money, Adika's comments concisely illustrate our point about the pervasiveness of uncertainty. Despite parting with potentially life-changing sums of money, there is no guarantee a player will accomplish their goal off the back of this commercial exchange. This constitutes a compounded form of uncertainty in the sense that there is no guarantee a club will sign the player – which is true of most, if not all football trials – and the 'opportunity' to migrate might not be all that it seems. Indeed, since 2010 there have been multiple stories from all four corners of the continent about players parting with large sums of money only to find that they were being duped by people purporting to be talent scouts (Mugote, 2019; Redfern, 2018; Richardson,

2020). This criminal behaviour can result in irregular forms of migration, which involves 'people who enter a country without the proper authority; people who remain in a country in contravention of their authority; people moved by migrant smugglers or human trafficking' (Koser, 2010: 183).

Crucially, an advantage of 'trying your luck' to overcome involuntary immobility and migrate through football – perhaps unlike in other areas of Ghanaian and African life more generally – is that it is not solely dependent on financial resources. There are at least two other factors that are capable of helping to remove or negotiate obstacles to spatial and social mobility: engagement with the spiritual realm, which borders on religiosity, and harnessing a distinguishable talent or skill. This is actually a sophisticated and nuanced understanding of agency and the life course, because luck and skill are usually viewed in binary terms (McKinnon, 2014). Therefore, rather than relying on a specific causal factor, namely wealth, this triumvirate provides young people in urban Ghana and other parts of the continent who are attempting to 'try their luck', with a means to make sense of and navigate football's migration infrastructures, which are as perplexing as they are miserly in providing places in the professional ranks of the game.

Spirituality: 'Never let your boots leave your eyes'

'Trying your luck' by engaging with the spiritual realm reflects how youth deploy their agency to realise their plans, and invoke a set of explanatory tools to decipher events in their (and other people's) footballing journey that appear inexplicable or random. To be clear, we are not referring to a rigid set of rules. Nor is the recourse to spiritual beliefs and practices in the context of African football migration unique to Ghanaian youth, as evidenced by the work of Kovač (2018) in Cameroon and Hann (2018) in Senegal. Anthropologists and African studies scholars have noted how reference to spiritual and supernatural causality in an African context are often wrongly conflated with primitivism and backwardness (Geschiere, 1997; Tazanu, 2018). This approach to understanding causality can be, and very often is, a reflection of adaptation to and a part of modernity, prevalent throughout the contemporary world (Bonnett, 2017; Meyer and Pels, 2003). More importantly, professional football is littered with examples of references to spiritual and religious causation (Armstrong, 2004b; Bloomfield, 2011; Fumanti, 2012). On this subject, Kurt Okraku, a former secretary of GHALCA, made a similar observation with regard to the prevalence of spiritual causality in the football industry:

> In our part of the world, religion plays a big part. For Europeans, maybe not a big part, but it does play a part, make no mistake about it. I have been to

> European clubs where religion is key. I have had chats with football people who really believe in the mystical world. It is not for fun that you go to [a big European club] and [the club's star player] wanted to be the last person to walk onto the pitch. It is not for fun that in the dressing room of [a big European club, the club's star player] had to sit on that chair in the little corner and nobody sits there, it is for a reason. (Interview, 14 February 2011)

Several theorists of celebrity culture contend that celebrities are the product of modern post-God societies, and the embodiment of neoliberal democracy and capitalism (Andrews, Lopes and Jackson, 2015; Rojek, 2006; van Krieken, 2012). We propose, similarly to Pype (2009), that in African contexts celebrity is not a secular counterpart and that it can and is found in social contexts where fame derives not merely through Rojek's (2001) typology of ascribed (e.g. lineage), achieved (e.g. sport or the arts) and celetoid produced (e.g. reality TV). Celebrities can also exist in modern societies where they are associated with possessing spiritual powers. This is significant in the case of African football more generally (Künzler and Poli, 2012; Njororai, 2014), and for Ghanaian football specifically, where players' sporting prowess makes them bona fide celebrities and simultaneously considered by large swathes of the public to be beneficiaries of spiritual assistance.

The belief among members of the public, including young players, that footballers benefit from spiritual support is reinforced, as Kurt Okraku notes above, by an awareness that professional players do engage in religious and superstitious practices. On this point, during conversations about his journey from Cameroon to France, Jules, a twenty-five-year-old Cameroonian semi-professional footballer residing in Paris, provided the following anecdote about how the spiritual realm is used by youth in Cameroon to help make sense of footballing success stories:

> For me, the thing I want to say is that I have heard a lot of young guys believe that players like [Samuel] Eto'o and [Didier] Drogba have some spiritual people behind them who help. I heard that a player like Eto'o fucks men to get more power. They are not gay but they fuck guys. I was very traumatised the first time I see or hear about this, how a man can do that? But they say when you do that you take the power of that man. Also, in Cameroon they say never let your boots leave your eyes. You should sleep with them under your pillow. It is like that. You don't just leave them everywhere for people to tamper with. (Interview, 10 July 2011)

There are several potential discussion points that emerge from this quote, not least the deplorable homophobic sentiments; however, we focus on how it illuminates our discussion of agency and causality. As indicated above, young people in a range of African contexts believe in the existence of invisible supernatural forces which interact with the material world and influence their life chances and everyday activities. It is in this context that youth come to believe that the likes of Eto'o and Drogba achieved fame and success through spiritual means. This is not indicative of irrational pre-modern cultural beliefs. Instead, it provides an entry point into understanding subjectivities informing their attempts to 'try their luck' and navigate uncertainty within the football industry's migration infrastructure. Put differently, despite speculating on their ability to 'make it' and 'become a somebody', young players are rarely sure if or when their defining moment will arrive. It therefore becomes imperative to ensure that any unforeseen elements that could prove detrimental to securing an opportunity to pursue a pathway abroad are neutralised or, even better, eradicated before they materialise. Many players believe that they can do so by actively seeking positive intervention from the spiritual and religious realm. But what does this look like in practice?

In Ghana, male youth seeking to migrate through football engage in various rituals ranging from prayer, fasting, vigils and the use of what is colloquially referred to as 'medicine'. Medicine is procured, often at some considerable cost, from local fetish priests known as ɔbosomfo (Nukunya, 2003; Ephirim-Donkor, 2016). While it is not considered good etiquette to press someone to disclose the full nature of their medicine, it was explained that in many cases it was a powder-like substance that could be rubbed onto the body or an object. More specifically, players place medicine on their feet, socks, football boots, inside their shin pads and goalkeeping gloves (if they played in that position). As referenced in the quote above from Jules, there was also an inverse use of this medicine, where it might be used to negatively impact an opponent's performances on the pitch and in doing so elevate one's own chances of success.

Whereas the use of medicine can be quite subtle, overt articulations of engagement with the spiritual realm are also evident. This can be seen in instances where players make the sign of the cross as they come onto the pitch or kiss a crucifix before the game begins; point to the sky to acknowledge God or prostrate themselves on the ground after scoring a goal; and pour water blessed by a Christian pastor over their heads before a match.

While individuals will have their own personalised set of practices, there are also often institutional dimensions to engagement with spirituality. For example, it is customary to see teams embrace and commence a collective prayer before, during (at the half-time interval) and after matches. At Barracks FC, the management made it compulsory for players to attend services at the local Pentecostal church on Sunday, Monday, Wednesday and Friday, sometimes for the duration of the night. Unfortunately, their observance of such religious practices did not stop them going on a five-game losing streak. In an attempt to improve results on the pitch, the players lengthened their usual fasts and kept longer vigils before matches. The response to the losing streak came to symbolise the ontological differences between the *Obruni* volunteer coaches and the club's local players and staff. *Obruni* is a term used by Ghanaians to describe a Western visitor to Ghana. An *Obruni* is usually racialised as white but the term can be used to refer to a Western foreigner more broadly. The *Obruni* volunteers at Barracks FC would often talk among themselves, and occasionally with one or two of the players, about the illogicality of belief in spiritual causality. It was suggested that staying up all night before a game and fasting could in fact be leaving the players tired and dehydrated, thus negatively impacting their performances and contributing to their losing streak. Conversely, many of the players explained how hard work and practice alone are not enough to win matches and/or 'make it' as a professional player, because there are too many unaccountable variables.

The plight of Barracks FC was common knowledge at other clubs, and many senior players at these teams were unsurprised by the decline in results. One player, Kwabena, explained that Barracks FC had courted controversy the previous season when they 'sacked' several key players because they failed to attend church:

> They had a striker and he scored for them in the lower divisions, now he is playing in Division One. They played a match and they scored a team 4-3, and he scored three of the goals. Then in the middle of the league they sack him because he didn't go to church. So why are they losing now? Because those that helped them qualify [for that division] they have sacked them ... They sacked all of the players, they got the experience to play for Second Division and that is why they qualified, because they can play. But now you are sacking them and using small boys from the academy to play. (Interview, 25 February 2011)

Kwabena's quote succinctly demonstrates how youth were well aware that medicine and entreating the spiritual realm can only take you so far. Yusuf, a thirty-year-old Nigerian footballer who was lured to Accra by a bogus agent with promises of a contract at a Premier League club, expressed this point as follows: 'If rubbing holy water alone on your head will make you win the game, then why bother going to training?' (interview, 20 February 2011). Kurt Okraku also articulated this position when explaining that a person cannot assume that religion alone will secure footballing success:

> First of all, we need to accept that football is a science. If you think you don't need to train and sitting in the church praying will get the result, then you are fooling yourself – you will never get the result. You can bring eleven world-renowned pastors and put them in a strip and on the pitch but they won't win. So let's get what must be done right and then back it up with the spiritual world. (Interview, 14 February 2011)

Kurt, Kwabena and Yusuf are all addressing the tension between striving for proprietorship of one's self and the notion that a person is to a large extent operated through spiritual powers (Meyer, 1998). They also point to an idea that circulates in everyday as well as academic domains, which is the perception that 'agents can create their own luck because people with more skill tend to have more opportunities to benefit from luck' (McKinnon, 2014: 558). It is therefore also important to acknowledge and illustrate how 'trying your luck' related to, and coalesced with, the notion of nurturing and drawing on an individual's footballing skill set.

Race: 'We naturally have quality'

The topic of natural talent and sporting ability was briefly touched upon in Chapter 4 when we highlighted that one of the reasons a career in professional football is considered more attractive than other vocations is linked to ideas of race and innate physical attributes. Back in the 1970s, Guttmann (1978) argued that the standardisation of rules within modern sport was influenced by the principle of equality and the attempt to establish fair and egalitarian competitive conditions. Despite this attempt to create a 'level playing field', the potential for what he called an 'inequality of results' remains. Given the supposedly egalitarian nature of modern sport, the presence of successful Black male athletes in certain sports, and not in others, is wrongly claimed to signify a correlation between race and sporting ability.

Arguments placing nature and not nurture at the centre of sporting success have, however, been refuted as a form of racist thinking (Spaaij, Farquharson and Marjoribanks, 2015; St Louis, 2003, 2004). They are reliant upon a 'heuristic illusory correlation' combined with 'overestimation bias', which leads to the conclusion that two issues – in this case, racial phenotype and athleticism – are related, and an overestimation of biological differences between groups as compared to within groups (Hughey and Goss, 2015; Rasmussen, Esgate and Turner, 2005). Nevertheless, the belief that Black West African males are physically predestined to excel in football, a form of palatable racism, is omnipresent in Ghana. Herbert Adika noted that, 'here people think we have the talent, that is the attitude, and they say "I know it so I can go for it", so they go thinking that if they put the ball down they can play' (interview, 28 March 2011). Similar sentiments were expressed during a joint interview with two seventeen-year-old Cameroonian football migrants that James conducted in Paris (interview, 28 July 2011):

JE: So the clubs want you because you are from West Africa?
Patrick: Yes, because they know we naturally have quality.
JE: So you think it is a natural quality in African players?

Pierre: Yes, we are naturally strong. It is a fact. Everywhere I went, I knew that. The agents in Europe already know that in West Africa there are good players, that if you go to West Africa you will find good players.

JE: What makes them good?

Pierre: Let me say, it is nature. Nature has made it so; there is no other way. Look, if you look at Africa and the big players today, you have Drogba, Muntari, Eto'o and Essien, and all of those players are from West Africa. So the agents already know that the good players come from West Africa.

The sentiments expressed above speak to the idea that 'racialised ascriptions do not always imply negative judgements; sometimes, they involve seemingly positive descriptions and expressions of admiration' (Engh, Settler and Agergaard, 2017: 80). Black West African males often racialised and emasculated in other fields have become immersed within a vision of a footballing hierarchy, which they believe places them at or very close to the top. Given the relatively small numbers who are able to obtain a career in professional – particularly European – football, the tendency to depict Black West African males and footballing prowess as one and the same is contrary to reality (Agergaard and Ungruhe, 2016; Poli, 2010a), and we address the topic of players being released from their clubs in the next section. Yet the aforementioned belief is, in many ways, reaffirmed by the concentration and prevalence of scouting networks and academies in this region (Darby, Akindes and Kirwin, 2007; Darby and Solberg, 2010; Hann, 2018; Poli, 2010a).

Pointing towards the unique qualities that West African players embody, Mads, a leading staff member of FC Midtjylland's academy, mentioned 'their strength, their balance and technical skills combined with their speed and their physical skills. They can run very, very fast. They can jump very, very high. And they are very strong and have a very good balance. And if you can make these things work together then you have a very good football player' (interview, 9 February 2016). This and similar views concerning the African sporting body are shared beliefs among scouts, coaches and academy staff in the region, and culminate in their insistence that 'African players are natural-born sportsmen', as a director of a European-run academy in Ghana put it (interview, 10 March 2010). Anthony Baffoe, a former Ghanaian international football player and secretary of the Professional Footballers Association of Ghana, did not attribute this situation to race, but when reflecting on the high-profile African migrant players of the 2000s he acknowledged the notoriety of West Africans in professional football: 'The western region [of Africa] is very, very successful. Nigeria, Côte d'Ivoire, Ghana, just look at the players. Muntari, Drogba, Gyan, the Touré brothers, Keita, Mikel, Obinna, you can just go on and on. It is incredible. You can go to Mali and there is also Kanouté' (interview, 10 April 2011).

The value of sporting bodily capital attributed to racialised and gendered bodies is in part socially constructed, as it is the social value attached to physical capacities such as speed and strength that is meaningful, not the capacities themselves. We will further examine this topic of the racialised African sporting body and how it evolves upon migration to Europe in Chapter 8. However, in order to better understand the situation in Ghana regarding how race influences migratory practices, it is necessary to look beyond the mantra of social construction. We need to engage with the issue of corporeality and understandings of how race and gender are spatially embodied practices. When viewed from the position of young aspirant players seeking to 'try their luck' in the football industry, race is not merely a social construct; it also has a clear and identifiable materiality that emerges from the site of the body itself. People are phenotypically different, and while phenotype does not necessarily refer to skin colour, it and other visible characteristics, such as clothing, hairstyle, piercings, height and weight, are recognised in real, everyday interactions and play a role in what people are able to do (Nayak, 2010; Slocum and Saldanha, 2016). It is worth noting here that the migration of female African players in the football industry and their competencies as athletes are constantly undermined by racially inscribed representations (Engh, Settler and Agergaard, 2017).

Youth seeking to 'try their luck' and migrate through football were aware of, and acted upon, certain beliefs attributed to bodily differences. Their bodies were not only inscribed with a particular projection of race and gender, they also informed agency. In this context, what happens to certain bodies and what those bodies are able to do, and the fact they tend to be white, pink, brown, yellow or Black in certain spaces and places, are important in order to understand how and why certain practices occur (Slocum and Saldanha, 2016; St Louis, 2004). Inscriptions are read, understood and influence perceptions of what is physically possible, and more importantly what is required in order to obtain a transfer abroad. Bodies become racialised not just through discourses but also by the ways in which actions and capacities are attributed to the body. These racialised actions and capacities are enabled and limited by the social-physical space in which bodies are located. We will draw on two further examples to elaborate this point, firstly the choice of field position that aspirant migrants opt to play in, and secondly the training practices that are employed.

It is not only choosing to play football that increases the prospect of successfully migrating but also which position you opt to play in. Ato, who at around 5 feet 8 inches was a relatively short, U-17 left-sided defender at Austin Texans FC, expressed this predicament when recounting his experience at an event that, although described as a 'friendly match', and while only involving players from his club, for all intents and purposes was an organised trial. It did not take place on their home pitch in Medina and was instead held on a well-maintained grass pitch at the University of Ghana Legon Campus in Accra. Rumours circulated about potential scholarship opportunities for selected players to travel to America and spend the summer training with a US college soccer team. Ato felt he put in a commanding performance with several well-timed interceptions, consistent overlapping runs and excellent distribution of the ball in the attacking third. His coach and the club owner agreed, as did his teammates, albeit some more begrudgingly than others. However, the visiting coach from the US did not select Ato. Instead, he picked two centre forwards, a decision that created considerable disquiet among the squad as neither of these players had performed well during the match, each squandering several scoring chances.

It is entirely possible that the US coach saw something in the performances that everyone else missed. It is also possible that his team already had ample cover in Ato's position. Yet Ato was adamant that he was not selected because of his choice of position. Put differently, Ato was alluding to the practice of 'stacking', where in the context of football it is argued that Black players are often placed, or encouraged to play, in certain playing positions (Alegi, 2010; Engh, Settler and Agergaard, 2017; Giulianotti, 1999; King, 2004; Melnick, 1988). Stacking is argued to be the outcome of racially informed stereotypes about what athletes are capable of, which informs where coaches and managers opt to play them. Whether or not Ato was actually a victim of stacking is not the point here. The point is that he perceived he was and, more importantly, young West African players believe that European scouts have a preference for certain playing positions (Esson, 2015b). Thus, an outcome of the practice of stacking is not merely discursive; it also materialises in the presence of players opting to play in certain positions, for example as defensive midfielders and attacking forwards whenever possible. This is due to the perception that scouts are actively seeking these types of players. The spatiality of race in this context is not simply 'one of grids of self/other dialectics, but one of viscosity, bodies gradually becoming sticky and clustering into aggregates' (Saldanha, 2006: 10).

It is not just where but also how the players believed they were expected to perform on the field of play that was important to their plans. Daniel, a senior team player and coach for Future Icons FC's U-17 team, highlighted this point and how it is believed that Ghanaian and African players more generally adapt their performance to please representatives from foreign teams. He gave the example of the Nigerian player John Obi Mikel, who was an attacking midfielder but while at Chelsea adopted a more defensive style: 'It is like he has lost everything because he used to be a creative player and now he is not because he thinks to get in the team he has to show that he is strong' (interview, 24 February 2011). Understanding expectations regarding how young would-be professional football players were expected to perform was important to their migratory aspirations. The owners, coaches and players at all three clubs explained how important it was to learn and apply the training methods used by European clubs, as it enabled them to understand scientific modes of causation – as alluded to above by Kurt Okraku – and complement the natural sporting ability of Black Ghanaian males. Richard, a U-17 player at Future Icons FC, gave an example of this point:

> Look at Baby Jet [Asamoah Gyan], for instance – he upgraded. When he was here at Liberty [Professionals FC] he was good, but over there the Europeans can take a Black player who is strong and then with their training add the skills and tactics to it to make him a better player. (Interview, 2 April 2011)

To this point, the coaches and players at Barracks FC explained how the presence of *Obruni* volunteer coaches was highly welcomed, as it allowed them to incorporate European training techniques. This involved studying certain aspects and details of the match and attempting to isolate practices and procedures that are considered to bring consistent success and improved performances, and employing specialist coaches and training methods specific to particular outcomes and scenarios on the pitch.

The *Obruni* volunteers did not explicitly describe Black Ghanaian males according to racial stereotypes that depicted them as aggressive, explosive, powerful, energetic and quick with an impulsive and wild side. The volunteers also did not state that any lapses in concentration or composure at critical moments in a game was attributable to naivety or deficient cognitive capabilities linked to race. Similarly, the Ghanaian players and coaches did not explicitly state that the *Obruni* were intelligent, tactically aware, determined and hard working. In this situation, race took shape not through an explicitly racialised sporting discourse, but from the physical gathering of bodies through which phenotype influenced connections to material objects, practices and processes (Saldanha, 2006; Slocum and Saldanha, 2016). These ideas were often unspoken yet embodied in the training practices that were introduced and employed. Nevertheless, no matter how hard a player 'tries their luck', through money, spiritual intervention or harnessing their bodily capital using Western training techniques, there is a chance that things will not go as planned. In the next section we focus on understanding how young people navigate one of, if not the key unwanted outcome in a young footballer's life: being asked to leave an academy.

Being 'sacked' from the elite game: shame and guilt

Chapter 1 brought attention to the wealth of literature on the migration of African players within the football industry. It is perhaps a slight idiosyncrasy of the field that so many studies and publications have been dedicated to the movement of players internationally, when the reality is that the vast majority of people who play football, including those youth who make it to an elite academy, are unlikely to go on and have a professional playing career, let alone do so outside their country of origin. This foregrounding in academic scholarship of those who are able to migrate in many ways mirrors the lopsided coverage of success stories in the mainstream news media, as well as the everyday conversations that take place in clubs and academies across the globe. This is not to say that people in the football industry are oblivious to this reality (see, e.g., Mason *et al.*, 2019). Our point is that in the context of Ghanaian football, it is a topic that borders on being taboo, a constant presence reverberating in the background like the humming of mosquitos when the sun goes down in Accra. Just like a mosquito's bite, 'release' or 'deselection' from a club can be sudden and painful even though one might know there is a chance it could happen. This time-space in a player's life is indicative of a 'vital conjuncture' (Johnson-Hanks, 2002). For players based at elite-level clubs, being released without securing a contract to continue their career with a Ghanaian or, ideally, overseas club is far from the optimum outcome. For this cohort, the description of this event in the local Ghanaian parlance as being 'sacked', as opposed to being 'released' or 'deselected' (the more commonly used phrases in Western contexts), attests to the sense of dejection and failure it elicits.

We should highlight that the ways in which the relationship between an academy and a player comes to an end is not uniform. Van der Meij, Darby and Liston (2017: 187) note that for 'sacked' players, their exit can happen at numerous points in the course of their academy training, but it typically takes one of three forms. Firstly, some players are 'sacked' before their contract expires and/or before their eighteenth birthday because they are deemed to be lacking the requisite technical, tactical and physical attributes to 'make the grade'. It is not uncommon for these players to be released back into the care of parents or guardians, especially when they are under sixteen years of age, and they often continue playing in the Colts league or with a comparable youth team. Some academies stay in contact with former youth players for a period after their release in a pastoral capacity due to a realisation that 'sacking' can, as we show below, have impacts on the emotional wellbeing of players. Others also maintain contact for material reasons, such as contributing to the player's school fees because, as shown in Chapter 5, the neoliberalisation of education in Ghana and other parts of Africa can act as a barrier to young people's ability to access schooling.

The second form 'sacking' can take is that the player is sold by the academy to a local Ghanaian club. Given the financial speculation that surrounds young players in Ghanaian football, there is usually interest from the buyer's side, although players are often less inclined to want to stay in the domestic leagues. Moreover, this option is often reliant on a player acquiring the requisite physical attributes to cope with the rigours of the domestic, adult game. This arrangement is managed between the player, with input from their family in some cases, the academy and the buying club, with the transfer registered at the GFA.

Thirdly, there are groups of players who themselves opt to leave the academy or reject a contract extension. They often do so because they view their place at an academy as constraining their scope of attaining spatial mobility. In the remainder of this chapter, we examine how being 'sacked' impacts a player's trajectory, specifically how this 'vital conjuncture' has ramifications for transnational (im)mobility, which in turn informs and affects their subsequent speculation on their future in the game.

Similarly to other studies of players being released from academies (Blakelock, Chen and Prescott, 2016; Brown and Potrac, 2009; Kelly, 2014), young Ghanaian academy players forge a social identity and sense of being that was tied to their football abilities. In Chapter 5 we introduced the notion of 'Mobile Africa', to illustrate both the pervasiveness of a culture of migration among youth across the continent and how this culture is now shaping aspirations to 'make it' in football. This is because young players see academies as vital to achieving spatial mobility to, in turn, realise social mobility. Being 'sacked' is, therefore, emotionally challenging and deeply disappointing. Young people in this situation often speak of feeling 'miserable', 'blown away' and as having their 'dream shut down' (van der Meij, Darby and Liston, 2017). Describing their feelings in this manner reflects 'how future hopes for mobility may be produced by and reinforce temporal emotions of present "stuckness" about painful socio-economic blockages to achieving life course norms' (Judge, Blazek and Esson, 2020: 3). One respondent who lost his academy place because of injury articulated his feelings in the following way:

> I felt very down, because I was thinking there would be no opportunity for me again. I was like, I am finished, because where do I get this chance again? If you don't pass through the academy, it will be really difficult for you to move outside the country. (Van der Meij, Darby and Liston, 2017: 188)

Earlier in the chapter we alluded to the fact that a transfer to a Ghanaian club was not the desired option for most players, and the quote above reflects the sentiments of players who found themselves in such a predicament with no prospects of a transfer abroad. For players in this situation at the elite academies, there is a possibility that they will end up in the Ghana Premier League, the highest level in the domestic game. While this is far from being their ideal destination, many view this as a potential conduit into professional football overseas as it offers a way to improve their visibility (Carter, 2011; Engh and Agergaard, 2015). Nonetheless, most players describe it as an undesirable and deflating outcome of their academy training. The general view is encapsulated by the following quote from a player who spent seven years at an academy only to be transferred to a club playing in the local leagues: 'I was expecting something big from the academy ... I never dreamed I would play in Ghana. My expectation is to travel and I am coming home. That was something I felt bad at' (van der Meij, Darby and Liston, 2017: 188). This and the previous quotes illustrate powerfully how involuntary immobility is experienced on an emotional level. This is an important point in terms of understanding how young people navigate this 'vital conjuncture'.

Emotions have long occupied an important place in classic sociological theory, with Durkheim, Weber, Marx, Simmel, Mead, Elias and Cooley among others demonstrating that emotions are social phenomena that are central to understanding the relations between the individual and society (Stets, 2010; Turner, 2009). There has, however, been a more recent interest in the role of emotions as they relate to young people's spatial mobility. For example, Chakraborty and Thambiah (2018) argue that emotions are both expressive and instrumental in migration: they are expressions of mobility experiences but they are also, as we have shown in Chapter 4, drivers behind young people's mobilities (see also Judge, Blazek and Esson, 2020). Furthermore, they call for a more substantive engagement with young people's emotions in work on migration and mobilities:

> There is a lack of engagement with children and young people's emotions and affectual realities often because emotions are implicitly subsumed rather than explicitly problematized or singularly inspected. (Chakraborty and Thambiah, 2018: 583)

The key emotion that players who had been 'sacked' felt was shame. In keeping with the broad thrust of Chakraborty and Thambiah's (2018) point above and Scheff's (2000) argument that shame warrants much more social scientific scrutiny, we contend that understanding how shame is elicited, manifested and responded to during this 'vital conjuncture' is crucial in making sense of how transnational immobility is experienced by Ghanaian players and how they seek to navigate through it by speculating on their ability to secure a place in the professional ranks of the game. Our conceptualisation of shame is informed by the work of the anthropologist Fessler (2004), who argues that shame is often induced by nonconformity to a social norm and involves a variety of shame-instigating events associated with guilt, embarrassment, shyness and subordination. Fessler's notion of 'classical shame events' is particularly important. He argues that these events involve 'a focus on a concern with others' actual or imagined negative evaluations; often stem from violation of a relatively important social standard; [and are] characterised by feeling small, wishing to avoid being seen by others' (Fessler, 2004: 218). This resonates with conceptualisations of shame that note its prevalence in sporting contexts (Tangney and Dearing, 2003) and clearly applies to how being 'sacked' from an academy is experienced.

It is important to point out here that shame is experienced differently depending on the individual involved and the strength of the social norm that has been violated. According to Retzinger (1991), these variations range from mild, transient embarrassment, to intense, long-lasting feelings of humiliation. The intensity and duration of this emotion among immobile players and the responses to it are intimately bound up with the intergenerational contract. To some extent, this reflects established conceptualisations of shame as arising from public exposure and disapproval of a misdemeanour or shortcoming alongside a more private response to a situation (Tangney and Dearing, 2003). Alongside personal disillusionment and disappointment, players interviewed in the study referred to the difficulties of facing family members who had invested materially and emotionally in their football development and move to an academy.

As illustrated in the previous chapter and elsewhere (van der Meij and Darby, 2014), this sort of investment was undertaken as part of a wider household livelihood strategy and on the assumption, if not expectation, that it would culminate in material and social benefits for the family (see also Besnier *et al.*, 2018; Dubinsky and Schler, 2019; Onwumechili and Akpan, 2019). Transnational immobility was, therefore, equated by players with a failure to live up to familial bonds of reciprocity and an inability to meet their obligations within the intergenerational contract, and the net result was strong, persistent feelings of shame. One of the issues that fed into this was a perception that their return to the family home would place a financial burden on the household. Unlike their peers in the Colts leagues, those at elite academies were in a position where the costs of their day-to-day needs – nutrition and accommodation, as well as their education – had been borne by the academy. Some felt a sense of guilt that upon their 'sacking' this responsibility was returned to their parents. As one player expressed it:

> I always depend on my parents because for now, they are taking care of me because I do not have a manager or club that say I can go to them for that

... So, it is not all that easy. And it is not all the time that they have the money to give. (Van der Meij, Darby and Liston, 2017: 188)

This reliance on parents and older family members was particularly problematic for former academy players who had reached an age at which they were expected to start reciprocating to their family. For example, one player who was released from an academy in his early twenties found it exceptionally difficult to move back into the family home. He had signed for a local club and because of the low wages at this level he felt he had become a burden on his family. As he explained, this caused some disquiet and resentment in the household:

> She [his mother] was struggling for me to play football, and if she sees me lying down without doing anything, she wouldn't be happy ... And I am in the house not doing anything. So when my senior brothers see me, they are not happy. (Van der Meij, Darby and Liston, 2017: 189)

In light of these perspectives, a player's release involves more than just personal disappointment at seeing their hopes of a professional football career suffer a major, potentially terminal setback. They quickly come to understand that they will be subjected to negative social evaluation by family members as well as by peers in their local communities. In this sense, their involuntary immobility is experienced as a 'classical shame event' in that it leads to a concern or fixation on real or imagined negative social evaluations by others. As is the case with all 'classical shame events', the behaviours, actions or strategies adopted by the players in responding to these events are often predicated on these evaluations. This not only influences how they deal with the immediate consequences of their release but also informs their perspectives on their future life and football-related trajectories. We now focus on these trajectories, specifically how internal migration became an option at this 'vital conjuncture' to realise international migration and its attendant benefits.

Internal migration for international migration

As noted in Chapter 1, Vigh's (2009) concept of 'motion squared' represents a useful analytical optic to make sense of how players navigate football's GPN and how they act in uncertain circumstances. It is particularly useful here to think through their release from an academy as they attempt to re-establish a place at an appropriate node within the game's GPN through which to resume their career. The termination of a player's relationship with an academy clearly creates a precarious and uncertain time-space for young players, one that is characterised by emotional, social and material challenges (van der Meij, Darby and Liston, 2017). Among those players who were 'sacked', it was possible to identify a set of navigation strategies that chimed with Fessler's (2004: 218) argument that responses to classical shame events involve 'wishing to avoid being seen by others' in order to minimise feelings of humiliation and shame. As we show below, some players make a decision not to return to the family home following their release. There is a geography to this decision, with players from rural areas and the regions away from the southern coast more inclined to take this course of action. This is because most players are keen to move to towns and cities along Ghana's coastal belt, but particularly to Greater Accra, the region surrounding the country's capital, due to a recognition of the more developed nature of the football infrastructure in these places. This is a strategic move, also designed to heighten their visibility through easier access to trials and tournaments where football agents, talent scouts or academies are actively recruiting players.

This type of internal migration is not a form of mobility available to everyone, and there are some players whose circumstances dictate that they have no option other than returning home. When they do, they often attempt to sidestep embarrassment and negative judgement from family and friends by maintaining a low social profile. As one player who was released because of a serious injury explained: 'within me, I know I am very hurt, but I don't tell them ... They would be laughing at you. So, I don't tell them till I got a second division team' (van der Meij, Darby and Liston, 2017: 189). The spectre of shame looms so large and intensely that some young players ask their parents to find another place for them to live in order to avoid the risk of meeting extended family members and experiencing 'shame events'. One player noted, 'I don't want to show myself to people that I have come to the house, because it is a big disgrace for me' (van der Meij, Darby and Liston, 2017: 189). While these actions might appear passive, especially when contrasted with the notion of 'trying your luck' discussed in the first part of this chapter, they are still legitimate forms of agency characterised by resilience. They offer players the scope to make sense of their 'vital conjuncture' and recuperate from its emotional and in some cases physical challenges.

The ability to adopt avoidance tactics was linked to social inequality, with some players lacking the social or material means to engage in these forms of agency when dealing with their 'sacking'. This meant they had to engage with family members, engagement that often exacerbated their personal disappointment and magnified their sense of shame for having failed to live up to their end of the intergenerational contract. Given that their status as an academy player had been a marker of kudos previously, their 'sacking' resulted in a loss of status among peers, which further compounded their emotional difficulties. If we consider the discussion in Chapter 5 on the cultures of migration tied to the notion of 'Mobile Africa', it is understandable that premature release from an elite academy, and the ensuing restraints on opportunities for spatial mobility, could negatively alter how players were viewed by their peers.

Some players experience this 'vital conjuncture', and its associated involuntary immobility, through a sense of shame and seek out ways to alleviate or mitigate against this emotion. Others confront their 'sacking' or transfer by attempting to find an acceptable exit. Perhaps tellingly, the continued pursuit of transnational mobility through football is strong among 'sacked' players as well as those who are transferred from their academy to a local Ghanaian club. The resolute belief across both groups of players in the possibility of 'becoming a somebody' through football, despite having not made the grade at academy level, is emblematic of the 'illusion of facility' that cultivates the culture of football migration that exists in Africa more generally (Poli, 2006a, 2006b). On the one hand, this 'illusion of facility' fuels unrealistic expectations that are likely to lead to further emotional turmoil. On the other, it does catalyse young players who find themselves at this 'vital conjuncture' having to deal with and respond to the emotional baggage associated with their release. For example, our participants who transferred to a domestic team viewed this 'vital conjuncture' not as an end point of their football aspirations but as a detour. While far from ideal, the domestic leagues were seen as a stepping stone to transnational mobility. This was explicit in the words of one participant:

> I have to be happy and then be praying for any opportunity again, so that I can move up there [Europe]. There is no money in Ghana league. You see, we are here, just a stepping stone ... we play for exposure, because some good agent will see you who is fine to help you ... and then take you somewhere. I am determined that I have to get some place by January. (Van der Meij, Darby and Liston, 2017: 190)

Thinking and acting in this way in order to overcome transnational immobility clearly correlates with the forms of social navigation that Vigh (2009) identified among aspiring migrants in Guinea-Bissau. But it also echoes the strategies employed by aspiring sport migrants more generally who, as Carter (2011) notes, seek out opportunities to make themselves 'visible' to sports teams in order to enhance their chances of producing mobility (see also Šašková, 2019).

Players who move from an academy to a local club in Ghana often do so with a pang of disappointment, but they believe that it could help them to realise transnational mobility. Given the increasing number of Ghanaian clubs that operate primarily as ventures to develop and sell players overseas, as outlined in Chapter 4, combined with the fact that some clubs have established strong transnational connections with European clubs, as detailed in Chapter 3, this is not an unreasonable scheme. In many ways, this desire to realise spatial mobility mirrors the disposition of their peers in the Colts leagues who are also 'trying their luck' against the odds to migrate through football.

Conclusions

Enacting transnational mobility via a contract with an overseas club, preferably in Europe, constitutes the most sought-after outcome of the considerable bodily, emotional and financial investments that young African football players make in their journey through youth football or academies. Yet it is also the one that is most difficult to secure. This chapter threw this disjuncture into sharp relief. By doing so, it offered insight on how African youth encounter, experience and negotiate the pursuit of football migration. We illustrated how young people deploy unique forms of agency, like 'trying your luck', to realise their aspirations for and expectations of transnational migration.

This chapter also teased out the subjectivities that enable young people to remain resolute in the pursuit of their football-related dreams despite the evidence pointing to the fact that the likely outcome of their efforts is involuntary immobility. One such form of evidence is being 'sacked' or released from an academy before securing terms with a foreign club. This moment constitutes a 'vital conjuncture' in the lives of players, one marked by 'shame' but also resourcefulness as players come to terms with and try to navigate their way through involuntary immobility. There are, of course, those who are able to leverage their footballing ability to secure passage abroad. The subsequent chapters undertake an exploration of the experiences of those who were able to migrate. They attend to how African players produce and try to sustain transnational mobility in a range of contexts, including Europe and South-East Asia, and examine how embarking on a career as a football migrant impacts on their post-playing-career trajectories.

7

Navigating liminality in foreign football industries

Introduction

When an almost-sixteen-year-old John came to Denmark in the early 2000s, he felt that he was taking the first step on the path to a successful football career abroad. He had benefited from a partnership agreement between his team, FC Maamobi, and FC Midtjylland that had been established a few years earlier. This partnership was part of an emerging business model that involved scouting African players at a young age, bringing them to Denmark as students and developing their abilities, initially during extended trials then subsequently as youth amateur players and – provided they were suitably skilled – as contracted professionals, before selling them on for a profit. Several times, members of the Danish club's staff came to Ghana to evaluate John's and his teammates' prospects of becoming professional players in Europe. When John was selected, he felt that he was close to realising what so many other boys of his generation imagine but fail to achieve: a professional football career abroad.

Though the Danish club assured him of the opportunity to further his education in a local school, his mother wanted him to pursue education in Ghana and to graduate from senior high school first before moving. On the contrary, John's father supported an immediate move to Denmark and argued that a professional career in international football may provide better chances in life than a local high-school certificate. While these conflicting points of view reflect increasingly shifting perceptions of the value of education in Ghanaian families, and particularly in relation to a career in football (see Chapter 5), John's family eventually concluded that moving to Europe for football could be a once-in-a-lifetime opportunity. Hence, John remembers, 'we all agreed that I should go'. This consensus was underpinned by the family's belief that in the event of the move to Denmark not going as hoped, as John put it, 'education, you can continue anytime you want to' (interview, 13 June 2016). That he was able to make this move before he turned eighteen, the age at which FIFA's RSTP permits international transfers (see

Chapter 3), was tied to an exception in Article 19 of the regulations that appeared to allow clubs to sign minors whose reason for relocating to Europe was to pursue their studies rather than football activities. With a student visa in hand, the Danish Immigration Service granted John a residence permit and the Danish Football Federation issued a player licence that enabled FC Midtjylland to register him as an amateur at their academy.

As far as John was concerned, he had started his career abroad. However, as we will show in this and the following chapter, it was a career that did not follow a linear trajectory or deliver the success he dreamt of. Notwithstanding some minor achievements on the pitch, the recurrence of setbacks, comebacks, fraud and failure added up to an ambivalent yet precarious experience over the coming years before he finally disappeared from the football scene. When Christian approached Mads, one of the academy's leading staff members in Denmark, years after John's departure from the club and asked about his whereabouts, it took a moment before John's name rang a bell. Then, a smile flickered over Mads's face. He remembered John with joy, praising the playmaker's talent and good character. He should have made a bigger name in football, said Mads, and wondered as to the reasons why John 'failed'. However, he had lost touch after John had finally left the country and was unaware of what had happened to him.

John's trajectory is not unique. Despite European clubs being sanctioned for violating Article 19 of the RSTP (De Marco, 2018), African footballers continue to move abroad at a young age. Indeed, some years after John's arrival in Denmark, FC Midtjylland and the Danish Football Federation received a strong warning from FIFA for infringing Article 19 in the case of six Nigerian minors who were brought to Denmark from another of Midtjylland's feeder clubs, FC Ebedei, ostensibly to study but who were also able to register at the club's academy (Court of Arbitration for Sport, 2009). Beyond this sort of movement of minors, young African players commonly move abroad after they have turned eighteen as part of official international transfers sanctioned by FIFA (Acheampong and Malek, 2019). Whether these young players migrate via an academy partnership, as in John's case, or with the help of intermediaries or as part of a self-organised journey, moving abroad is evidently a key node in their career trajectory and, as outlined in Chapter 5, marks the moment when a young person's dream of 'becoming a somebody' seemingly materialises. However, arriving in Europe, South-East Asia or elsewhere is far from the end point of a player's journey. Rather, reaching what is often perceived in young players' imaginations as the football Eldorado is seldom the ticket to a smooth and successful future career trajectory (Ungruhe and Esson, 2017).

For most players, their initial sojourn to Europe does not come with the security of a long-term playing contract. Many are instead invited for trials or signed on short-term contracts or agreements such as loans and are immediately required to prove their abilities to 'make it' in European or Asian football (Agergaard and Ungruhe, 2016). Hence, leaving the African continent rarely results in a player attaining a sense of career security; rather, it leads to a continuation of uncertainty, albeit in different geographical contexts. In the best-case scenarios, careers eventually accelerate. However, the majority of players do not succeed and many are left to rethink their ambitions and recalibrate their strategies to become a professional footballer abroad. By elaborating on players' lived experiences in their early encounters with football industries outside Africa, this chapter scrutinises the crucial meaning of this period between leaving Africa and securing terms abroad for their future career trajectory.

We begin by accounting for the diverse nature of these initial moves, which encompass seemingly straightforward transfers and more unconventional trajectories to Europe. We interrogate how a range of actors, such as intermediaries and clubs, influence players' efforts to enact football-related mobility, and evaluate the opportunities and obstacles experienced along the way. We then move beyond the prominent Africa–Europe nexus and elaborate on illustrative case studies of African players en route to South-East Asia, the most popular alternative destination for young African footballers (Akindes, 2013). While this serves to identify some regional particularities in the migration process abroad, we analyse the experiences of these players and the rather marginalised position of power they hold in the South-East Asian football industry. Our treatment of all of these themes draws further on the concept of social infrastructure outlined in Chapter 1 and used in Chapters 4 to 6 in addition to the concept of precarity (see During, 2015). Precarity is used here and in the following chapters to refer to both the structural challenges of problematic working conditions in the football industry as well as to players' subjective experiences and handling of uncertainty, risk and their spatialities, temporalities and ambivalences (Agergaard and Ungruhe, 2016) in an age of 'millennial capitalism' (Comaroff and Comaroff, 2000).

Making it to Europe: conventional paths and obstacles

Embarking on conventional routes through clubs' scouting networks, with the help of registered player agents or via a professional academy or club partnership, is indicative of what Lanfranchi and Taylor (2001) have coined 'moving with the ball'. These routes typically involve serious trials, training placements or direct transfers, and probably form the most promising trajectories through football's GPN (see Poli, 2010c). As was outlined in

Chapter 2, most players, for varying reasons, first move to teams outside the 'big five' leagues of England, Spain, Germany, France and Italy, such as those in Scandinavia, Benelux or southern and eastern Europe. Some of these initial moves include following long-established migration routes with colonial ties, favourable entry and visa regulations, or a modest sporting level that allows the player to adjust more easily to European football and gradually develop their careers (Acheampong and Malek, 2019; Poli, 2010a; Scott, 2015). As illustrated in Chapter 3, a promising, conventional route is via the academy node. Some West African academies and clubs such as ASEC Mimosas, Liberty Professionals FC and Right to Dream that are widely known for their professional management, scouting network and staff, serve as stepping stones to Europe and have indeed initiated the successful careers of players like Yaya Touré, Michael Essien and Mohammed Kudus.

The success stories of the disproportionately low numbers of players who have 'made it' cannot overshadow the fragile and at times problematic business practices in the partnerships between clubs and academies. Many of these links are based on personal relationships between leading staff members rather than on institutionalised agreements. When these relationships become fraught or are ended, they often cease to become a viable conduit for transnational mobility into the professional football industry. As discussed in Chapter 3, this was the case following the death of Liberty Professionals FC's chairman and technical director Alhaji Sly Tetteh in September 2011. Since then, Liberty has not been able to re-consolidate its coordinating role in African football migration, and its status as a leading national institution for talent development in the early 2000s, when it produced players such as Michael Essien and Asamoah Gyan, has waned. Another example of the fragility of the transnational connections that academies create can be seen in the decision by the Red Bull organisation to close its Ghanaian academy in 2013, just six years after it opened. While the academy had struggled to produce players for its parent club, academy players saw their hopes for the future as being reliant on the access to high-quality infrastructure and links to European football that Red Bull Ghana offered. When it closed, the young players became disheartened and disillusioned, although the re-opening of the facility as WAFA and its subsequent success in opening up pathways to the European game reignited the enthusiasm and commitment of many of these players (Darby, Esson and Ungruhe, 2018; Kainz, 2015).

Partnerships between clubs and academies also do not guarantee an upward career trajectory for every player who moves to Europe. On the contrary, most of the Ivorian players who initially came to Europe through the relationship between ASEC Mimosas and KSK Beveren ultimately moved to lower divisions in Belgium and France or were unable to remain in professional football after their contracts expired. Many disappeared from the football industry and had to make a living outside of the game (Schwarz, 2010). Others had to return to Africa with little to show for their endeavours and few options to continue with professional football or alternative livelihoods. The case of Ali, who moved from FC Ebedei, FC Midtjylland's Nigerian partner club, to the Danish academy under a similar partnership programme to the aforementioned John in the early 2000s, underlines the existential pressure players experience in their efforts to avoid such an outcome. Upon arrival, the sixteen-year-old found himself competing for a contract with three other West African trialists. As he recalled, 'we were all warned' that the Danish club intended to only offer contracts to three of the four and that 'we should be a step ahead [of the local players] for us to stay in Denmark' (interview, 30 March 2016). Mads, from FC Midtjylland's academy staff, confirmed this, outlining the high-stakes nature of the annual trial process:

> Normally, three or four players [from FC Ebedei's academy] are invited for try-outs and will be here for the [maximum of] ninety days ... They come up here, and are told from the beginning that, 'You are invited to Europe for a try-out. ... No matter how the try-out goes, no matter how good you are or how bad you are, all of you are going back to Nigeria on that date.' Then ... the club [FC Midtjylland] will decide if one, two [or] three will be re-invited. They can get a new ninety-day visa, and if the timing is good then they are invited [with the visit timed such that] within the three months that they are here the second time they will turn eighteen. And then we can write or offer the contract. (Interview, 9 February 2016)

Based on his experiences of this sort of extended trial, Ali astutely observed that as an 'African-born coming to Europe at that age, you should have something extra in order for you to make it to the top ... it's a big challenge because if you have this kind of opportunity and you [don't] make it then you never know when you get this kind of opportunity again' (interview, 30 March 2016). As things transpired in his case, Ali successfully navigated his trial and was first registered as an amateur with FC Midtjylland's U-19 team before signing a professional contract. While obviously a talented footballer, there was also a high degree of serendipity involved in this outcome. Not long after he moved, the alignment of the very same arrangement through which he had been recruited with Article 19 of FIFA's RSTP was questioned. As discussed earlier, this led to FC Midtjylland being formally reprimanded by FIFA, effectively closing this route into European football. Ali's case was not among those which were investigated by FIFA or the Court of Arbitration for Sport and the ruling had no implications for him (Court of Arbitration for Sport, 2009). However, other players who believed they had gained a foothold in the European football industry via this partnership had different experiences from those of Ali and their encounters offered very different prospects. The trajectory of John's career illustrates this vividly.

When John was sent back home after his first stay in Europe with FC Midtjylland, his life was turned upside down. As an academy player in Denmark, he was combining football with part-time education in the tenth grade of a Danish public school and participated in extra lessons in Danish. Soon after his arrival he suffered an injury that prevented him from training and playing matches during the first few months of his stay. Yet he managed to recover and play the two remaining matches before the winter break. In one of the games, he scored twice during a victory over their rivals Aarhus GF. John thought that he was progressing well and looked forward to continuing in the academy team for the meantime and in the longer term getting a professional contract when he turned eighteen or nineteen. After he spent Christmas with a Ghanaian family in Denmark and returned to the club to resume training he was called for a meeting with the academy staff. He was informed that he had to leave the academy for sporting reasons. 'I panicked', he remembered. 'I cried a lot ... I wasn't aware that I would be kicked out of the academy ... it just came to me out of the blue' (interview, 13 June 2016).

While John's sudden and involuntary release resembles practices in West African academies (see Chapter 6), failing to succeed in Europe and being forced to return home constitutes a different, even more existential challenge. The date of return was already set for January. 'I was shocked, disappointed [and] asking myself so many questions', he said. 'I quit school in Ghana too to chase my dream. Now I've fallen' (interview, 13 June 2016). As an academy player, he only received pocket money and board from the club, and leaving Denmark immediately meant that he could not complete the school term. Hence, without having accrued significant financial or educational capital, he returned to Ghana having to reignite his football ambitions from scratch. Similar to other players whose hopes and prospects were tied to partnership arrangements between African and European clubs that ultimately did not enable their transfer 'outside' (Poli, 2006a), John found himself in a very precarious situation.

While the relatively few successful career paths of African players who benefit from club partnerships may at first sight point to linear pathways through football's GPN, John's case illustrates that young players under contract with academies or partner clubs of European teams in Africa have little say in their own career trajectories (Darby, 2007b; Poli, 2006b). This was also evident in Kingsley's case. Short and slightly built, Kingsley was a talented player in his youth and eager to move to Europe to play professional football. In search of the best stepping stone to achieve this, he moved to various clubs in Ghana and neighbouring Togo and was eventually recommended to Red Bull Ghana by a former coach, who took on a coordinating role. Following a successful one-month trial, Kingsley, who was eighteen years old at the time, became a member of Red Bull Ghana's U-19 academy squad. Since he was informed by staff members that the academy aimed to produce players for the European market, in keeping with the culture of speculation around player mobility discussed in Chapter 4, Kingsley saw this as the best opportunity to build a career abroad. In his first year with the team, he was voted the academy's best player in his age group and he attracted the interest of several Ghanaian Premier League clubs. However, Red Bull decided to take him to the parent club in Salzburg for a month-long training placement to test his skills in a European environment. While he was not happy that a possible move within Ghana was blocked, he was eager to showcase his abilities in Austria. However, his experience did not extend beyond training with Salzburg's U-17 and U-15 teams while two of his teammates, who came with him to Austria, were sent to trials with other Austrian clubs. Kingsley felt that he was being given contradictory information about the purpose of his trip to Austria by staff members at Red Bull. His concerns that he was not being given a proper opportunity were realised when he was eventually told that he was too small to play in Austria and that there would not be any trials arranged for him.

Kingsley lost confidence in Red Bull's approach. Of their focus on producing players for the parent club, he noted: 'If they are sending us to one place where they are looking for a type of player, they are killing us. ... On the field someone can run fast and he could play in England, another can play in Portugal, so you have to watch and you have to know your market.' Kingsley did not see any reason to stay for another two weeks and returned to Ghana after half of the anticipated period. 'It was a lesson for me', he recalled. After he returned from Austria, he wanted to leave the academy but claimed that he was told that he was still under contract. He did not know what Red Bull planned for him and made a number of assertions about the academy that he felt illustrated how his ambitions were being constrained:

> The previous year [Asante] Kotoko came for me and if they [Red Bull] allow me to go I would be in the national U-20 squad. While I'm here I will not get anywhere because the GFA is not on good terms with this academy. When they invite the players, Red Bull don't allow us to go ... I know that an academy is a long-term programme. You do your training. We are being camped here and we train twice per day for two hours. We don't go anywhere and it is dull. They told us that it is a programme. (Interview, 28 August 2010)

Indeed, a year after his experience in Austria, Kingsley, then aged twenty, was still at the Red Bull academy, and no options to move either internally or internationally had materialised. Kingsley's case does not just reflect an isolated experience of a disillusioned player. It rather points to protectionist practices in how academies often engage with their players over their futures, particularly where a European partner is involved. As discussed in Chapter 3, these types of partnership arrangements invariably involve European clubs investing in an African academy with a view to securing first refusal on the most talented players, and this raises questions about the autonomy of players vis-à-vis the commercial interests of academies and clubs. This is an issue that came to prominence when a number of Western media outlets carried a series of exposé-type stories involving the Ghanaian academy Right to Dream. It is worth expanding on this, not least because it reveals a further set of complications for academy players seeking to play professionally in Europe.

In December 2018, a consortium of European investigative journalists working with the Football Leaks platform published a series of allegations about aspects of the relationship between the English Premier League club Manchester City, the Ghanaian academy Right to Dream and the Danish Superliga club FC Nordsjælland. As we detailed in Chapter 3, an agreement was signed in 2010 between Manchester City and Right to Dream. In return for an annual investment of almost one million euros, Manchester City had the right to exercise an option to sign players from the academy once they turned eighteen. With Right to Dream's purchase of FC Nordsjælland in late 2016, this agreement was extended to cover FC Nordsjælland, and there was a clause inserted into the contract that appeared to give Manchester City a degree of control over the onward transfer of Right to Dream graduates at the Danish club, particularly those players that they wanted to exercise an option on. In those cases, FC Nordsjælland was obliged, according to the contract, to 'use its best endeavours to effect the transfer of the player's registration to MC [Manchester City] for nil consideration' (Haslov and Brock, 2018a). The allegation made in the German news magazine *Der Spiegel* and the Danish daily *Politiken* was that this contravened FIFA's rules around third-party influence in the transfer of players, and aspersions were cast that players were being maltreated and given little control over decisions surrounding their onward transfers either from Right to Dream or FC Nordsjælland (*Der Spiegel*, 2018; Haslov and Brock, 2018a).

While Manchester City remained mute, Right to Dream publicly addressed the allegations and engaged openly with the journalists involved in the exposé. In an interview with the Danish journalists who first published the allegations, Tom Vernon, the founder of Right to Dream and then chairman of FC Nordsjælland, argued that the clause had not only recently been removed from the contract with Manchester City for reasons not linked to the media stories but had also never been operationalised in practice (see

Haslov and Brock, 2018b). This intervention from Vernon did not stop the media interest in the issue, mainly because even if the clause had not been used, and it had been removed, that did not negate the point that its existence in the first place was problematic in terms of its potential implications for player agency. In the face of further stories published in *Politiken*, FC Nordsjælland responded with its own press release in which it set out the precise terms of relations with the English club and, critically for our discussion here, the extent to which players had a say in their onward transfer:

> Manchester City FC was not guaranteed anything else in return apart from the opportunity to offer 18-year-old players a contract when they left the academy: Just like any other club can. It was then, as it is today, the player himself who can decide 100% where he wishes to play and who he wants to sign a contract with. All players that were offered to continue their careers with Manchester City FC were offered contracts on what we believe were market terms. A total of 12 players have moved on to Manchester City FC through the 20 years Right to Dream has existed. All 12 are still active as professional football players today. Nine of them have represented their country since they moved to Manchester City FC. (FC Nordsjælland, 2018a)

Faced with continued negative reporting in late 2018, FC Nordsjælland released a nine-thousand-word dossier setting out its full response, which contained testimonies from former academy players and their family members attesting to their full involvement in a consultative decision-making process around future trajectories, either in football or pursuing educational opportunities offered through Right to Dream's partner schools in the US. What this dossier also alluded to though were nefarious practices at the African end of football's GPN involving a network of Ghanaian intermediaries who had been offering Right to Dream players financial inducements, or conversely threatening them and their family members, to break their contract with the academy in order to enter into representation arrangements with these talent speculators. The detail is further illustrative of the difficulties young African academy players face in navigating what they hope will be a path to the European game, and is therefore worth quoting at length:

> There is a small group of former students who have all ended up in an unfortunate position of being vulnerable to manipulation from a Ghanaian network that has for several years tried to shut down RIGHT TO DREAM, in order to get hold of the talented players for their own financial gain. A network consisting mainly of four people, all of whom are part of a police investigation in Ghana that has been ongoing for 14 months on 'trafficking of African players'. A network that has previously unsuccessfully tried to spread similar charges in Ghana as well as trying to bribe young female students to make false allegations of sexual abuse, which RIGHT TO DREAM can document. Several employees, and their families, at RIGHT TO DREAM have

been threatened by the four main characters of this network. RIGHT TO DREAM estimates that this group of vulnerable students, who are controlled by promises of rewards or threats, consists of between 10–15 players, of which *Politiken* has now brought articles with five of these. All five can be directly linked to the four individuals in the agent network. (FC Nordsjælland, 2018b)

In a series of interviews that we conducted in June and November 2018, the chairman, chief executive officer and legal counsel of FC Nordsjælland pointed to the regulatory terrain within which these sorts of intermediaries operated, and particularly FIFA's decision to liberalise the football agent licensing system, detailed in Chapter 2, as being central in creating these complications in the trajectories of young African footballers.

At the time of writing, over two years after the allegations about the agreement between Manchester City, Right to Dream and FC Nordsjælland were first made, FIFA does not appear to have formally pursued this matter and no sanctions have been imposed. In a separate, unrelated case, FIFA reprimanded and imposed a fine of 370,000 Swiss francs on Manchester City in August 2019 for several breaches of Article 19 of the RSTP. One of these involved two Right to Dream students who played for the club in friendly matches as part of their trial before they turned eighteen and who subsequently signed for the club in 2012 and 2013, respectively (BBC Sport, 2019a; Jackson, 2019). Ironically, the outcome of this case highlights further regulatory barriers in terms of young African players' access to the professional game. Article 19 contains a number of exceptions to the ban on the international transfers of minors.

The most prominent exception of Article 19 is that players within the EU or the European Economic Area are permitted to move internationally provided the signing club makes appropriate provision for their training, education and welfare. No such exception applies to players not resident in Europe, a scenario that limits African players' access to the elite echelons of the European game and to clubs who are equipped to offer them the same sort of welfare, educational and training provisions that are deemed by FIFA to be appropriate. This raises questions around the extent to which these rules enable parity of treatment for young players from different geographical locales within football's GPN. Indeed, Yilmaz *et al.* (2020) have argued that these exceptions, and other elements of the RSTP, not only treat young players differently depending on where they were born but also run counter to a number of articles of the United Nations Convention on the Rights of the Child.

Without a formal FIFA investigation being initiated, it is impossible to attest to the veracity or otherwise of the media allegations around the contractual relations between Manchester City, Right to Dream and FC Nordsjælland.

At the very least though, this case and that of other transnational development pathways discussed in this section raise important questions about the tensions between players' aspirations, autonomy and ability to manoeuvre to consolidate their position in football's GPN and the commercial, business-focused interests of academies and clubs. Nonetheless, joining an academy that has a transnational partnership or arrangement with a European club is an attractive proposition for young African players because they appear to, and oftentimes do, offer the most talented players direct, frictionless routes into the professional game (Poli, 2010d). However, there are also wrinkles and roadblocks involved in traversing this path. The cases discussed above, involving the sudden withdrawal from talent development in Africa, the inability to sustain structures and networks to develop players and facilitate their moves abroad, organisational agreements that have been construed as restricting players' movement to clubs of their choice, and the vagaries of the application of FIFA's international transfer regulations are illustrative of this. The outcomes and lived realities for players, including in some of those cases discussed above, who may have considered transnational arrangements as the most conventional, advantageous route to achieving their ambitions, are often problematic, leading instead to immobility, a recalibration of career plans and, for some, the pursuit of more unconventional routes through the game's GPN. It is to these that this chapter now turns.

Following unconventional paths to Europe

Despite the many obstacles and failures that players following conventional routes experience, the relatively few glittering success stories continue to inspire the fantasies of aspiring African talents. By their very existence, football academies and club partnerships help to cultivate and nourish the dreams of young footballers all over Africa, but access to these comparatively privileged nodes is rather limited. Right to Dream, for instance, organises 'justifies' that attract about eighteen thousand young trialists annually. Among them, only around fifteen are picked and offered a place at the academy (Darby, Esson and Ungruhe, 2018). In light of these figures, it is not an exaggeration to state that all over Africa, footballers aiming to move abroad lack sufficient exposure, visibility and the right connections in the football business to help them translate their aspirations to reality. Yet, as we show in the examples that follow, despite the exceedingly long odds of 'making it' in European football, they remain confident in their abilities, resolute and, critically, creative in the strategies that they employ and the actions they take to increase their visibility and connections (Besnier *et al.*, 2018; Hann, 2020; Ungruhe and Esson, 2017).

For those who find themselves on the fringes of the more formalised nodes of football's GPN in Africa, what are these strategies and how do players make them work? In order to attract the attention of potential suitors, players increasingly post videos on social media demonstrating their technical ability and highlights from matches or trials. Our conversations with young players and observations at trials revealed that they often travel considerable distances to attend scouting tournaments and events. They also seek to connect with coaches, agents and African migrant players abroad via the Internet to widen their network of potential coordinators in the football business. Players seeking a move abroad also try to utilise relationships with former teammates who have gone before them and been recruited by European clubs, asking them to connect them to gatekeepers and insiders who might help facilitate spatial mobility (Agergaard and Tiesler, 2014; Elliott and Gusterud, 2018; Elliott and Harris, 2015; Elliott and Maguire, 2008). For most players it remains uncertain and speculative whether and when the hours and money spent on these practices will ever pay dividends.

Waiting and working towards the right opportunity is often an experience of trial and error and involves a great degree of dedication, patience, flexibility, knowledge about the football industry and its opportunities and pitfalls, as well as a sense of adventure and an ability to cope with frustration and setbacks (van der Meij, Darby and Liston, 2017; Ungruhe, 2016; Ungruhe and Büdel, 2016). Embarking on unconventional, less formalised routes chasing the dream of a career in European football can, in many senses and almost paradoxically, be considered the norm rather than the exception. Players' strategies are multiple and varied. They range from competing for a trial with a European club on a reality TV show, such as the popular *MTN Soccer Academy* in Ghana which paved the way for players like Gideon Baah (HJK Helsinki and Red Bull New York), to travel to Europe on tourist visas and looking for clubs independently.

There are also accounts of refugees who have made it to professional football, such as the Gambian winger Bakery Jatta, who secured a contract with the German club Hamburger SV in 2016. As of early 2021, Jatta was still playing for the club, even though his actual identity was a topic of debate in the German media. This situation has led to official investigations by German immigration authorities (Burghardt, 2021). There are also a few notorious, albeit amusing, examples of players who successfully secured contracts with professional clubs despite their skills being far from the required level. The most prominent in this regard was Ali Dia from Senegal, whose creativity (with the truth), helped him reach the upper echelons of the European game. Dia had played as an amateur in the lower leagues in France and Germany and had had a number of failed trials in England before signing for a non-league club, Blyth Spartans. His unlikely recruitment by Southampton in the English Premier League came about following a recommendation from an intermediary claiming to be the Liberian superstar George Weah, at the time the most famous African player in Europe. Dia himself added to the connivance by claiming to be a free-scoring Senegalese international. Though he had spent most of his career at an amateur level he eventually benefited from several player absences in the Southampton team, and a complete lack of oversight on the part of the then manager, Graeme Souness, to sign a contract with the club. He soon gained infamy for his fifty-three-minute appearance in a league match against Leeds United in the 1996/97 season, during which his limited football abilities were revealed to the world (Menery, 2015).

The examples of Jatta and Dia also depict the problematic layers of economic and political inequalities in the global football industry and between the Global South and Global North more generally (Ungruhe and Büdel, 2016; Esson, 2020). Their stories are exceptional and should be juxtaposed with the widespread vulnerability and burdens that most African football migrants face. Indeed, when embarking on journeys to Europe, many players experience fraud and failure. The frequent media reports that label African football migrants as victims of trafficking or of a new slave trade may paint a dramatic picture and misinterpret the degree of exploitation in the football industry (Esson, 2015a). However, exploitation does exist and is the lived reality for some migrant players. As we depicted in Chapter 4, this is often related to a problematic infrastructure of actors who unscrupulously indulge in speculation to benefit from young footballers' talent.

The football industry, at least at the elite end, is highly lucrative, attracting dubious figures at a range of points in the GPN who seek to take advantage of the widespread hopes but limited possibilities among African youth for football-related mobility. Young players in particular are often lured by fake agents with false promises and pay them for opportunities such as trials with European clubs that never materialise (Drywood, 2016; Esson and Drywood, 2018; Hawkins, 2015). Others are abandoned by these intermediaries the moment organised trials have proved unsuccessful and the player is deemed of no further financial benefit (Darby, Akindes and Kirwin, 2007; Donnelly and Petherick, 2004). Once in Europe, these players usually experience a very precarious existence with uncertain social and material prospects. They find themselves without a contract, connections or a place to stay, alongside an expiring visa and limited financial means (Büdel, 2013; Ungruhe, 2018a). That being said, media narratives of victims and heroes oversimplify the experiences encountered by the majority of African football migrants. Players' trajectories play out in more nuanced ways than this prominent dichotomy suggests, and in many cases involve players demonstrating creativity to navigate the constraints on their desired spatial and social mobility through football. This is especially visible in the trajectory of Demba, a young Cameroonian player who navigated a succession of obstacles to secure a professional contract in European football. His story is worth expanding on in some detail.

Growing up in a suburb of the country's capital, Yaoundé, and playing football on the streets in his neighbourhood since early childhood, Demba joined his first local club while attending primary school. He was eleven years old when he took part in what was depicted as an exhibition tournament organised by a well-established football academy, but what was in reality a trial for a place at said academy. Demba attracted the attention of the scouts and was among the lucky few to be invited for a formal trial at the academy in Douala, a few hundred kilometres away from his hometown. He impressed once again and was offered a place at the academy, locating him at a node in football's GPN that could increase his visibility. Demba was eager to play football in a professional environment, even if this meant moving away from his family. The rocky pitches in his neighbourhood were unsuited to his style or attributes. In such a setting, technique and passing skills were subordinated to a physical style based on strength and endurance, and during training the emphasis was on running rather than playing with the ball. The academy was different. The playing fields and training sessions were of a much higher standard and the coaches from France and Switzerland focused on a more technical style of play.

Demba believed that a place in the academy could take him closer to a professional career in Europe. Providing a further example of the role of the family in a player's career choices, a key theme of Chapter 5, his parents were consulted and accepted the offer, not least because it included a scholarship for the academy's own school, as well as living expenses and accommodation. While playing for the academy's various junior teams, Demba was able to concentrate on his education and graduate from school with a baccalaureate at the age of sixteen. Despite showing academic promise, rather than furthering his education Demba was keen to pursue his dream of a football career in Europe. He left the academy, but it was proving exceptionally difficult for him to get the necessary visa to travel. He got in contact with a football agent from Yaoundé who offered to use his connections to the Russian embassy to get him a visa. Without a direct invite from a club for a trial or contract offer, they decided to apply for a student visa. In 2006, while still a minor, Demba was accepted for a bachelor's course in economics at a university in Moscow, and received the requisite visa from the embassy.

Once in Moscow, Demba's agent promised to look for a professional club for him. Demba explained, 'I always wanted to get out of Cameroon.

Studying abroad was just my plan B ... but if I cannot get to Europe directly through football, I have to try the university.' His parents supported his plans to study and provided funds for the plane ticket, fees and accommodation in Russia. Demba had to pay the equivalent of a few hundred US dollars for his agent's service. However, after arriving in Moscow, Demba found he was no longer able to contact the agent, which seemingly confirmed that he had been duped into thinking that an opportunity in Russian football was a possibility. Shortly after his arrival, he witnessed a murder in the subway when a group of young men stabbed a Black man to death. 'I was totally shocked', he recalled. 'I didn't know anybody and was scared to go out of the apartment. I was thinking, "What am I doing here with football? Shall I go back to Cameroon?"' In articulating his doubts about his move to Russia, he concluded, 'It was really bad' (interview, 28 November 2010).

Soon after the incident, however, he regained confidence and resolved to make the best of his legal status as a foreign student. Demba started language classes at the university, met and befriended other exchange students and began playing football with other African migrants on a public pitch. He discovered that quite a few of them had been brought to Moscow by the same agent and had had similar experiences. For most of these individuals, their visas had expired and they were constantly under threat of being detained by the authorities and expelled from the country. However, despite their precarious position, they were able to act as coordinators and put Demba in contact with individuals at a Moscow-based top-flight club who invited him for trials. He was not offered a contract, but was given the chance to continue training with the reserve team. He accepted this offer, hoping that being around a professional football environment would not only improve his game but also increase his visibility. Hence, he was content to stay in Moscow to combine his studies with his ambition to play professional football (interview, 28 November 2010).

At this juncture in Demba's life, to which we will return in Chapter 8, his future was highly uncertain. The fraudulent interaction with the purported agent revealed his marginalised position in the social infrastructure of football's GPN, one that left him unable to consolidate his status in the Russian game. Yet securing a university place and student visa enabled him to hold out for an opportunity in football, and despite the setbacks he experienced, he continued to actively work towards a career in Europe. At first sight, there may have been an element of naivety involved in holding on to his belief in a better future through football regardless of the actual prospects of this materialising. However, Demba's actions in seeking to enhance his visibility and broaden his options were replete with what Johnson-Hanks (2005) has conceptualised as 'judicious opportunism'. This is by no means unique to Demba. His story is illustrative of the opportunism, flexibility and resolve that the many young African players who pursue what might be considered unconventional career pathways exhibit in order to cope with and negotiate precarious experiences in their pursuit of such a highly prized future. As we have illustrated above, the same can be said for those whose aspirations of a football career abroad are fashioned in more conventional nodes of football's GPN. The sorts of travails, hardships and uncertainties that frequently accompany initial encounters with the European football industry are also evident for those players who move to emerging football destinations beyond Europe. For the remainder of this chapter, we explore how African players seek to navigate entry into football in South-East Asia, and we do so mainly through the experiences of two Ghanaian players whose career course we followed closely.

Outside Eldorado: African football migration to South-East Asia

European leagues, and particularly the 'big five', are the dream destination for African footballers. However, with the game's increasing professionalisation and commercialisation in many parts of the world since the mid-1990s, the migration of African players has become an almost global phenomenon. Among the many and diverse locations where African footballers ply their trade, South and South-East Asia stand out and form an increasingly important node in football's GPN beyond the Africa–Europe nexus (Akindes, 2013; Poli, 2010a). Following the movement of a few African pioneers to these regions between the late 1970s and early 1990s (see Chapter 2), clubs began to recruit African footballers in a more systematic fashion from the late 1990s onwards. The expanded media coverage of European football in Asian countries, frequent promotional pre-season tours by European teams in the region and, critically, the first hosting of the FIFA World Cup on Asian soil when the tournament was held in South Korea and Japan in 2002 have all boosted football's popularity throughout the continent (Cho, 2013, 2016).

These developments led to a drive to expand, invest in, professionalise and improve standards of play across the region. For several reasons, African players were identified as offering much potential in helping Asian leagues and clubs achieve their objectives. Given the growth in media coverage of European football in Asia, local clubs and investors had witnessed the growing presence and value of African players in the European game. The success of Senegal on Asian shores during the 2002 World Cup, in which they beat the then world champions, France, in the opening game before being narrowly defeated by Turkey at the quarter-final stage, was also likely to have whetted the appetite of clubs for African talent. Critically though, beyond their abilities, African players were affordable and were generally willing to migrate and play in emerging leagues and for clubs that could not yet offer a professional infrastructure in terms of management, coaching and training facilities. In addition, African players seemingly embodied a different style of physicality and technique that not only bolstered the competitiveness of clubs but was also attractive to the growing football-consuming public in Asia (Abe, 2018; Akindes, 2013).

In turn, African players benefited from liberal rules on the number of foreign players permitted in Asian leagues (Poli, 2010a), easier access to visas (Akindes, 2013; Rehal, 2015) and burgeoning African communities in a number of South-East Asian nations that established close links to their home countries (Pelican and Schwarz, 2015). With African pioneers like David Williams and Roger Milla already putting Asia on the map of potential destinations for footballers from Africa (Mukharji, 2008; Akindes, 2013), the region grew in popularity and the number of African players in the various leagues increased markedly in the new millennium (Akindes, 2013; Poli, 2010a). At times and in some leagues, such as Cambodia's top division, the C-League, African players made up 50 per cent of all foreign players (Abe, 2018). None of this is to say that migrating to Asia is a seamless, uncomplicated route into professional football. Rather, as we now illustrate, it is one wrought with difficulties and hardships.

In the case of South-East Asia, African players often need to embark on rather unconventional journeys to secure a trial or a contract, not least because a lack of finances and connections militates against scouting players directly in African settings. Aspiring migrant footballers therefore tend to depend on peer networks or fellow African players based in South-East Asia who may recommend them to their clubs (Akindes, 2013; de Latour, 2010; Rehal, 2015). The pay-in-advance services of intermediaries are also often sought out to secure trials or contracts, but this is a risky path given the preponderance of unscrupulous talent speculators operating in what is an emerging and largely unregulated business in the region (Akindes, 2013; de Latour, 2010; Poli, 2010a; Rehal, 2015). Whether organising their trips themselves or relying on an agent's mediation, players often pay a considerable amount of money for flight and visa costs and are seldom aware of the many uncertainties and struggles that frequently follow. Players often arrive on short-term tourist visas, which are cheaper and easier to acquire compared to working visas. However, this informal practice means that players are under pressure to secure contracts immediately and to become eligible for more permanent working visas (Rehal, 2015). If their visas expire, African players face considerable fines or even jail, and are often abandoned by their intermediaries with no means to pay for the return ticket home (Akindes, 2013). Hence, facing these consequences, players have little room for manoeuvre and are at the mercy of the intermediaries or a club to secure their stay. The lived experiences of these challenges encountered in the early migration process are articulated in Isaak's story.

Isaak was a talented midfielder from Ghana whose dream was to play professionally in Europe. Compared to many of his age group who shared his ambitions, his chances of succeeding looked promising. Playing for Ghana's U-17 national team, the Black Starlets, he enjoyed greater visibility and built relations with relevant figures in the football industry. In particular, his relationship with the team manager of the Black Starlets was critical in opening up the possibility of securing a contract with a club abroad. In 2012, the year Isaak turned eighteen, the manager asked him if he wanted to play in Thailand. The manager was in touch with a Ghanaian footballer based in Thailand who was also trying to establish himself as a player agent and saw an opportunity to act as a conduit for young Ghanaians to transfer to Thai clubs. Given his desire to become a professional player and in light of the association between spatial and social mobility, discussed in Chapter 5, Isaak was eager to go.

Despite having no knowledge about the country or its football industry, Isaak trusted his team manager that a move to Thailand was a good opportunity to build a career abroad. According to the Ghanaian player now serving as his agent, all arrangements and logistics had been taken care of. He would deal with the paperwork, including the visa, book the flight, arrange board and lodging and organise trials and training with several professional clubs. Isaak would only need to compensate him for his expenditures and service upon signing a contract with a Thai club. Isaak's parents and his elder brother, seeing the arrangement in terms of a household livelihood strategy, were supportive and encouraged him to travel to Thailand.

Shortly after the Thai authorities had issued a three-month tourist visa, Isaak began his journey. Together with seven other Ghanaian players to whom the agent had promised similar deals, he boarded a plane to Bangkok and looked forward to what he thought was the biggest and most promising step in his career so far. However, after the agent had picked them up from the airport and brought them to the accommodation he had rented for them, it quickly became clear that the promised trials had not been organised. As Isaak saw it, 'everything was a lie'. He described the reality of what he, and his compatriots faced:

> We were seven players in a small room. No windows, no air condition[ing], nothing. I was the youngest, so I had to sleep on the floor. Nobody cared about me ... there was nowhere to go, so we stayed in the room all day. At times, no food for me for the whole day. (Interview, 15 February 2020)

Isaak had embarked on the journey with only ten US dollars in his pocket. He had spent this on a local sim card and credit and he was now financially dependent on the goodwill of his fellow players. 'I was really suffering', he said. 'I remember one time I woke up and I started to cry because I was so hungry, without food.' Though some years had passed between these events and our interview, he found it hard to talk about his experience. He sighed and paused. Then, after a moment of silence he concluded, 'It was really, really tough'.

The agent continued to appease the players with promises that trials would happen and asked for their patience. Isaak, as with many African players who hope to succeed in the game, found consolation in prayer (see Chapter 6): 'When I pray, I become so strong, I don't fear anything. I can do anything I want.' However, the act of praying was helpful on another level. He remembered one particular evening in the room with his fellow players: 'We were together. We were supposed to contribute money for the dinner. And I have no money. I was praying. You know, Muslims, when we pray, you can't stop us. So the guys were waiting for me to pay my share. Just fifteen [Thai] baht, or twenty [around 0.37–0.50 euros]. I was done with prayers. But if I stop praying, they will ask me [for my share of the money]. So, I kept on praying for about an hour.' Afterwards he ate the leftovers from his roommates' meals.

Isaak was clearly in a difficult predicament and grew desperate. Nevertheless, he did not want to give up and he feared returning home empty-handed and with no realistic prospects of re-embarking on a professional career abroad. 'Some of the guys wanted to go home', he said, but 'no matter what I am not going back home. I am going to do my best. Because there is nothing at home.' He also did not talk with his parents about his hardship. 'I always protect them', he explained, clearly eager that they should not worry about him. Instead, he turned to his brother at home for help. He was willing to support Isaak and sent him money via the agent's bank account. However, Isaak never received the funds. The agent told him that the account was blocked and that he could not make any withdrawals from it. Isaak suspected him of stealing the money but refrained from questioning him as he feared that doing so would risk the little chance of getting a trial or a contract in the country. Despite the impasse he was facing, Isaak did not lose hope: 'I was just waiting for the right opportunity. I was just concentrated.'

Indeed, an opportunity did eventually arise. Two months after their arrival in Thailand, the agent informed the players about an upcoming trial with a semi-professional fourth-division club. Isaak was full of hope, even though he was one of ten African players trying to get a contract. 'When the coach saw me, he started to laugh' – he felt Isaak was too small to compete in the game. Yet Isaak quickly impressed the coach and was rewarded with a contract for the upcoming season. He received a monthly salary of around twenty-five thousand baht (approximately 625 euros) in addition to a room in the club house, and the club also organised his visa and work permit for one year. However, from his salary he had to compensate the agent who had facilitated his journey to Thailand. For six months, Isaak paid him twenty thousand baht [approximately 500 euros] back every month to cover his expenditures for the flight ticket, his tourist visa, accommodation and services associated with his trial. Then, after having paid his dues, Isaak ended his relationship with the agent.

Though he was happy to have moved closer to achieving his dream of professional football abroad, Isaak felt that going to Thailand 'wasn't the right move'. Despite the hardships he faced in the first months, Isaak played at a level that was neither seen nor recognised in the global football industry. 'I was dreaming about Europe all the time but, unfortunately, I ended up here', he concluded. As he saw it, 'I was deceived' (interview, 15 February 2020). Isaak's story points to the problematic social infrastructure around African football migration to South-East Asia. First, his disillusionment and the hardships he experienced over his journey show the subordinate position of power of migrating players and the difficulties this creates in attempting to consolidate their status. Relying on intermediaries to open up opportunities through trials or personal contacts while competing with others for what are limited spots on team rosters leaves players with little room to navigate their next and crucial career step.

During Christian's research stay in Thailand in early 2020, it became clear that the practice of inviting multiple players for trials at the same time is widespread among clubs and intermediaries in the region. By coordinating for whom and when a trial materialises, intermediaries and club officials consolidate their position of power in the business. Though this scouting practice is still highly speculative, it reduces their risk of failure: even if only one player out of several succeeds, their speculation has paid off. This strategy transposes all the risks of failure onto the individual players who, if they are not recruited, either have to return home or are left to negotiate their own path in the South-East Asian football industry. This highlights the precarities associated with being an 'entrepreneur of self', as discussed in Chapter 5. In Isaak's case, rather than consolidating his status as a promising player on an international level, his speculative move to the region led to him losing the visibility that he had accrued as a member of Ghana's U-17 national team. This visibility could have enabled a move to a more recognised node in the football industry, and the fact that it was diminished by moving to a lower-tier Thai league likely limited his options in terms of his future career trajectory.

Cases such as Isaak's are widespread among young African players in South-East Asia (Abe, 2018; Akindes, 2013; Rehal, 2015) and point to what Poli (2010b, 2010c) conceptualised as 'trafficking through football'. Yet it would be inaccurate to state that every single move to South-East Asia turns out to be a disillusioning, precarious experience, as the following outline of Jordan's move demonstrates. When Jordan moved to Thailand in 2012, he was still a minor. Only fourteen years of age and playing for a team in one of Ghana's Colts leagues, he was approached by Ken, a Ghanaian footballer who plied his trade at a first-tier club in Thailand but spent his holidays at home in Ghana. Before Ken returned home for his close season break, his coach asked him to look for young Ghanaian players for the club's academy, and Ken identified Jordan as someone with the talent to succeed there and become a professional footballer. Despite his young age, Jordan felt ready. 'If I have the chance I will go', is how he recalled his early mindset and ambition to play abroad. 'It's my dream to play outside', he confirmed (interview, 15 February 2020). His mother did not want him to leave, but Ken assured her that the club would take good care of her son and provide board, lodging and schooling if he succeeded in his trial. However, the family were told that they had to pay for the flight and the visa. Jordan's elder brother was convinced that this was a unique opportunity for his talented young sibling and indeed the entire family, and they agreed to pay the costs.

The club sent all the requisite documents for the processing of the visa. In order to circumvent Article 19 of the RSTP, the club indicated that the primary reason for Jordan's sojourn to Thailand was to pursue education and that he was under the care of Ken and staff members of the club. On his arrival, Jordan came together with six other young footballers from Ghana who all hoped to get a place in the club's academy. When the head coach of the academy team saw Jordan for the first time, he thought he was too small to compete with the other players in the team, a situation that resonates with Isaak's experience. However, Jordan and one other player impressed during the trials and were chosen to join the academy, while the other five players had to return to Ghana. For Jordan, everything seemed to be materialising as he was promised and hoped for. When he began to play for the academy team, he shared a room with the other Ghanaian talent, received regular meals and began schooling. Despite a few initial challenges in his new socio-cultural environs (see Chapter 8), he enjoyed the professional training facilities at the club and playing for the academy team. Occasionally, he also took part in international youth tournaments in Europe. Given these benefits, he felt he was on track to becoming a professional footballer in the near future.

While we continue to examine Jordan's career course in the next chapter, his initial success cannot overshadow that a player's migration to the region is a risky endeavour. His success in winning a place at the club's academy meant that five other Ghanaian players were not successful and had to return home, possibly to 'try their luck' again. Nevertheless, while stories similar to those of Jordan's, still a minor when he moved to Thailand, and Isaak's initial experiences, have evoked allegations of a widespread practice of human trafficking of African footballers to the region (Edwards, 2015; Luedi, 2018), players' capacity to navigate the challenges they encounter should not be underestimated. Both Jordan's and Isaak's ability to perform during their initial trials, despite their respective coaches' doubts, illustrate this. Furthermore, while Jordan was taken good care of, Isaak's resilience and ability to find spiritual consolation allowed him to negotiate the difficult predicament he found himself in. These abilities and practices reveal migrant players as agentive individuals who, despite the various obstacles that confront them, exhibit a 'judicious opportunism' (Johnson-Hanks, 2005), one that enables them to hold on to, and continue to pursue, their hopes of 'making it' as professional players and 'becoming a somebody', no matter how small the likelihood of this being achieved.

Conclusions

This chapter has drawn attention to the diverse pathways and players' experiences as they negotiate initial transnational moves to Europe and South-East Asia, and the implications that these have for their future career trajectories. While some conventional routes promise a smoother career trajectory abroad, such as when players benefit from being located at an African academy with direct, institutional links with a European club, these are not a guaranteed ticket to success. Whether following such conventional pathways or rather less formalised routes, the ability to navigate uncertain, unpredictable terrain is a key asset for all African players. Despite their subordinate position of power compared to other actors in the game, such as clubs, academies, agents and other intermediaries, many players nevertheless exercise considerable resilience and learn to cope with the constraints they encounter in the initial period of their moves abroad.

Securing and consolidating a position as a professional player is undoubtedly difficult and requires long-term commitment and financial, physical and emotional investment. Continuing to speculate on their physical capital, skills and talent in this initial stage of a potential professional career abroad should not be seen then as an act of naivety or despair, but rather as a belief in one's abilities and a strategic pursuit of the futures they envisage. In addition, the cases presented here have underlined that coordinating actions are not necessarily bound to a powerful position in the GPN. As Demba's trajectory in particular shows, investing in developing social relations with peers and fellow players may facilitate links to other actors in the game that can help consolidate one's position as a footballer.

Nevertheless, this chapter has also illustrated how power imbalances in the social infrastructure of football's GPN often leave players in a marginalised position. Many experience fraud or are left with few opportunities to achieve their aspiration to 'make it' in professional football. This is due to the realities of a highly competitive and commercialised industry and a tension between the interests of these powerful actors and those of the player. This tension is visible in both Europe and South-East Asia. In this way, players moving to these destinations share similar experiences of a challenging liminality. Regardless of the type of route pursued or the destination, negotiating and navigating a first migratory move beyond Africa does not just constitute a transient moment of uncertainty but can also become a precarious state of 'in-between' that may last several months or years and that can have significant consequences for players' future career courses. In the next chapter we continue to highlight the experiences of African players in Europe and South-East Asia by elaborating on how they approach and navigate the challenges and precarities they encounter from the point at which their careers in European and South-East Asian professional football materialise. We do so by continuing to elaborate on the experiences of players discussed in this chapter, such as John, Demba, Isaak and Jordan, while also introducing other players that we engaged with during our research.

8

Hope and precarity in transnational football careers

Introduction

In February 2020, shortly before most football leagues in the world were suspended due to the accelerating COVID-19 pandemic, Jordan, the Ghanaian player we introduced in the previous chapter who had joined an academy in Thailand aged just fourteen, gathered with his teammates to finalise preparations for the upcoming season. As they went through their final training session before the start of the regional third-division programme, they were relaxed and looking forward to their first match the following day. This year marked Jordan's third season as a professional with the club. At the age of nineteen, after five years in the academy, he had made the step up to the senior team. According to Ken, the Ghanaian player who facilitated Jordan's move, the league he was playing in would be a good platform to establish himself in professional football. Here, he said, Jordan could learn to compete among experienced players and would be visible to more established teams looking for new recruits.

Ken was certain that Jordan could progress from this level. 'He is serious, he can make a difference', he said, before offering the qualification that 'he has to work hard' (interview, 19 February 2020). Indeed, his ability and work ethic impressed during the final pre-season training session. Jordan also had no difficulties following his assistant coach's instructions in Thai, as he performed the passing and shooting exercises with accuracy and assurance. Jordan was certainly a talented player; it seemed that he had adjusted well to the demands of local professional football and was well prepared to progress to a higher level.

Irrespective of a player's talent and dedication, the path to a sustained and successful professional career abroad is often long, arduous and uncertain. From the accounts of John, Demba, Jordan and Isaak outlined in Chapter 7, and indeed, the biographical vignette featuring Nii Lamptey which opened this book, we know that trajectories similar to those of Sadio Mané, Samuel Eto'o, Michael Essien or other iconic African players are confined to a fortunate, outstanding few. In short, linear and upward career trajectories within football's GPN are the exception rather than the norm among African players in Europe and South-East Asia (Poli, 2010a; Büdel, 2013; Ungruhe and Büdel, 2016). Even reaching a modest level in a professional league abroad remains out of reach for most. Yet, at first glance, players' mere presence in Europe or South-East Asia appears to open doors and increases their chances of carving out a career. Playing in these territories typically enables access to professional infrastructures, such as modern training facilities, highly qualified coaching staff and physiotherapists. This infrastructure can help improve a player's technique, tactical awareness, physical condition and performances. Media attention and scouting networks that extend into peripheral European and Asian football leagues ostensibly offer greater visibility and can even serve as a stepping stone to higher-profile leagues and lucrative contracts.

In this chapter, using 'thick' ethnographic descriptions, we examine the career experiences of a selection of African players in Russia, Germany, Scandinavia and Thailand as they navigate complex and intersecting structural, geographic, socio-cultural and sporting challenges. This illustrates how African migrant players act and are acted upon within the social infrastructure of the football industry in these settings. In detailing players' experiences in new socio-cultural, political and economic environments, we show how the structural conditions and actors they encounter relegate them to subordinate positions of power and expose them to racialisation and racism. Our analyses here, and particularly with reference to the career courses of John, Demba and Jordan, also illustrate that despite what is often a premature end to their careers, African players continue to maintain the hope of 'making it' and 'becoming a somebody'.

Encountering and navigating the challenges of foreign fields

From the accounts presented in Chapter 7, and indeed the details of Nii Lamptey's career that opened this book, it is clear that many African players find entering foreign football fields challenging. They often learn quickly that media portrayals of a glittering industry are far removed from the harsh day-to-day realities of playing in a lower-tier, small-town club somewhere in the peripheries of Europe or South-East Asia. The structural conditions that they encounter and that engender low wages and short-term precarious contracts (see Poli, 2006a, 2006b) hamper the ability of African players to consolidate their position socially and materially. Often, their difficulties are exacerbated by the fact that they are also experiencing their first stay away from home, and their first direct encounter with an unfamiliar sporting and cultural setting and climate (see also Šašková, 2019). In addition, migrant players usually move alone, without the company of parents, family members, wives or children. Hence, many struggle on their own and become dependent on the goodwill and often limited efforts of intermediaries, clubs or teammates to help them settle into their new environment in and beyond football (Ungruhe and Agergaard, 2020c).

When John experienced a northern European winter for the first time, the novelty of cold affected his performance considerably. 'It was very difficult. It was snowing, it was very cold. It's kind of stressing, you know, before [I] even practise my toes are already frozen. I can't even shoot the ball so hard' (interview, 13 June 2016). With support from the club, better preparation and access to appropriate clothing, players usually learn to cope and eventually reach their full potential. However, as Edward, another Ghanaian player who moved to Scandinavia, recalls, this may take time, sometimes too much time. Indeed, his inexperience with the local climate had a damaging impact on his career course. In 2009, at the age of twenty, Edward had just moved from his Ghanaian team to a recognised Ivorian academy with established links to European agents and clubs. Through these channels he was offered a trial with a Finnish second-tier club that was looking for a right full-back. Edward impressed staff and officials and secured a loan contract after the first day of his trial. However, when the season started, he found it difficult to show his full potential.

Despite other issues such as being the only Black player in the team and feelings of loneliness given his limited social contacts outside the training ground, Edward remembered that 'the most challenging was the weather. … [It] was very, very cold'. This led him to become 'very, very nervous' about being able to perform. It took Edward almost half a year and the transition to the milder spring and summer seasons before he acclimatised. However, his club had already made a decision about his future. When the loan period ended, Edward was not considered for a permanent deal and, in the absence of other offers, he had to return to Ghana (interview, 23 May 2016).

Aside from the colder climate, language barriers and limited options to become acquainted with their new environment often negatively affect both players' sporting inclusion and their wider social participation. This was apparent in Jordan's early experiences in Thailand. Though he enjoyed good care in the Thai academy he moved to from Ghana, he faced many difficulties in adjusting to his new location: 'In the first month I thought, "No, I cannot stay here" … I couldn't eat their food. I used to take bread and Coca-Cola every morning, afternoon and evening. I was sick, I felt stomach pains, I could not sleep. Even the smell of their food, I wanted to vomit.' During this initial period, he also found it hard to communicate and socialise with his fellow players since not many of them spoke English. 'It wasn't easy for me', he recalled. Jordan described feeling lonely and out of place, feelings doubtless compounded by his tender age at the time (fourteen). As a consequence, he struggled to show his abilities on the pitch. However, he was reluctant to give up on his dream: 'I said to myself, "I want to make it here. It is not the right time to go home."' Over several months, he slowly got acquainted with his new environs. He learnt to read and write Thai, began to develop a taste for the local food and started to socialise with his Thai teammates. Feeling more settled, he was soon able to perform on the pitch at a much higher standard (interview, 15 February 2020).

Beyond the emotional toll of struggling to adjust, players' experiences of unfamiliarity and social exclusion may also put their careers at risk. The following two cases of African footballers who entered German football in the mid-1990s illustrate this clearly. When twenty-two-year-old Habib participated with his Senegalese team in a town twinning tournament in a German city, his performance led to an offer from a local semi-professional club in the German fourth tier. Habib accepted, happy to move to a European football team. However, as he recalled of his first months in Germany, 'many things were not as I had imagined them. You may think, "Europe is paradise" … but first I had to deal with the language which I did not speak. … My family was not around and I could not really talk to people.' When his teammates questioned his performances during training, he was unable to explain his decision making. 'All this made it hard [for me]. I couldn't make it' (interview, 3 November 2010). His struggles led to him being loaned to a club in an even lower division.

While Habib was successful at his new club, it remained uncertain at that point whether he would be able to re-enter the higher level he had played at. He was unable to continue his language course and therefore did not improve his German skills during his year-long loan. Living in a small town compounded his lack of social interaction. With almost no one around him who spoke French, he found it hard to establish contacts within or outside the team and felt uncomfortable hanging out with people to improve his language skills. Only after finishing the season and returning to his first club in Germany did he gradually acquire the communication skills required to interact with teammates and establish relationships which helped him to perform in German professional football.

Felix, a Ghanaian who was signed by a German Bundesliga club in the mid-1990s after impressing the club's scouts at an international youth tournament, had a similar experience to Habib. The then eighteen-year-old trained with the club's senior team during the week and played for its junior side at weekends. As a Ghanaian youth national team player, he also frequently travelled to play international matches and attend extended training camps. This made it difficult for him to forge connections with and secure acceptance from his club colleagues. With limited social contacts with fellow players, and no other social relations in his new surrounds, he left his apartment only to attend training sessions. 'The first year was very hard', he recalled. He dealt with his social isolation through regular telephone calls home to family and friends: 'I had a monthly phone bill of around four thousand marks [about two thousand euros].' Often, he called his mother in Ghana and discussed giving up professional football and returning home. But his mother convinced him to stay and to struggle through. It took a year before he finally felt comfortable. Regular invites from his coach to join him and his family for dinner contributed, as did Felix's decision to reduce his participation in national youth team training camps in Ghana. These adjustments helped him become more socially integrated in the team, and this also led to an upturn in his performances (interview, 24 March 2011).

These accounts point to important questions about the extent to which African players' wellbeing, social inclusion and transitions into foreign climes are adequately catered for in the context of the social infrastructure of European and South-East Asian football. Regarding Europe, it is possible that the experiences outlined above may not have occurred in countries such as France or Portugal where there is a longer tradition of clubs recruiting African footballers, and fewer challenges in terms of language (Cleveland, 2017; Taylor, 2006). However, professional clubs in other countries such as Sweden, Italy and Germany did not start to implement reliable player welfare structures and policies until the 2000s (Scott, 2015; Mauro, 2016; Ungruhe, 2018a). From then onwards, players' social and sporting struggles were better acknowledged, albeit as part of a realisation that improving welfare could make players more productive and, in turn, increase a team's likelihood of success (Acheampong and Malek, 2019; Otto, 2009). Hence, this increasing attention towards players' wellbeing is often far from an altruistic move, but rather serves the sporting and economic interests of clubs. Some clubs have created specific administrative roles and hired retired footballers to help foreign players manage their transition, social integration and day-to-day affairs. As in the case of Massimo Mariotti, who has served as an 'integration commissioner' for the German teams Borussia Dortmund, VFB Stuttgart and Schalke 04, they also play a role in educating players about the history, traditions and fan culture of clubs (Asmussen, 2019).

Many clubs' efforts to aid migrant players' adjustment depend on the personal commitment of a staff member or teammate (Spatz, 2008), who in many ways take on a coordinating role within the game's social infrastructure. However, those clubs with African partnerships often have a more systematic approach towards supporting their African players' social inclusion and enhancing their capacity to deal with the demands of life and football in Europe. This is rooted in a recognition of the challenges that African players face in making the transition to Europe. As Tom Vernon, the Chief Executive Officer of the Right to Dream Group, put it: 'I think history, recent history has shown that it's very difficult for players coming directly from an African academy without any experience of European football, then go directly into first team football' (interview, 19 June 2018).

To counteract this, a partner club's values, training methodologies and style of play are often introduced and taught to players while they are still residing in the African academy. Furthermore, and as was noted in Chapter 7, clubs such as FC Midtjylland and FC Nordsjælland also invite talents from their partner academies – FC Ebedei (Nigeria) and Right to Dream (Ghana), respectively – for extended training placements so that they can become acquainted with the club's facilities, staff and life in Denmark more generally. As alluded to in Chapter 3, FC Nordsjælland established an 'international academy' programme which involves players from Right to Dream training at the Danish club for up to three months at a time, sometimes twice per year. The players also compete in youth tournaments as part of a combined team with their FC Nordsjælland contemporaries, and in doing so they get first-hand experience of European football and life in general. This initiative is clearly informed by the business model of the club, which is partially about easing the transition of Ghanaian players into Danish football, transferring them at the end of their first professional contract and thus accruing a bigger financial return on their investment, which can then be reinvested into the academy in Ghana. According to Jan Laursen, FC Nordsjælland's former Sports Director and since January 2021 club chairman, the international academy is beneficial to a player's career development in two ways. It creates a platform for the player to build and sustain transnational football careers and enables them to make more informed decisions about their potential career trajectories. Laursen emphasised this latter point, arguing that, 'I think it's very important they come here as much as possible from quite an early age. Also, to find out it's somewhere they want to go, so that they don't feel forced to go' (interview, 22 October 2018). As Mads, a leading staff member at FC Midtjylland's academy noted, when a partner academy player is finally signed, his transition to foreign climes and wider social inclusion is often further supported by arranging for him to live with a local family or fellow migrant players. This helps him negotiate day-to-day challenges off the pitch (interview, 9 February 2016).

In contrast, many other clubs, particularly those on the European periphery or in lower divisions, do not have the means, expertise or ambition to implement these sorts of approaches. Hence, African players who move to such clubs often need to find their own way. As the examples earlier illustrated, this absence of reliable coordinators at the club level is often problematic. However, having fellow African or other foreign nationals among one's teammates is often helpful in terms of being able to learn from their experiences, to discuss ideas and share knowledge about practical matters such as transport, banking or laws and regulations in their country of residence, as well as more intangible issues such as unknown cultural values. Indeed, some players who are able to consolidate their status abroad assume roles as coordinators of fellow African players' social inclusion and wellbeing. For example, in Thailand, a group of mature Cameroonian players initiated a social media group chat among their fellow countrymen. As Vincent, one of their number, explained, this provided a means to stay in touch and informed about their compatriots' wellbeing and any challenges that they experienced. When instances of hardship occurred, group members were able to provide emotional and material support. This was clearly expressed by Vincent: 'When you are here you have nobody. Your family is far … Therefore, we decided, when somebody needs help, we can all give, maybe [up to] five hundred baht [approximately 12.50 euros] each.' Since the group was set up, they had been able to contribute to players' hospital bills, fines for visa overstay or even return flights back home (interview, 18 February 2020).

These practices underline the fact that African footballers also navigate challenges abroad collectively (Akindes, 2013; Rehal, 2015; Ungruhe, 2020). In addition, many players utilise transnational relations to their families and friends at home to ease and mediate the difficulties associated with living in a new environment. Often, parents are asked for advice and consolation in times of social isolation or sporting disappointments, as Felix's example revealed. Seeking encouragement from close relatives can reanimate players' hopes, nourish their belief in their football abilities and, in doing so, embolden them to persevere. This transnational practice represents a continuation of wider familial participation in the football migration process. As discussed in chapters 5 and 6, family members often take part in the speculation around a player's career by financing his journey, often in the hope that they will benefit from his future success. However, their role does not conclude at the point at which their son or sibling departs their home country. Rather, through their ongoing support, they continue to help to consolidate his position as a professional footballer abroad.

In addition to challenges relating to climate, language and social inclusion, many African players face difficulties in adjusting to different styles of play abroad. This is because perceptions and stereotypes about playing styles that are attributed to specific countries or regions often oversimplify how the game is played. Perceptions and stereotypes also fail to account for hybridity, and how tactical systems and approaches tend to be temporally fluid and responsive to tactical innovations and the valorisation of 'new' methodologies. Playing styles develop under specific socio-cultural and political conditions, and are reproduced by players, coaches, commentators and fans over time. An apparent proclivity for physicality and long balls in English football, a reliance on organisation and efficiency in German football or tiki-taka in Spain, are prominent examples of this. However, when essentialised and detached from the original historical context in which they were developed or attributed, these ideas can become self-fulfilling. As such, they continue to influence how supporters, media commentators and players, including African migrants, interpret how the game should be played in particular locales (Ungruhe, 2014).

There is also a materiality in how young Africans learn to play the game, and the aesthetic it produces. As Alegi (2010: 32) observed about emerging African football in the colonial period: 'Material poverty, lack of equipment … and inadequate facilities influenced vernacular styles of play'. In the second decade of the twenty-first century, beyond the comparatively limited number of pristine pitches available in the continent's elite academies, these conditions, and a desire to 'stand out' to talent speculators, academies and clubs that might help them achieve their dream, continue to produce a particular African grassroots football aesthetic. This is characterised by an emphasis on ball control, creativity, improvisation and displays of individual talent over the sort of team play, discipline and collective organisation that are considered prerequisites in the professional game abroad. This adds a further layer of complication for young African players' adjustment to foreign fields.

In Thai football, African players frequently expressed difficulties meeting coaches', fans' and teammates' expectations on the pitch. After Isaak's team lost 4-2 in the opening match of the 2020 season of the regional third division, he expressed displeasure with his colleagues' performance: 'The way they play is not my style. They want to pass and run but I can dribble. I can dribble and take out the defenders. But they don't want me to dribble' (interview, 16 February 2020). Indeed, while Isaak was constantly involved in the action, he did not appear to be supported by his teammates when he took possession of the ball and tried to initiate an attack by running with it. When talking about this incident with Abed, a fellow Ghanaian footballer who has played in Thailand for several years, he intimated that Isaak had not yet understood what was expected from him. Abed outlined these expectations and some of the issues that they created for African players in the following terms:

> As an African player you need to work hard. You need to work double. You have to do what coach tells you, keep your position, pass and circulate the

ball. But then, you will never succeed because that is what the Thais do and they will say, 'Why are you paying the African so much money? I can do the same.' So as an African you have to run all over the pitch, get the ball from the defenders and take it to the opponent's half, dribble, defend, score. You have to lead their game, you have to prove you are outstanding. If not, you will never succeed here. (Interview, 16 February 2020)

Several other African players in the country corroborated Abed's interpretation while at the same time pointing to the potentially injurious physical and mental demands of trying to meet the level of expectation placed on them over an extended period of time.

In European football, African players encounter similar issues that hinder their performances on the pitch and, therefore, opportunities to consolidate their position in the football industry there. When nineteen-year-old David moved to a Norwegian club for a one-year loan deal in winter 2005, he struggled to adapt on the field. Though his Ghanaian team had produced several players who had embarked on successful careers with clubs all over Europe, he was not prepared for the way football was played in Norway. 'Ghanaians like technique', he suggested, and 'are skilful, we like to go on the ball and to play technical.' Pointing, perhaps a little flippantly, to the direct and physical style of play he encountered at his new club, he stated that 'it was difficult to understand how they play because most of their games are all long balls. So, at the beginning, I think [for] two to three months, it was difficult for me, but as I studied how they played I got into the system.' However, he only played a couple of matches and was often left out of the matchday squad. Almost inevitably, the club were not interested in turning David's loan contract into a more permanent deal and he was forced to return to Ghana to try to re-invigorate his career (interview, 5 June 2016).

The sporting exclusion that frequently emanates from African players struggling to adjust to new methodologies of playing can have severe consequences for the realisation of career ambitions, as we see in the case of David. But even for those players at clubs that exercise a little more patience, on-field issues can further marginalise players and exacerbate the off-field struggles they are likely to be going through. Combined, the challenges of a different climate, a foreign language, alien socio-cultural practices and a different style of playing football often contribute to an overwhelming and precarious experience, particularly at the outset of migrant careers abroad. Some do succeed and are able to navigate these issues and with the support of clubs, fellow players and transnational ties to family and friends at home, better enabling them to consolidate their position and further their overseas careers. However, many African players are unprepared for such encounters and their lack of knowledge and experience likely hinders them from maximising their full potential when they migrate to pursue a life in professional football (Agergaard and Ungruhe, 2016). Given that African players often arrive in Europe or South-East Asia on trial, via loan deals or under other short-term agreements, they need to demonstrate their full potential right from the start (see Chapter 7). Failure to do so may result in a rather abrupt end to their attempts to succeed abroad. Some of the aforementioned challenges, namely the different playing styles and specific roles attributed to African players on the pitch, point to a problematic, racialised discourse regarding African expatriates in the global football industry. In the following section, we further elaborate on this and scrutinise the discourses, structures and practices of racialisation and racism encountered by African migrant players in Europe.

Racialisation and racism in European football

Notwithstanding the multi-faceted, intersecting challenges African players face in transitioning to foreign climes, they remain attractive recruitment targets for many professional clubs in Europe. That this is the case is due in no small measure to the fact that they can be signed cheaply. However, evaluations of their value to a European team extend beyond the financial and are also underpinned by popular conceptions of African players' (and other Black footballers') difference that circulate widely in the European football industry. They are articulated and reproduced by football fans, talent speculators, coaches and other actors in the industry, and tend to cohere around the alleged physical prowess of players of African origin and their 'natural' possession of particular football attributes. Stereotypes about the abilities of African players and Black footballers more generally are reinforced by media discourses that both implicitly and at times explicitly portray them as having 'natural' ability, being predisposed to trickery, creativity and improvisation, and as possessing strength and speed but being simultaneously playful, unpredictable, undisciplined and naive (Engh, Settler and Agergaard, 2017; Farrington *et al.*, 2017; Scott, 2015; Ungruhe, 2014).

These ideas are undergirded by European evolutionary worldviews and racial tropes constructed during pre-colonial and colonial times to justify subjugation and economic exploitation on the continent. However, not only do they ignore the materiality of the diverse attributes exhibited by African players in Europe that we pointed to earlier, but they also overlook the political context within which local styles of play developed across colonial Africa. As we showed in Chapter 2, football was diffused to local populations as a way of encouraging conformity to the colonial order and an acceptance of white European domination. However, male African youth and young men used the game for their own ends as a means to gain prestige and to negotiate social status among their peers. They did so, in part, by combining a tough, urban masculine physicality with trickery, improvisation and dribbling. In culturally appropriating the game in this way, they established a counter-model to colonial intentions which ensured that football became a platform for anti-colonial sentiments and nation-building efforts in the aftermath of independence (Alegi, 2002; Darby, 2007a, 2013a).

The emphasis on technique as a counter-weight to colonial ideas and the colonial image of Africans as playful, wild and unsophisticated have contributed to stereotypes about African footballers. Reports on football in Africa regularly generalise and romanticise it as childish and immature, qualities which allegedly distinguish it from the more sophisticated, organised and calculated version of the game found in Europe (Ungruhe, 2014). While recruitment at the top of the European game reflects careful scouting and assessment of African players that goes beyond searching for what are stereotypically perceived to be distinctively African qualities, these racial and ethnic ascriptions do circulate widely and constitute shared social knowledge in the European football business. For example, coaches and football officials sometimes explain their admiration for the supposedly natural talents that Africans possess with recourse to statements such as, 'African players exhibit so much playfulness and so much pleasure in the game', or 'Africa is a gold mine of love for the ball, elegance and passion for playing' (Thielke, 2009: 122 and 44, translated from the original German by the authors).

As we have already shown in Chapter 6, racialised ideas about football talent are also widely acknowledged and reproduced by African and other Black players themselves (Esson, 2015b; Ungruhe, 2014). Ascriptions of being immature, undisciplined and reliant on 'natural' traits clearly diminish these players. However, some draw on the idea of a distinctive African football aesthetic as a form of ethnic 'self-charismatisation', or the (over-) emphasis of specific and extraordinary attributed skills, qualities and abilities (Soeffner, 1997: 65–67; Zifonun, 2010), which helps them in the process of securing and sustaining a career in Europe. By acknowledging that ascriptions of being playful, trick-loving, elegant or powerful are certainly much-admired assets that allegedly distinguish them from others, African and Black players often routinise, rather than explicitly articulate, these traits in their individual play in order to meet the expectations of European clubs, coaches, fans and the media. The process of self-charismatisation is not so much a deliberate and collective action of players, one that would point to a marginalised group's 'strategic essentialism' (Spivak, 2012). Rather, it creates an embodied form of ethnic capital – one, however, which is not a passive asset but is continuously reproduced in dialogue with European actors in the game.

Players' self-charismatisation does not negate the need to incorporate alleged European qualities such as result orientation and team play in order to be successful (see King, 2004). Sharing 'knowledge' about an African style of play by performing and, even more crucially, interpreting certain actions on the pitch as an expression of an 'African' style assures European actors in the game of their image of it and acknowledges the expected role that African players need to play in order to succeed in Europe (Müller, 2010). While this process of self-charismatisation may be exaggerated and does not reflect the actual abilities of a player, it has been internalised by them to accrue sporting recognition and, in the process, improve their standing in contract negotiations, or to establish their place on a team (Ungruhe, 2014). However, there are problematic implications for African and other Black players of engaging in this process of self-charismatisation. By buying into and conforming to stereotypical notions of what it is to be genuinely African on the football field, these players can inadvertently reinforce a colonial worldview in the European game that depicts them as being naive, immature, wild and backward. These connotations have historically served to produce discriminatory practices and create inequalities within the game, leading as they have to a view that African and other Black players lack the intelligence or sophistication to play in positions that require strategic, cognitive abilities (Cleveland, 2017; Lanfranchi and Taylor, 2001; see Chapter 6). While this perception has changed over time, not least because of the greater influx of Africans into the European game since the 1990s, the image of these footballers as immature remains prominent.

The fact that such racialisation is not restricted to African players but includes Black players more generally, pointing to their alleged skills and abilities as 'natural' features, again reproduces problematic ideas of a given white superiority. This was evident in an incident that involved the Black German international Antonio Rüdiger, who was born and grew up in Germany. During a UEFA Champions League fixture in the 2015/16 season, the commentator and former Italian international Stefano Eranio criticised an error by the then AS Roma defender during his team's 4-4 draw against Bayer Leverkusen. Following Rüdiger's failed attempt to play the offside trap, ultimately resulting in Leverkusen's second goal, Eranio said: 'Black players in the defensive line often make these mistakes because they're not concentrating. They are powerful physically, but when it is time to think … they often make this type of error' (*Guardian*, 2015). Eranio's statement caused an outcry in the media, leading to his dismissal by the Swiss TV station RSI. Eranio felt misunderstood and sought to defend himself by saying: 'Rüdiger read the situation badly because Black players are not accustomed to paying attention to certain details. If they were as detail-oriented as us, then they'd dominate the spot, because they have everything in terms of strength and technique' (*Guardian*, 2015). Eranio's explanation may have been an attempt to qualify the racist connotations of his initial statement, but in referencing Black otherness and unsophisticated behaviour, it only served to compound the racist tone of his initial description of the incident. Indeed, following his line of argument, Rüdiger and other Black players would have a natural disadvantage compared to their white counterparts when trying to succeed in European football.

Consequently, to follow this line of argument, while what are seen as specifically African qualities are desired in European football, African players also need to mature and embody 'European qualities' such as discipline, tactical understanding and a more calculated approach to results. Hence, it is the combination of supposed African and European skills and attributes that leads to success. This point was made explicitly by Charles Akonnor, former head coach of the Black Stars and an ex-Ghanaian international whose club career took him to Germany, Denmark and Cyprus: 'If an African player has an African style and adds some European skills, then he will be a star' (interview, 11 March 2010). These sentiments are shared by many African players. When a former professional footballer from West Africa was looking back on his professional career in Germany between 2000 and 2010, he commented: 'I've learnt a lot here, tactics, discipline', while contrasting this to his experiences in Africa, which he claimed were more about self-expression and enjoyment (interview, 8 April 2011). Gerald Asamoah, a former Black German international born in Ghana underlined this view: 'African players lack discipline, systematic order and seriousness. I myself have learnt this not before being in Germany' (Fritsch, 2013, translated from the original German by the authors).

African academies and African-European club partnerships have incorporated this view and placed an emphasis on teaching their talents supposedly European skills from a young age to increase the likelihood of producing players who are able to succeed in European competitions (Ungruhe, 2014). Young academy players in West Africa, eager to comply with the wishes of those who potentially hold the key to their future, tend to uncritically accept this. As one fifteen-year-old told us: 'As an African footballer ... the key is discipline. If you don't have the discipline, even if you are the best player here, you are not going to play. ... If you are disciplined it can take you anywhere. ... I know it's through discipline and hard work because that's what [the academy] is looking for' (interview, 27 April 2010).

Such processes of racialisation that reinforce otherness and produce discriminatory practices against African players reflect wider structural inequalities along racial lines in European countries and ultimately constrict

African players' opportunities to consolidate their position in the game there. As we have argued, in contributing to the precarious power imbalances and dependencies inherent in African football migration, racialisation also creates a scenario whereby African players must conform to European expectations in order to succeed. Self-charismatisation is required to prevail in football, to secure better deals and reduce the risk of immobility. Thus, African players need to perform 'double work' by executing perceived African virtues and combining them with what are portrayed as European skills (Agergaard and Ungruhe, 2016; Ungruhe, 2014). Players who are able to navigate this double work may consolidate their status in professional European football and, in the best-case scenario, go on to achieve global stardom (see Künzler and Poli, 2012). However, successful self-charismatisation and the concomitant consolidation of careers comes at a cost because it reaffirms and perpetuates racialised tropes around African physical and intellectual capabilities, and in doing so contributes further to the inequalities faced by African migrant players (Agergaard and Ungruhe, 2016; Ungruhe, 2014; van Sterkenburg, Peeters and van Amsterdam, 2019). This occurs despite a general trend of growing hybridity and diversity in playing styles that migrants contribute to in leagues all over the world.

The precarity induced by processes of racialised othering and self-charismatisation becomes even more apparent in instances where African players experience overt racism in the game from fans, opponents or, as in the case of Nii Lamptey while playing for Greuther Fürth, from teammates. For many years, football governing bodies, clubs and associations ignored open forms of racism in the European game. Fortunately, this has gradually changed, albeit unevenly and not necessarily at the pace required to completely eradicate it from football. In Germany, for instance, it was only during the 1990s that a rising awareness of racism in the game led to measures and policies to tackle the problem. For some years, these were successful to the extent that open forms of racism towards Black players significantly declined in stadiums. Yet racism in football, particularly among specific groups of supporters, continued in the country and, indeed, all across Europe, both in the stands and latterly via social media (Engh, Settler and Agergaard, 2017; Scott, 2015; Ungruhe, 2014).

Time and again, African players in Europe are confronted with racist insults and denigration. In northern Europe, Scott's (2015) work reveals numerous examples of African and Black players in general being subjected to overt racist abuse and more subtle, institutionalised forms of racism at all levels of the game in Sweden since the early 2000s. In England, alongside African football migrants, Black players of all origins, with or without an individual history of migration, have long been victims of racism (Back, Crabbe and Solomos, 2001). A study published in 2019 by the English football equality and inclusion organisation Kick It Out revealed persistent and increasing levels of racial discrimination in the game both at the professional and the grassroots level (Kick It Out, 2019). For instance, Manchester United's Paul Pogba and Marcus Rashford, along with Chelsea's Tammy Abraham and Reading's Yakou Méïté, all faced racial insults on social media after missing penalties for their respective teams during league matches in the 2019/20 season. In light of this, social media platforms were criticised for not taking sufficient measures to counter these assaults (Fifield, 2019). Their inaction has continued to have serious implications for Black players in England where, at the time of writing, levels of racially motivated hate crimes against these players have risen to unprecedented levels (Liew, 2021).

Belgian striker Romelu Lukaku transferred to Milan-based club Internazionale ahead of the 2019/20 season, and during his first matches he repeatedly faced racist insults from opposition fans. The lack of appetite on the part of the Italian football authorities to deal with racism was very much in evidence following an incident during a Serie A match in Cagliari when Lukaku was targeted with monkey chants. Following the game, the Italian football association sanctioned the Sardinian club for fans throwing bottles but not for racial discrimination, which would have led to a more severe punishment (PA Media, 2019). In Germany, the aforementioned Hamburger SV winger Bakery Jatta, who was confronted with allegations in the media that he plays under a false identity and had violated immigration laws when he sought asylum after travelling from Gambia (see Chapter 7), was booed by opposition fans during a match in the 2. Bundesliga against Karlsruher SC in the 2019/20 season. It was reported that the publicity around Jatta's case caused general hostile sentiments towards refugees in Germany (BBC Sport, 2019b).

Following these incidents, and the widespread media attention they elicited, football associations, clubs, supporters' groups and players have expressed an intent to urgently intensify the fight against racism in European football. Furthermore, in 2020 the Black Lives Matter movement became a prominent voice in seeking to address not only open forms of racism in football but also racialised discourses and forms of structural discrimination in the game that work to denigrate and disadvantage Black players. However, there is much to do with clubs and club owners seemingly overwhelmed with the problem of racism and either unwilling or unsure how to address it. For instance, following the racist treatment of Excelsior Rotterdam footballer Ahmad Mendes Moreira by supporters of FC Den Bosch during a match in the Dutch second-tier Keuken Kampioen Divisie on 16 November 2019, the club initially and predictably trivialised the incident, reflecting the institutional, structural nature of racism in football (Harmsen, Elling and van Sterkenburg, 2019). Following criticism of the club's reaction by academics, FC Den Bosch's chairman Jan-Hein Schouten reached out for external support to fight racism among its supporters (*Teller Report*, 2019).

Time will tell if growing awareness, a collective approach and stronger sanctions to tackle overt and more veiled racism in the game will be successful and lead to a more hospitable environment for African and indeed Black footballers more generally. In the absence of progress in this direction, processes of racialisation and racism will likely continue to give rise to the most existential precarious experience for African players, one that in many ways can fundamentally challenge their sense of identity and self-assurance. This, combined with the other structural, socio-cultural and environmental challenges that they confront in the global football industry, can determine players' football careers, livelihoods and future life courses. In the remainder of this chapter, we draw on the experiences of a number of African players including John, Demba and Jordan, who we introduced in the previous chapter, in order to illustrate how African players navigate the multiple and intersected precarities we have identified in this chapter and work to consolidate their careers in the European and South-East Asian football industries.

Navigating career trajectories in Europe and South-East Asia

John

When John was released from FC Midtjylland's academy and returned to Ghana, he at first felt out of place. In Denmark he believed he was on the way to realising his ambitions of a career in European football. Now he felt deprived of an opportunity that so many of his peers dream of but rarely get close to. While his family received him back with open arms, proud of what he had achieved in migrating to Europe, some of his friends and others in the community where he was living reacted to him differently. What John experienced resonates with the accounts of youth players in Ghana 'sacked' from their academy, as discussed in Chapter 6. 'Some people were talking a lot of trash about my failure and all that in the community', he recalled. 'But back in the days they never knew I was in the academy. They were thinking I was making money straightforward. They didn't know I was ... trying to develop, then get a first team contract and all that.' He was approached on numerous occasions and asked for financial help but he was in no position to offer this. This created tensions and many did not understand how someone who they believed had played football in Europe was not able to give: 'some were like, "Oh you went there, you came back with nothing". They didn't know I was only getting pocket money at the end of the month.' He felt ashamed and bemoaned his fate. 'This is not what's supposed to happen', he said (interview, 13 June 2016).

The outcome of his short-lived stay in Denmark thrust John from a consolidating position back to one of speculation. He was not ready to give up on his dream of succeeding in European football. Still relatively young at sixteen years of age, he felt that he still had something to accomplish. John resumed schooling, and also re-joined his local team and quickly regained his confidence. Indeed, his performances for the rest of the season were so outstanding that he was called up for the U-17 national team. After participating in the 2005 U-17 World Cup in Peru he received an offer from a professional club in a different part of Ghana. He decided to leave his community and quit school again to fully concentrate on football. At first, his parents were upset about his decision not to complete senior high school but they accepted his decision, not least when he explained his thinking in the following way: 'now I'm in the game and I wanna put the failure of Midtjylland behind me ... so I need all the concentration' (interview, 13 June 2016).

At the time, this seemed to be the right move. After some months with his new club, John was approached by a Danish coach who was a former staff member of FC Midtjylland. The coach was utilising his connections in Ghanaian football to scout players for his new club, which also played in the Danish Superliga. When he came across John and saw him perform, he arranged a trial. When the visa had been issued by Danish authorities, John did not hesitate to accept the invitation. He impressed to such an extent that he was offered a five-year contract with the Danish club's first team after it had negotiated the conditions of the transfer with John's club in Ghana. Despite John's previous disillusioning experience in Denmark, he saw the opportunity of returning to Scandinavia to play in the Danish Superliga, albeit for a lower-rated club than FC Midtjylland, as key to his aspirations of establishing himself as a professional footballer. In explaining his decision to accept the offer, he commented: 'Though it's not a place you can expect to make millions, it's still a place to develop your football career when given the chance' (interview, 13 June 2016). He had just turned eighteen and was back in the European game, ready to make a more substantive impact than he had two years previously.

From the outset, his prospects looked promising. John had returned to a country he was already familiar with and enjoyed living in a bigger, cosmopolitan city. His new club were keen that he integrated into the club and Danish society more generally and helped him to undertake a Danish language course. They also found him accommodation in the city centre close to the training ground. Despite his young age, he quickly became an established first team regular. A salary of around three thousand euros per month allowed him to support his family at home. John paid school fees for his younger sister and supported his ageing parents who did not have a regular income. He also cared for some friends in his hometown, fulfilling what he considered as an obligation to help: 'I was able to give them something that they were expecting' (interview, 13 June 2016). He also sent used football kits from his club to his hometown in Ghana and added money to this where possible. In doing so, he revived his standing in the local community and met the widespread responsibility among African footballers who have consolidated their position in the game to meet familial obligations and give back to their local community (Acheampong, Bouhaouala and Raspaud, 2019).

After two seasons, John's career course began to falter. The club hired a new coach who preferred other players and John was asked to look for a new club. He was loaned to a Danish second-tier club but failed to make any impact. After the end of the one-year loan period, his former club did not want him back and he was sent to its reserve team in which he played out the following season. In the meantime, John had not been called up to the Ghanaian national team for his age group. He decided to leave Denmark to revive his career. He had already given up the Danish language course and was eager to 'try his luck' in Eastern Europe. An agent originating from the region had approached John some time before and offered his services to find him a club there and secure a more profitable deal for him than he had in Denmark. John had no experience dealing with intermediaries in the football business, but he believed that the agent could help him to revive his career and consolidate his status in European football.

At first, things went well for John. After his Danish club agreed to terminate his contract so that he could move on a free transfer, John signed a lucrative one-year contract with a club in Eastern Europe. He impressed in the first-tier competition right from the start, and felt that he was back on his feet again. The only thing that worried him was the xenophobic climate in the country. John did not feel safe or welcome when walking the streets. On one occasion while out socialising with an African friend, he had direct experience of a racially motivated attack: 'I was with one guy, we were attacked. He was beaten up by my own fans', he recalled. 'They didn't beat me up because I was playing for their club. They know me [and] they were like, "You just stay here". [But] the other Black guy, they beat him up. … I was really, really scared' (interview, 13 June 2016).

This incident and wider racism and xenophobia in the country weighed heavily on his mind, but John put any thoughts of leaving aside when the then top-tier league champions expressed an interest in signing him. With only a few months remaining on his club contract, he was anticipating another free transfer. His agent negotiated the deal and John signed for the following season. By this stage in his career, he was in his mid-twenties and looked forward to featuring for his new team in European club competition, seeing this as a platform on which he could enhance his profile and reputation in European football. At this juncture, it seemed that he had fully consolidated his status in professional football and that his career would continue on an upward trajectory. However, before the season ended and he was about to move he got seriously injured in a match. This misfortune ultimately dealt his career a terminal blow:

> When I got injured, that was when the problem started. There was no insurance … no proper treatment like in Denmark … you have to fight for everything. It's more like you have to take care of yourself. I didn't know that, so it was really, really bad. (Interview, 13 June 2016)

Though the transfer to the new club went ahead, John felt abandoned from day one. According to him, they refused to make provision for his rehabilitation or to pay his salary, and John was forced to cover his medical expenses from his own pocket. His agent was of no help. 'He cares for himself [rather] than me. He only wants to get his money', John explained. Without any support or knowledge about possible steps to take, he grew increasingly uncomfortable and after eighteen months in the country he decided to leave. He returned to Ghana, and despite his hopes of reviving his career abroad he was unable to do so (interview, 13 June 2016).

Christian got in touch with John a few years after his return to Ghana, shortly before the end of a research trip. They met on one of those late mornings in mid-June when heat and humidity create unpleasant, sticky conditions. John picked Christian up from the small but busy bus station north of Accra's centre and they walked a few minutes until they reached his residence. It was the family's house in which John had grown up and had returned to after his years in Europe playing professional football. The air was filled with noise and dust from the nearby busy road when they entered the room he occupied. He turned on the old fan and quickly went to his mother's room to grab a plastic chair and a glass of water for Christian. John sat down on the thin mattress lying on the concrete floor. The room was barely furnished. A few faded posters of famous footballers decorated the unpainted walls; clothes and magazines were scattered all over the floor.

Before Christian had even gone through the formalities of explaining the subject of his research, obtaining John's consent for the interview and pressing 'record' on his Dictaphone to start their conversation about his international football career, it was obvious that John's high hopes of 'becoming a somebody' through football had proved fruitless. Back home in Ghana, all attempts to revive his career had floundered. Though he had recovered from his injury he had not played serious football for some time. All visa applications for European countries had been denied, all approaches to former teammates and other actors in the football business failed, and he was unable to secure a decent contract with a local club. He had begun to think about alternatives to playing football, of getting an education, investing in businesses, attending a coaching course, becoming a scout or getting married. Yet nothing was concrete. 'I don't have money', he explained, 'I'm living more like a *kobolo* … and sometimes I sit down, I just don't know where to start from.' For the meantime, his parents were supporting him financially in addition to providing a place to stay. Some good friends encouraged him to forget about the past and move on in life. For others though, he is a failure. John told Christian that he tries not to listen to the gossip, yet he cannot shake off the shame of returning from Europe empty-handed and not having become 'a somebody' (interview, 13 June 2016).

John's career had taken a few dramatic turns that moved him from a position of speculation to consolidation and back again. This points to a common experience among African footballers in the game's GPN; trajectories to and in Europe are rarely linear and are rather dominated by precarities (Ungruhe, 2018a; Ungruhe and Büdel, 2016). Sporting failure, fraud and ill-judged decisions frequently coalesce with the wider set of challenges experienced by African players in Europe that we addressed earlier and ultimately culminate in social immobility. Back in Ghana for the second time, John seemed to have lost it all: status, means and prospects. Unable to meet the social and economic demands of an 'intergenerational contract' (Kabeer, 2000) or become a 'social giver' (Martin, Ungruhe and Häberlein, 2016), his football migration trajectory had failed both as a 'household livelihood strategy' (van der Meij and Darby, 2017) and as a vehicle for his individual ambitions of achieving social recognition and acceptable male adulthood (Ungruhe and Esson, 2017).

Despite all of this, portraying John as entirely a victim of the football business would oversimplify his efforts at reaching and staying in the professional game in Europe. In many ways, his precarious experiences turned out to be ambivalent (see Agergaard and Ungruhe, 2016). While the unwanted outcome of his first stay abroad opened doors to a career in the national team, his unsuccessful loan period at a Danish second-tier club eventually led to a more profitable contract in a different country. The dramatic turn that his career then took in Eastern Europe put an end to the prospect of fully realising his hopes and furthering his achievements in the game. Potentially, his career could have proceeded differently if he had not suffered that serious injury just before moving to his new employers or had had adequate medical insurance. Without the injury, he could have featured in

European club competition, enhanced his visibility and potentially transferred to the elite echelons of the European game. This is, of course, conjecture. Nonetheless, it points to African football migrants as engaged in what could be described as a tightrope walk with just a thin line between success and failure (see also Behrends, 2002).

Demba

The career arc of Demba, the Cameroonian player we introduced in the previous chapter, took a different path to John's, albeit it was one that was also far from linear. While studying in Moscow, his persistence in seeking out opportunities in the local game there paid off. He got in touch with a referee who had his own football academy in Moscow and was eager to help Demba to consolidate his career. Using his own contacts, he organised a trial with an ambitious club in Novgorod, a few hundred kilometres from where Demba was living at the time, which featured in a regional division in the fourth tier, the highest amateur level in the country. Demba, still a minor then, impressed and the club offered him a short-term contract which he was happy to sign, partially because moving to Novgorod also allowed him to continue his studies at the local university.

Demba stayed for a year and helped the team to win promotion to the third tier, the lowest professional level in Russia. However, rather than continuing at this level in Russia, he decided not to renew his contract and to look for opportunities outside the country. His reasons were both football and family related: 'I found it difficult to stay in Russia, because I could only play in a small league', he explained. 'Russia was a good start but I wanted to promote my career. ... Also, I have a brother in Germany and an uncle in France and I wanted to move closer to my family' (interview, 28 November 2010). However, once again, in order to facilitate his move to a setting that he felt provided him with better options to further his football career, he drew on his educational assets.

With the help of his brother, Demba applied to a university in northern Germany. He secured a place to study economics and received a student visa. While he was attending a German language course at the university and holding down a number of part-time jobs, he was also trying to reignite his football career with an ambitious local club. Although his trials with the club's junior team were successful, he had to wait for six months to be properly registered by the regional Northern German Football Association. In the meantime, while he worked to provide all the required documents for this, he was able to train and play friendly matches for the club. He officially joined for the second half of the 2007/08 season and his performances at the second-highest junior level of German football resulted in a call-up to Cameroon's U-20 national side. Demba also received offers from the reserve teams of two German Bundesliga clubs. He seemed within touching distance of securing a professional contract in one of Europe's most prestigious leagues. However, during Cameroon's preparations for the FIFA U-20 World Cup in Egypt in 2009, he developed shin splints, an injury which stopped him playing football for eight months.

Demba's injury meant that he could neither attend the U-20 World Cup nor sign for either of the two German clubs that had expressed interest in him. A great opportunity to increase his visibility and further consolidate his status as a professional footballer was lost. A year later, when he had fully recovered from the injury, he left the team he had been playing for and joined the senior side of a fifth-tier club in northern Germany that offered him a contract that would secure his livelihood and allow him to give up his part-time jobs. As he saw it, 'This is better than before, because studying, having a job and going to training everyday was quite exhausting'. Nonetheless, he recognised that despite his best efforts to balance study, work and football, he had been unable to consolidate his status in the German game. His priorities began to shift and he grew more discerning about offers to play professional football. As he explained: 'I got the chance to play for premier league clubs in other European countries. But then, I would have to stop my studies or learn a new language in order to be able to study'. He went on to say that 'studying was my plan B but now I would say it's 55 per cent football and 45 per cent education' (interview, 28 November 2010).

At the time of our interview in November 2010, Demba was twenty-one. Still playing as a striker, he had heard nothing from either of the two Bundesliga clubs that had previously expressed interest in signing him, and he was no longer eligible for the Cameroon U-20 national team. Reflecting on his struggles to become a professional footballer in Europe, he said:

> I have two little cousins in Cameroon who play football. Now I always tell them to concentrate on their education. When you come to Europe [as a footballer] and you get an injury, you won't be able to do anything. How can you survive? It is very important to have a second option if football doesn't work. (Interview, 28 November 2010)

Despite his more circumspect perspective on the likelihood of earning a living through professional football, he continued to harbour dreams of 'making it'. 'As long as there is hope, I cannot give up', he said, adding that to achieve his ambition, 'I need to work harder every day during training' (interview, 28 November 2010). By early 2021, Demba's hope had not materialised and at the age of thirty-one nor was it likely to. After temporary spells with fourth- and fifth-tier clubs in northern Germany, he moved to a sixth-tier side in 2016 and has played there since. Football had now become a leisure-time activity and his priorities had shifted towards a job related to his education.

In Demba's trajectory, we see hopeful, prudent yet courageous endeavours enacted in a state of ongoing uncertainty. As we outlined in Chapter 7, his encounters with fraudulent actors during his initial move to Russia, his subsequent sense of social isolation, his witnessing of a fatal, racially motivated attack and subsequent concerns about spending time outside his apartment not only induced subjective feelings of precarity but also informed his later doubts about pursuing football. Nonetheless, a strong sense of self-identification as a footballer with potential to play professionally kept him on this career pathway. This was not based on naive imaginations of what the future may hold. Rather, it reflected his dexterity and resilience in navigating opportunities that offered some prospect of signing for a professional club. This was writ large in his approach to his studies. By his own admission, his education served as his 'plan B', but taking up university places in Russia and Germany also enabled moves that might have enhanced his visibility in the European football industry, and potentially helped him reproduce his spatial and social mobility. However, rather than suggesting that Demba's trajectory is therefore an exceptional case, we argue that it exemplifies African football migrants' general sense of creativity and flexibility in the context of precarious migration processes.

Jordan

The relaxed atmosphere and a good performance during the final training session before the kick-off of the 2020 season of the Thai regional third division raised expectations for the upcoming match the next day. Despite the best efforts of a group of ten supporters that followed Jordan's team to away games, the almost empty stadium lacked atmosphere and this seemed to transmit to his team's performance. Their play was ponderous and Jordan struggled to initiate any meaningful attacks. The opposition fared little better and the game was only decided in the final five minutes. After losing its tall central defender due to injury, Jordan's team conceded two headed goals. After the match, Jordan could not hide his frustration. He did not blame himself or his teammates though. As he saw it, preparations for the match were not professional, elaborating that:

> We left [the team's base in north-eastern Thailand] around midnight and we arrived here [in Bangkok] early morning. But we couldn't enter the hotel rooms, only after noon. So, we had to sit and wait, but how to relax properly? Then, it was already 2 p.m., we went for training. So, no time to relax either. (Interview, 16 February 2020)

Jordan was happy to have made his first steps in professional Thai football with the team, but he felt it was time to move on. The season had just started and the transfer window was already closed, but he hoped that he could secure a move to a better, more ambitious club for the second half of the season. However, COVID-19 thwarted his plans. The global acceleration of the pandemic in March 2020 put football competitions all over the world on hold and led to an indefinite suspension of the lower professional leagues in Thailand. It was a time of growing uncertainty for Jordan and many other players, particularly in these lower levels. At first, expecting that football would recommence soon, Jordan's club respected their players' contracts. Nonetheless, his earnings decreased given that he was missing out on potential win bonuses and other incentives that contribute substantially to a player's pay at this level. Jordan accepted the conditions, partly because he also believed that the league would resume soon, and partly due to a lack of alternative options. But with tightened governmental measures to control the pandemic introduced in the country, it was announced that the lower professional leagues were to be cancelled, with a new season (2020/21) scheduled to start in October. This put many clubs under immense financial strain, resulting in pressure to terminate the contracts of their players, particularly those of comparatively well-paid foreigners (Amelia, 2020; Football Tribe, 2020; Newsbeezer, 2020).

In the course of these events, Jordan's club informed their players that their contracts would be cancelled but that they would negotiate new agreements when the league resumed. Jordan was disillusioned and unwilling to accept this somewhat vague offer. 'I will move from this team. They are not professional', he said. Feeling that he deserved better treatment, he expressed some bitterness for what he considered to be the sacrifices he had made for the club: 'If you have an injury, they still expect you to play. They expect more from us [Africans]'. Directly referencing the marginal position that African players have in Thai football, he went on, 'When you are born Black it is a problem for you'. Citing several instances where he felt that he had suffered for the team, he was clearly upset that his loyalty had not been reciprocated (interview, 16 February 2020; social media conversations, 14 April and 13 May 2020).

Jordan left the team and lived off his savings. He did not have a family in Thailand to care for, but he was still expected to support his mother and siblings at home in Ghana. The moment he moved to Thailand he felt a heightened sense of responsibility and obligation towards his family. Although salaries at the level at which he was playing did not facilitate a luxurious lifestyle, he had become, in his own words, the *de facto* 'head of the family'. As such, his family looked to him for support: 'they check your club website and see you are playing football there. They expect something from you'. He went on to detail how his regular remittances back to Ghana were being spent: 'I pay 50 per cent school fees for my sister's child who goes to private school and I helped my mum to build a house in Ghana.' This kind of support was difficult to maintain in his current situation, he admitted. While he felt that he would have to reduce what he sent home, he still believed that he had no choice but to keep supporting them. Because of this and given that he maintained aspirations to consolidate his career in Thailand before moving on to a more lucrative segment of the football industry, returning home was not an option for him. He trained on his own to keep himself fit and reached out to connect with fellow players and coaches to maintain visibility. 'I am working hard. I am ready', he said, remaining hopeful that he would be able to revive his career when the leagues in Thailand resumed (interview, 15 February 2020; social media conversations, 14 April and 13 May 2020).

Nonetheless, Jordan was aware of his marginalised position and limited options to act. In light of the uncertainty around how the pandemic would evolve and impact on football and life in general, he, like many other players in similar situations, found consolation in spirituality (see chapters 6 and 7). He replied to Christian's questions about his plans and opportunities by saying 'It's in God's hands' and 'the Lord will provide' (social media conversations, 5 June and 3 July 2020). In August 2020, a light appeared on the horizon. While clubs had started to prepare for the upcoming season and began to sign players, Jordan and also Isaak, whose contract got cancelled for similar reasons, managed to use their connections to secure trials and eventually sign one-year contracts with third-tier clubs in the Bangkok metropolis and Eastern region, respectively. Jordan felt relieved to be on the verge of re-establishing his career and began to aspire once more for a consolidated position. The club he had moved to were ambitious and sought promotion to the national second-tier division in the upcoming season. He started the campaign with high hopes, believing that his new club would be a platform to take his career to the next level (social media conversations, 17 and 21 August 2020). However, with a further wave of COVID-19 in late 2020, the Football Association of Thailand was forced to terminate the regional group stage of the season abruptly. Jordan's team was positioned in the lower half of the league table, far from a possible promotion to the Thai League 2. Hence, from early January 2021 onwards the club suspended team training and stopped paying players' salaries. Once again, Jordan was forced to live off his savings while awaiting the start of a new season later in the year. The same fate befell Isaak at his club. At the point at which we completed this book in April 2021, their further career trajectory was once again uncertain. It remained unclear whether they would be able to renew their contracts and re-join their respective teams or whether they would need to re-embark on the struggle to find a new team and place in the lower ranks of professional football in Thailand to start from again (social media conversation, 3 April 2021).

Jordan's trajectory during the pandemic exemplifies the contemporary precarious status of many African players abroad. Those playing at a lower professional level in global football's periphery are confronted with issues such as salary cuts, premature contract termination and sudden invisibility, while social obligations to support families at home (who are usually also affected by the pandemic) continue. On the other hand, Jordan's experiences also show how players have navigated this predicament in order to regain visibility and consolidate their status. Jordan was able to do this because his long-standing experience as a footballer in Thailand had equipped him with important connections in the local football business that helped engineer opportunities to obtain a new contract. However, we are yet to see whether his career will indeed advance in the ways he hoped or how the COVID-19 pandemic will impact on the many other African players located in the game's peripheral leagues.

Our preliminary findings indicate that COVID-19 has increased the pressure on football labour migrants, particularly those at lower professional levels where clubs are forced to minimise costs and reduce squad size. Further, as other studies and reports have revealed, the pandemic has generally led to an increase in the percentage of loans and other short-term agreements in global professional football (Cáceres, 2020; Poli, Ravenel and Besson, 2020a, 2020b). A reversal of this trend is not (yet) in sight. It is likely, therefore, that the pandemic will accelerate competition among African migrant players seeking to succeed in football around the world. This is particularly problematic in the South-East Asian context where, prior to the pandemic, many African players were already labouring in very precarious circumstances without a contract or legal status in their host country (Akindes, 2013; Rehal, 2015). While COVID-19 put many anticipated careers and hopes on hold, it also took away daily opportunities to meet and connect with people in the social infrastructure of Thai football that might help to increase one's visibility. It has also closed up the ability of players to supplement their incomes by participating in private football tournaments, which have all come to a halt due to lockdown measures and social distancing. In these circumstances, African players, particularly those without contracts, increasingly struggle to meet their daily needs and obligations to family and to secure their legal status. Critically for their ability to negotiate or maintain their status as professional footballers, the continued impact of the pandemic has moved many to a more marginal position of power in the football industry.

Conclusions

African players' career trajectories in European and South-East Asian football are enmeshed in a number of precarities. Yet, while 'making it' abroad seldom leads to a smooth and successful career pathway, the popular image of fallen African players as victims of the global football industry distorts how pathways actually evolve. Rather, we have shown the nuances within their trajectories and how African football migrants act and are acted upon in GPN settings that involve various conflicting interests and unequal power relations (Carter, 2013). Certainly, African players seeking to secure and sustain a career are in one of, if not the, most vulnerable position. They are frequently lacking resources and relations while competing with thousands of others for a very limited number of opportunities. In the process, they must also negotiate and meet multiple expectations from families, agents, clubs and coaches, as well as those that are self-imposed. This position exposes them to various forms of discrimination in the form of less lucrative or problematic contract conditions (Poli, 2006a, 2006b), fraud (Darby, Akindes and Kirwin, 2007; Esson *et al.*, 2020) and racialisation (Engh, Settler and Agergaard, 2017). Thus, most African players' careers are dominated by an ongoing uncertainty that often leads to downward mobility in the business and an earlier exit from their football career than they would have hoped (Poli, 2010a). This situation is likely to continue as long as COVID-19 impacts professional football.

The chapter also illustrated how structural vulnerabilities articulate with players' individual endurance and resilience. The hope that leads to 'trying your luck' as a young footballer, discussed in Chapter 6, is often transformed into a form of 'judicious opportunism' (Johnson-Hanks, 2005) that opens up new opportunities to act under experiences of precarity. Border-crossing relations and activities, players' embodied belief in their ability to succeed and the desire to make their migration project valuable for themselves, their family and wider community frequently mitigate the disillusionment and setbacks that they often face. In short, these actions and approaches provide relief and offer prospects that keep players going despite the numerous barriers and exhausting detours they encounter. Staying in the game and keeping the hope of 'making it' alive gives meaning to the struggle, regardless of how precarious the present may be.

9

Post-playing-career transitions and struggles

Introduction

Matchday nineteen of the 2016 season in a local sixth-tier division in east central Sweden began with a show of strength from the division's leading team, the Northern All Stars. On a pleasant day in early October, they were playing their last home game of the campaign and were dominating their opponents right from the kick-off. With just one match remaining the following weekend, a win would bring them within touching distance of promotion. The players seemed capable of dealing with the pressure, and their superior technical skills and team play put them firmly in the ascendancy. At half-time, they led by four goals to nil, and all was set for an easy win. As Christian watched the match, he was not overly surprised by their performance. The team featured a group of African former professional footballers who had ended their careers in Sweden and remained in the country. Playing together provided an opportunity to stay in touch with friends, strengthen the local African diasporic community and remain active in the game. They also had a long-term goal of reaching the top level of Swedish football, the Allsvenskan. Thirty-five-year-old Chi was one of the players who harboured such aspirations. However, he was struggling with an injury that had prevented him from playing for some time. Chi took his absence from pitch as an opportunity to coach the team during this season. On this day though, there was not much for him to do. During the half-time break he simply praised the players for their performance and encouraged them to remain focused.

Despite their lead, the second half began with the Northern All Stars under pressure. The ex-professionals, all aged at least in their thirties, seemed exhausted. The game had suddenly changed. Their technically elaborate game gave way to long balls punted deep into their opponents' half that no one chased but that offered a temporary respite from the relentless attacks they were facing. The opposing team's younger and faster players took advantage of the situation and scored an early goal. Chi could not control his temper. He began to shout at and argue with his players, nervous about giving away what seemed only ten minutes earlier to be a comfortable lead. The team continued to struggle but eventually managed to add to their tally through a somewhat fortuitous shot from distance. Chi and the substitute players celebrated, confident that the victory was assured. Indeed, the opposing team lost confidence and the rest of the game was played out without further incident. When the referee finally blew the whistle to end the match everyone associated with the Northern All Stars – players, coaches and supporters – felt relieved. Their 5-1 win secured a two-point lead at the top of the table and many were already celebrating what they considered to be the formality of clinching the championship title the following week.

Chi looked forward to progressing through the league system. Due to his injury, he had given up on playing the game professionally but he hoped to continue playing at a level commensurate with his abilities and condition. In this respect, the Northern All Stars were the perfect fit for him. However, his long-term aspiration was to gain coaching experience and become a professional coach, and he saw the opportunity to work with a talented group of players at a higher level as an important step in establishing a reputation and climbing the coaching ladder. Chi was once a promising player but the recurring injuries, as well as a number of ill-conceived transfers that resulted in his career stagnating, prevented him from realising his full potential. Despite struggling with downward mobility in the game from his mid-twenties onwards, he continued to focus on 'becoming a somebody' through football. As consequence, he stopped exploring alternatives to professional football that might have opened up a less precarious livelihood and career path.

When Chi ended his professional career at the age of thirty-one, with no further education or vocational training, employment options were scarce. Nonetheless, he was reluctant to return home. In Sweden, he took a variety of part-time, menial jobs to sustain himself, his wife and child. Without the financial means and connections that could have paved the way to a coaching career in Swedish football, he began to work as a delivery driver for a fast-food outlet and secured hourly paid, irregular work for a removal company. While this earned him a modest living, it was far from what he imagined and expected when he came to Sweden as a promising football talent. At the time of the interviews, Chi was in his mid-thirties and had learnt that re-entering professional football as a coach and securing upward social mobility through the game was far from an easy undertaking (interviews, 1 October and 10 November 2016).

Chi's precarious transition and uncertain post-playing career is not unique. For many African players abroad, approaching the end of their playing days is a challenging 'vital conjuncture' (Johnson-Hanks, 2002). While some manage to translate their career success into consolidating productive future life courses, others, especially those whose professional careers did not materialise as anticipated, continue to experience a precarious existence (Agergaard and Ungruhe, 2016; Ungruhe and Agergaard, 2020b). When players step out of the spotlight of a short-lived professional career, many are quickly forgotten. The media has carried some remarkable and unusual stories of the post-playing-career trajectories of former African players such as the Liberian icon George Weah, who serves as president of his country, or the Cameroonian Benoît Assou-Ekotto, who was (wrongly) believed to have established a career in the adult film industry when he retired from the game. However, the whereabouts and life courses of most former migrant African footballers remain widely unknown (Ungruhe and Agergaard, 2020b).

In order to better understand the meaning and impact of African footballers' migration projects, we consider it critical to shed light on how they approach, experience and navigate their post-playing-career trajectories and livelihoods. Thus, after situating our discussion within the extant literature on career transitions in sport, this chapter interrogates how former players continue to negotiate an envisaged social mobility through the professional game and evaluates how they come to terms with their career achievements and failures. This enables us to conceptualise African migrant footballers' quest for social mobility as an ongoing transnational process that occurs throughout their life course, from the forming of their migratory aspiration, to their careers abroad and finally into their post-playing-career lives. The second part of the chapter compares their options and decisions in terms of whether to remain abroad or return home after their careers end.

Approaching career retirement and facing (occupational) precarity

As noted in Chapter 1, post-playing-career transitions and trajectories have only emerged as an important topic in studies on African football migration from the second decade of the new millennium (see Acheampong, 2019; Berthoud, 2017; Kyeremeh, 2020; Ungruhe and Agergaard, 2020a, 2020b). The dominant focus on the structural and socio-cultural conditions of migration practices, and players' aspirations as well as their experiences abroad, has highlighted the role, status and perceptions of active athletes rather than those of retired sportspeople. The disregarding of African footballers' experiences when their playing careers come to an end reflects a more general trend in sport-related research. The bulk of the literature that addresses athletes' post-playing careers are situated in psychology and place a strong emphasis on Western contexts (Stambulova and Ryba, 2014). This limited focus has resulted in European and North American perspectives being treated as a universal norm (Ryba and Stambulova, 2013) that seldom considers the experiences of athletes from African settings or the Global South more generally (Berthoud and Poli, 2011; Grundlingh, 2015; Tshube and Feltz, 2015; Ungruhe and Agergaard, 2020a).

A growing body of psychological studies on career transitions has called for a 'culturally informed approach' (Ryba and Stambulova, 2013: 1). Qualitative methodologies have been added to complement the dominant positivist-induced methods in the field. While the empirical focus for the emerging qualitative research remains on Western settings (Ryba and Stambulova, 2013; Stambulova, 2016), this literature has highlighted players' lived experiences, diversity and cross-cultural practices in dealing with the conclusion of their active career in sport. Qualitative perspectives have also helped in analysing athletes' post-playing-career transitions and trajectories with respect to the various social, legal, political and economic domains in which athletes act and are acted upon (Stambulova, Ryba and Henriksen, 2020). The emphasis on athletes as 'whole persons' has enabled post-playing careers to be conceptualised as non-linear, complex and as taking unusual turns. As we show in this chapter, this is particularly relevant with respect to African migrant footballers.

An increasing number of sociological studies likewise emphasise athletes' post-playing-career transitions and trajectories in Europe and North America. This work has examined the ways in which structural conditions, most notably institutionalised racism, limit opportunities for migrant and Black and minority ethnic athletes to access coaching positions both within the football industry and beyond, following their retirement from their playing career (Agergaard and Ungruhe, 2016; Bradbury, 2013; Bradbury, Lusted and van Sterkenburg, 2020; Bradbury, van Sterkenburg and Mignon, 2018; Campbell, 2020; Curran, 2015; Ungruhe and Agergaard, 2020b). The sociological studies have also pointed to the role of migrant athletes' transnational relations and activities in navigating the obstacles they face after retiring from sport. Emotional support from parents, relatives and friends, and engaging in promising economic activities have all been shown to be important in this regard (Ungruhe and Agergaard, 2020a).

Given the numerous and continuous precarities faced by African footballers during their careers abroad, the fact that they experience challenging post-playing-career transitions and trajectories should come as no surprise. African migrant football players are not unique in experiencing difficult career 'afterlives'. In fact, many professional athletes all over the globe face uncertain future career paths and experience a declining social status after their sporting career has come to a conclusion (Park, Lavallee and Tod, 2013). This is particularly visible in the global football industry and is closely linked to the inability of many players to accrue sufficient financial means to facilitate their post-playing-career plans. A study by the international players' union FIFPro (2016) with fourteen thousand professional footballers worldwide revealed that three-quarters of these players received average wages of less than four hundred US dollars a month during their playing careers. To some degree, differing levels of salaries and living costs in different parts of the world helps to put this level of pay into perspective. That being said, FIFPro's findings are not limited to situations in low-income countries. A study among former professional footballers in Germany found that 20–25 per cent were living on minimum social welfare at some point when their career came to an end (Ritzer, 2011). Receiving only the minimum wage as active players leaves little room to save for the post-playing-career life stage or to adequately bridge times of unemployment and/or job-seeking. This is particularly problematic since about three-quarters of professional footballers end their careers without qualifications or job training (FIFPro, 2016).

In general, while the provision of opportunities for pursuing education or alternative job training by clubs, national governing bodies and national player unions is patchy at best, and virtually non-existent at lower levels of football around the world, footballers themselves frequently seek to make provision for their retirement from playing by pursuing improved professional contracts that offer better pay. The stress and challenges that this can pose, with the hoped-for rewards often failing to materialise to a sufficient degree, restrict footballers' financial capital and options for smooth and successful post-playing-career transitions. Combined, career precarities in the form of low salaries and the subordinate role of players' education and job training in the football industry generally account for widespread precarious post-playing-career life courses among former professional footballers (Agergaard and Ungruhe, 2016; FIFPro, 2016; Ungruhe and Agergaard, 2020b).

Preparing for post-playing-career lives

Transitioning to life after professional sport is a problematic endeavour for many athletes in the global football industry, but migrant footballers seem to be particularly challenged. Among them, African players in Europe and elsewhere are especially vulnerable. Generally, given low wages over the course of their careers in comparison to the average professional player in European football, irregular trajectories and recurring and often long periods of unemployment (Büdel, 2013; Poli, 2006a; Ungruhe, 2018a), African players are seldom able to accumulate sufficient finances for a comfortable retirement (Ungruhe and Agergaard, 2020b). Despite these constraints, some players opt to spend their rather limited means to try to maintain a lifestyle characterised by the X-Way, with its emphasis on conspicuous consumption (see also Chapter 5). This lifestyle is often facilitated through generous credit lines with banks, meaning the luxury cars and designer clothes associated with these players are typically purchased via loans. Yet posting pictures of one's car(s) or clothes on social media to be consumed in their country of origin, conveys and perpetuates an image of a successful migrant, and raises the player's social status among family members and friends (Ungruhe and Agergaard, 2020a). Nevertheless, in addition to other expenditures such as paying generally higher living costs in Europe and supporting family and friends at home, funding an appetite for a lifestyle characterised by conspicuous consumption further limits players' finances and complicates their preparations for their futures (Berthoud and Poli, 2011; Ungruhe and Agergaard, 2020a), particularly when bank loans come due or are cut when a playing contract expires.

Limited financial means form only part of the challenge in planning for a future beyond playing. The precarious, short-term contractual arrangements that African players frequently enter into in order to gain a foothold in the professional football industry demand that they focus their time and energies into developing their football-related abilities. Hence, as the reflections of players such as John have highlighted in the two previous chapters, African players tend to speculate almost exclusively on securing upward career mobility in professional football. On this basis, many African footballers believe that if they succeed in consolidating their position in the game, the upward social and economic mobility achieved is lasting and may even enable them to become coordinators in the industry at some point in the future. In contrast, however, players often refer to the realisation of their mobility and success in football as being in 'God's hands', as Jordan, whose career trajectory in South-East Asia was examined in the previous two chapters, put it. Pointing to their own limitations and dependencies in terms of 'making it' as professional players, they also recognise that embarking on productive, fulfilling post-playing-career life courses is often beyond their control, too.

The implications of a single-minded focus on upward mobility through football at the expense of exploring possible alternatives becomes evident in the case of unsuccessful or mediocre career trajectories mired in precarity. The story of Emmanuel, thirty-three at the time of our interview, underlines this. Emmanuel was born and raised in Ghana and spent most of his career playing for various Scandinavian teams at the first- and second-tier level. However, several injuries during the early stages of his career hindered him from making a lasting impact in the game. Contracts were seldom renewed, and from his mid-twenties onwards his career moved in a downward arc. Although he was aware for a long time that it might be useful to get an education, Emmanuel kept his focus exclusively on football. He opted to prioritise recovering from his recurring injuries and plotting a move to a top league in Europe, which he remained confident would eventually be realised. His hopes did not materialise. When Emmanuel was finally forced to end his professional career at the age of twenty-seven, he was ill-prepared to consolidate his post-playing livelihood. Emmanuel had not acquired any qualifications or experiences that could provide an alternative to football, and he was left to contemplate a precarious future. While he decided to pursue the notion of a coordinating role in Ghanaian football by becoming a scout, it proved difficult to turn this idea into practice because he first needed to find a job to replace his salary from football. As he commented: 'At the end of the day, you've got to find a way of living, you know? There's no other way.' Thus, following his retirement from the game, he remained in Scandinavia and took up a physically demanding job as a parcel courier with a private company, a role that he found 'very, very hard' (interview, 6 November 2016).

It is important to note here that some players do actively strive for an education alongside their playing careers, but it is often difficult for them to access suitable courses or job training. In the global football industry, education is predominantly provided through football academies or educational partnerships between professional clubs and schools or colleges. As such, these opportunities are primarily directed towards players of school age, often in order to meet legal requirements (see Chapter 5, and John's and Jordan's references to their education abroad in Chapter 7). At the senior level, meanwhile, facilitating education or job training is an exception rather than the norm among professional clubs (FIFPro, 2016). Even in the EU where policies such as the guidelines on the dual careers of athletes (European Commission, 2012) and funding schemes like Erasmus+ provide resources to implement dual-career activities and programmes, dual-career opportunities are not the norm in the continent's professional football industry (Breslin *et al.*, 2019). Rather, given the priority placed on sporting success and economic gain in the industry, clubs' focus is on the development and utilisation of a player's abilities on the pitch (see FIFPro, 2016; Ungruhe and Agergaard, 2020c).

In Scandinavian countries, however, where clubs offer modest salaries compared to many other European countries, there is more of a focus on athletes' education alongside their careers. A range of clubs and the national football associations there acknowledge the limited economic prospects offered through a career in the domestic game. Reflecting a widespread cultural approach in Scandinavian countries to develop 'whole human beings' in and beyond sport, dual-career policies have been designed to ease the challenges of post-playing transitions (Agergaard, 2016). However, whereas such dual-career programmes often benefit local players, they do not accommodate the specific needs of migrant players from outside the EU by, for example, providing tuition or training in English or French. As a consequence, migrant players who enter Scandinavia beyond their school age appear to be considered only as full-time professionals rather than as 'whole human beings' who may need an education or job training to prepare for their post-playing-career life courses (Agergaard, 2016).

Beyond the specific Scandinavian context, there are additional reasons that make pursuing dual careers impractical for African players abroad. As outlined in Chapter 5 in relation to the Ghanaian context with its high rates of unemployment among young people, some players and parents question the benefits of education for future employability and do not pursue formal study beyond the primary or lower secondary-school level (see Esson, 2013; Gough et al., 2019; Palmer, 2009; Rolleston and Oketch, 2008). In addition, regular, consistent school attendance in many African settings, including Ghana, is far from the norm and many pupils' educational experiences are often characterised by alternating periods of in-school tuition and non-attendance (Langevang, 2008; see Chapter 5). Even for those migrant players who attend school before they move abroad, their experiences often leave them underqualified to enrol or excel in educational programmes in other countries. Given that many African players migrate at a comparatively younger age than their peers from other parts of the world (Poli, 2006a), many do not possess the formal qualifications required to access dual-career provision (Agergaard and Ungruhe, 2016).

Another outcome of being a migrant is unfamiliarity with support systems in destination countries. Thus, there are players who would have pursued opportunities to gain skills and qualifications alongside their playing careers but were not aware of the possibility of doing so while playing professionally (Ungruhe and Agergaard, 2020b). This is particularly problematic since suitable dual-career opportunities have been identified as the key factor for successfully navigating retirement from playing among African athletes (Tshube and Feltz, 2015). Taking this into account, the implementation of educational programmes in a number of elite West African academies, perhaps most notably at Right to Dream, which has developed a number of educational partnerships with schools and colleges in the US and UK (see Chapter 3), may help those who enter the ranks of professional football abroad to better navigate alternative careers. However, the number of players benefiting from this is rather limited compared to the overall number of African footballers abroad.

Even where migrant players progress through nodes in football's GPN that allow them to attend school alongside their football training, such as in the cases of John and Jordan (see chapters 7 and 8), the long-term benefit is uncertain. Learning the local language in order to qualify for further education or job training is a difficult activity to combine with the demands of a professional playing career, not least where a player's transnational mobility involves frequent changes of clubs and countries (Agergaard, 2016; Ungruhe and Agergaard, 2020b). Likewise, when Ali, whose move from FC Ebedei to FC Midtjylland was highlighted in Chapter 7, was promoted from the Danish club's academy to its professional senior team at the age of eighteen, he found it difficult to continue with schooling. He attended the tenth grade of a Danish public school but was only able to graduate in English language. He was aware that an education would increase his chances of success in life and wanted to learn Danish and continue his school career. Ali explained how his emphasis on gaining a good education was the product of growing up in a household where education was positioned as key for achieving social mobility: 'My parents, they believe ... that the way to success is getting educated' (interview, 20 March 2016). However, in order to succeed in the European game, Ali felt that he had to focus on football first. He rationalised this in the following way:

> We trained very early in the morning, and sometimes we trained in the afternoon, too. So playing for the first team is not the same as playing in the academy. In the first team there is a lot of pressure and [you need] a lot of commitment ... So then it's up to me to choose a position [and] I decided, "Okay, this [football] is really what I want, and then I have to go for it, 100 per cent". (Interview, 20 March 2016)

Recurring injuries ultimately ended his ambitions and he finally had to quit professional football at the age of twenty-seven. Having informally acquired Danish language skills over the years it was only then that he managed to re-embark on education with the aim of getting a university entrance qualification. He continued to play at a semi-professional level, which helped him to generate a little extra income. However, while he was confident that 'once you are educated you can be anything in life', it remained far from certain whether his ambition to secure employment in football management would come to fruition (interview, 20 March 2016).

Ali's trajectory points to the dynamics of the social infrastructure around which football migration, and footballers' post-playing-career trajectories, cohere. As a young academy player, he speculated on securing a professional career in European football, but influential individuals at his Danish club also coordinated opportunities for his life after football by facilitating his education. However, due to the demands of his playing career, the comparatively marginalised status of education at the senior level of the game and his club's withdrawal from its coordinating role at this stage, he did not invest sufficiently in planning for his post-football-playing life. As he faced a premature end to his career, he clearly thought more about what he would do and how he would consolidate his status when he stopped playing. His parents' faith in education influenced his outlook and he re-engaged with education. Nonetheless, this account of Ali's career reveals that postponing plans for retirement from playing is a risky endeavour that has the potential to create downward social mobility. However, as we will show now, this is common practice among African football migrants.

Postponing retirement and 'judicious opportunism'

Regardless of their age or fitness level, it is a common strategy among African players to delay their retirement from playing for as long as possible. When thirty-year-old players state, 'I don't see age to be a factor' (Edward, interview, 23 May 2016) and '[y]ou can be forty and still be playing' (David, interview, 5 June 2016), they are referencing a racialised but common view among West African footballers that their alleged physical prowess equips them for long careers (see Chapter 6). While they point to and take inspiration from iconic players such as Roger Milla, Didier Drogba, Michael Essien and Samuel Eto'o who played professionally until their late thirties or even early forties, these prolonged careers are not the norm among African football migrants specifically or professional football players more generally. Indeed, as we have illustrated, African players often experience shorter careers than their European counterparts, albeit the reasons for this often relate more to the structural conditions of the football industry in Europe rather than differences in respective physical capabilities (Angeli, 2010).

For African players other than those at the elite end of the European game, speculating on the possibility of a prolonged career is a risky strategy, not least because it is dependent on avoiding serious injury and maintaining a high level of fitness over an extended period of time. As we saw earlier in this chapter, for example, Chi's efforts to prolong his career were undone by injury, and having ended up in precarious jobs and without qualifications he regretted that he had not prepared better for life after professional football: 'I was so blinded with football … I wasn't seeing, I wasn't looking deep into society. I was just more eager about my career.' Looking back with the benefit of hindsight, he suggested that learning to become more fluent in Swedish and acquiring qualifications either in coaching or in a field outside the football business would have provided a better livelihood for him and his family than persevering with playing (interview, 10 November 2016).

At the time though, despite recurring injuries, frequent transfers to clubs in different countries and at lower levels, less playing time and more modest salaries, Chi was unwilling to think about alternatives to football. He maintained his belief in his ability to prevail in the game and accepted offers from smaller clubs because they allowed him to keep playing and, as he saw it, offered a route back to a higher level and better contracts. It was only when he met a friend's father who asked him what he did for a living that he began to have doubts about football as a suitable path. 'I said, "I play football"', Chi recalled. But the man did not believe him. '"No, I mean your job"', the friend's father insisted, '"nobody plays football for a living. What do you do for a job?"' Chi was shocked. 'If you are not playing in the Allsvenskan … where your name is in the newspaper, they don't ever see you to be working'. While this exchange gave him cause for reflection, he continued with his football career (interview, 10 November 2016).

When Chi joined a third-tier club located a three-hour bus and train journey away from where he lived with his family, he first took the long commute as an unavoidable burden he had to accept. However, his salary was too little to sustain himself and his family. 'I started having problems with finances, couldn't pay [bills] in time', he recalled. 'It became a real horrific situation.' He left the team in the mid-season transfer window to sign a short-term contract with another third-tier club closer to his residence and was able to secure terms that eased his financial situation a little. After the season ended, he intended to negotiate a new deal but with the club no longer able to afford his salary, he was asked to play for free. Unable to find a different club that would offer him an adequate contract, he grew disillusioned: 'I just got frustrated and tired of the whole thing and … started thinking about doing something else with myself'. By then, at the age of thirty-one, Chi had finally reconsidered his ambitions in professional football and he began to think about alternatives. He wanted to remain involved in the game, not least because he felt that he 'didn't have a full run' in his career and believed that he 'still [had] a lot to give to the game'. Thus, while a full-time playing career had been replaced with working in demanding jobs in the removal and delivery business, he retained his connection to football through his involvement in the amateur game with his African friends. As outlined in the vignette that opened this chapter, this had sparked an interest in coaching, and he came to see this as an important first step en route to building a different career in the game (interview, 10 November 2016).

Chi's case, and those of his fellow migrants recounted in this book, clearly demonstrate that players engage in an all-consuming, single-minded effort to gain entry into football markets abroad and to consolidate their position in the professional game. This strategy for securing their future livelihoods and those of family members, and transitioning from youth-hood to acceptable, masculine adulthood is inherently risky. This risk is accentuated because once players embark on this path, they typically do so with absolute, unwavering commitment and focus. As David put it: 'as a professional, you must offer 100 per cent' (interview, 5 June 2016). This simple yet stark insight encapsulates the mindset and subjectivities of many African players who see their possibilities of success, not only during their playing careers but also afterwards, as being bound up with their own abilities, efforts, luck and fate.

As we illustrated in Chapter 5, youth and young men in Africa become an 'entrepreneur of self', in a Foucauldian sense, by utilising their bodily capital as part of a strategy to enact spatial mobility through football, achieve social mobility and 'become a somebody'. Chapters 7 and 8 showed that being an 'entrepreneur of self' does not end when they leave Africa but rather continues to undergird their transnational football-related endeavours and careers. However, in these chapters, we have revealed that being an 'entrepreneur of self' is a problematic, yet ambivalent approach among African football players to circumvent unfavourable conditions for self-realisation and social mobility at home, and the structural obstacles that give rise to non-linear migration routes and career pathways in football's GPN, such as fierce competition, short-term contracts and low wages.

When African football migrants combine the subjectivity of being an 'entrepreneur of self' with a sense of 'judicious opportunism' (Johnson-Hanks, 2005), they are better able to reconcile the pursuit of a utopian dream. This also gives meaning to their struggles and allows them to deal with the precarities they face by reproducing their hope and self-affirmation as a migrant and a footballer. However, when players approach the end of their careers and their sporting, economic and social ambitions have not materialised as anticipated and their future lives become more uncertain than ever, these 'entrepreneurs of self' appear to act less judiciously. As they age or struggle with injuries, their decreasing bodily capital and steadily diminishing prospects of consolidating their position in the football industry become more obvious. Despite (or perhaps because of) this, rather than investing in and planning for their post-playing livelihoods, many ignore the inevitable and instead continue to speculate by increasing their efforts to sustain their playing careers. For those nearing the end of their career, 'judicious opportunism' often backfires and the ambivalences of being an 'entrepreneur of self' finally give way to a harsh reality in which holding on to the hope of a successful professional football career becomes meaningless as their precarious post-playing-career life course unfolds.

Transnational relations, social obligations and preparing for life after football

Navigating post-playing-career lives and livelihoods is not solely a rational process involving individuals making decisions and taking actions that they feel are in their own or their immediate family's best interests. Rather, it is a complicated, border-crossing affair that is underpinned by the often-ambivalent transnational conditions, relations and experiences that African players are tied into and that influence almost every stage of their journey from clubs or academies in Africa to international football fields (Ungruhe and Agergaard, 2020c). For instance, while social norms of being valuable to one's home community do not end after a migrant player's retirement from professional football, a football migrant's adult masculine identity remains connected to his potential, willingness and actual practice of 'giving back' (Acheampong, Bouhaouala and Raspaud, 2019) and fulfilling the intergenerational contract (see chapters 5 and 6). Hence, whereas a player's successful transition to a respectable career and livelihood may secure social recognition at home, failure to do so can lead to downward social mobility. In this section, we explore how players navigate these transnational relations to meet their own and sustain others' expectations of their lives after professional football.

When eighteen-year-old Michael moved to a club in the Swedish Allsvenskan on a short-term loan, it raised high expectations with his parents. In reflecting back on what this meant for the family, his father referenced how his son's move enabled him to meet his household obligations at a relatively young age: 'We knew for sure if he [Michael] gets to Sweden it will be new because we took him as the breadwinner for the family' (interview, 29 June 2016). Although Michael only received about two thousand euros per month, a comparatively modest salary in professional football terms, and was based in a country with high living costs, he managed to support his family by sending between four hundred and five hundred euros home each month. This covered his retired parents' living costs to a great degree. When his mother became severely ill Michael also took care of the medical bills. However, Michael was not able to reproduce his status as a migrant professional player. He returned to Ghana and later moved on a number of short-term contracts to clubs in Europe and northern Africa. He was neither able to make a lasting impact nor secure a lucrative contract at any of the clubs he played for and the modest salaries he received made it increasingly burdensome to continuously support his family. As he recounted, 'There wasn't much left to do other things'. Critically, meeting his familial obligations also prevented him from pursuing education or training, or making investments that could have secured a livelihood when he retired from the game (interview, 20 April 2016).

Michael had plans to buy a farm in Ghana that would provide a home and a business for him and his family. However, the costs involved in his mother's medical treatment ended that ambition. In early 2021, Michael was thirty-one and there was no prospect of him re-embarking on a playing career abroad. He had returned to Ghana five years previously for a short spell with a local Premier League club, but since then he had been without a team. Even though his playing career had effectively ended, his plans for life after football remained vague. He continued to be his family's primary breadwinner, supporting them from the modest savings he was able to accrue during his career, but this was not adequate to meet his own or other people's expectations, nor was it enough to consolidate upward social mobility to a sufficient and lasting degree. As his father saw it, by the end of his career, 'he also has to build a house' that would secure the family's future livelihood (interview, 29 June 2016). However, this was not on the horizon as Michael admitted: 'I had that dream that if I get to Europe, I'll be able to buy houses, I'll be able to buy cars, invest and maybe help out the many people in need'. He concluded by saying, 'I would have wished for more', words that reflected his regret at being unable to actualise his own and his family's high hopes for his career abroad (interview, 20 April 2016).

As Michael's emphasis on consumption and care indicate, meeting such expectations serves several purposes. Supporting family members with remittances as part of a household livelihood strategy (van der Meij and Darby, 2017) enables players to consolidate their position as 'social givers' (Martin, Ungruhe and Häberlein, 2016). At the same time, meeting social obligations by acquiring or building a house for their parents or wider family (as well as purchasing cars and other high-end imported goods) also visibly materialises migrant players' success in the public sphere and further builds upon their social status at home. Eventually, this practice provides them with some degree of material security at the end of their playing careers. This is illustrated vividly by Nana, a former migrant player who suggested that, having secured a contract abroad, 'the first thing every Ghanaian will do ... [is to] try to have two, three houses' (interview, 9 May 2016). Almost every player who participated in our research had such a plan in mind and, indeed, many had managed to build or buy a house in their country of origin over the course of their careers. Even in the numerous cases where players struggled to actualise their career ambitions, meet their own and others' expectations, and support their family, ending their career with a house at home was a priority.

Other players who were more successful in their careers, such as Ali, were able to make provision for a family home in Africa. When he signed his first professional contract as an eighteen-year-old, he regularly sent half of his monthly income of about two thousand euros home to his family to pay for their daily livelihood and his siblings' education. In explaining his remitting, he commented: 'I lived with my parents [who] tried to put me through the life ... how can I help them, what can I do for them to get it better, to make it?' (interview, 30 March 2016). Alongside this support, he also bought a plot of land at home and started to build a house. Due to his limited financial means this was not a straightforward process and took seven years to complete. While Ali remained abroad as he continued his football career, his family maintained the property and used it as their residence.

The significance of a migrant player building or buying a house in their country of origin extends beyond the purely financial or practical. While it symbolises a player's success abroad, it carries forward an image of a caring and present son who fulfils the intergenerational contract of mutual support between parents and children in West Africa (Kabeer, 2000; Smith and Mazzucato, 2009). Becoming 'social givers' in this way helps migrant players realise social maturity and enhances their status in their community of origin (see also Kuuire *et al.*, 2016; Page and Sunjo, 2018). As such, building a house may replace other investments such as in education or training in the quest to provide for future life courses (see Ungruhe and Agergaard, 2020c).

Given the uncertain post-playing-career trajectories of African former players, it is questionable whether a sole focus on a house is sufficient in planning for the future. For Ali, and many others, investing in football to the complete exclusion of education was a risky, highly speculative decision that restricted opportunities following their retirement from the game. For some, this pays off. But as we have shown in this chapter and elsewhere in the book, the harsh realities of the football business create significant precarities for African football migrants, not just during their playing days but also long into their futures. Moreover, the transnational dimension of their post-playing-career transitions and trajectories can also contribute to anxious and uncertain futures, particularly where they fail to live up to social obligations and expectations at home or display symbols typically associated with a successful career abroad. In these cases, former players experience the shame of failure and experience downward social mobility in the places and communities that they departed to pursue their professional football career abroad (van der Meij and Darby, 2016; Kleist, 2017).

Staying abroad or returning home?

Ending a career abroad and the transnational dimension of post-playing-career lives brings to the fore the question of where former migrant professionals intend to reside. For most African football migrants, the question of staying abroad or returning home is far from a straightforward individual decision. Rather, it involves complex considerations connected to multifarious personal, social, legal, political and economic motives and entanglements. These include: job prospects; the degree of social inclusion in the host society; health; personal safety; educational aspirations for one's children; a desire to live closer to relatives and ageing parents; legal residence and citizenship; social status at home and abroad; and aspirations to give back to one's home society. All of these issues intersect and complicate migrant players' decisions about whether to remain living abroad, return home or to combine both.

A common feature of this decision relates to what option offers the best prospects to remain working in the game after their playing career comes to an end. Starting a career as a coach, player agent or scout emerged as the primary occupations that former migrant players aspired to. In South-East Asia it is common practice among former and some still active players to work as scouts or intermediaries and search for talent in their countries of origin or elsewhere in Africa. At times, as in the case of Ken, the Ghanaian player and intermediary who facilitated Jordan's move to Thailand (see chapters 7 and 8), they do this during their off-season holiday or they are sent by their clubs specifically for this purpose. Others, such as the intermediary who brought Isaak to Thailand (see Chapter 7), will often invite a small number of local players for trials, negotiate with their clubs and parents and make travel arrangements. While their remuneration from clubs is usually performance-based and depends on a successful player signing, they also often charge invited players for their services in facilitating their trials and transfers. Particular scouts and intermediaries often operate in an unscrupulous manner and with little consideration for the welfare of young players, but they are generally important actors in the games' social infrastructure. By facilitating intercontinental player migration, they connect the African and South-East Asian football industries and reproduce a GPN built on the ongoing speculation of African talent and South-East Asian clubs' interest in signing these players at minimal cost.

In addition to these practices, former African players who played professionally in South-East Asia are increasingly recruited as youth coaches at academies and local clubs. Sam's trajectory illustrates this trend. His journey from Ghana into the Thai football industry was turbulent and far from linear. By his mid-twenties, he had experienced fraud during an encounter with an intermediary who promised him a contract in Europe, new hope when he was offered a trial in Thailand and disappointment when a contract with a Thai club failed to materialise. He finally enjoyed upward social mobility in the game by moving from clubs in the third and second tiers to Thailand's top league. However, Sam enjoyed only a short period of success at this level, and after suffering a severe injury during preparations for his first season with his new club, his career came to a sudden end. As with many of his compatriots in the region, he tried to revive his career by moving to a lower-division club but his efforts were to no avail. Sam had to stop playing at the age of twenty-seven and at precisely the moment when his overseas career in the professional football industry seemed about to accelerate (interview, 21 February 2020).

It was never Sam's plan to stay in Thailand indefinitely and he was about to return home. However, his last club asked him to stay and work as an assistant to the head coach. Reflecting on why he was made this offer, Sam commented, 'They said I can communicate and control the team'. In view of a lack of alternatives, Sam accepted the offer. At first, he admitted, 'I was very sad when I could not come back anymore [as a player]. I always wished I was in the game. Sometimes I cried, I was not sleeping' (interview, 21 February 2020). However, he quickly demonstrated a talent for coaching and was appointed the head coach for the club's junior teams from the U-14 level upwards. Some of his young charges went on to play for clubs in Thailand's top league and the respect and gratitude that they expressed to him enhanced his confidence and encouraged him to continue his coaching career. He embarked on a number of coaching courses and acquired his first Asian Football Confederation coaching licence (AFC C licence) in 2017. He continued with his coaching education and began working towards obtaining the AFC Professional Coaching Diploma, which enables holders to coach at the highest level in Asian football.

None of this is to say that his coaching experiences were without challenges. Indeed, he pointed to what he perceived to be racially motivated cheating by officials during games involving teams he was coaching: 'as a Black coach here you face a lot of challenges. It is very hard. Sometimes the referee favours the opponent team because of my colour. They rob us totally.' Despite these barriers, he aspired to achieve in the coaching domain what he was unable to as a player: success at the very top. In articulating this, and with reference to the various actors in Thai football, he said, 'I want to challenge them and show that I can do it' (interview, 21 February 2020).

Whether Sam's future evolves as hoped or not, he had already been successful in consolidating his status after his active career came to an end. By coaching local players who have gone on to play in Thailand's top tier, he demonstrated his abilities to take on a coordinator role in Asian football. However, while coaching careers at the higher levels of the global football industry are typically characterised by short-term contracts, immense pressure to deliver and high turnover, the fact that African coaches experience additional, racially charged challenges in Thai football adds to the uncertainty of Sam's and other African players' coaching trajectories in the country. Hence, as Sam put it, returning home is always on the horizon, but only if he can reproduce the social standing that he had acquired in Thailand back in Ghana: 'I want to go to Ghana and show my country that I have learned, what I have achieved' (interview, 21 February 2020).

Despite Sam's trajectory, opportunities to coach or work as a scout in the South-East Asian football business are generally rather limited. Other viable football-related livelihood options are equally scarce. By playing football or futsal at private tournaments, former players may be able to generate some income, but this does not represent a sustainable livelihood. While it is common practice to look for alternatives outside football, formal jobs are often unavailable as migration regulations restrict the issuing of work permits for foreign nationals. Therefore, several migrant players attempt to get a foot in the import-export business as independent traders, arranging for consumer goods to be shipped to Africa for sale. However, this offers only infrequent income and certainly not at the level required for a decent livelihood. While many former players remain and look for employment opportunities in Asia, others decide to return home to seek better opportunities there.

For former migrant players from Africa who have played in Europe, opportunities to remain in the game following their retirement from playing are even scarcer. Whereas a growing number have obtained internationally recognised licences to coach at a professional level, they face a number of intersecting constraints at the micro-, meso- and macro-levels in seeking to secure such positions (see Bradbury, Lusted and van Sterkenburg, 2020). For instance, Sam's account of how teams with Black coaches appear to be disadvantaged during games in Thailand points to routine discrimination on the pitch. This and similar incidents at the micro-level are likewise visible in European football (Bradbury, Lusted and van Sterkenburg, 2020; Gearity and Metzger, 2017). On the societal macro-level, national regulations regarding migrants' rights of residence also limit former African players' opportunities to build a career in coaching. Working solely as a coach at the semi-professional level in a country where a migrant has not secured citizenship does not entitle them to legal residency. However, without gaining experience at this level, securing work as a coach in professional football, and thereby qualifying for residency rights, is unlikely. Moreover, when a coaching contract is terminated, it can invalidate the legal basis for a residence permit and a migrant coach is then often unable to maintain the professional network and visibility that might enable them to secure another coaching position in the country they were working in.

Beyond legal constraints, the general lack of access to the networks that are frequently required to open doors to coaching jobs in the higher echelons of the game is also prohibitive for former African players aspiring to a coaching career (Bradbury, 2020; Bradbury, van Sterkenburg and Mignon, 2018). Most crucially, however, are the aforementioned structural barriers, specifically processes of racialisation and institutionalised forms of racism that operate on the organisational meso-level. For instance, the lack of racial diversity among the members of European clubs' boards of directors has been shown to limit opportunities for non-white coaches (Bradbury, 2013). Efforts to address the exclusion of Black, Asian and minority ethnic coaches, such as the implementation in the English Football League of the 'Rooney Rule', which requires clubs to interview at least one non-white candidate for vacant coaching jobs, have failed to make an impact (Mezahi, 2020). Crude racial stereotypes about the intellectual capabilities of Black people and their supposed innate propensity to excel in sport-related roles that require physical prowess undergird this situation and act to restrict opportunities for African (and other Black) former players from accessing coaching positions in professional football (Bradbury, 2013; Campbell, 2020).

Research carried out by Bradbury (2013), which revealed that only 1 per cent of coaches in European football are Black or from a minority ethnic group, highlights the extent of this issue. Hence, only a few outstanding African migrant players, such as Mário Wilson from Mozambique who managed Benfica to the Portuguese championship in 1976, have managed to successfully land coaching positions with prestigious European clubs (Cleveland, 2017). Examples in the new millennium include the Ivorian former international Kolo Touré, who was appointed assistant coach at Glasgow giants Celtic in 2017 and then at Leicester City in 2019, and the Ghanaian ex-international Otto Addo, who became assistant coach at Borussia Dortmund in 2019, following similar roles at Hamburger SV, FC Nordsjælland and Borussia Mönchengladbach. Michael Essien, Ghana's most famous football export, joined the coaching staff of FC Nordsjælland following a spell as player-coach with the Azerbaijani team Sabail. Opportunities to act as head coach for European teams have been far scarcer, although the former Nigerian international Ndubuisi Egbo led FK Tirana to the Albanian league title in the 2019/20 season, while in Belgium the former Senegalese international Mbaye Leye took over as the new head coach of Standard Liège in December 2020. Others have landed coaching jobs outside Europe, such as the Ghanaian Edward Ansah, who has been a member of the coaching staff at the Indian second-tier club Churchill Brothers SC since the 2018/19 season. In addition, Nigeria's Michael Emenalo's post-playing career, which included positions as technical director for Chelsea FC (2011–17) and AS Monaco (2017–19), is a unique example of a successful trajectory beyond coaching. While these examples may indicate the possibility of a particular group of very successful former players making it in the global football industry, they also underline the absence of opportunities at the top level of the game for most African former professional footballers. Indeed, of those African former players who coach in Europe, the vast majority work at an amateur or semi-professional level and without realistic prospects of climbing the ladder (Ungruhe and Agergaard, 2020a).

Given the barriers in European football, former players who return home seem to have better options to stay in the game than those who remain abroad. Iconic coaches such as the late Stephen Keshi, who in 2013 won the Africa Cup of Nations with the Nigerian national team, the Super Eagles, and others who came later such as Charles Akonnor (Ghana) and Aliou Cissé (Senegal), have paved the way for a growing number of returnees to achieve coaching positions with first-tier clubs or national teams in Africa. Aspiring returnees usually build on relations with former teammates in their respective home countries to access the coaching business. It is common among former migrant footballers to meet once or twice a week to play football for fun, with players using this opportunity to talk about shared experiences, past 'glories', recent developments in local and global football as well as possible jobs in the business. This is how Evans managed to embark on a coaching career. When he returned to Ghana from a career in Europe and Asia that took him to well-known clubs in Belgium and Turkey at his peak, he was unable to secure a job for two years. He tried to become a West African scout for one of his former European clubs but failed to land the role. When a media business that he invested in collapsed, his future became precarious and he became reliant on his shrinking savings to support himself and his family. Without any concrete plans for the future, Evans had to reduce living costs and adjust his lifestyle. As he explained, 'After the game things go down and you get to a state [when] you cut the cord according to your size'. This was a hard lesson for him. 'You don't want to go down', he admitted, 'but in Ghana you realise reality' (interview, 12 May 2016).

Two years after his return, Evans's fortunes appeared to improve when he was approached by a fellow former international player at a self-organised football gathering and asked whether he was interested in becoming his assistant at a local second-division club. Though coaching was not his first choice, Evans accepted the offer given the lack of alternative options. At this time, he did not possess any coaching experience or qualifications. As a player, however, Evans was known for his ability to lead a team, which, in the eyes of his former teammate, made him suitable for the job. He quickly adjusted to his new role: 'When I joined and I went to the grounds with the team, and I saw how the boys were coached and how the boys were playing, I thought, "I have a lot in me that I can impact into these boys" … That's how I became a coach. Then I started to get serious'. Hence, soon after his appointment, he took a coaching course in Ghana and started the process of acquiring the introductory qualification, the CAF C licence (interview, 12 May 2016).

After his first season as an assistant coach, Evans was offered the opportunity to replace the departing head coach. He accepted the post and further enhanced his curriculum vitae by obtaining the CAF B and A licences, which entitled him to coach at the highest level in CAF competitions. He quickly built a strong reputation in coaching circles and moved on to work at some of the most well-renowned clubs in West Africa. This was enabled by maintaining close connections with head coaches he had worked with previously; when they were appointed by a new club, he usually followed them. Besides working at the club level, Evans also extended his profile by working as an assistant coach in the GFA. Following several assistant jobs with the national U-17 and U-20 squads, he was appointed the head coach for one of Ghana's national youth teams (interview, 12 May 2016).

It should be noted that a coaching career in an African setting could be considered as even more challenging than in other locations. In several ways, African coaches suffer from structural disadvantages in Africa and protectionist policies in the global football industry. On the one hand, coaching jobs in African football are no less transient and similarly bound to immediate success as elsewhere in the business. Salaries are lower and the level of global visibility that coaches working in Africa might accrue and use to pursue a coaching career abroad is minimal. On the other, if African players have not obtained their licences in Europe (or under the Asian or South American associations' regulations), coaching opportunities abroad are rather restricted because CAF coaching licences are much less recognised – they do not qualify the holders for positions in European football or other attractive destinations in the global industry (Mezahi, 2020). For these reasons, coaching in Africa is often considered as a subordinate post-playing-career choice and remains a precarious endeavour for most returnees (see Ungruhe and Agergaard, 2020a).

An alternative to a coaching career that enables retired players to remain in the game involves them forming their own clubs or academies upon return. The Ghanaian Abedi Pelé, who founded Nania FC (see Chapter 3), and the Malian Salif Keita, who established the Jeunesse Sportive Centre, are among the most prominent examples. Running their own clubs or academies as business ventures provides opportunities for a wider and potentially more profitable occupation than coaching or scouting. As discussed in Chapter 3, former players usually establish and operate clubs and academies with the intention of identifying, developing and exporting local talent to clubs overseas and, in the process, continuing to earn a livelihood from football. As such, they act as critical coordinators in the game, creating a node at the African end of football's GPN that further reproduces the cycle of local talents' aspirations, possible transfers and careers abroad (Acheampong, Bouhaouala and Raspaud, 2019; Darby, 2013b; Darby, Akindes and Kirwin, 2007).

Beyond those academies that are export-oriented and form part of the local football business in West Africa, some former players have invested in or established football academies with more philanthropic intentions. Some returning players do this because they want to be viewed as socially engaged public figures in their home countries and communities (Acheampong, 2019; Kyeremeh, 2020). In addition to Nii Lamptey and his Glow-Lamp Soccer Academy in southern Ghana (see Introduction), his fellow former Ghanaian international Peter, who embarked on a lucrative career in the Middle East after a short stay in Scandinavia, set up a more charity-inflected football academy when he returned home. Peter described his investment in this venture, located in a less-developed neighbourhood of Accra, in the following terms: 'I play football and I have to bring something up to the society. Our academy is for needy children who want to play football. And they don't have the help. It's an academy for the society, for the poor' (interview, 4 May 2016). While Peter stressed the purpose of the academy as a social facility, he also wanted to provide good facilities for talented young players to develop their abilities and, hence, improve the local game. For returning footballers, 'giving back to society' (Acheampong, 2019) in this way represents a means to combine the display of success abroad with a desire to meet social obligations to one's community or society. This transforms a former player's status as a migrant and professional footballer into longer-lasting social recognition in their home setting.

Between two worlds: transnational precarity and the impossibility of return

In contrast to those who return to their countries of origin, other former players are reluctant or feel unable to follow this path (Ungruhe and Agergaard, 2020a). Given the expectations and obligations surrounding their sojourns to football fields abroad, many fear the shame of returning empty-handed and the downward social mobility that this would elicit. This is evident in the experiences of Ibrahim, who went to Scandinavia as a young academy player and decided to remain abroad when his career came to an abrupt end. We begin this final section of the chapter by unpacking Ibrahim's trajectory before returning to that of Chi, who had been coaching the Northern All Stars in the Swedish sixth tier following a disappointing end to his playing career. Both vividly illuminate the implications of transnational precarity faced by former migrant African players when their careers come to an end.

During the course of his career, Ibrahim suffered several severe injuries that hampered his breakthrough as a footballer. At one point, after another of these setbacks, he thought that his career was 'totally finished. Without any education, I didn't go to school. I didn't have anything.' He feared that his contract would not be renewed and that his club would just send him 'back to Africa'. Rather than admit failure and return without any prospects,

Ibrahim chose to stay in Scandinavia and survived on state benefits for some time. While he was unable to return to playing, he managed to secure an apprenticeship as an assistant nurse, which guaranteed him a stable though relatively poor income. The fact that his salary when he was fully qualified would be modest, and not at the level he envisaged when he first came to Scandinavia to play football, made returning home problematic. In particular, he feared the overwhelming demand from family and friends. '[I]n Africa', he suggested, 'you need more, you know? The family around you, friends who will come for the help.' He went on to highlight the implications of the weighty and unrealistic expectations that he felt would be placed on him as someone who had played professional football in Europe: 'If you are not lucky the money run[s] out … [friends] don't understand that you're in Europe, that you cannot help them.' With the pressures of social obligations to give back to family, peers and his wider community, he expressed doubts about the possibility of a productive, fulfilling post-playing-career life at home, posing the rhetorical question, 'How are you going to live?' (interview, 6 November 2016).

Similar to the experiences of those who are unable to engineer a move abroad or attract interest from potential suitors in the football industry, returning home empty-handed or without the means to support family and peers at the end of a career in the professional game 'outside', constitutes a 'classical shame event' that can evoke lasting feelings of guilt and subordination (Fessler, 2004). Despite being able to enact spatial mobility through football, an inauspicious return and a slow loss of financial and cultural capital at home could eventually lead to a form of 'social death' (Vigh, 2006b; see also Chapter 5). Under such circumstances, many players, including Ibrahim, remain abroad partly in order to avoid the emotional stress, shame and loss of face that would inevitably come with not being able to meet familial and societal expectations and obligations at home (Kleist, 2017), but also so that they can retain some of the cultural cache and status that being in Europe, and ostensibly as a professional footballer, allows them to accumulate at home. Hence, for many, the 'vital conjuncture' (Johnson-Hanks, 2002) at the threshold between a playing career and future livelihood paths does not entail a real choice in terms of whether to stay abroad or return home.

While remaining abroad insulates players like Ibrahim from experiencing shame at home, societal expectations to meet social obligations to kin and friends continue and often contribute to financial struggles and a transnational form of precarity. Most people in Ibrahim's hometown believed that he was still an active professional player in Denmark even though he had retired. 'It's only me and the family that know I'm not playing the higher level', he said. 'My friends still ask me for money, you know, to help them with their family and their kids' school fees and all that.' Despite his own financial struggles, he continued to support them, albeit at a significantly reduced level than he had during his playing career. 'I only help with the important things', he explained, such as in the case of health issues within a friend's family or for educational reasons. Ibrahim also stopped buying consumer goods for friends and family back in Ghana. This resulted in some of his friendships cooling off. 'They think you don't want to help them', he explained, 'that you are happy [in Europe]'. The sting in this criticism for Ibrahim was the implication that he had become greedy and had forgotten where he came from (interview, 6 November 2016).

Ibrahim's experiences clearly illustrate that while reducing remittances and support for family and friends at home is necessary to limit the precarity that former players face as they try to support themselves and dependents living with them, this can negatively impact their social standing and relations in African settings. This does not elicit the same levels of intense shame felt by unsuccessful players who make the decision to return home after their playing days have ended, but it does reproduce financial difficulties for those who remain abroad. By meeting social obligations at least to some degree, former players are engaged in a form of transnational navigation designed to consolidate their local status as 'social givers' at home while at the same time minimising the financial precarities that this may impose on their lives abroad.

This discrepancy between one's image at home and one's actual abilities and livelihood abroad point to what Nieswand (2014) has conceptualised as 'status paradox'. This is a state characterised by simultaneously belonging to a higher social class in the home country and to a lower class in the destination country. While this is widespread among West African migrants more generally (Coe, 2020), it is plainly evident in the subjectivities and experiences of African migrant footballers, not least because of the popular, but erroneous, assumption that the global football industry facilitates excessive wealth and luxurious lifestyles for all those who participate in it (Darby and van der Meij, 2018). Linked to the concept of social infrastructure, migrant players' status paradox reveals the relational spatial dynamics in their quest for social mobility. While, in their transnational relations with home, they adopt roles as 'social givers' and help to consolidate the lives of those in their extended family as well as friends and peers, their post-playing-career lives abroad are characterised by continuous speculation and uncertainty about their future livelihoods. In the long run, the continuous practice of giving may indeed exacerbate the precarious life courses of former migrant footballers abroad. Hence, when what are for most African migrant players short-lived, transient and poorly paid playing careers come to an end, precarity becomes a transnational experience that links their economic challenges and uncertain future lives abroad with the persistence of social norms at home and the difficulties this creates for the prospect of returning to one's country of origin.

In light of these consequences of African migrant footballers' status paradox, Chi expressed his frustration in the following manner: 'Most of us … were living lies … when they [migrant footballers] go back to Africa they want to show off. They lie to these boys back there: "I live in a mansion", "I drive the biggest car", "My club gives me a billion, a billion dollars"'. He went on to argue that, 'They [people at home] start believing [it] like: "It's kind of easy over there. Even the worst player that goes over there comes back with a lot of money." But it's not like that. We built that lie … and it became a stigma'. The outcome of this stigma, as Chi articulated it, was that it would create a 'whole lot of pressure' at home for returning football migrants (interviews, 1 October and 10 November 2016). As a consequence, Chi was not prepared to contemplate moving back home empty-handed and risking his social status there, no matter how precarious his life in Europe had become.

Conclusions

Matchday twenty of the 2016 season in the local sixth-tier division in east central Sweden: the Northern All Stars made it. It was a closer run thing than expected, but a 4-2 away win against the bottom-placed team in the league secured the title and promotion to the fifth tier of the Swedish game for the 2017 season. The players celebrated on the pitch with their supporters, friends and families, relieved to have made a modest step towards their goal of reaching the Swedish Allsvenskan. In the seasons that followed, the team achieved a further promotion, but with the increase in playing standards in the higher divisions, they had a long way to go to achieve their ambitions. The same could be said of Chi. At the time of writing, he was still involved in coaching the team and had earned some additional coaching qualifications. He had also begun a role as an assistant coach for a local women's team who play in the Swedish third tier. His hopes of becoming a professional coach and finally achieving upward and lasting social mobility through football have not diminished. However, his ambitions are yet to be realised and, as with his playing career, his prospects remain highly uncertain.

Uncertainty is what characterises most African former football migrants' lives. Success and failure, setbacks and new hopes contribute to a complex and dynamic challenge to produce a decent, sustainable livelihood during and after a professional football career. In this way, the vignette that opened and closed this chapter, recounting the Northern All Stars' struggles on the final two matchdays of the 2016 season, can be read as a metaphor for a player's journey in the professional football industry. This journey starts with optimism and hope and involves navigating fears of failure and overcoming varied obstacles. It frequently results in what are at best modest accomplishments and offers much in the way of uncertainty as initial ambitions are chased, recalibrated and often left unfulfilled. Hence, while the end of African footballers' playing careers seemingly form the concluding stage in their migratory trajectories, their journeys and struggles continue, and as with their efforts to enact and reproduce mobility through football, they remain rooted in complex transnational dynamics.

Caught between the structural constraints of the football business and their own and others' at times unrealistic expectations about the promise of a professional career abroad, African football migrants often experience post-playing transitions and life courses as precarious processes and enduring, uncertain journeys. Yet neither conditions of precarity nor upward social mobility achieved through football are fixed determinants of (former) players' life courses. Indeed, the post-playing-career life course that Nii Lamptey embarked on, defined by a commitment to be socially responsible and 'give back' (see Introduction and Acheampong, 2019), which secured him considerable respect in Ghanaian society, may represent an example and offer hope to the numerous active and former African migrant players who struggle with their journeys in and out of the global football industry.

Conclusion

As Paul's taxi pulled out of the gates of Nii Lamptey's house to take him to Kotoko International Airport and his flight home at the end of a month of fieldwork, he felt a mixture of exhilaration, gratitude and some sadness that what was an enlightening and productive period of research had come to an end. The trip had begun well. The morning after his late-night arrival, he walked from his hotel to the official press centre for the 2008 Africa Cup of Nations, located in Accra's International Conference Centre, a stone's throw from the Ohene Djan Sport Stadium, named after Ghana's first Director of Sports. The press centre had been chaotic the day before. A power outage had caused the accreditation system to crash and irate journalists, eager to have their press passes in hand, harangued beleaguered staff who could do little to process their electronically pre-submitted applications. When Paul entered the same cavernous hall a day later, the scene could not have been more serene; power and a sense of order had been restored. With the help of Tunde Adelakun, a UK-based Nigerian journalist and editor of *New African Soccer Magazine*, Paul left the building fifteen minutes later with press credentials hanging from a lanyard around his neck. The 'ALL VENUES' access that press accreditation granted would prove to be invaluable for networking, building relationships and recruiting participants willing to share their insights into African football migration. Indeed, it was during a press event for the Cameroon national team at the Accra Novotel that Paul first met Nii Lamptey.

Attending tournament matches and escaping the rather stultifying and staid surrounds of the official press areas to mix with supporters in the stadium and its immediate environs also facilitated serendipitous exchanges and conversations that led to access to the amateur youth level of the game in Ghana and to informal academies. Over the ensuing weeks players both young and retired, coaches, academy owners and directors, FIFA licensed agents and other actors who operated or had a stake in the various nodes of the Ghanaian end of football's GPN generously shared their perspectives and insights. Nii Lamptey's name had come up in conversations on a number of occasions, and after reading newspaper stories about his career and his post-playing life, Paul, and subsequently Christian, sought out opportunities to speak with him. They were both convinced that this would be invaluable in better understanding the aspirations, experiences and trajectories of African football migrants. And so it transpired. The interviews with Lamptey, during which he laid bare the high and low points of his whole career from aspiring youth player to benevolent and socially conscious retired player, did not disappoint. When Paul's meeting with Lamptey ended, he was left with a series of research leads and questions to follow up, but unfortunately the demands of professional and personal life temporarily suspended pursuing these. Nonetheless, the meeting seemed a perfect way to bookend the first of what became a series of fieldwork visits to Ghana over the course of the next decade and that ultimately led to the collective effort of writing this book.

In the Introduction, we chronicled Lamptey's biography and set out how it offered insights into the themes and issues we have explored across these pages. His career experiences are to varying degrees symptomatic of those of many other African footballers in the global football industry. Often though, Africa's tremendous contribution to the global game is reduced to the impact of iconic players. Pioneering figures such as Arthur Wharton and Albert Johanneson, world-class players such as George Weah, Michael Essien and Didier Drogba who graced the game more recently, as well as contemporary global icons such as Mo Salah and Sadio Mané have undoubtedly contributed immeasurably to football's international appeal and cultural status. However, the lives and careers of these well-known players, often represented in the media via a meteoric 'rags-to-riches' narrative, provide only a glimpse into what African football migration entails and how it has impacted the global game.

The global football industry is deeply shaped by the many lesser-known or less successful African players whose careers take circuitous, unconventional paths. They leave their mark in quieter, more modest ways in leagues beneath the top level of the game and without garnering international acclaim nor featuring regularly in the sports headlines of the many countries where they play. Even those who aspire and work towards landing a contract with a professional club in Europe, Asia or elsewhere but without success, also leave indelible traces on the global football industry and how it operates. But these players are also acted upon by this industry, fuelling their migration projects and tying them into multiple dependencies and subordinate positions of power that deeply influence their trajectories. Even if an African player meets all the sporting prerequisites to pursue a successful career in European football, outstanding talent, the desired physical attributes and a track record of high-level performances do not necessarily translate into success.

The arc of Nii Lamptey's and many other African players' career courses vividly illustrates how aspiration and exceptional talent cannot shield a player from a precarious and non-linear career trajectory. Hence, when Lamptey reflects, 'the way I started, maybe I should have ended [up] playing for Arsenal or Real Madrid [but] it did not happen that way' (interview, 17 February 2010), he speaks for thousands of gifted African players who come to Europe or South-East Asia with high hopes and great expectations that are ultimately unfulfilled. As we have shown in this text, for the vast majority who pursue football migration and an imagined but quixotic future as a player in the rarefied echelons of the elite professional game, the outcome is frustrating, crushing immobility or brief, stunted transnational careers at the margins of the industry. At their journey's end, transnational or not, a fresh cycle of young, talented, ambitious footballers emerges and insert themselves into various nodes of football's GPN with the same hopes and dreams of 'making it' as their predecessors.

This book was never intended as an accompaniment to the numerous media reports that illustrate the extraordinary success stories of African football celebrities. It also was not meant to be another contribution to oft-used, and overly simplified, depictions of African mediocrity. Nor did it seek to perpetuate the narrative of African football and footballers as passive victims of unequal power relations within the global football industry. Rather, the book was concerned with uncovering how and why African players aspire to and enact transnational mobility through football and interrogating their accomplishments as well as the dependencies, hardships and disappointments they face along the way. We aimed to do so by examining how African football migration is locally rooted, facilitated, driven and experienced, and through exploring the consequences of these processes and experiences for African players and global football alike. This enabled us to generate fresh perspectives on how football migration structures, projects and processes work on a daily basis and evolve over time.

The ambitious research questions at the centre of this book, set out in the Introduction, allowed us to comprehensively unpack the complexity of African football migration at a range of temporal stages. The GPN model, outlined in Chapter 1, provided a useful framework to map the structural, macro-level features of African football migration and how African players have become embedded in the global football industry. In Chapter 2 we used this model to tease out how this process has evolved historically, how it is geographically patterned internationally and what regulatory structures and processes facilitate and inhibit it. Our historical overview of African football migration illustrated that African players have been migrating across national borders to play in foreign fields around the world for over a century. This is significant because it qualified popular perceptions that the presence of African players in foreign leagues is a modern phenomenon. It also revealed that Africans, and more specifically those from West Africa, constitute one of the primary sources of football labour in the European football industry and are becoming increasingly numerous in the South-East Asian game. In mapping out its spatial dimensions, we illustrated that the mobility of African players has been characterised by complex shifting geographical patterns. Flows of players between colonies, especially in West and North Africa, and clubs in the metropole, were found to have predominated during the colonial era. Post-colonial patterns of player migration, especially since 2000, have, however, become much more diffuse and diverse. This chapter also showed how players' career trajectories are enabled and constrained by a fluctuating and multi-faceted regulatory environment governing international migration both within football and more generally.

The intensification and lengthening of the outflow of African talent reflects expanding opportunities associated with the wider globalisation of the game and its professionalisation in what might be considered peripheral football regions. However, it is also a consequence of a transformation of the African game from a community resource and a vehicle for local and national pride to one that has increasingly become oriented around producing talent for the export market. In Chapter 3 we added the meso-level to our structural overview of the GPN that African players enter and navigate in their pursuit of transnational mobility and a professional football career abroad. We did so by setting out the key nodes of the African football export industry. Notably, the chapter detailed the increasingly prominent role of football academies in the production and export of players and our analyses uncovered the varied approaches and rationales that underpin these critical institutions.

While chapters 2 and 3 emphasised the macro- and meso-level in African football, the remaining chapters examined the articulations between these and the micro-level in order to better understand the lived experiences of African football players over their whole career course. Chapters 4 to 6 focused on how local nodes of football's GPN are negotiated and experienced by young Ghanaian footballers. Chapter 4 situated these processes socio-temporally by conveying how continuity and change associated with Ghanaian football migration interacts with the social realignments, economic liberalisation and globalising dynamics of contemporary West Africa. Utilising theorisations of 'social infrastructure' (McFarlane and Sliver, 2017; Simone, 2004) in this and subsequent chapters, we showed that football migration in Ghana emerges from and through the practices of a multitude of actors, institutions and networks that often have a vested interest in the movement of players within Ghana and 'outside'.

Chapter 5 explained how African youth rationalise their entry into the game and their aspirations for spatial mobility through football. In revealing the economic and cultural drivers that influence their decisions to pursue football as a professional career and a potential source of transnational migration, we showed how the subjectivities and dispositions of aspirant footballers are best understood when contextualised within a wider culture of migration, conceptualised as 'Mobile Africa' (de Bruijn, van Dijk and Foeken, 2001; Ungruhe, 2016). Our discussion also illustrated how the decision to enter the football industry constitutes a neoliberal-inspired form of biographical planning to 'become a somebody' (see Langevang, 2008) and attain respectable male adulthood, referred to locally as living the X-Way. Key to realising this aspiration is adopting the form of an 'entrepreneur of self' (Foucault, 2008). Finally, we demonstrated how the development of such perspectives on football by Ghanaian youth and members of their family leads to players' football migration projects becoming a household livelihood strategy and a way to fulfil intergenerational obligations to family and meet wider expectations around social giving.

In Chapter 6 we illuminated young Ghanaian players' encounters in and experiences of local youth and academy nodes of football's GPN. Our use of a 'social navigation' (Vigh, 2009) approach allowed us to outline the tactics and strategies deployed by youth as they attempt to make their way through a competitive and uncertain footballing landscape. 'Trying your luck' was introduced as a way to theorise these attempts. Unlike other areas of Ghanaian life, 'trying your luck' by migrating through football is not reliant upon money alone. Instead, it is perceived as being dependent upon maximising one's bodily capital, in keeping with acting as a resourceful 'entrepreneur of self' and utilising the spiritual realm. As this chapter argued, enacting football-related migration, preferably to Europe, constitutes the most sought-after outcome of the considerable bodily, emotional and financial investments that young African football players make in their journey through youth football or academies. However, it is also an outcome that is difficult to secure. Despite their hopes and expectations around transnational migration, the reality for the vast majority of players is 'involuntary immobility' (Carling, 2002). We explored this unwanted but normative outcome of African players' pursuit of transnational football migration and detailed how they encounter, respond to and seek to overcome it. These experiences were positioned within the context of the intergenerational contract and familial expectations around reciprocity. This allowed us to foreground the overlooked role that 'shame' plays in understanding how players come to terms with and navigate their way through this 'vital conjuncture' in their lives (Johnson-Hanks, 2002).

Exploring why and how African youth rationalise their entry into the game and their aspirations for spatial mobility through football enabled us to extend debates beyond the field of sports studies. One overarching and significant way in which we did so relates to our engagement with two, often interlinked discourses allied with studies of 'African migration' and 'African youth'. More specifically, both fields are dominated by a discursive emphasis on crisis, which fuels the image of Africa as a continent of failure and inferiority. Discourses around African migration internationally often revolve around attributions of scarcity, poverty, hardship and hopelessness (Beauchemin, 2018; Flahaux and de Haas, 2016). Meanwhile, since the last two decades of the twentieth century, if not before, young people in African settings have been categorised as a troubled population living with and in deficit. This labelling has been applied to particular groups including working children, street children and youth, and victims of child trafficking, as well as to a whole generation of socially immobile youth. This labelling creates an image of enduring social, political and economic exclusion, which is manifested in popular conceptualisations of 'being stuck' (Sommers, 2011), 'persistent marginalization' (Resnick and Thurlow, 2015) and probably most prominently in the (mis)application of Honwana's (2014) conceptualisation of 'waithood'. This strand of work implicitly acknowledges the enduring and durable observation of Africa's 'lost generation' (Cruise O'Brien, 1996). The reproduction of this narrative in public and academic discourses has led to what we call an 'African crisism', the inclination to think of Africa through a prism of crisis.

As outlined in Chapter 1, some academic studies have called for a more nuanced picture of African migration and the experiences of youth in African contexts in order to illustrate how young people aspire to and creatively navigate challenging social, political and economic environments through spatial mobility (Christiansen, Utas and Vigh, 2006; Honwana and De Boeck, 2005; Langevang, 2008; Martin, Ungruhe and Häberlein, 2016; Thieme, 2018). It is at this nexus between the aspiration to be spatially mobile and the realisation of international mobility that this book makes a key contribution. We demonstrated that when young male African talents hold on to football as the ticket to secure livelihoods and respectable social adulthood, despite the exceptionally limited chance of realisation, it is not an expression of naivety or despair. Rather, their subjectivities and attendant forms of agency such as 'trying your luck' are the embodiment of the notion of 'Mobile Africa' (de Bruijn, van Dijk and Foeken, 2001). Furthermore, the embedded culture of migration in their home societies is increasingly constitutive of a need to strive resourcefully to 'become a somebody' in environments where neoliberal capitalism has made this difficult to actualise.

Holding on to the hope of migration through football therefore gives meaning to young men's struggles, and as this sense of hope circulates more widely and intensively among male youth in African settings it powerfully reaffirms the belief that a career in professional football is possible. In this way, hopes of 'becoming a somebody' through migration are socially negotiated and continuously reproduced. Hence, far from romanticising their migration projects as heroic struggles, our account of the experiences of aspirant and actual migrant footballers offers a conceptual corrective to the tendency to view young people in African settings via a lens of 'African crisism'. Instead, we have underlined the productive quality of young people's transnational lives and trajectories, be they imagined or achieved.

The final three chapters analysed African footballers' mobilities into, and out of, the football industry in Europe and South-East Asia. In Chapter 7, through 'thick' ethnographic descriptions we detailed the initial cross-border journeys of a number of African players, the nature of their experiences and trajectories and how they navigate these. We focused on the varied ways that mobility to European football transpires before examining the first steps of African players into South-East Asia. Our analyses revealed how these transnational moves are facilitated and hindered by clubs, intermediaries and talent speculators, family members, social relations with other Africans abroad and, critically, by the levels of resilience and self-belief that players themselves can muster. Our accounts here also illustrated that while players' pathways are multifarious, rarely linear and often involve a state of liminality, uncertainty and precarity, their efforts in attempting to consolidate their position in the football industry are replete with agency and, in particular, 'judicious opportunism' (Johnson-Hanks, 2005).

In concentrating on those African players who have been able to produce and reproduce transnational mobility to leagues in Europe and South-East Asia, Chapter 8 uncovered novel insights on how the dream of playing abroad matches up with the reality of being a professional 'outside'. We showed that the actual, rather than the envisaged, experience is fraught with difficulties. Adjusting to and being accepted in new locales that are perceived as culturally, socially and climatically different from those from which migrant players departed bring a range of challenges. Of particular significance here is the fact that African migrant players' professional and personal lives, particularly in Europe, are frequently tainted by racialisation and racism. In outlining how they respond to this, we showed how they engage in processes of 'self-charismatisation'. This involves migrant players' requirement to acknowledge racial stereotypes about African bodily skills and abilities and use them to meet local expectations about what they should bring to the field. While this may aid their adjustment to and acceptance within the European game, we argued that it nevertheless reproduces stereotypical depictions of African inferiority. By picking up again with some of the players we introduced in the previous chapter and detailing their onward trajectories within European and South-East Asian football, our empirical material offered original insights not only into how they act in these settings and under these circumstances but also how they are acted upon within the 'social infrastructure' of the football industry.

The final chapter elucidated how African migrant players' careers come to an end, and how they plan for and manage this eventuality and respond to the struggles that it brings. One of the most significant issues that all professional athletes face is what to do when they retire from sport or when their career is brought to a premature end. For African migrant footballers, this problem, and how it is negotiated, is complex. Many of these players experience precarious careers and this often leads to precarity when these careers come to an end. The absence of educational or vocational qualifications and the dearth of dual-career support, common among African football migrants, seriously limits their post-playing-career options and ability to secure a sustainable livelihood. The anxieties that this creates are compounded by concerns that uncertain, financially challenged futures will diminish the hard-fought social status that they have been able to accrue by enacting transnational mobility and playing football professionally, even at levels of the game that are far from elite.

Those who have been prudent during their career and who have the financial means often deal with and embark on their post-playing-career futures by continuing to act transnationally and in ways that enable them to reproduce their social standing. As is clear from Chapter 9, investing in businesses and, particularly, real estate in origin contexts during their playing careers and afterwards is a key way in which they attend to their future needs. But at the same time, these transnational acts also enable them to meet local, culturally embedded expectations around social giving and providing for kin, friends and the wider community. In so doing, social status is maintained or potentially elevated, leading to a consolidated position. The significance of social giving for a migrant player's social standing at home is reflected in the fact that those who experience precarious livelihoods abroad after their retirement from playing nevertheless engage in transnational giving activities to try to convey the image of a successful migrant. All of these dynamics play out in former migrant players' decisions about whether to remain abroad or return to their country of origin to pursue their futures, and it is clear from this chapter that this is far from an uncomplicated choice.

In summarising how this book extends knowledge and understanding of African football migration and the lifeworlds of African migrant footballers and those who aspire to but are unable to produce transnational mobility through football, we would point to five key advancements. Firstly, our findings set out a comprehensive interdisciplinary picture that incorporates the intersecting macro-, meso- and micro-level currents that contour and influence the migratory imaginaries and projects of African football players. Secondly, and informed by our long-term, ongoing relationships and engagement with African players and other actors in African football migration, we have situated their perspectives, subjectivities and experiences at the centre of our analysis. In doing so, we have detailed the spatiality of their experiences as they negotiate a diverse array of transnational, cultural and institutional settings in pursuit of their professional, personal and familial ambitions.

The third key contribution relates to the long-term, temporal perspective we offer through this book. This exposed the whole career course of African players from the point they come to understand the game as a route to accomplishing myriad intersecting economic, social, cultural and sporting ambitions, through to their entry into professional football markets abroad, their exit from these and, finally, their post-playing-career trajectories. It also shed light on the junctures where careers deviate from their planned path and where doors to deeply desired career opportunities and progression are slammed shut, resulting in immobility, a return home or an enduring, liminal existence for African players in the interstices of football industries and societies overseas. By applying a long-term perspective and following football talents over their life courses, this book articulated the conceptual benefits of a holistic approach to young people's mobilities. This approach highlights migration as part of young people's biographical projects of being and becoming, in which they act and are acted upon, and in which 'vital conjunctures' open new horizons or entail closures that are subject to intra- and intergenerational negotiations.

Our fourth contribution is that by showing ethnographically how the historical, political, economic and social dynamics of African contexts connect with and shape the experiences of players in destination settings, we uncovered the multiple transnational dimensions in players' imaginaries and professional and personal life courses. Finally, as indicated in the previous passages, this book highlighted the intellectual benefits of examining African football migration, and sport migration more generally, in an interdisciplinary manner. Here, the conceptual and methodological approaches from different disciplines were not disaggregated and applied to understand particular moments in the player's life course or stages of the migratory process. Instead, we integrated and embedded them throughout our analysis to produce a book that rigorously and cogently expounds the imagined, unprocured and enacted spatial mobility of African football players. This allowed the multifarious meanings young African people attach to transnational migration, and the complex implications of their (im)mobilities for their personal and professional life trajectories, to be explicated in novel ways.

In setting out how this book extends the knowledge base on African football migration, we are not claiming to have produced the final word. There is clearly still much to be done in fully elucidating the transnational (im)mobilities of African football players. As we noted in the preface, more work is needed on the aspirations, experiences and transnational trajectories of African women footballers. The small, but important body of scholarship on these issues (see Chapter 1) has highlighted similarities and differences between men's and women's ambitions in and encounters with professional football abroad. However, it has also revealed the importance of accounting for and understanding the gendered particularities of African football migration. While overseas transfers of female players from Africa are far from comparable to those of men, there is every possibility that the increasing growth, investment and media coverage associated with the professional women's game in Europe will continue to widen opportunities. This, combined with the transnational careers and visibility of icons of the African women's game, such as the South African Thembi Kgatlana, Gaëlle Enganamouit from Cameroon and, particularly, the Nigerian women's team captain, Barcelona star and four-time African Women's Player of the Year Asisat Oshoala, will likely fuel migratory aspirations among the growing number of female youth in Africa playing football. Analyses of how these aspirations unfold, whether they translate into spatial mobility or lead to involuntary immobility, and the experiences of and meanings attached to these outcomes, represents a critical research agenda moving forward.

There are other empirical blind spots on African football migration that require investigation and that, if pursued, will ensure the field neither stagnates nor becomes narrowly focused. For example, there is considerable scope for the geographical coverage of the research to expand. We already know much about how migration is embedded within football industries and cultures in West Africa, particularly Ghana, but much less about how it is understood and pursued elsewhere on the continent. In keeping with one of the primary concerns of this book, we would encourage scholarship that seeks to localise African football migration by explicating its meaning in the varied cultural contexts in which it is enacted or constrained. We have seen the emergence of research exploring the flows and experiences of players to South-East Asia, including in this book. However, there is a need to interrogate further how African players move to and experience the growing number of leagues around the world that have come to be seen as viable entry routes to more lucrative nodes in the professional football industry or temporary destinations in a process of step-migration.

The impact of changes in migration regulations both within and beyond football, not least those imposed by Brexit and FIFA's ongoing reforms of its rules governing international transfers, need to be unpacked in future research on players' career trajectories. While we devoted a full chapter to the post-playing-career lives of migrant players, much more work is required to understand the long-term social, cultural and economic implications of a career in the professional game abroad. In particular, former African migrant players' ambitions to coach professionally in the overseas destinations in which they played and the ways in which their access to this profession is constrained by race are important issues to consider moving forward. As we illustrated in Chapter 9, a small number of former African players are making inroads into this profession, but research is needed to examine their coaching journeys and how their ongoing trajectories might challenge the racial stereotypes that continue to limit opportunities for African and other Black coaches.

The intersections between migration and development should also feature prominently in future work, as should a concern for whether the rights of African children, as enumerated in the United Nations Convention on the Rights of the Child, are promoted or impinged upon in their encounters with the global football industry. Finally, no future-oriented research agenda on African footballers' (im)mobilities, and on both migration and sport migration more generally, would be complete without examining the impact of the global COVID-19 pandemic with its attendant lockdowns, restrictions on international travel and challenges to the economic sustainability of professional sports teams and leagues.

In pursuing these new directions, we encourage scholars to be open to concepts and ideas beyond their own disciplinary proclivities. Interdisciplinarity has enabled rich insights in this book and we are convinced that it can be the bedrock of novel, rigorous theorisation in the future that enhances our understanding of African football migration and at the same time illuminates wider processes of youthhood, agency, migration, transnationalism and development in Africa. In pursuing an interdisciplinary research agenda, we also advocate a systematic, longitudinal, multi-sited methodological approach that meaningfully engages with those African youth, both male and female, who aspire to and produce transnational migration through football. The prospect of living with COVID-19 into the future and the possibility of periods where our own mobilities as researchers might be constrained need not curtail such an approach. Researchers, and for that matter aspiring African migrant players, will need to become more technologically savvy in how they navigate their respective fields. Online, digital methodologies have long offered a useful way of unpacking complex social and cultural issues (Pink *et al.*, 2015). Their increasing use in migration studies (Leurs and Prabhakar, 2018), and as a method for uncovering the dynamics of sport migration and 'understanding the experiences of those "in hard to reach" places and those "on the move"' (Thorpe and Wheaton, 2021: 2), points to potentially productive methodological routes for studying African football migration. Irrespective of the methods employed, it is critical in our view that the experiences, perspectives and voices of African football migrants, aspiring and actual, are foregrounded and privileged in the same way that they have been in this book.

Bibliography

Abe, T. (2018), 'African football players in Cambodia', in S. Cornelissen and Y. Mine (eds), *Migration and Agency in a Globalizing World* (London: Palgrave Macmillan), pp. 231–45

Acheampong, E. Y. (2019), 'Giving back to society: evidence from African sports migrants', *Sport in Society*, 22:12, 2045–64

——— (2020), 'The journey of professional football career: challenges and reflections', *Journal of Sport and Social Issues*, online first, 1–18, https://doi.org/10.1177/0193723520958341

Acheampong, E. Y., M. Bouhaouala, and M. Raspaud (2019), *African Footballers in Europe: Migration, Community, and Give Back Behaviours* (London and New York: Routledge)

Acheampong, E. Y., and B. Malek (2019), 'African footballers' life cycles according to the analysis of transfer value along their career path: a case study of Ghanaian players', *Sport in Society*, 22:12, 2024–44

Adam, C., and A. Devillard (2008), 'Comparative study of the laws in the 27 EU member states for legal immigration including an assessment of the conditions and formalities imposed by each member state for newcomers', *European Parliament Think Tank*, www.europarl.europa.eu/thinktank/en/document.html?reference=IPOL-LIBE_ET(2008)393281 [accessed 13 February 2021]

Adams, S. (2018), 'Odartey Lamptey: former soccer star grinding the next soccer stars', GhanaWeb, 24 August, www.ghanaweb.com/GhanaHomePage/SportsArchive/Odartey-Lamptey-Former-soccer-star-grinding-the-next-soccer-stars-679222 [accessed 13 February 2021]

Adamu, M. (2020), '"Death" of colts football; Hearts and Olympics' sufferings', *Footy Ghana*, https://footy-ghana.com/2020/06/death-of-colts-football-hearts-and-olympics-sufferings/ [accessed 11 July 2020]

Adepoju, A. (1998), 'Linkages between internal and international migration: the African situation', *International Social Science Journal*, 23, 145–55

——— (2006), 'Leading issues in international migration in sub-Saharan Africa', in D. Gelderblom, N. Roux, and J. Mafukidze (eds), *Views on Migration in Sub-Saharan Africa: Proceedings of an African Migration Alliance Workshop* (Cape Town: HSRC press), pp. 25–47

Adinkrah, M. (2012), 'Better dead than dishonored: masculinity and male suicidal behavior in contemporary Ghana', *Social Science & Medicine*, 74:4, 474–81

Agergaard, S. (2016), 'When globalisation and migration meet national and local talent development', in U. Wagner, R. K. Storm and K. Nielsen (eds), *When Sport Meets Business: Capabilities, Challenges, Critiques* (London: Sage), pp. 30–42

―――― (2018), *Rethinking Sports and Integration: Developing a Transnational Perspective on Migrants and Descendants in Sports* (London and New York: Routledge)
Agergaard, S., and V. Botelho (2014), 'The way out? African players' migration to Scandinavian women's football', *Sport in Society*, 17:4, 523–36
Agergaard, S., and T. V. Ryba (2014), 'Migration and career transitions in professional sports: transnational athletic careers in a psychological and sociological perspective', *Sociology of Sport Journal*, 31:2, 228–47
Agergaard, S., and N. C. Tiesler (2014), *Women, Soccer and Transnational Migration* (London and New York: Routledge)
Agergaard, S., and C. Ungruhe (2016), 'Ambivalent precarity: career trajectories and temporalities in highly skilled sports labor migration from West Africa to Northern Europe', *Anthropology of Work Review*, 37:2, 67–78
Ahmed, M. (2020), 'Coronavirus threatens €10bn hit to football transfer market', *Financial Times*, www.ft.com/content/067a3eeb-e915-48af-8384-94fdc495cf59 [accessed 18 February 2021]
Akindes, G. A. (2010), 'Transnational Television and Football in Francophone Africa: The Path to Electronic Colonization?' (doctoral thesis, Ohio University), https://etd.ohiolink.edu/apexprod/rws_etd/send_file/send?accession=ohiou1273678991&disposition=inline [accessed 27 April 2021]
―――― (2013), 'South Asia and South-East Asia: new paths of African footballer migration', *Soccer & Society*, 14:5, 684–701
Akpan, U. (2020), 'Elite local leagues and transnational broadcast of European football', in C. Onwumechili (ed.), *Africa's Elite Football: Structure, Politics, and Everyday Challenges* (London and New York: Routledge), pp. 34–44
Akyeampong, E. (2018), 'African socialism; or, the search for an indigenous model of economic development?', *Economic History of Developing Regions*, 33:1, 69–87
Alacovska, A., T. Langevang, and R. Steedman (2020), 'The work of hope: spiritualizing, hustling and waiting in the creative industries in Ghana', *Environment and Planning A: Economy and Space*, online first, 1–19, http://dx.doi.org/10.1177/0308518X20962810
Albertini, R. von, and A. Wirz (1982), *European Colonial Rule, 1880–1940: The Impact of the West on India, Southeast Asia, and Africa* (Oxford: Clio Press)
Alegi, P. (2002), 'Playing to the gallery: sport, cultural performance, and social identity in South Africa, 1920s–1945', *International Journal of African Historical Studies*, 35:1, 17–38
―――― (2010), *African Soccerscapes: How a Continent Changed the World's Game* (Athens, OH: Ohio University Press)
Amankwaa, E. F., J. Esson, and K. V. Gough (2020), 'Geographies of youth, mobile phones and the urban hustle', *Geographical Journal*, 186:4, 362–74
Amelia (2020), 'A series of Thai players to be sacked because of the COVID-19 epidemic', *Sports 442*, https://sports442.com/en/308-a-series-of-thai-players-to-be-sacked-because-of-the-covid-19-epidemic-d197569.html [accessed 14 February 2021]
Amusa, L., and A. Toriola (2010), 'The changing phases of physical education and sport in Africa: can a uniquely African model emerge?', *African Journal for Physical Health Education, Recreation and Dance*, 16:4, 666–80
Andersson, R. (2014), *Illegality, Inc.: Clandestine Migration and the Business of Bordering Europe* (Oakland: University of California Press)

Andrews, D. L., V. B. Lopes, and S. J. Jackson (2015), 'Neymar: sport celebrity and performative cultural politics', in P. D. Marshall and S. Redmond (eds), *A Companion to Celebrity* (Hoboken: John Wiley & Sons, Inc.), pp. 421–39

Angeli, T. (2010), '"Die meisten verschwinden irgendwann von der Bildfläche" (Interview with Raffaele Poli)', *Beobachter*, 11, 22–23

Ansell, N., F. Hajdu, L. van Blerk, and E. Robson (2018), '"My happiest time" or "my saddest time"? The spatial and generational construction of marriage among youth in rural Malawi and Lesotho', *Transactions of the Institute of British Geographers*, 43:2, 184–99

Appadurai, A. (1994), 'Commodities and the politics of value', in S. Pearce (ed.), *Interpreting Objects and Collections* (London and New York: Routledge), pp. 76–91

Arango, J. (2004), 'Theories of international migration', in D. Joly (ed.), *International Migration and the New Millennium* (Aldershot: Ashgate), pp. 15–36

Armstrong, G. (2004a), 'The migration of the black panther: an interview with Eusébio of Mozambique and Portugal', in G. Armstrong and R. Giulianotti (eds), *Football in Africa: Conflict, Conciliation and Community* (Basingstoke: Palgrave Macmillan), pp. 247–63

―――― (2004b), 'The lords of misrule: football and the rights of the child in Liberia, West Africa', *Sport in Society*, 7:3, 473–502

Asmussen, E. (2019), 'Lange BVB, jetzt Schalke: Er hilft den S04-Stars bei der Integration', *Reviersport*, https://reviersport.de/artikel/lange-bvb-jetzt-schalke-er-hilft-den-s04-stars-bei-der-integration/ [accessed 14 February 2021]

Ayamga, E. (2019), 'Inside the Liberty Academy: the talent factory that shaped Ghana's finest talents', *These Football Times*, https://thesefootballtimes.co/2019/09/05/inside-the-liberty-academy-the-talent-factory-that-shaped-ghanas-finest-talents/ [accessed 20 February 2021]

Back, L., T. Crabbe, and J. Solomos (2001), *The Changing Face of Football: Racism, Identity and Multiculture in the English Game* (Oxford: Berg)

Bair, J. (2008), 'Analysing global economic organization: embedded networks and global chains compared', *Economy and Society*, 37:3, 339–64

Bakewell, O. (2010), 'Some reflections on structure and agency in migration theory', *Journal of Ethnic and Migration Studies*, 36:10, 1689–708

Bale, J. (2004), 'Three geographies of African footballer migration: patterns, problems and postcoloniality', in G. Armstrong and R. Giulianotti (eds), *Football in Africa: Conflict, Conciliation and Community* (Basingstoke: Palgrave Macmillan), pp. 229–46

Bale, J., and J. Sang (1996), *Kenyan Running: Movement Culture, Geography, and Global Change* (London: Frank Cass and Co.)

Baller, S. (2014), 'Urban football performances: playing for the neighbourhood in Senegal, 1950s–2000s', *Africa: Journal of the International African Institute*, 84:1, 17–35

Barimah, N. Y. (2017), '"Reintroduce Academicals football team"', *Graphic Online*, www.graphic.com.gh/sports/football/reintroduce-academicals-football-team.html [accessed 13 February 2021]

Barreaud, M. (1998), *Dictionnaire Des Footballeurs Étrangers Du Championnat Professionnel Français: 1932-1997* (Paris: Editions L'Harmattan)

Bayart, J.-F., S. Ellis, and B. Hibou (1999), *The Criminalization of the State in Africa* (Oxford: James Currey)

BBC News (2018), 'Ghana dissolves football association after cash gifts scandal', 8 June, www.bbc.com/news/world-africa-44406535 [accessed 18 February 2021]

BBC Sport (2017), 'Chinese Super League limits foreigners', 16 January, www.bbc.co.uk/sport/football/38636082 [accessed 20 February 2021]
—— (2019a), 'Man City avoid ban for transfer breach', 13 August, www.bbc.co.uk/sport/football/49337051 [accessed 19 February 2021]
—— (2019b), 'German sides withdraw objections over Gambia's Jatta', 4 September, www.bbc.co.uk/sport/football/49577693 [accessed 14 February 2021]
Beauchemin, C. (2018), 'Introduction', in C. Beauchemin (ed.), *Migration between Africa and Europe* (Cham: Springer), pp. 1–10
Beech, H. (2014), 'World Cup mystery: why is China so horrible at soccer?', *Time*, https://time.com/2869357/world-cup-mystery-why-is-china-is-so-horrible-at-soccer/ [accessed 20 February 2021]
Behrends, A. (2002), *Drahtseilakte. Frauen aus Nordghana zwischen Bildung, Beruf und gesellschaftlichen Konditionen* (Frankfurt/Main: Brandes und Apsel)
Berthoud, J. (2017), 'Devenir, être et avoir été un footballeur camerounais. Des arrêts de carrière en tension' (doctoral thesis, University of Lausanne), https://core.ac.uk/download/pdf/159143244.pdf [accessed 7 June 2018]
Berthoud, J., and R. Poli (2011), 'L'après-carrière des footballeurs professionnels en Afrique du Sud', *Staps*, 94, 25–38
Besnier, N. (2015), 'Sports mobilities across borders: postcolonial perspectives', *International Journal of the History of Sport*, 32:7, 849–61
Besnier, N., D. G. Calabrò, and D. Guinness (eds) (2020), *Sport, Migration, and Gender in the Neoliberal Age* (London and New York: Routledge)
Besnier, N., D. Guinness, M. P. Hann, and U. Kovač (2018), 'Rethinking masculinity in the neoliberal order: Cameroonian footballers, Fijian rugby players, and Senegalese wrestlers', *Comparative Studies in Society and History*, 60:4, 839–72
Bezuidenhout, A., and S. Buhlungu (2011), 'From compounded to fragmented labour: mineworkers and the demise of compounds in South Africa', *Antipode*, 43:2, 237–63
Black, D. R. (2010), 'The ambiguities of development: implications for "development through sport"', *Sport in Society*, 13:1, 121–9
Black, R., R. King, and R. Tiemoko (2003), 'Migration, return and small enterprise development in Ghana: a route out of poverty' (presented at the International Workshop on Migration and Poverty in West Africa, Citeseer), xiii, 1–22
Blakelock, D. J., M. A. Chen, and T. Prescott (2016), 'Psychological distress in elite adolescent soccer players following deselection', *Journal of Clinical Sport Psychology*, 10:1, 59–77
Blazek, M., and M. Windram-Geddes (2013), 'Editorial: thinking and doing children's emotional geographies', *Emotion, Space and Society*, 9:1, 1–3
Bleck, J., and A. Lodermeier (2020), 'Migration aspirations from a youth perspective: focus groups with returnees and youth in Mali', *Journal of Modern African Studies*, 58:4, 551–77
Bloomfield, S. (2011), *Africa United: How Football Explains Africa* (Edinburgh: Canongate Books)
Boer, W. (2006), 'Football, mobilization and protest: Nnamdi Azikiwe and the goodwill tours of World War II.', *Lagos Historical Review*, 6, 39–61
Bonnett, A. (2017), 'The enchanted path: magic and modernism in psychogeographical walking', *Transactions of the Institute of British Geographers*, 42:3, 472–84
Boswell, C. (2008), 'Combining economics and sociology in migration theory', *Journal of Ethnic and Migration Studies*, 34:4, 549–56

Botelho, V. L., and S. Agergaard (2011), 'Moving for the love of the game? International migration of female footballers into Scandinavian countries', *Soccer & Society*, 12:6, 806–19

Brackenridge, C. (2010), 'Children's rights in football: welfare and work' (presented at the Centers and Peripheries in Sport: International Conference on Sports, Malmö University, Sweden), https://core.ac.uk/download/pdf/336712.pdf [accessed 27 April 2021]

Bradbury, S. (2013), 'Institutional racism, whiteness and the under-representation of minorities in leadership positions in football in Europe', *Soccer & Society*, 14:3, 296–314

—— (2020), '"Fit for doing but not fit for organising": racism, stereotypes and networks in coaching in professional football in Europe', in S. Bradbury, J. Lusted, and J. van Sterkenburg (eds), *'Race', Ethnicity and Racism in Sports Coaching* (London and New York: Routledge), pp. 22–42

Bradbury, S., J. Lusted, and J. van Sterkenburg (eds) (2020), *'Race', Ethnicity and Racism in Sports Coaching* (London and New York: Routledge)

Bradbury, S., J. van Sterkenburg, and P. Mignon (2018), 'The under-representation and experiences of elite level minority coaches in professional football in England, France and the Netherlands', *International Review for the Sociology of Sport*, 53:3, 313–34

Brannagan, P. M., and R. Giulianotti (2015), 'Soft power and soft disempowerment: Qatar, global sport and football's 2022 World Cup finals', *Leisure Studies*, 34:6, 703–19

Breslin, G., K. Ferguson, S. Shannon, T. Haughey and S. Connor (2019), 'Player Transition Out of Football to Protect Wellbeing: A Dual Career Identity Study', Ulster University, School of Sport, https://uefaacademy.com/wp-content/uploads/sites/2/2019/07/2019_UEFA-RGP_Final-report_Breslin-Gavin.pdf [accessed 23 April 2021]

Broere, M., and R. van der Drift (1997), *Football Africa!* (Oxford: Worldview Publishing)

Brown, C. K. (1996), 'Gender roles and household allocation of resources and decision-making in Ghana', in Elizabeth Ardayfio-Schandorf (ed.), *The Changing Family in Ghana* (Accra: Ghana Universities Press), pp. 21–41

Brown, G., and P. Potrac (2009), '"You've not made the grade, son": de-selection and identity disruption in elite level youth football', *Soccer & Society*, 10:2, 143–59

Bruijn, M. de, R. van Dijk, and D. Foeken (2001), 'Mobile Africa: an introduction', in M. de Bruijn, R. van Dijk, and D. Foeken (eds), *Mobile Africa: Changing Patterns of Movement in Africa and Beyond* (Leiden: Brill), pp. 1–8

Büdel, M. (2013), 'An ethnographic view on African football migrants in Istanbul', *Ankara Üniversitesi SBF Dergisi*, 68:1, 1–20

Burghardt, P. (2021), 'Die Causa Bakery Jatta schweißt den HSV zusammen', *Süddeutsche Zeitung*, www.sueddeutsche.de/sport/bakery-jatta-hsv-1.5191384?reduced=true [accessed 13 February 2021]

Cáceres, V. J. (2020), 'Transfer-Bilanz: Die Leihe als Zeichen der Krise', *Süddeutsche Zeitung*, www.sueddeutsche.de/sport/transfer-bilanz-die-leihe-als-zeichen-der-krise-1.5057954 [accessed 14 February 2021]

Campbell, P. (2020), *Education, Retirement and Career Transitions for 'Black' Ex-Professional Footballers: From Being Idolised to Stacking Shelves* (Bingley: Emerald)

Carling, J. (2002), 'Migration in the age of involuntary immobility: theoretical reflections and Cape Verdean experiences', *Journal of Ethnic and Migration Studies*, 28:1, 5–42

Carr, M. (2015), *Fortress Europe: Inside the War Against Immigration* (London: Jurst & Company)

Carswell, G., and G. De Neve (2013), 'Labouring for global markets: Conceptualising labour agency in global production networks', *Geoforum*, 44, 62–70

Carter, T. F. (2011), *In Foreign Fields: The Politics and Experiences of Transnational Sport Migration* (London: Pluto Press)

—— (2013), 'Re-placing sport migrants: moving beyond the institutional structures informing international sport migration', *International Review for the Sociology of Sport*, 48:1, 66–82

Castles, S., and M. Miller (1998), *The Age of Migration: International Population Movement in the Modern World* (London: Macmillan Press)

Chakraborty, K., and S. Thambiah (2018), 'Children and young people's emotions of migration across Asia', *Children's Geographies*, 16:6, 583–90

Chepyator-Thomson, J., and E. Ariyo (2016), 'Out of Eastern Africa: an examination of sport labour migration in the post-independence era', *International Journal of the History of Sport*, 33:15, 1826–46

Chipande, H. (2016), 'The structural adjustment of football in Zambia: politics, decline and dispersal, 1991–1994', *International Journal of the History of Sport*, 33:15, 1847–65

Cho, Y. (2013), 'Introduction: football in Asia', *Soccer & Society*, 14:5, 579–87

—— (2016), *Football in Asia: History, Culture and Business* (London and New York: Routledge)

Christiansen, C., M. Utas, and H. Vigh (eds) (2006), *Navigating Youth, Generating Adulthood: Social Becoming in an African Context* (Uppsala: Nordic Africa Institute)

CIES (2020), 'Atlas of migration: association of origin of expatriate players', CIES Football Observatory, https://football-observatory.com/IMG/sites/atlasmigr/ [accessed 13 February 2021]

Cleveland, T. (2017), *Following the Ball: The Migration of African Soccer Players across the Portuguese Colonial Empire, 1949–1975* (Athens, OH: Ohio University Press)

Cobblah, T. (2011), 'Knee-jerk reaction', GhanaWeb, 26 August, www.ghanaweb.com/ GhanaHomePage/features/Knee-Jerk-Reaction-217116 [accessed 13 February 2021]

Coe, A., and J. Wiser (2011), 'Ghanaians footballers stranded in Mauritius', *Modern Ghana*, 4 August, www.modernghana.com/sports/343568/ghanaians-footballers-stranded-in-mauritius.html [accessed 9 July 2020]

Coe, C. (2012), 'Growing up and going abroad: how Ghanaian children imagine transnational migration', *Journal of Ethnic and Migration Studies*, 38:6, 913–31

—— (2020), 'Social class in transnational perspective: emotional responses to the status paradox among Ghanaian migrants', *Africa Today*, 66:3–4, 160–78

Coe, N., P. Dicken, and M. Hess (2008), 'Global production networks: realizing the potential', *Journal of Economic Geography*, 8:3, 271–95

Coe, N., and M. Hess (2013), 'Global production networks, labour and development', *Geoforum*, 44, 4–9

Coe, N., and D. Jordhus-Lier (2011), 'Constrained agency? Re-evaluating the geographies of labour', *Progress in Human Geography*, 35:2, 211–33

Coe, N., and H. Yeung (2019), 'Global production networks: mapping recent conceptual developments', *Journal of Economic Geography*, 19:4, 775–801

Collins, J. (2005), 'New directions in commodity chain analysis of global development processes', *Research in Rural Sociology and Development*, 11, 3–17

Comaroff, J., and J. L. Comaroff (2000), 'Millennial capitalism: first thoughts on a second coming', *Public Culture*, 12:2, 291–343

Cornelissen, S., and E. Solberg (2007), 'Sport mobility and circuits of power: the dynamics of football migration in Africa and the 2010 World Cup', *Politikon*, 34:3, 295–314

Court of Arbitration for Sport (2009), 'CAS 2008/A/1485 FC Midtjylland A/S v. FIFA' (Court of Arbitration for Sport), https://jurisprudence.tas-cas.org/Shared%20Documents/1485.pdf [accessed 19 January 2021]

Cowley, J. (2005), 'Vieira', *Observer Sport Monthly*, 63, 17–21

Cruise O'Brien, D. (1996), 'A lost generation? Youth identity and state decay in West Africa', in R. Werbner and T. Ranger (eds), *Postcolonial Identities in Africa* (London and New York: Zed Books), pp. 55–74

Curran, C. (2015), 'Post-playing careers of Irish-born footballers, 1945–2010', *Sport in Society*, 18:10, 1273–86

Dabscheck, B. (2004), 'The globe at their feet: FIFA's new employment rules – I', *Sport in Society*, 7:1, 69–94

——— (2006), 'The globe at their feet: FIFA's new employment rules – II', *Sport in Society*, 9:1, 1–18

Darby, P. (2000a), 'Football, colonial doctrine and indigenous resistance: mapping the political persona of FIFA's African constituency', *Culture, Sport, Society*, 3:1, 61–87

——— (2000b), 'The new scramble for Africa: African football labour migration to Europe', *European Sports History Review*, 3:1, 217–44

——— (2002), *Africa, Football and FIFA: Politics, Colonialism and Resistance* (London and New York: Routledge)

——— (2005), 'Africa and the World Cup: politics, Eurocentrism and resistance', *International Journal of the History of Sport*, 22:5, 883–905

——— (2006), 'Migração para Portugal de jogadores de futebol africanos: recurso colonial e neocolonial', *Análise Social*, 179, 417–33

——— (2007a), 'African football labour migration to Portugal: colonial and neo-colonial resource', *Soccer & Society*, 8:4, 495–509

——— (2007b), 'Out of Africa: the exodus of elite African football talent to Europe', *WorkingUSA*, 10:4, 443–56

——— (2010), '"Go outside": the history, economics and geography of Ghanaian football labour migration', *African Historical Review*, 42:1, 19–41

——— (2013a), '"Let us rally around the flag": football, nation-building, and pan-Africanism in Kwame Nkrumah's Ghana', *Journal of African History*, 54:2, 221–46

——— (2013b), 'Moving players, traversing perspectives: global value chains, production networks and Ghanaian football labour migration', *Geoforum*, 50, 43–53

Darby, P., and S. Agergaard (2018), 'Dreams to reality? Right to Dream, FC Nordsjælland and female football migration from Ghana to Denmark' (presented at the Congress of the European College of Sport Sciences, University College Dublin, Republic of Ireland)

Darby, P., G. A. Akindes, and M. Kirwin (2007), 'Football academies and the migration of African football labor to Europe', *Journal of Sport and Social Issues*, 31:2, 143–61

Darby, P., J. Esson, and C. Ungruhe (2018), 'Africa: SDP and sports academies', in H. Collison, S. Darnell, R. Giulianotti, and D. Howe (eds), *Handbook of Sport for Development and Peace* (London and New York: Routledge), pp. 419–29

Darby, P., and E. Solberg (2010), 'Differing trajectories: football development and patterns of player migration in South Africa and Ghana', *Soccer & Society*, 11:1–2, 118–30

Darby, P., and N. van der Meij (2018), 'Africa, migration and football', in J. Nauright and M. Amara (eds), *Sport in the African World* (London and New York: Routledge), pp. 94–109

Darkwah, A. (2013), 'Keeping hope alive: an analysis of training opportunities for Ghanaian youth in the emerging oil and gas industry', *International Development Planning Review*, 35:2, 119–34

David, P. (2004), *Human Rights in Youth Sport: A Critical Review of Children's Rights in Competitive Sport* (London and New York: Routledge)

De Marco, N. (2018), 'Transfers, agents and minors', in J. Anderson, R. Parrish and B. Garcia (eds), *Research Handbook on EU Sports Law and Policy* (Cheltenham: Edward Elgar), pp. 382–409

Der Spiegel (2018), 'Venture capital: how clubs maximize profits by exploiting young African talent', *Der Spiegel*, 9 November, www.spiegel.de/international/business/venture-capital-how-clubs-maximize-profits-by-exploiting-young-african-talent-a-1237618.html [accessed 19 February 2021]

Dicken, P., P. Kelly, K. Olds, and H. Yeung (2001), 'Chains and networks, territories and scales: towards a relational framework for analysing the global economy', *Global Networks*, 1:2, 89–112

Donnelly, P., and L. Petherick (2004), '"Workers" playtime? Child labour at the extremes of the sporting spectrum', *Sport in Society*, 7:3, 301–21

Drywood, E. (2016), '"When we buy a young boy…": migrant footballers, children's rights and the case for EU intervention', in L. Lusman and H. Stalford (eds), *The EU as a Children's Rights Actor* (Leverkusen: Verlag Barbara Budrich), pp. 191–219

Dubinsky, I., and L. Schler (2017), 'Mandela Soccer Academy: historical and contemporary intersections between Ghana, Lebanon, and the West', *International Journal of the History of Sport*, 33:15, 1730–47

——— (2019), 'Goal dreams: conflicting development imaginaries in Ghanaian football academies', *Journal of Modern African Studies*, 57:2, 247–72

Dubois, L. (2010), *Soccer Empire: The World Cup and the Future of France* (Berkeley: University of California Press)

During, S. (2015), 'Choosing precarity', *South Asia: Journal of South Asian Studies*, 38:1, 19–38

Edwards, P. (2015), 'Underage African footballers "trafficked" to Laos', BBC News, 21 July, www.bbc.co.uk/news/world-africa-33595804 [accessed 13 February 2021]

Elliott, R., and E. Gusterud (2018), 'Finding the back of the net: networks and migrant recruitment in Norwegian football', *International Review for the Sociology of Sport*, 53:1, 69–83

Elliott, R., and J. Harris (eds) (2015), *Football and Migration: Perspectives, Places, Players* (Abingdon: Routledge)

Elliott, R., and J. Maguire (2008), 'Thinking outside of the box: exploring a conceptual synthesis for research in the area of athletic labor migration', *Sociology of Sport Journal*, 25:4, 482–97

Engh, M. H. (2014), 'Producing and Maintaining Mobility: A Migrant-Centred Analysis of Transnational Women's Sports Labour Migration' (doctoral thesis, Aarhus University)

Engh, M. H., and S. Agergaard (2015), 'Producing mobility through locality and visibility: developing a transnational perspective on sports labour migration', *International Review for the Sociology of Sport*, 50:8, 974–92

Engh, M. H., F. Settler, and S. Agergaard (2017), '"The ball and the rhythm in her blood": racialised imaginaries and football migration from Nigeria to Scandinavia', *Ethnicities*, 17:1, 66–84

Enria, L. (2018), *The Politics of Work in a Post-Conflict State: Youth, Labour and Violence in Sierra Leone* (Melton: James Currey)

Ephirim-Donkor, A. (2016), *African Religion Defined: A Systematic Study of Ancestor Worship among the Akan* (Lanham: University Press of America)

Esson, J. (2013), 'A body and a dream at a vital conjuncture: Ghanaian youth, uncertainty and the allure of football', *Geoforum*, 47, 84–92

——— (2015a), 'Better off at home? Rethinking responses to trafficked West African footballers in Europe', *Journal of Ethnic and Migration Studies*, 41:3, 512–30

——— (2015b), 'You have to try your luck: male Ghanaian youth and the uncertainty of football migration', *Environment and Planning A: Economy and Space*, 47:6, 1383–97

——— (2015c), 'Escape to victory: development, youth entrepreneurship and the migration of Ghanaian footballers', *Geoforum*, 64, 47–55

——— (2016), 'Football as a vehicle for development: lessons from male Ghanaian youth', in N. Ansell, N. Klocker, and T. Skelton (eds), *Geographies of Global Issues: Change and Threat* (New York: Springer), pp. 145–62

——— (2020), 'Playing the victim? Human trafficking, African youth, and geographies of structural inequality', *Population, Space and Place*, 26:6, e2309

Esson, J., E. F. Amankwaa, and P. Mensah (2020), 'Boys are tired! Youth, urban struggles, and retaliatory patriarchy', *Transactions of the Institute of British Geographers*, 46:1, 193–207

Esson, J., P. Darby, E. Drywood, C. Mason, and S. Yilmaz (2020), *Children Before Players: Current Risks and Future Research Agendas* (London: UNICEF UK)

Esson, J., and E. Drywood (2018), 'Challenging popular representations of child trafficking in football', *Journal of Criminological Research, Policy and Practice*, 4:1, 60–72

European Commission (1995), 'Professional football: European Court rules in the Bosman case', press release, 15 December, https://ec.europa.eu/commission/presscorner/detail/en/IP_95_1411 [accessed 27 April 2021]

——— (2009), *Study on Sports Agents in the European Union* (Brussels: European Commission)

——— (2012), 'EU Guidelines on Dual Careers: Recommended policy actions in support of dual careers in high-performance sport', https://ec.europa.eu/assets/eac/sport/library/documents/dual-career-guidelines-final_en.pdf [accessed 27 April 2021]

——— (2020), 'Guidance note – Research on refugees, asylum seekers and migrants', https://ec.europa.eu/research/participants/data/ref/h2020/other/hi/guide_research-refugees-migrants_en.pdf [accessed 13 February 2021]

Fair, L. (1997), 'Kickin' it: leisure, politics and football in colonial Zanzibar, 1900s–1950s', *Africa*, 67:2, 224–51

Farrington, N., L. Hall, D. Kilvington, J. Price, and A. Saeed (2017), *Sport, Racism and Social Media* (London and New York: Routledge)

Fates, Y. (2004), 'Football in Algeria: between violence and politics', in G. Armstrong and R. Giulianotti (eds), *Football in Africa: Conflict, Conciliation and Community* (Basingstoke: Palgrave Macmillan), pp. 41–58

FC Nordsjælland (2018a), 'Announcement from FCN and RTD', https://fcn.dk/wp-content/uploads/2018/11/announcement-from-fcn-and-rtd.pdf [accessed 19 February 2021]
——— (2018b), 'Udmelding fra Right to Dream', https://fcn.dk/2018/12/udmelding-fra-right-to-dream/ [accessed 19 February 2021]
Ferguson, J. (2006), *Global Shadows: Africa in the Neoliberal World Order* (Durham, NC, and London: Duke University Press)
Fessler, D. (2004), 'Shame in two cultures: implications for evolutionary approaches', *Journal of Cognition and Culture*, 4:2, 207–62
FIFA (2020a), *Global Transfer Market Report 2020: Men's Professional Football* (Zurich: FIFA), pp. 1–84, https://img.fifa.com/image/upload/ijiz9rtpkfnbhxwbqr70.pdf [accessed 18 February 2021]
——— (2020b), *Regulations on the Status and Transfer of Players – June 2020 Edition* (Zurich: FIFA), https://resources.fifa.com/image/upload/regulations-on-the-status-and-transfer-of-players-june-2020.pdf?cloudid=ixztobdwje3tn2bztqcp [accessed 18 February 2021]
Fifield, D. (2019), 'Romelu Lukaku says "we're going backwards" in fight against racism', *Guardian*, 2 September, www.theguardian.com/football/2019/sep/02/romelu-lukaku-racism-going-backwards-inter-cagliari-calls-action [accessed 14 February 2021]
FIFPro (2016), *Global Employment Report: Working Conditions in Professional Football* (Hoofdorp: Fédération Internationale des Associations de Footballeurs Professionnels)
Finn, B., and S. Oldfield (2015), 'Straining: young men working through waithood in Freetown, Sierra Leone', *Africa Spectrum*, 50:3, 29–48
Flahaux, M.-L., and H. de Haas (2016), 'African migration: trends, patterns, drivers', *Comparative Migration Studies*, 4:1, 1–25
Football Tribe (2020), 'How are Thai clubs coping with COVID-19? Muang Loei United's experience', Football Tribe Asia, 8 June, https://football-tribe.com/asia/2020/06/08/how-are-thai-clubs-coping-with-covid-19-muang-loei-uniteds-experience/ [accessed 14 February 2021]
Foucault, M. (2008), *The Birth of Biopolitics: Lectures at the Collège de France, 1978–1979*, trans. G. Burchell (Basingstoke: Palgrave Macmillan)
Frank, A. G. (1969), *Capitalism and Underdevelopment in Latin America* (New York: Monthly Review Press)
Fridy, K. S., and V. Brobbey (2009), 'Win the match and vote for me: the politicisation of Ghana's Accra Hearts of Oak and Kumasi Asante Kotoko football clubs', *Journal of Modern African Studies*, 47:1, 19–39
Friedland, W. (2011), 'Reprise on commodity systems methodology', *International Journal of Sociology of Agriculture and Food*, 9:1, 82–103
Fritsch, O. (2013), 'Nicht alle Rassisten werfen Bananen', *Die Zeit*, 21 January, www.zeit.de/sport/2013-01/gerald-asamoah-rassismus-ballack [accessed 14 February 2021]
Fumanti, M. (2012), 'Black chicken, white chicken: patriotism, morality and the aesthetics of fandom in the 2008 African Cup of Nations in Ghana', *Soccer & Society*, 13:2, 264–76
Gallwey, M. (2018), 'The odd couple: going through the unique relationship between Red Bull and football', *Footall Chronicle*, https://footballchronicleco.wordpress.com/2018/10/22/the-odd-couple-going-through-the-unique-relationship-between-red-bull-and-football/ [accessed 17 February 2021]

Gearity, B. T., and L. T. Metzger (2017), 'Intersectionality, microaggressions, and microaffirmations: toward a cultural praxis of sport coaching', *Sociology of Sport Journal*, 34:2, 160–75

Geest, S. van der (2016), 'Will families in Ghana continue to care for older people? Logic and contradiction in policy', in J. Hoffman and K. Pype (eds), *Ageing in Sub-Saharan Africa: Spaces and Practices of Care* (Bristol: Policy Press), pp. 21–42

Gereffi, G. (1994), 'The organisation of buyer-driven global commodity chains: how U.S. retailers shape overseas production networks', in G. Gereffi and M. Korceniewicz (eds), *Commodity Chains and Global Capitalism* (Westport: Praeger), pp. 95–121

——— (1995), 'Global production systems and third world development', in B. Stallings (ed.), *Global Change, Regional Response: The New International Context of Development* (Cambridge: Cambridge University Press), pp. 100–42

——— (1996), 'Global commodity chains: new forms of coordination and control among nations and firms in international industries', *Competition and Change*, 1:4, 427–39

——— (1999), 'International trade and industrial upgrading in the apparel commodity chain', *Journal of International Economics*, 48:1, 37–70

——— (2001), 'Shifting governance structures in global commodity chains, with special reference to the Internet', *American Behavioral Scientist*, 44:10, 1617–37

Gereffi, G., and M. Korzeniewicz (eds) (1994), *Commodity Chains and Global Capitalism* (Westport: Praeger)

Geschiere, P. (1997), *The Modernity of Witchcraft: Politics and the Occult in Postcolonial Africa* (Charlottesville and London: University of Virginia Press)

Ghana Soccernet (2019), 'Ghana FA elections: Kurt Okraku reveals plans of reviving colts football', 22 October, https://ghanasoccernet.com/ghana-fa-elections-kurt-okraku-reveals-plans-of-reviving-colts-football [accessed 12 July 2020]

GhanaWeb (2019), 'McDan Colts football tournament kicks off', 16 September, www.ghanaweb.com/GhanaHomePage/SportsArchive/McDan-Colts-football-tournament-kicks-off-781426 [accessed 13 July 2020]

Ghanaian Times (2020), 'Gyan to initiate campaign to revive colt football', www.ghanaiantimes.com.gh/gyan-to-initiate-campaign-to-revive-colt-football/ [accessed 12 July 2020]

Gibbon, P., and S. Ponte (2005), *Trading Down: Africa, Value Chains, and the Global Economy* (Philadelphia: Temple University Press)

Giulianotti, R. (1999), *Football: A Sociology of the Global Game* (Cambridge: Polity Press)

Glanville, B. (2007), 'Obituary: Bill Perry', *Guardian*, 8 October

Gleeson, M. (1996), 'The African invasion', *Kick-Off: African Cup of Nations 1996 Fans Guide*, January, p. 106

Goldblatt, D. (2007), *The Ball Is Round: A Global History of Football* (London: Penguin Books)

Goodfellow, T. (2020), 'Political informality: deals, trust networks, and the negotiation of value in the urban realm', *Journal of Development Studies*, 56:2, 278–94

Gough, K. V. (2008), '"Moving around": social and spatial mobility of youth in Lusaka', *Geografiska Annaler: Series B, Human Geography*, 90:3, 243–55

Gough, K. V., and T. Langevang (2016), *Young Entrepreneurs in Sub-Saharan Africa* (London and New York: Routledge)

Gough, K. V., T. Langevang, P. W. K. Yankson, and G. Owusu (2019), 'Shaping geographies of informal education: a Global South perspective', *Annals of the American Association of Geographers*, 109:6, 1885–902

Grätz, T. (2010), 'Introduction: mobility, transnational connections and sociocultural change in contemporary Africa', in T. Grätz (ed.), *Mobility, Transnationalism and Contemporary African Societites* (Newcastle: Cambridge Scholars Publishing), pp. 1–18

Gray, G. (2010), 'Scout (Saatchi & Saatchi EMEA)' [video], YouTube, uploaded 18 July 2010, www.youtube.com/watch?v=1jmqeLNCDJc [accessed 7 July 2020]

Groves, A. (2012), 'Molding and moving bodies in a neoliberal world: African football labor migrants in Egypt' (master's thesis, American University in Cairo)

Grundlingh, S. M. (2015), *After the Triumph: An Anthropological Study into the Lives of Elite Athletes after Competitive Sport* (Bloemfontein: University of the Free State)

Guardian (2015), 'Former Italy winger Stefano Eranio sacked over racist comments', *Guardian*, 22 October, www.theguardian.com/football/2015/oct/22/stefano-eranio-sacked-racist-comments [accessed 14 February 2021]

Guinness, D. (2018), 'Corporal destinies: faith, ethno-nationalism, and raw talent in Fijian professional rugby aspirations', *HAU: Journal of Ethnographic Theory*, 8:1, 314–28

Guttmann, A. (1978), *From Ritual to Record: The Nature of Modern Sports* (New York: Columbia University Press)

Haan, A. de, and B. Rogaly (2002), 'Introduction: migrant workers and their role in rural change', *Journal of Development Studies*, 38:5, 1–14

Haas, H. de (2008), *Migration and Development: A Theoretical Perspective* (Oxford: University of Oxford), pp. 1–61, file:///Users/gyjhne/Downloads/WP9%20Migration%20and%20Development%20Theory.pdf

—— (2010), 'The internal dynamics of migration processes: a theoretical inquiry', *Journal of Ethnic and Migration Studies*, 36:10, 1587–617

Hammar, T., and K. Tamas (1997), 'Why do people go or stay?', in T. Hammar and G. Brochmann (eds), *International Migration, Immobility and Development: Multidisciplinary Pespectives* (Oxford: Berg), pp. 1–20

Hann, M. P. (2018), 'Sporting Aspirations: Football, Wrestling, and Neoliberal Subjectivity in Urban Senegal' (doctoral thesis, University of Amsterdam), https://pure.uva.nl/ws/files/30399861/Thesis.pdf [accessed 27 April 2021]

—— (2020), 'The dream is to leave: imagining migration and mobility through sport in Senegal', in N. Besnier, D. G. Calabrò, and D. Guinness (eds), *Sport, Migration, and Gender in the Neoliberal Age* (London and New York: Routledge), pp. 185–212

Hansen, K. T. (2005), 'Getting stuck in the compound: some odds against social adulthood in Lusaka, Zambia', *Africa Today*, 51:4, 3–16

Hardman, K. (2008), 'Physical education in schools: a global perspective', *Kinesiology*, 40:1, 5–28

Harmsen, F., A. Elling, and J. van Sterkenburg (2019), *Racisme, sociale kramp en innerlijke drijfkrachten in het betaaldvoetbal* (Be.People, Mulier Insituut and Erasmus University Rotterdam), pp. 1–17, www.kennisbanksportenbewegen.nl/?file=9708&m=1571231919&action=file.download [accessed 27 April 2021]

Haslov, L., and J. L. Brock (2018a), 'City can cherry-pick African talents at Danish top flight club – for free!', *Politiken*, https://politiken.dk/sport/fodbold/art6830967/Manchester-City-can-cherry-pick-African-talents-at-Danish-top-flight-club-%E2%80%93-for-free [accessed 13 February 2021]

——— (2018b), 'FC Nordsjællands ejer om City-aftale: »Uden disse partnerskaber er det sikkert, at Right to Dream ikke ville eksistere i dag«', *Politiken*, https://politiken.dk/sport/fodbold/art6828832/%C2%BBUden-disse-partnerskaber-er-det-sikkert-at-Right-to-Dream-ikke-ville-eksistere-i-dag%C2%AB [accessed 13 February 2021]

Haß, J., and S. Schütze (2019), 'New spaces of belonging: soccer teams of Bolivian migrants in São Paulo, Brazil', in A. Feldmann, X. Bada, and S. Schütze (eds), *New Migration Patterns in the Americas* (Cham: Palgrave Macmillan), pp. 317–36

Hawkey, I. (2009), *Feet of the Chameleon: The Story of African Football* (London: Portico)

Hawkins, E. (2015), *The Lost Boys: Inside Football's Slave Trade* (London: Bloomsbury)

Hear, N. van, O. Bakewell, and K. Long (2018), 'Push-pull plus: reconsidering the drivers of migration', *Journal of Ethnic and Migration Studies*, 44:6, 927–44

Henderson, J., P. Dicken, M. Hess, and H. Yeung (2002), 'Global production networks and the analysis of economic development', *Review of International Political Economy*, 9:3, 436–64

Hernández-Carretero, M., and J. Carling (2012), 'Beyond "kamikaze migrants": risk taking in West African boat migration to Europe', *Human Organization*, 71:4, 407–16

Hoffman, J., and K. Pype (2016), *Ageing in Sub-Saharan Africa: Spaces and Practices of Care* (Bristol: Policy Press)

Honwana, A. (2014), '"Waithood": youth transitions and social change', in D. Foeken, T. Dietz, L. de Haan, and L. Johnson (eds), *Development and Equity: An Interdisciplinary Exploration by Ten Scholars from Africa, Asia and Latin America* (Leiden: Brill), pp. 28–40

Honwana, A., and F. de Boeck (2005), *Makers and Breakers: Children and Youth in Postcolonial Africa* (Oxford: James Currey)

Hopkins, T., and I. Wallerstein (1977), 'Patterns of development of the modern world system', *Review*, 1:2, 111–45

——— (1986), 'Commodity chains in the world economy prior to 1800', *Review*, 10:1, 157–70

Howard, N., and J. Boyden (2013), 'Why does child trafficking policy need to be reformed? The moral economy of children's movement in Benin and Ethiopia', *Children's Geographies*, 11:3, 354–68

Hughey, M. W., and D. R. Goss (2015), 'A level playing field? Media constructions of athletics, genetics, and race', *ANNALS of the American Academy of Political and Social Science*, 661:1, 182–211

Jackson, J. (2019), 'Manchester City fined by FIFA over recruitment of players under 18', *Guardian*, 13 August, www.theguardian.com/football/2019/aug/13/manchester-city-fined-fifa-player-recruitment [accessed 19 February 2021]

Jeffrey, C. (2010), 'Geographies of children and youth I: eroding maps of life', *Progress in Human Geography*, 34:4, 496–505

——— (2012), 'Geographies of children and youth II: global youth agency', *Progress in Human Geography*, 36:2, 245–53

Johansen, A. J. (2013), 'Football Nomads: The Determinants of Kenyan Football Migration' (master's thesis, University of Copenhagen)

Johnson-Hanks, J. (2002), 'On the limits of life stages in ethnography: toward a theory of vital conjunctures', *American Anthropologist*, 104:3, 865–80

—— (2005), 'When the future decides: uncertainty and intentional action in contemporary Cameroon', *Current Anthropology*, 46:3, 363–85

Jones, M. (2006), 'Arsenal face FIFA investigation', BBC News, 27 June, http://news.bbc.co.uk/1/hi/programmes/newsnight/5037494.stm [accessed 17 February 2021]

Jónsson, G. (2008), 'Migration Aspirations and Immobility in a Malian Soninke Village', working paper, International Migration Institute, University of Oxford, www.migrationinstitute.org/publications/wp-10-08 [accessed 27 April 2021]

—— (2011), 'Non-Migrant, Sedentary, Immobile, or "Left Behind"? Reflections on the Absence of Migration', working paper, International Migration Institute, University of Oxford, www.oxfordmartin.ox.ac.uk/downloads/academic/wp-11-39-non-migrant-sedentary-immobile-or-left-behind.pdf [accessed 27 April 2021]

Jua, N. (2003), 'Differential responses to disappearing transitional pathways: redefining possibility among Cameroonian youths', *African Studies Review*, 46:2, 13–36

Judge, R. C., M. Blazek, and J. Esson (2020), 'Editorial: transnational youth mobilities: emotions, inequities, and temporalities', *Population, Space and Place*, 26:6, e2307

Kabeer, N. (2000), 'Inter-generational contracts, demographic transitions and the "quantity-quality" tradeoff: parents, children and investing in the future', *Journal of International Development*, 12:4, 463–82

Kainz, M. (2015), *Red Bull Ghana, Global Value Chains and the Grabbing of Land and Resource: A Case Study on the Embedment of European Football Academies in Western Africa* (Vienna: Vienna Institute of International Dialogue and Cooperation)

Kalir, B. (2005), 'The development of a migratory disposition: explaining a "new emigration"', *International Migration*, 13:4, 167–96

Kandel, W., and D. S. Massey (2002), 'The culture of Mexican migration: a theoretical and empirical analysis', *Social Forces*, 80:3, 981–1004

Kaper, J. (2019), *Nii Lamptey: De vloek van Pelé* (Netherlands: Benka Uitgeverij)

Kaplinsky, R. (2001), 'Globalisation and unequalisation: what can be learned from value chain analysis?', *Journal of Development Studies*, 37:2, 117–46

Kelly, P. (2013), 'Production networks, place and development: thinking through global production networks in Cavite, Philippines', *Geoforum*, 44, 82–92

Kelly, S. (2014), 'The migration of Irish professional footballers: the good, the bad and the ugly', in R. Elliott and J. Harris (eds), *Football and Migration: Perspectives, Places, Players* (New York and Abingdon: Routledge), pp. 76–92

Kick It Out (2019), 'Discrimination reports in football rise by a third', 24 July, www.kickitout.org/news/discrimination-reports-in-football-rise-by-a-third [accessed 14 February 2021]

King, A. (2003), *The European Ritual: Football in the New Europe* (London and New York: Routledge)

King, C. (2004), 'Race and cultural identity: playing the race game inside football', *Leisure Studies*, 23:1, 19–30

King, R. (2012), 'Theories and Typologies of Migration: An Overview and a Primer', Willy Brandt Series of Working Papers in International Migration and Ethnic Relations (Malmö University)

Klein, A. (2007), 'Towards a transnational sports studies', *Sport in Society*, 10:6, 885–95

―― (2011), 'Sports labour migration as a global value chain: the Dominican case', in J. Maguire and M. Falcous (eds), *Sport and Migration: Borders, Boundaries and Crossings* (London and New York: Routledge), pp. 88–101

―― (2014), *Dominican Baseball: New Pride, Old Prejudice* (Philadelphia: Temple University Press)

Kleist, N. (2017), 'Disrupted migration projects: the moral economy of involuntary return to Ghana from Libya', *Africa*, 87:2, 322–42

Klute, G., and H. P. Hahn (2007), 'Cultures of migration: introduction', in H. P. Hahn and G. Klute (eds), *Cultures of Migration: African Perspectives* (Münster: LIT Verlag), pp. 9–30

Konadu-Agyemang, K. (2000), 'The best of times and the worst of times: structural adjustment programs and uneven development in Africa: the case of Ghana', *Professional Geographer*, 52:3, 469–83

Koser, K. (2010), 'Dimensions and dynamics of irregular migration', *Population, Space and Place*, 16:3, 181–93

Kovač, U. (2018), 'Foootball, Pentecostalism, and Transnational Aspirations in Cameroon Football' (doctoral thesis, University of Amsterdam)

Krieken, R. van (2012), *Celebrity Society* (London and New York: Routledge)

Künzler, D., and R. Poli (2012), 'The African footballer as visual object and figure of success: Didier Drogba and social meaning', *Soccer & Society*, 13:2, 207–21

Kuuire, V. Z., G. Arku, I. Luginaah, M. Buzzelli, and T. Abada (2016), 'Obligations and expectations: perceived relationship between transnational housing investment and housing consumption decisions among Ghanaian immigrants in Canada', *Housing, Theory and Society*, 33:4, 445–68

Kwafo, E. N. Y. (2019), 'Developing Colt Football Will Improve Ghana Football – Coach Kwesi Appiah', *Modern Ghana*, 8 August, www.modernghana.com/sports/949323/developing-colt-football-will-improve-ghana-footba.html [accessed 12 July 2020]

Kyeremeh, E. (2020), 'Exploring the return migration experience of football migrants: a case study of Ghanaian footballers', *African Geographical Review*, 39:3, 224–39

Lamptey, G. (2021), 'More about George', George Lamptey [personal website], www.georgelamptey.com/more-about-george [accessed 18 February 2021]

Lanfranchi, P., and M. Taylor (2001), *Moving with the Ball: The Migration of Professional Footballers* (Oxford: Berg)

Langevang, T. (2008), '"We are managing!" Uncertain paths to respectable adulthoods in Accra, Ghana', *Geoforum*, 39:6, 2039–47

Langevang, T., and K. V. Gough (2009), 'Surviving through movement: the mobility of urban youth in Ghana', *Social and Cultural Geography*, 10:9, 741–56

Latour, E. de (2010), 'Joueurs mondiaux, clubs locaux. Le Football d'Afrique en Asie', *Politique Africaine*, 118, 63–84

Lema, B. (1989), 'Sport in Zaire', in E. A. Wagner (ed.), *Sport in Asia and Africa: A Comparative Handbook* (New York and London: Greenwood Press), pp. 229–47

Lembo, C. (2011), 'FIFA transfer regulations and UEFA player eligibility rules: major changes in European football and the negative effect on minors', *Emory International Law Review*, 25, 539–85

Leurs, K. H. A., and M. Prabhakar (2018) 'Doing digital migration studies: methodological considerations for an emerging research focus', in R. Zapata-Barrero and E. Yalaz (eds), *Qualitative Research in European Migration Studies*, IMISCOE Research Series (Cham: Springer), pp. 247–66

Levitt, P., and N. G. Schiller (2004), 'Conceptualizing simultaneity: a transnational social field perspective on society', *International Migration Review*, 38:3, 1002–39

Liew, J. (2021), 'English football is consumed by racism and hatred. Can the cycle be broken?', *Guardian*, 8 February, www.theguardian.com/football/2021/feb/08/english-football-is-consumed-by-racism-and-hatred-can-the-cycle-be-broken [accessed 13 February 2021]

Lindholm, J. (2016), 'Can I please have a slice of Ronaldo? The legality of FIFA's ban on third-party ownership under European union law', *International Sports Law Journal*, 15:3–4, 137–48

Lloyd, C. B., and A. J. Gage-Brandon (1993), 'Women's role in maintaining households: family welfare and sexual inequality in Ghana', *Population Studies*, 47:1, 115–31

Luedi, J. (2018), 'Southeast Asia's African football slaves', *Diplomat*, 15 February, https://thediplomat.com/2018/02/southeast-asias-african-football-slaves/ [accessed 13 February 2021]

Lund-Thomsen, P. (2013), 'Labour agency in the football manufacturing industry of Sialkot, Pakistan', *Geoforum*, 44, 71–81

Maguire, J., and M. Falcous (2011), 'Introduction: borders, boundaries and crossings: sport, migration and identities', in J. Maguire and M. Falcous (eds), *Sport and Migration: Borders, Boundaries and Crossings* (Abingdon and New York: Routledge), pp. 1–12

Mahjoub, F. (2003), 'Bientot un Championat Professionel a la Senegalaise', *Jeune Afrique L'Intelligent*, 20 July, pp. 22–24

Mangan, J. A. (1998), *The Games Ethic and Imperialism: Aspects of the Diffusion of an Ideal* (London: Frank Cass and Co.)

Manzo, K. (2007), 'Learning to kick: African soccer schools as carriers of development', *Impumelelo: The Interdisciplinary Electronic Journal of African Sports*, 2, 1–13

Marcus, G. E. (1995), 'Ethnography in/of the world system: the emergence of multi-sited ethnography', *Annual Review of Anthropology*, 24:1, 95–117

Marsaud, O. (2001), 'ASEC Mimosas, pépinière des talents ivoiriens: les talents de l'ASEC Mimosas', *Afrik Foot*, 6 February, www.afrik-foot.com/asec-mimosas-pepiniere-des-talents-ivoiriens [accessed 17 February 2021]

Martin, J., C. Ungruhe, and T. Häberlein (2016), 'Young future Africa – images, imagination and its making: an introduction', *AnthropoChildren*, 6, 1–18

Martin, P. (1991), 'Colonialism, youth and football in French Equatorial Africa', *International Journal of the History of Sport*, 8:1, 56–71

Mason, C., P. Darby, E. Drywood, J. Esson, and S. Yilmaz (2019), 'Rights, risks and responsibilities in the recruitment of children within the global football industry', *International Journal of Children's Rights*, 27:4, 738–56

Massey, D. S., G. Arango, A. Hugo, A. Kouauci, A. Pellegrino, and J. E. Taylor (1993), 'Theories of international migration: a review and appraisal', *Population and Development Review*, 19:3, 431–66

Mauro, M. (2016), *The Balotelli Generation: Issues of Inclusion and Belonging in Italian Football and Society* (Bern: Peter Lang)

McDougall, D. (2008), 'The scandal of Africa's trafficked player', *Observer*, 6 January, pp. 50–55

McFarlane, C., and J. Silver (2017), 'Navigating the city: dialectics of everyday urbanism', *Transactions of the Institute of British Geographers*, 42:3, 458–71

McGee, D. (2015), 'Navigating Bodies, Borders and the Global Game: An Ethnography of Youth, Football and the Politics of Privation in Ghana, West Africa' (doctoral thesis, University of Toronto)

McGrath, S. (2013), 'Fuelling global production networks with slave labour? Migrant sugar cane workers in the Brazillian ethanol GPN', *Geoforum*, 44, 32–43

——— (2018), 'Dis/articulations and the interrogation of development in GPN research', *Progress in Human Geography*, 42:4, 509–28

McKinnon, R. (2014), 'You make your own luck', *Metaphilosophy*, 45:4–5, 558–77

McQuaid, K., J. Esson, K. V. Gough, and R. Wignall (2020), 'Navigating old age and the urban terrain: geographies of ageing from Africa', *Progress in Human Geography*, online first, 1–20, https://doi.org/10.1177/0309132520948956

Meagher, K. (2005), 'Social capital or analytical liability? Social networks and African informal economies', *Global Networks*, 5:3, 217–38

Meij, N. van der (2015), 'Family Matters in African Football Migration: An Analysis of the Role of Family, Agency and Football Academies in the Mobility of Ghanaian Football Players' (doctoral thesis, Ulster University)

Meij, N. van der, and P. Darby (2014), '"No one would burden the sea and then never get any benefit": family involvement in players' migration to football academies in Ghana', in R. Elliott and J. Harris (eds), *Football and Migration: Perspectives, Places, Players* (London and New York: Routledge), pp. 159–79

——— (2016), '"They eat football, they drink football, they do everything football": intra-family negotiations and recruitment into football academies in Ghana', *Studi Emigrazione: An International Journal of Migration Studies*, 203:3, 457–74

——— (2017), 'Getting in the game and getting on the move: family, the intergenerational contract and internal migration into football academies in Ghana', *Sport in Society*, 20:11, 1580–95

Meij, N. van der, P. Darby, and K. Liston (2017), '"The downfall of a man is not the end of his life": navigating involuntary immobility in Ghanaian football', *Sociology of Sport Journal*, 34:2, 183–94

Melero, V., and R. Sorion (2012), 'The dilemma of third-party ownership of football players', *EPFL Sports Law Bulletin*, 10, 41–44

Melnick, M. J. (1988), 'Racial segregation by playing position in the English football league: some preliminary observations', *Journal of Sport and Social Issues*, 12:2, 122–30

Menery, S. (2015), 'The search for Ali Dia, legendary football hoaxster turned Houdini', *Bleacher Report*, https://bleacherreport.com/articles/2551248-the-search-for-ali-dia-legendary-football-hoaxster-turned-houdini [accessed 13 February 2021]

Meneses, J. P. (2013), *Niños Futbolistas* (Barcelona: Blackie Books)

Meyer, B. (1998), 'Commodities and the power of prayer: Pentecostalist attitudes towards consumption in contemporary Ghana', *Development and Change*, 29:4, 751–76

Meyer, B., and P. Pels (2003), *Magic and Modernity: Interfaces of Revelation and Concealment* (Redwood City: Stanford University Press)

Mezahi, M. (2020), 'Why are there no African coaches in Europe's top football leagues?', *African Arguments*, 23 July, https://africanarguments.org/2020/07/why-are-there-no-african-coaches-in-europes-top-football-leagues/ [accessed 14 February 2021]

Mugote, M. S. (2019), '"Fake" Cameronian football agent arrested in Kenya', *Sports Corna*, 19 December, http://sportscorna.com/index.php/2019/12/19/fake-cameronian-football-agent-arrested-in-kenya/ [accessed 9 July 2020]

Mukharji, P. B. (2008), '"Feeble Bengalis" and "big Africans": African players in Bengali club football', *Soccer & Society*, 9:2, 273–85

Müller, J. (2013), *Migration, Geschlecht und Fußball zwischen Bolivien und Spanien, Netzwerke – Räume – Körper* (Berlin: Reimer)

Müller, M. (2010), 'Ethnische und funktionale Differenzierung: Zur Relevanz ethnisch-nationaler Zuschreibungen im Profifußball', in M. Müller and D. Zifonun (eds), *Ethnowissen. Soziologische Beiträge zu ethnischer Differenzierung und Migration* (Wiesbaden: VS Verlag), pp. 339–421

Murray, B. (1996), *Football: A History of the World Game* (Aldershot: Scolar Press)

Narkortu Teye, P. (2020), 'Mohammed Kudus: Ajax Amsterdam announce deal for Ghana prodigy', *MSN*, https://bit.ly/3j7zMvr [accessed 13 February 2021]

Nayak, A. (2010), 'Race, affect, and emotion: young people, racism, and graffiti in the postcolonial English suburbs', *Environment and Planning A*, 42:10, 2370–92

Ndee, H. (1996), 'Sport, culture and society from an African perspective: a study in historical revisionism', *International Journal of the History of Sport*, 13:2, 192–201

Ndiaye, K. (2001), 'Human traffic: Senegal', *African Soccer*, May, pp. 12–13

Newsbeezer (2020), 'All you need to know: when does the 2020 Thai League start?', 14 August, https://newsbeezer.com/thailandeng/all-you-need-to-know-when-does-the-2020-thai-league-start/ [accessed 14 February 2021]

Nieswand, B. (2014), 'The burgers' paradox: migration and the transnationalization of social inequality in southern Ghana', *Ethnography*, 15:4, 403–25

Njororai, W. W. S. (2009), 'Colonial legacy, minorities and association football in Kenya', *Soccer & Society*, 10:6, 866–82

—— (2014), 'Iconic figures in African football: from Roger Milla to Didier Drogba', *Soccer & Society*, 15:5, 761–79

—— (2019), 'Organizational factors influencing football development in East African countries', *Soccer & Society*, 20:1, 168–88

Nukunya, G. K. (2003), *Tradition and Change in Ghana: An Introduction to Sociology* (Accra: Ghana Universities Press)

Nyamnjoh, F. B. (2013), 'Fiction and reality of mobility in Africa', *Citizenship Studies*, 17:6–7, 653–80

Nyamnjoh, F. B., and B. Page (2002), 'Whiteman Kontri and the enduring allure of modernity among Cameroonian youth', *African Affairs*, 101:405, 607–34

Obeng-Odoom, F. (2013), *Governance for Pro-Poor Urban Development: Lessons from Ghana* (London and New York: Routledge)

OECD (2020), *What Is the Impact of the COVID-19 Pandemic on Immigrants and Their Children?* (Paris: Organisation for Economic Co-operation and Development), www.oecd.org/coronavirus/policy-responses/what-is-the-impact-of-the-covid-19-pandemic-on-immigrants-and-their-children-e7cbb7de/ [accessed 18 February 2021]

Oldenburg, S. (2019), 'Dead end? Young mototaxi drivers between being stuck, bridging potholes and building a future in Goma, Eastern Congo', *Cadernos de Estudos Africanos*, 37, 63–87

Oliver, B. (2008), 'Big interview: Nii Odartey Lamptey', *Observer*, 3 February, www.theguardian.com/football/2008/feb/03/africannationscup2008.africannationscup1 [accessed 13 February 2021]

Onwumechili, C. (ed.) (2020), *Africa's Elite Football Structure, Politics, and Everyday Challenges* (London and New York: Routledge)

Onwumechili, C., and U. Akpan (2019), 'Nigeria: as football labour scrambles, what about family?', *Sport in Society*, 23:7, 1119–35

Onwumechili, C., and J. Perry (2020), 'The rise of football academies', in C. Onwumechili (ed.), *Africa's Elite Football Structure, Politics, and Everyday Challenges* (London and New York: Routledge), pp. 45–56

Opoku Amoako, Y., (2021), 'WAFA transfer two key players to RB Salzburg', *GhanaGuardian.com*, https://ghanaguardian.com/wafa-transfer-two-key-players-to-rb-salzburg [accessed on 22 April 2021]

Ornstein, D. (2008), 'Charlton focus on Ivorian future', BBC Sport, 15 February, http://news.bbc.co.uk/sport1/hi/football/teams/c/charlton_athletic/7244803.stm [accessed 13 February 2021]

Otto, C. (2009), 'Integration ist mehr als Dienstwagen und Wohnung', *Die Zeit*, 16 September, www.zeit.de/sport/fussball/2009-09/wolfsburg-martins-stiel-ismael-integration [accessed 14 February 2021]

PA Media (2019), 'Cagliari fined for fans throwing bottles but not racist abuse of Lukaku', *Guardian*, 17 September, www.theguardian.com/football/2019/sep/17/cagliari-serie-a-avoid-sanction-fans-racist-abuse-romelu-lukaku [accessed 14 February 2021]

Page, B., and E. Sunjo (2018), 'Africa's middle class: building houses and constructing identities in the small town of Buea, Cameroon', *Urban Geography*, 39:1, 75–103

Palmer, R. (2009), 'Formalising the informal: Ghana's National Apprenticeship Programme', *Journal of Vocational Education & Training*, 61:1, 67–83

Pannenborg, A. (2010), 'Big men, big gains? The involvement of African club officials in the transfer of players', *African Historical Review*, 42:1, 63–90

Papada, E., A. Papoutsi, J. Painter, and A. Vradis (2020), 'Pop-up governance: transforming the management of migrant populations through humanitarian and security practices in Lesbos, Greece, 2015–2017', *Environment and Planning D: Society and Space*, 38:6, 1028–45

Park, S., D. Lavallee, and D. Tod (2013), 'Athletes' career transition out of sport: a systematic review', *International Review of Sport and Exercise Psychology*, 6:1, 22–53

Pelican, M. (2014), 'Urban lifeworlds of Cameroonian migrants in Dubai', *Urban Anthropology and Studies of Cultural Systems and World Economic Development*, 43:1–3, 255–309

Pelican, M., and T. Schwarz (2015), 'Space for informal activities', Reflections on migration in the Global South – voices from around the world (Global South Studies Center, University of Cologne), https://kups.ub.uni-koeln.de/6403/1/voices022015_reflections_on_migration_in_the_global_south.pdf [accessed 19 February 2021]

Philips, N., R. Bhaskaran, D. Nathan, and C. Upendranadh (2014), 'The social foundations of global production networks: towards a global political economy of child labour', *Third World Quarterly*, 35:3, 428–46

Phillips, T. (2017), 'China aims for football glory with academy based on Barcelona's', *Guardian*, 6 March, www.theguardian.com/world/2017/mar/06/china-to-open-football-academy-modelled-on-barcelonas-la-masia [accessed 20 February 2021]

Pink, S., H. Horst, J. Postill, L. Hjorth, T. Lewis, and J. Tacchi (2015), *Digital Ethnography: Principles and Practice*. (London: Sage Publications)

Poli, R. (2005), 'The football players trade as a global commodity chain: Transnational networks from Africa to Europe' (presented at the Workshop on Social Networks of Traders and Managers in Africa, University of Bayreuth, Germany), https://core.ac.uk/download/pdf/20641197.pdf [accessed 27 April 2021]

―――― (2006a), 'Africans' status in the European football players' labour market', *Soccer & Society*, 7:2–3, 278–91

―――― (2006b), 'Migrations and the trade in African football players: historic, geographic and cultural aspects', *Africa Spectrum*, 41:3, 393–414

―――― (2010a), 'African migrants in Asian and European football: hopes and realities', *Sport in Society*, 13:6, 1001–11

―――― (2010b), 'Agents and intermediaries', in S. Chadwick and S. Hamil (eds), *Managing Football: An International Perspective* (Oxford: Butterworth Heinemann), pp. 201–16

―――― (2010c), 'The migrations of African football players to Europe: human trafficking and neo-colonialism in question' (presented at the Football for Development Conference, Vienna, Austria), https://docplayer.net/24472715-The-migrations-of-african-football-players-to-europe.html [accessed 27 April 2021]

―――― (2010d), 'Understanding globalization through football: the new international division of labour, migratory channels and transnational trade circuits', *International Review for the Sociology of Sport*, 45:4, 491–506

Poli, R., L. Ravenel, and R. Besson (2015), *Exporting Countries in World Football*, CIES Football Observatory, https://football-observatory.com/IMG/pdf/mr08_eng.pdf [accessed 27 April 2021]

―――― (2020a), *The Effects of the Pandemic on the Demography of Players in Europe*, CIES Football Observatory, https://football-observatory.com/IMG/sites/mr/mr59/en/ [accessed 26 April 2021]

―――― (2020b), *The Real Impact of COVID on the Football Players' Transfer Market*, CIES Football Observatory, https://football-observatory.com/IMG/sites/mr/mr58/en/ [accessed 26 April 2021]

Porter, G., K. Hampshire, A. Abane, E. Robson, A. Munthali, M. Mashiri, et al. (2010), 'Moving young lives: mobility, immobility and urban "youthscapes"', *Geoforum*, 41, 796–804

Power, A. (1974), *Conversations with James Joyce* (London: Millington)

Pype, K. (2009), 'Media celebrity, charisma and morality in post-Mobutu Kinshasa', *Journal of Southern African Studies*, 35:3, 541–55

Quansah, M. (2001), 'Human traffic: Ghana', *African Soccer*, May, pp. 14–15

Quartey, P. (2009), *Migration in Ghana: A Country Profile 2009* (Geneva: International Organization for Migration)

Rasmussen, R., A. Esgate, and D. Turner (2005), 'On your marks, get stereotyped, go! Novice coaches and black stereotypes in sprinting', *Journal of Sport and Social Issues*, 29:4, 426–36

Ratele, K. (2008), 'Analysing males in Africa: certain useful elements in considering ruling masculinities', *African and Asian Studies*, 7:4, 515–36

Redfern, P. (2018), 'Fake UK football agents kill dreams of young Africans', *Daily Nation*, 25 April, www.nation.co.ke/kenya/sports/football/fake-uk-football-agents-kill-dreams-of-young-africans-36350 [accessed 9 July 2020]

Rednege, K. (1998), *The Complete Encyclopaedia of Football* (London: Colour Library Direct)

Rehal, S. R. (2015), 'Caught between a rock and a hard place: realities of African soccer players in the Philippines', *Asia Pacific Journal of Sport and Social Science*, 4:1, 7–18

Resnick, D., and J. Thurlow (eds) (2015), *African Youth and the Persistence of Marginalization: Employment, Politics, and Prospects for Change* (New York and London: Routledge)

Retzinger, S. M. (1991), *Violent Emotions: Shame and Rage in Marital Quarrels* (London: Sage Publications)

Rial, C. S. (2016), 'From "Black Kaká" to gentrification: the new motilities of expatriate Brazilian football players', in J. Gledhill (ed.), *World Anthropologies in Practice: Situated Perspectives, Global Knowledge* (London: Bloomsbury Publishing), pp. 77–91

Ricci, F. M. (2000), *African Football Yearbook* (Rome: Prosports)

Rice-Coates, R. (2017), 'Nii Lamptey: the next Pelé whose life descended into turmoil', *These Football Times*, 18 August

Richards, P. (ed.) (2005), *No Peace, No War: An Anthropology of Contemporary Armed Conflicts* (Melton and Ohio: James Currey and Ohio University Press)

Richardson, J. (2020), 'Football con: newly prominent TTM warn against "fake trial" scams', *South African*, 15 June, www.thesouthafrican.com/sport/ttm-warn-fake-trial-scams/ [accessed 9 July 2020]

Rigg, J. (2007), 'Moving lives: migration and livelihoods in the Lao PDR', *Population, Space and Place*, 13:3, 163–78

Rintaugu, E. G., A. Mwisukha, and V. Onywera (2012), 'Analysis of factors that affect the standard of soccer in Africa: the case of East African countries', *Journal of Physical Education & Sport*, 12:1, 135–39

Ritzer, U. (2011), 'Ausgekickt, rausgekickt', *Süddeutsche Zeitung*, 5 August, www.sueddeutsche.de/geld/arbeitslose-fussballer-ausgekickt-rausgekickt-1.1128276 [accessed 14 February 2021]

Rojek, C. (2001), *Celebrity* (London: Reaktion Books)

——— (2006), 'Sports celebrity and the civilizing process', *Sport in Society*, 9:4, 674–90

Rolleston, C., and M. Oketch (2008), 'Educational expansion in Ghana: economic assumptions and expectations', *International Journal of Educational Development*, 28:3, 320–39

Rossi, G., A. Semens, and J. F. Brocard (2016), *Sports Agents and Labour Markets: Evidence from World Football* (London and New York: Routledge)

Roth, C. (2008), '"Shameful!" The inverted intergenerational contract in Bobo-Dioulasso, Burkina Faso', in S. Alber, S. van der Geest, and W. Reynolds (eds), *Generations in Africa: Connections and Conflicts* (London: Transcation Publishers), pp. 47–70

Ryba, T. V., and N. Stambulova (2013), 'The turn towards a culturally informed approach to career research and assistance in sports psychology', in N. Stambulova and T. V. Ryba (eds), *Athletes' Careers Across Cultures* (London and New York: Routledge), pp. 1–16

Salazar, N. B. (2011), 'The power of imagination in transnational mobilities', *Identities*, 18:6, 576–98

Saldanha, A. (2006), 'Reontologising race: the machinic geography of phenotype', *Environment and Planning D: Society and Space*, 24:1, 9–24

Šašková, Z. (2019), "From zero to hero": the life of Sierra Leonean football players in Scandinavia' [blog], Mats Utas (personal website), 10 November, http://matsutas.com/migration/from-zero-to-hero-the-life-of-sierra-leonean-football-players-in-scandinavia-by-zora-saskova/ [accessed 23 April 2021]

Schapendonk, J., and G. Steel (2014), 'Following migrant trajectories: the im/mobility of sub-Saharan Africans en route to the European Union', *Annals of the American Association of Geographers*, 104:2, 262–70

Scheff, T. J. (2000), 'Shame and the social bond: a sociological theory', *Sociological Theory*, 18:1, 84–99
Schieder, D., and G.-H. Presterudstuen (2014), 'Sport migration and sociocultural transformation: the case of Fijian rugby union players in Japan', *International Journal of the History of Sport*, 31:11, 1359–73
Schiller, N. G., L. Basch, and C. Blanc-Szanton (1992), 'Transnationalism: a new analytic framework for understanding migration', *Annals of the New York Academy of Sciences*, 645:1, 1–24
Schokkaert, J. (2016), 'Football clubs' recruitment strategies and international player migration: evidence from Senegal and South Africa', *Soccer & Society*, 17:1, 120–39
Schokkaert, J., J. Swinnen, and T. Vandemoortele (2012), 'Mega-events and sports institutional development: the impact of the World Cup on football academies in Africa', in A. Zimbalist and W. Maennig (eds), *International Handbook on the Economics of Mega Sporting Events* (Cheltenham: Edward Elgar), pp. 314–35
Schwarz, C. (2010), 'KSK Beveren – Das belgische Sprungbrett der Ivorer', *Transfermarkt*, 22 October, www.transfermarkt.de/ksk-beveren-das-belgische-sprungbrett-der-ivorer/view/news/47812 [accessed 22 October 2010]
Scott, C.-G. (2015), *African Footballers in Sweden. Race, Immigration, and Integration in the Age of Globalization* (New York: Palgrave Macmillan)
Sienu, S. T. (2019), 'Refreshing news for juvenile football as GFA absorbs player registration fees', *Football Made in Ghana*, 28 November, https://footballmadeinghana.com/2019/11/28/refreshing-news-for-juvenile-football-as-gfa-absorbs-player-registration-fees/ [accessed 6 August 2020]
Simone, A. (2004), 'People as infrastructure: intersecting fragments in Johannesburg', *Public Culture*, 16:3, 407–29
——— (2005), 'Urban circulation and the everyday politics of African urban youth: the case of Douala, Cameroon', *International Journal of Urban and Regional Research*, 29:3, 516–32
Slocum, R., and A. Saldanha (2016), *Geographies of Race and Food: Fields, Bodies, Markets* (London and New York: Routledge)
Smith, L., and V. Mazzucato (2009), 'Constructing homes, building relationships: migrant investments in houses', *Tijdschrift Voor Economische En Sociale Geografie*, 100:5, 662–73
Soeffner, H. G. (1997), *The Order of Rituals: The Interpretation of Everyday Life* (New Jersey: Transaction Publishers)
Sommers, M. (2011), *Stuck: Rwandan Youth and the Struggle for Adulthood* (Athens, GA: University of Georgia Press)
Spaaij, R., K. Farquharson, and T. Marjoribanks (2015), 'Sport and social inequalities', *Sociology Compass*, 9:5, 400–411
Spatz, S. (2008), *Profisportler und ihre Integration in Mannschaftssportarten am Beispiel Fußball* (Bayreuth: University of Bayreuth)
Spivak, G. C. (2012), *In Other Worlds: Essays In Cultural Politics* (London and New York: Routledge)
St Louis, B. (2003), 'Sport, genetics and the "natural athlete": the resurgence of racial science', *Body & Society*, 9:2, 75–95
——— (2004), 'Sport and common-sense racial science', *Leisure Studies*, 23:1, 31–46
Stambulova, N. (2016), 'Athletes' transitions in sport and life: positioning new research trends within the existing system of athlete career knowledge', in R. Schinke, K. McGannon, and B. Smith (eds), *International Handbook of Sport Psychology* (London and New York: Routledge), pp. 519–34

Stambulova, N., and T. V. Ryba (2014), 'A critical review of career research and assistance through the cultural lens: towards cultural praxis of athletes' careers', *International Review of Sport and Exercise Psychology*, 7:1, 1–17

Stambulova, N., T. V. Ryba, and K. Henriksen (2020), 'Career development and transitions of athletes: the International Society of Sport Psychology Position Stand revisited', *International Journal of Sport and Exercise Psychology*, online first, https://doi.org/10.1080/1612197X.2020.1737836

Sterkenburg, J. van, R. Peeters, and N. van Amsterdam (2019), 'Everyday racism and constructions of racial/ethnic difference in and through football talk', *European Journal of Cultural Studies*, 22:2, 195–212

Stets, J. E. (2010), 'Future directions in the sociology of emotions', *Emotion Review*, 2:3, 265–68

Stuart, O. (1995), 'The lions stir: football in African society', in S. Wagg (ed.), *Giving the Game Away: Football, Politics and Culture on Five Continents* (London and New York: Leicester University Press), pp. 24–51

Tangney, J. P., and R. L. Dearing (2003), *Shame and Guilt* (New York and London: Guilford Press)

Taylor, M. (2006), 'Global players? Football, migration and globalization, c.1930–2000', *Historical Social Research*, 31, 7–30

Tazanu, P. M. (2018), 'Of polluted spirits and compromised identity: Pentecostal depictions of causality and the repositioning of human agency in Cameroon', *Journal of Asian and African Studies*, 53:6, 970–83

Teller Report (2019), 'In an open letter FC Den Bosch chairman asks for help in the fight against racism', *Teller Report*, 22 November, https://bit.ly/3zarecO [accessed 14 February 2021]

Teye, J. (2020), 'What will international migration in West Africa look like after COVID-19?', *Open Democracy*, 16 December, www.opendemocracy.net/en/pandemic-border/what-will-international-migration-west-africa-look-after-covid-19/ [accessed 18 February 2021]

Thielke, T. (2009), *Traumfußball. Geschichten aus Afrika* (Göttingen: Die Werkstatt)

Thieme, T. A. (2018), 'The hustle economy: informality, uncertainty and the geographies of getting by', *Progress in Human Geography*, 42:4, 529–48

Thorpe, H., and B. Wheaton (2021), 'Young Gazan refugees, sport and social media: understanding migration as a process of becoming', *International Migration Review*, online first, https://doi.org/10.1177/0197918320988247

Thorsen, D. (2006), 'Child migrants in transit: strategies to assert new identities in rural Burkina Faso', in C. Christiansen, M. Utas, and H. Vigh (eds), *Navigating Youth, Generating Adulthood: Social Becoming in an African Context* (Uppsala: Nordic Africa Institute), pp. 88–114

Tiemoko, R. (2004), 'Migration, return and socio-economic change in West Africa: the role of the family', *Population, Space and Place*, 10:2, 155–74

Transfermarkt (2021a), 'Major League Soccer – Players from Ghana, 2021', https://transfermarkt.com/major-league-soccer/gastarbeiterdetail/wettbewerb/MLS1?saison_id=2020&land_id=54 [accessed 17 February 2021]

——— (2021b), 'USL Championship – Players from Ghana, 2021', https://transfermarkt.com/usl-championship/gastarbeiterdetail/wettbewerb/USL/galerie/0?saison_id=2020&land_id=54 [accessed 17 February 2021]

Tshube, T., and D. L. Feltz (2015), 'The relationship between dual-career and post-sport career transition among elite athletes in South Africa, Botswana, Namibia and Zimbabwe', *Psychology of Sport and Exercise*, 21, 109–14

Turner, J. H. (2009), 'The sociology of emotions: basic theoretical arguments', *Emotion Review*, 1:4, 340–54

Twum-Baah, K. A. (2005), 'Volume and characteristics of international Ghanaian migration', in T. Manuh (ed.), *At Home in the World? International Migration and Development in Contemporary Ghana and West Africa* (Accra: Sub-Saharan Publishers), pp. 55–77

Twum-Danso, A. (2009), 'Reciprocity, respect and responsibility: the 3Rs underlying parent-child relationships in Ghana and the implications for children's rights', *International Journal of Children's Rights*, 17:3, 415–32

UNESCO (2010), *The State of Social Science in Sub-Saharan Africa* (Paris: UNESCO), pp. 1–44, https://unesdoc.unesco.org/ark:/48223/pf0000190659 [accessed 24 May 2020]

Ungruhe, C. (2010), 'Symbols of success: youth, peer pressure and the role of adulthood among juvenile male return migrants in Ghana', *Childhood*, 17:2, 259–71

—— (2011), 'Migration, marriage and modernity: motives, impacts and negotiations of rural-urban circulation amongst young women in northern Ghana', in A. Daniel, K. Fink, L. Kroeker, and J. Schütze (eds), *Women's Life Worlds 'In-Between'* (Bayreuth: University of Bayreuth), pp. 58–79, https://core.ac.uk/download/pdf/33805313.pdf#page=69 [accessed 20 February 2021]

—— (2014), '"Natural born sportsmen": processes of othering and self-charismatization of African professional footballers in Germany', *African Diaspora*, 6:2, 196–217

—— (2016), 'Mobilities at play: the local embedding of transnational connections in West African football migration', *International Journal of the History of Sport*, 33:15, 1767–85

—— (2018a), 'Ein prekäres Spiel. Erfahrungen von Risiken und Unsicherheit unter afrikanischen Profifußballern in Deutschland', in J. Haß and S. Schütze (eds), *Ballspiele, Transkulturalität und Gender: Ethnologische und altamerikanistische Perspektiven* (Berliner Blätter: Ethnographische und Ethnologische Beiträge, 77), pp. 94–114

—— (2018b), *Lasten tragen, Moderne befördern: Wanderarbeit, Jugend, Erwachsenwerden und ihre geschlechtsspezifischen Differenzierungen in Ghana* (Münster: LIT Verlag)

—— (2019), 'Beyond agency's limits: "street children's" mobilities in southern Ghana', *Cadernos de Estudos Africanos*, 37, 41–61

—— (2020), 'A lesson in composure: learning from migrants in times of COVID-19', Medical Anthropology at UCL, 7 May, https://medanthucl.com/2020/05/07/a-lesson-in-composure-learning-from-migrants-in-times-of-covid-19/ [accessed 14 February 2021]

Ungruhe, C., and S. Agergaard (2020a), 'Migrant athletes and the transformation of physical capital: spatial and temporal dynamics in West African footballers' approaches to post-careers', *European Journal for Sport and Society*, online first, https://doi.org/10.1080/16138171.2020.1863706

—— (2020b), 'Postcareer precarity: occupational challenges among former West African footballers in northern Europe', in T. Cleveland, T. Kaur and G. A. Akindes (eds), *Sport in Africa, Past and Present* (Athens, OH: Ohio University Press), pp. 190–206

—— (2020c), 'Cultural transitions? Transcultural and border-crossing activities among sport labor migrants', *Sport in Society*, 23:4, 717–33

Ungruhe, C., and M. Büdel (2016), 'Im Spiel bleiben: Ethnologische Perspektiven auf Fußballmigrationen aus Afrika', *Zeitschrift für Ethnologie*, 141:1, 81–99

Ungruhe, C., and J. Esson (2017), 'A social negotiation of hope: male West African youth, "waithood" and the pursuit of social becoming through football', *Boyhood Studies*, 10:1, 22–43

Ungruhe, C., U. Röschenthaler, and M. Diawara (2019), 'Introduction: young people working for better lives in West and Central Africa', *Cadernos de Estudos Africanos*, 37, 9–16

Ungruhe, C., and M. B. Schmidt (2020), 'Why are East African players absent in European football? Localizing African football migration along structural constraints, colonial legacies and voluntary immobility', *Journal of Sport and Social Issues*, 44:5, 397–420

Vasili, P. (1995), 'Colonialism and football: the first Nigerian tour to Britain', *Race and Class*, 36:4, 55–70

Versi, A. (1986), *Football in Africa* (London: Collins)

Vertovec, S. (2009), *Transnationalism* (London and New York: Routledge)

Vigh, H. (2006a), *Navigating Terrains of War: Youth and Soldiering in Guinea-Bissau* (New York and Oxford: Berghahn Books)

—— (2006b), 'Social death and violent life chances', in C. Christiansen, M. Utas, and H. Vigh (eds), *Navigating Youth, Generating Adulthood: Social Becoming in an African Context* (Uppsala: Nordic Africa Institute), pp. 31–60

—— (2009), 'Motion squared: a second look at the concept of social navigation', *Anthropological Theory*, 9:4, 419–38

Waage, T. (2006), 'Coping with unpredictability: preparing for life in Ngaoundere, Cameroon', in C. Christiansen, M. Utas, and H. Vigh (eds), *Navigating Youth, Generating Adulthood: Social Becoming in an African Context* (Uppsala: Nordic Africa Institute), pp. 61–87

Wallerstein, I. (1974), *The Modern World System* (New York: Academic Press)

—— (1979), *The Capitalist World Economy* (Cambridge: Cambridge University Press)

Watts, M., and D. Goodman (1997), 'Agrarian questions: global appetite, local metabolism: nature, culture and industry', in D. Goodman and M. Watts (eds), *Globalising Food: Agrarian Questions and Global Restructuring* (London and New York: Routledge), pp. 1–35

White, A. (2009), 'Internal migration, identity and livelihood strategies in contemporary Russia', *Journal of Ethnic and Migration Studies*, 35:4, 555–73

Whitehead, A., I. M. Hashim, and V. Iversen (2007), *Child Migration, Child Agency and Inter-Generational Relations in Africa and South Asia* (presented at the Children and Youth in Emerging and Transforming Societies conference, Oslo, Norway), https://assets.publishing.service.gov.uk/media/57a08c94ed915d622c001433/Whitehead_et_al.pdf [accessed 27 April 2021]

Wignall, R. (2016), 'From swagger to serious: managing young masculinities between faiths at a Young Men's Christian Association Centre in the Gambia', *Journal of Religion in Africa*, 46:2–3, 288–323

Wignall, R., K. McQuaid, K. V. Gough and J. Esson (2019), '"We built this city": mobilities, urban livelihoods and social infrastructure in the lives of elderly Ghanaians', *Geoforum*, 103, 75–84

Wilson, T. D. (2010), 'The culture of Mexican migration', *Critique of Anthropology*, 30:4, 399–420

Wrigley-Asante, C. (2011), 'Women becoming bosses: changing gender roles and decision making in Dangme West District of Ghana', *Ghana Journal of Geography*, 3, 60–87

Yilmaz, S., J. Esson, P. Darby, E. Drywood, and C. Mason (2020), 'Children's rights and the regulations on the transfer of young players in football', *International Review for the Sociology of Sport*, 55:1, 115–24

Zifonun, D. (2010), 'Ein "gallisches Dorf"? Integration, Stadtteilbindung und Prestigeordnung in einem "Armenviertel"', in D. Zifonun and M. Müller (eds), *Ethnowissen. Soziologische Beiträge zu ethnischer Differenzierung und Migration* (Wiesbaden: VS Verlag), pp. 311–27

Index

academies *see* football academies; Ghanaian football academies
Addo, Otto 214
Addo, Samuel 94
Adebayor, Emmanuel 72
Adika, Herbert 87, 88, 128, 133
Adjovi-Boco, Jimmy 72
Afful, Harrison 56
Africa Cup of Nations 2, 4, 6, 41, 48, 88, 215, 222
'African crisism' 36–7, 227–8
African migration
  culture of migration 34–5, 111–12, 139, 226
  illicit forms 7–8, 19, 20, 59, 116–17, 129, 154–5
  involuntary immobility 20, 112, 113, 125, 127, 140, 141–4, 145, 226–7
Agbomadzi, Blessing Shine 95
agency
  and financial resources 127–9
  labour agency 28–9, 31–2
  migrant players 13, 22–5, 46–7
  planning and strategic decision-making 22–3, 24
  race and sporting ability 133–7
  self-belief 144, 159–61, 167, 228
  social navigation 32–3, 37, 125, 127, 144, 226
  and spirituality 129–33
  'trying your luck' 126–37, 226, 227–8
agents *see* football agents
Agergaard, Sine xvi
Aguas, Jose 47
Ajax Amsterdam 75, 78

Akindes, Gerard A. 54
Akonnor, Charles 181, 215
Algeria, football migrants 45, 48, 51
Alizé Elite Foot 72
Altas of Migration 50–1
Amenumey, Evans 90, 95
Anagblah, Jordan 87, 88, 98–9
RSC Anderlecht 7–8
Angola, football migrants 46–7
Ansah, Edward 214
Appadurai, Arjun 97, 98
Appiah, Stephen 90
Arsenal FC 71
ASEC Mimosas Academy 70–1, 149–50
Ashimeru, Majeed 75
Assou-Ekotto, Benoît 198
Asuming, King James 91, 95
Attuquayefio, Cecil Jones 40–1, 44, 48–9
Austin Texans FC 99–100, 107, 136
Austria, Red Bull Salzburg 74–5, 152–3

Baah, Gideon 157
Baffoe, Anthony 89, 134–5
Bakambu, Cédric 56
Balogoun, Tesilimi 48
Barracks FC 92, 99, 100, 107–9, 115, 131–2
Barry, Boubacar 70–1
Bayor, Adjoa 90
Belgian Congo, football migrants 48
Belgium, football migrants 6, 7–8, 48, 49, 53, 70–1, 149–50
Bell, Joseph-Antoine 48

Index

Ben Barek, Larbi 45
Benfica 47, 68, 214
Besnier, Niko 127
'big men' 76, 89, 91, 92–3
Boateng, Derek 76
Bocande, Jules 48
Boka, Arthur 70
Britain
   football migrants 47–8
   Nationality Acts (1914, 1948) 48
Brokken, Karel 74

Caliendo, Antonio 8–9
Cameroon
   academy 159
   football migrants 45, 50, 133–4, 159–61, 175, 189–91
   migratory flows 51, 53, 54
Carter, Thomas F. 22, 26
case studies
   Ali (Denmark) 150, 204–5
   Chi (post-playing career) 196–7, 205–6, 220
   Demba (Cameroon) 159–61, 189–91
   Didzi (fraudulent contract offer) 115–18
   Emmanuel (post-playing career) 201–2
   Evans (post-playing career) 215–16
   Habib and Felix (Germany) 172–3
   Ibrahim (former player) 217–19
   Isaak (Thailand) 163–5, 176–7
   John (Denmark) 146–7, 151, 171, 184–9, 201
   Jordan (Thailand) 166–7, 169, 171–2, 191–4, 201
   Ken (coach and intermediary) 166, 169
   Kingsley (Red Bull) 151–3
   Mensah (football commitment) 104–5, 109–11, 113–14
   Michael (family support) 208–9
   Sam (coaching in Thailand) 211–12
   see also Lamptey, Nii Odartey
celebrity
   role models 7, 13, 105, 110, 169–70, 205, 223
   and spiritual powers 130–1
Central Africa, migratory flows 52

Chakraborty, Kabita 140
Charlton Athletic FC 47, 71
children, early informal exposure to football 66–7
China, migratory flows 55–6
CIES, Football Observatory 50–1
Cissé, Aliou 215
citizenship regulations 47, 49, 56–7, 213
Cleveland, Todd 25
coaches, pivotal intermediaries 100, 102, 117–18
coaching
   in Ghana 215–16
   post-playing career 11, 196–7, 206, 220
   in South-East Asia 211–13
Collège Africain Sports-Études (CASE) 71–2
colonial era 42–8, 178–9
Coluna, Mario 47
Confédération Africaine de Football (CAF) 49
Congo, TP Mazembe 52
corruption
   financial inducements 62, 153–4
   football trials 101–2, 128–9, 164–5
   fraudulent contract offers 115–17, 160
   West African referees and officials 91
Côte d'Ivoire
   football academy 70–1, 149–50
   football migrants 45, 51, 53, 149–50
COVID-19 xi–xiii, 91, 192–4, 232
culture of migration 34–5, 111–12, 139, 226

Denmark
   extended training placements 77–8, 174
   FC Midtjylland 75, 134, 146–7, 150–1, 174
   football academies 75, 77–8
   football migrants 146–7, 151, 171, 185–6
Dia, Ali 157–8
Diambars Institute 72–3
Djan, Ohene 68, 85

drivers of migration
  becoming an 'entrepreneur of self' 111, 113–14, 207
  culture of migration 34–5, 111–12, 139, 226
  gaining social status 38, 110–11, 112, 200–1, 209
  helping the family 113–14
  predisposing drivers 105–6
  professional football in Europe 81–2, 104–5
  role models of football success 7, 13, 105, 110, 169–70, 205, 223
  the X-Way (Extraordinary Way) 112–13, 118, 200–1
  see also football migration
Drogba, Didier 56, 105, 130–1, 205, 223
Dubinsky, Itamar 75–6, 95

East Africa, migratory flows 52–3, 54–5
FC Ebedei 147, 150, 174
Eboué, Emmanuel 70–1
education
  FIFA study rules 146–7
  football academy provision 72–3, 76–7, 88, 102, 138–9, 159
  limited dual career provision 202–5
  parental wishes 5, 120–1, 146
  PE (physical education) 67
  precarity from lack of education or vocational qualifications 5, 9, 11, 229
  as route to social mobility 5
  student visas 146–7, 159, 160, 189, 190, 191
  study combined with football placements 45, 48, 166
  study overseas 160, 189, 190, 191
  versus football 106–9
Egbo, Ndubuisi 214
Egypt, football migrants 47, 51
Emenalo, Michael 214
England
  football migrants 47–8, 157–8
  preferred destination 53
  racism in football 182–3
'entrepreneurs of self' 111, 113–14, 207
Eranio, Stefano 180–1

Essien, Michael 76, 105, 149, 169–70, 205, 223
Eto'o, Samuel 130–1, 169–70, 205
Europe
  academies as feeder pathways 73–5, 100–1, 146–8
  football migrants 53, 59
  post-playing careers 213–15
  preferred destination 53
European Court of Justice (ECJ), Bosman ruling 57–8
Eusebio (da Silva Ferreira) 47
exploitation, football migrants 8–9, 60, 116–17, 158, 163–5, 167

family
  conflicts and concerns over football 4–5, 119–22, 146
  driver of migration 113–14
  effects of losing academy place 141–3
  encouragement and support 118–19, 159, 175
  football migration as household livelihood strategy 23, 38, 114, 117–18, 209–11
  intergenerational contract 38–9, 121–2, 141–2, 208–10, 218–19, 229
  remittances home 186, 193
  responsibility and social adulthood 21, 37, 192–3
  role of older sibling 116, 117, 120
Feyenoord Fetteh Football Academy 73–5
FIFA
  African successes 93–4
  FC Midtjylland reprimand 147, 150
  Manchester City Article 19 fine 155
  no action on Football Leaks allegations 155
  Regulations on Working with Intermediaries (RWI) 61–2, 155
  transfer of minors 59–60
  transfer regulations (RSTP) 41, 59–60, 97–8, 146–7, 155
  U-16 World Championship 6–7
  U-17 World Championships/Cup 4, 69, 94, 185
  World Cup (2002) 161–2
  World Cup (2006) 76

Fofana, Youssuf 70
football academies
  access to professional game 156
  Aspire Academy (Qatar) 55
  challenging partnerships with clubs 148–56
  compensation payable to clubs 31, 60
  concerns and problems 156
  Côte d'Ivoire 70–1
  educational and social aspects 72–3, 76–7, 88, 102, 138–9, 159
  exploitation of minors 60
  extended training placements 77–8, 174
  global production network 65, 66–78, 216
  informal sector 78–80
  post-playing career 216–17
  recruitment age 68, 74
  recruitment process 64–5, 70
  significance 67–8
  trials *see* football trials
  variability and complexity 68–70
  see also Ghanaian football academies
football agents
  exploitation 8–9, 163–5
  fake agents 158
  FIFA regulations 61–2, 155
  fraudulent offers 115–17, 159–60
  Ghana police investigation 154–5
  online encounters 116–17
  South-East Asia 162–3
  see also talent speculators
football industry
  financial speculation 59, 61, 80, 94–5, 97–8
  training compensation paid to clubs 31, 60
  see also global production network (GPN)
football migrants
  access to professional infrastructures 170
  'becoming a somebody' 84, 105, 111, 117–19, 123, 131, 147–8, 187–8, 227–8
  conventional paths and obstacles 148–56
  'entrepreneurs of self' 111, 113–14, 207

exploitation 8–9, 60, 116–17, 158, 163–5, 167
as financial assets 31
involuntary return home 141–2, 143, 187–8
player integration measures 173–4
playing style differences 175–8
precarity and uncertainty 13, 20, 24, 53, 159–60, 194, 195
resilience 13, 167–8
self-belief 144, 159–61, 167, 228
self-charismatisation 179–80, 228–9
social challenges of adjustment 8, 10, 160, 170–5, 228–9
unconventional paths 156–61
see also agency
football migration
  colonial era 44–8
  future research 231–3
  history 42–50
  internal migration 21, 34–5
  intra-continental 49–50
  spatial distribution 20, 50–6, 81, 225
football trafficking 116–17, 158, 167
football transfers *see* player transfers
football trials
  coaches and family involvement 117–18
  fraud and controversy 101–2, 128–9, 164–5
  and playing position 136
  tournaments 64–5
  West African 'justifies' 74, 101–2, 156
Forson, Amankwah 75
France
  football migrants 45–6, 48, 51, 56, 72–3
  national team 45
  preferred destination 53
Francis, Gerry 47
Future Icons FC 107, 136–7, 137–8

Génération Foot 72
geography, of football migration 20, 50–6, 81, 225
Germany
  African stereotypes 181
  football migrants 86, 157, 172–3, 189–91

player integration measures 173
preferred destination 53
racism in football 182, 183
Gervinho 56, 70–1
Ghana
   kobolo (good-for-nothing) 5, 87
   political and economic instability 4, 87, 89
Ghanaian football
   Academicals 68, 88
   academies *see* Ghanaian football academies
   amateur league costs and fees 96
   'big men' 76, 89, 91, 92–3
   clientelism 92–3
   corruption 91, 92
   crisis and dysfunctionality 91–2, 93
   domestic game 48–9, 86–7
   FC Maamobi United 75, 146
   football success 4, 6, 41, 88
   Ghana (Amateur) Football Association (GAFA/GFA) 85, 89, 95–6
   history 85–9
   low salaries 93
   migratory flows 15, 48, 51, 54
   and national identity 43, 85–6
   national team (Black Stars) 8, 40, 41, 86, 90, 181
   popularity 4
   professionalisation 89–91
   profit motive 9, 89, 94–5, 97–103, 115
   'small boys' 95–6
   women's success 89–90
   youth football *see* Ghanaian youth football
Ghanaian football academies 73–8
   access to education 76–7, 88, 102, 138–9
   effects of losing academy place 138–46
   Glow-Lamp Academy and School 2, 11, 217
   Kumasi Sports Academy (KUSA) 91, 95
   Liberty Professionals FC 40, 76, 149
   local projects 75–6
   MTN Soccer Academy 157
   Nania FC 82, 216
   pathways to Europe 73–5, 100–1, 146–8
   as philanthropy 216–17
   Red Bull Ghana 73–5, 149, 152–3
   transfers to local domestic clubs (earlier) 139–40
   Unistar 94
   see also Right to Dream Academy
Ghanaian youth football
   Austin Texans FC 99–100, 107, 136
   Barracks FC 92, 99, 100, 107–9, 115, 131–2
   business opportunity 94–5
   'card dealers' 100
   Colts League 90–1, 95, 96
   costs and fees 96
   Future Icons FC 107, 136–8
   inappropriate practices 92–3
   'manager' contracts 99–100
   players as a potential source of capital 97–102
   prison match 124–5
   registration card 98–9
   registration fees 96
global production network (GPN)
   academy node 65, 67–78, 216
   football industry 29–30
   football production and export nodes 66–7
   intermediaries 60–1, 211
   players as commodities 97–102
   post-playing node 82
   theory 27–9
   West African node 42, 44
   workers' agency 28–9, 31–2
global value chain (GVC) 27–8
Gueye, Babacar 72
Guillou, Jean-Marc 70, 71
Guttmann, Béla 47
Gyamfi, Charles Kumi 86
Gyan, Asamoah 56, 76, 90, 105, 137, 149

Havelange, João 93
Henderby, Gareth 74
Henshaw, Etim 48
history
   football migration 42–50
   Ghanaian football 85–9

India, football migrants 50, 54
injury 187, 188–9, 190
intergenerational contract 38–9, 121–2, 141–2, 188, 208–10
Internet 116–17
see also social media
involuntary immobility 20, 112, 113, 125, 127, 140, 141–4, 145, 226–7
Italy
  preferred destination 53
  racism in football 183

Jatta, Bakery 157, 183
Johanneson, Albert 47, 223
Johnson-Hanks, Jennifer 27, 107

Kalaba, Rainford 52
Keita, Salif 48, 216
Kenya, migratory flows 53, 54–5
Kern, Herman 74
Keshi, Stephen 7, 8, 214–15
Klein, Alan 26, 30
KSK Beveren 70–1, 149–50
Kudus, Mohammed 78, 149
Kuffour, Ernest 94
Kumasi Sports Academy (KUSA) 91, 95

Lama, Bernard 72
Lamptey, George 89
Lamptey, Nii Odartey
  career trajectory 223, 224
  childhood footballing success 5
  childhood neglect and ill-treatment 4–5
  European club career stalls 8
  exploitative agent 9–10
  Glow-Lamp Academy and School 2, 11, 217
  introduction to football 4
  lack of formal education 5, 9, 11
  lower-level leagues 10
  national youth squad 6–7
  peripatetic career 89
  post-playing career 10–11
  racist abuse 10, 182
  return to Ghana 10
  signs for Anderlecht 7–8
  youthful achievements 1, 2

language
  difficulties 10, 171–2
  local language learning 160, 186, 203–4
Laursen, Jan 78, 174
Leye, Mbaye 214
Liberia, football migrants 54
Liberty Professionals FC 40, 76, 149
Lukaku, Romelu 183
Lusophone Africa, football migrants 46

FC Maamobi United 75, 146
Madjer, Rabah 48
Malaysia, football migrants 54
Mali
  football migrants 45, 48, 51, 53
  Jeunesse Sportive Centre 216
Manchester City FC
  player contracts 153–4, 155–6
  Right to Dream collaboration 77, 153, 154, 155
  RSTP Article 19 fine 155
Mané, Sadio 169–70, 223
Martins, Obafemi 56
masculine adulthood 13, 21, 37–8, 111
Matateu (Lucas Sebastião Fonseca) 47
Mensah, Gideon 75
Mensah, Jonathan 56
Mensah (young footballer)
  helping his family 113–14
  ICT studies 105
  individual responsibility 110–11
  prioritisation of football over education 109
  U-17 youth team 104–5
FC Metz 72
FC Midtjylland 75, 134, 146–7, 150–1, 174
migrants *see* football migrants
migration *see* African migration; drivers of migration; football migration
Mikel, John Obi 136–7
Milla, Roger 48, 50, 205
Mokone, Steve 47
AS Monaco FC 70, 71–2
Moreira, Ahmad Mendes 183
Morocco, football migrants 45, 51
Mozambique, football migrants 46–7
Muntari, Sulley 76

Nania FC 82, 216
nationalism, and football 43
neoliberalism 12–13, 25
Nepal, football migrants 54
Netherlands
    FC Den Bosch racism 183–4
    football academies 73–5
    football migrants 8
Nigeria
    FC Ebedei 147, 150, 174
    football academies 75
    football migrants 48, 50, 51, 54
Nkrumah, Kwame 43, 85, 86, 87
FC Nordsjælland 77–8, 153–6, 174
North Africa, migratory flows 51
Norway, football migrants 73, 177

Okraku, Kurt 92, 129–30, 132–3
Oshoala, Asisat 231
Ouégnin, Roger 70, 71
Owusu, Daniel 75

Paintsil, John 76
Pappoe, Emmanuel Addoquaye 76
Pelé, Abedi 6, 82, 87, 89, 216
Pereira, Costa 47
Perry, Bill 47
Pfister, Otto 9
Philippines, migratory flows 54
player transfers
    fees 78
    FIFA regulations 41, 59–60, 97–8, 146–7, 155
    Football Leaks allegations 153–5
    Portugal 46–7
playing styles 175–8
Poli, Raffaele 50, 97
Portugal
    colonial era training 68
    football migrants 46–7, 53, 56
    national team 47
    player transfers 46–7
post-colonial era 43–4, 48–50
post-playing career
    in Africa 214–16
    continuing in football 11, 91, 211–16
    in Europe 213–15
    expectations from home 141–3, 193, 209–10, 218–19
    'give back' 11, 13–14, 21, 72–3, 216–17, 221
    GPN node 82
    investment in real estate and houses 209–10
    limitations 229
    limited provision for alternative careers 202–5
    motives for return 21
    precarity 196–200, 217–20
    preparation 200–5
    scholarship 198–9
    in South-East Asia 211–13
    staying abroad or returning home 210–17
    unwillingness to contemplate retirement 197, 205–7
precarity
    definition 148
    football migrants 13, 20, 24, 53, 159–61, 194, 195
    post-playing career 196–200, 217–20
    and racism 182–3

Qatar, Aspire Academy 55
Quarshi, Emmanuel 6

race
    Black Lives Matter xiv–xv
    colonial worldview 180–1
    de-racialisation 46
    European skills 181
    players' self-charismatisation 179–80, 228–9
    power imbalances 181–2
    and sporting ability 133–7, 178
    stereotypical view of Black players 181
racism
    Eastern Europe 186
    from teammates 10
    from the terraces 10, 182–4
    Lamptey's experience 10
    need for action 183–4
    in social media 182, 183
Razak, Abdul 6
Red Bull 73–5, 149, 152–3
refugees 157
regulation 25–6, 56–62

Regulations on the Status and Transfer of Players (RSTP) 41, 59–60, 97–8, 146–7, 155
Regulations on Working with Intermediaries (RWI) 61–2, 155
religion 129–33, 164
research methods
  confidentiality 15–16
  digital methodologies 233
  ethnographic approach 14–16
  fieldwork 15–16
  interdisciplinary approach 26–7, 230, 232
  longitudinal observation 14
  long-term perspective 230
  micro- or meso- versus macro-level approach 21–5
  multiple settings 14
  networking 222–3
  see also scholarship
Right to Dream Academy
  extended training placements 77–8, 174
  Football Leaks allegations 153–6
  intermediary irregularities 62, 154–5
  'justifies' 156
  Manchester City collaboration 77, 153, 154, 155
  FC Nordsjælland acquisition 77–8, 153
  philosophy 76–7
  professionalism 149
  transnational links 77–8
  US links 56
role models 7, 13, 105, 110, 169–70, 205, 223
Romaric 70–1
Rüdiger, Antonio 180–1
Russia, football migrants 160–1, 189

Sackey, Alberta 90
sacking
  career perseverance 184–6
  emotional responses 138–42
  for failure to attend church 132
  reliance on family 141–2
  three forms 138–9
Salah, Mo 223
salaries 42, 51, 55–6, 56, 58, 93, 200

Santana, Joaquim 47
Schler, Lynn 75–6, 95
scholarship
  football migration 19–27
  post-playing career 198–9
  see also research methods
Schouten, Jan-Hein 184
Seck, Saer 72
self-belief 144, 159–61, 167, 228
self-charismatisation 179–80, 228–9
Senegal
  football academies 71–3, 79
  football migrants 45, 48, 53
  navétanes teams 71
shame
  on being 'sacked' 140–1, 142, 143–4
  of returning empty-handed 188, 217, 218
  status paradox 18, 218–20
Singapore, migratory flows 54
Singuluma, Given 52
Sinkula, Nathan 52
social becoming 37–8, 105–6, 112
social giving 21, 37, 229
social infrastructure 33–4
social media
  football trafficking 116–17
  player support groups 175
  promotional videos 15
  racism 182, 183
social navigation 32–3, 37, 125, 127, 144, 226
social status 38, 110–11, 112, 200–1, 209
  status paradox 18, 218–20
social wellbeing 170–5
socio-cultural conditions 24, 32
South Africa, football migrants 47, 52
South-East Asia
  African players' precarity 194
  challenges for players 162–7
  coaching opportunities 211–13
  football migrants 50, 161–7
  football's popularity 161
  migratory flows 54–5
  regulations 162
Spain, migratory flows 51, 53
statistics, migration flows 51

Sweden, football migrants 196–7, 208–9, 220

talent speculators 79–80, 84, 85, 128–9, 154–5, 162–3
see also football agents
television 44
Tetteh, Alhaji Sly 76, 149
Tetteh, Samuel 75
Thailand
   academy 166–7
   coaching opportunities 211–12
   COVID-19 192, 193–4
   football migrants 164–5, 166–7, 169, 171–2, 191–4
   football playing style 176–7
   migratory flows 54, 163–5, 169, 175
   reliance on intermediaries 163–5
Thambiah, Shanthi 140
Thiam, Idrissa 72
Touré, Kolo 214
Touré, Mady 72
Touré, Yaya 70–1, 149
TP Mazembe 52
transfers see player transfers
trials see football trials
Tunisia, football migrants 45, 51

U-16 World Championship 6–7
U-17 World Championships/Cup 4, 69, 94, 185
UEFA (Union of European Football Associations), '3+2' rules on non-nationals 57–8
United Arab Emirates (UAE), migratory flows 55
United States, football migrants 40, 56, 136
FC Utrecht 75

van der Meij, Nienke xvi, 23
Vernon, Tom 62, 76–7, 153–4, 174
Vieira, Patrick 72–3
Vigh, Henrik 32, 33, 113, 127, 142, 144, 226

visibility 107, 144, 165, 170
vital conjunctures
   concept 27, 230
   following sacking 138–45
   post-playing livelihood 218–19
   window for obtaining visibility 107, 144

Weah, George 158, 198, 223
Wenger, Arsène 71
West African Football Academy (WAFA) 75–6
Wharton, Arthur 48, 223
Wientjes, Henri 75
Williams, David 50
Wilson, Mário 214
women's football
   in Africa xiii–xiv
   commercial possibilities 95
   experiences 21
   future research 231
   Ghana successes 89–90
   icons 231
   and race 135
World Cup (2002) 161–2
World Cup (2006) 76

X-Way (Extraordinary Way) 112–13, 118, 200–1

Yeboah, Tony 6, 89
Youcef, Haruna 6
young people
   individual responsibility 109–11
   marginalisation 36
   negative depiction 36–7, 227
   socio-cultural context 35–6
   youth leagues 67
   see also Ghanaian youth football

Zaire, control of international transfers 48, 49
Zambia, migratory flows 52
Zimbabwe, migratory flows 52

EU authorised representative for GPSR:
Easy Access System Europe, Mustamäe tee 50,
10621 Tallinn, Estonia
gpsr.requests@easproject.com

www.ingramcontent.com/pod-product-compliance
Lightning Source LLC
Chambersburg PA
CBHW051605230426
43668CB00013B/1985